P.404
P.430

Platt Düütsch

LOW GERMAN

A BRIEF HISTORY
OF
THE PEOPLE
AND
LANGUAGE

1998

Platt Düütsch Press
10748 100th Street
Alto, Mich. 49302

Library of Congress Catalog Card Number 98-091589

International Standard Book Number 0 - 9665502 - 0 - X

Published in the United States of America

DEDICATED

to my parents

Carl Stockman and
Edna Marie Sophia Emma (Meyer) Stockman

for teaching me what's right

and for teaching me Platt Düütsch

CONTENTS

TABLE OF CONTENTS CONTINUED.

TABLE OF CONTENTS CONTINUED.
Chapter Six Continued:

TABLES

ILLUSTRATIONS

PREFACE

This book is a "Volks Buch"; which means it is a people's book. It is written for the enjoyment and use of anyone interested in the Low German language. It is not a technical book, although it was impossible to avoid using some technical terms. However, the casual user may ignore many, if not all, the technical terms. It is not a scholarly endeavor, since the author has no scholarly background in languages. That is also why it does not contain footnotes or a lot of technical references. Scholarly books can, despite their importance, be tedious for the average reader. Such books do contain much useful and interesting information, and it is unfortunate that only other scholars can enjoy them. The rest of us, meanwhile, remain that much less informed.

It is the intent of this book to discuss the Low German people and their language, from a historical perspective, with the hope that additional knowledge will generate additional insight and interest. This is a brief historical exercise, covering only some of the highlights. It is hoped that increased interest may generate increased support for efforts to preserve the language and the history. The information may encourage, and enable, people to read and write the language. Speaking, and more importantly writing, the language is the key to preserving it. This will be covered in detail in the concluding chapter.

Today, in the absence of one standard verson of the Low German language, there exist a variety of dialects which, in total, may be thought of as comprising a Low German *verbal* language. All the wonderful books available in Low German today are written in 'a' dialect, making them difficult for other Low Germans to enjoy. Each such book or poem, by and large, can be read and enjoyed only by those few people who have learned to read 'that' dialect. Thankfully there is a good deal of similarity between the verbal dialects, but the ease with which one can understand another dialect *verbally* doesn't help when one confronts the spelling differences in *written* dialects. The discussion in this book concerning various written dialects, which addresses their spelling differences, may help to reduce this problem.

Any detailed discussion of Low German, such as this book, has to adopt *one* dialect as the thread with which to weave a comprehensive view of the whole language. The dialect used here will be explained, so that people can relate to it from their own dialectical perspective. The basic dialect used in this book can be referred to as North Saxon. To those for whom this dialect is unfamiliar, this book contains information and some guidance for relating it the other major dialects. This is probably impossible to do adequately, due to the many spelling differences amongst the various dialects. As regards the subject of dialects in general, this book is above all dedicated to the *language* itself, while recognizing also that all the dialects are equally valid and important components of the language. Every dialect is as important to the author, though certainly not as familiar, as his own.

Please see the map in the Introduction Chapter for the relative location of the North Saxon dialect, within the community of dialects. The North Saxon dialect area reaches from near the Danish border down to the City of Hannover. This also happens to be the approximate area where the original Old Saxon-Low German-Platt Düütsch speaking people were located when the language first appeared.

Regionally speaking, the author's dialect derives from the southern, or southeastern part of the Lüneburger Heide; the Südheide. In terms of "local" dialect, it stems from the rural areas around the communities of Walsrode and Visselhövede.

This dialect, along with many others dialects, was brought to America by northern German emigrant farmers in the middle 1800's. Thus, having been handed down from generation to generation, it is grounded in a 150 plus year old dialect. The author learned to speak this dialect as a child, growing up on a farm in Northwestern Ohio. This is the same way that thousands of people throughout the Midwest learned their own dialect. This book is a salute, along with a "goden dag", to all of them.

Significant numbers of north German emigrants who traveled to America settled in the midwestern states of Ohio, Indiana, Illinois, Missouri, Kansas, Texas, Nebraska, South Dakota, Iowa, Minnesota and Wisconsin. Some that arrived at the Port of New York also settled in the State of New York, rather than make the arduous journey further west. In this emigration process, it so happens that all of the various Low German dialects found then in Germany wound up being transplanted somewhere within the above mentioned states of the United States of America.

Except in the case of daughter colonies, where some of the settlers in one area moved on to settle parts of the midwest, each Low German settlement was hardly aware that the others existed. There was, for over 100 years, virtually no contact between the various Low German settlements. They were only aware of their own small settlement, and the dialect spoken by their family, friends and neighbors. To them their dialect was all there was to Low German. For example, all but a few Ostfrisian speaking settlers were aware of the existence of Pommern, Hannoverian, or Westphalian speaking settlers. And vice versa, of course. They might even be located in the same state, and not be aware of each other. They were unaware that there was even such a thing as a Pomerania, Kingdom of Hannover or Kingdom of Westphalia. Many of them had slowly lost touch with their own dialect, never aware of the richness and variety of the history of the Low German language. Some retained their dialect in everyday use, but didn't know that Low German had been such a prominent language throughout the several centuries of the Hansa period. Only in the past five or six years has this kind of information become available to most of the Low German speaking people in America.

To compound the matter, the Low Germans in America had (have), for the most part, lost touch with other Low German speakers living in Germany. Only recently has contact "across the big pond" begun to be re-established. And nearly every American fortunate enough to visit Germany and speak Low German with the native Low

Germans there has encountered the same comment. The German will shake his finger and say, "You talk just like my grandparents talked." Without consciously thinking about it, the American speaks a version of a particular Low German dialect that existed over a hundred years ago in northern Germany or Poland. The version brought over by the emigrants, and now spoken in the middle of America, reflects largely a Low German language that is older than that which is currently spoken in Germany.

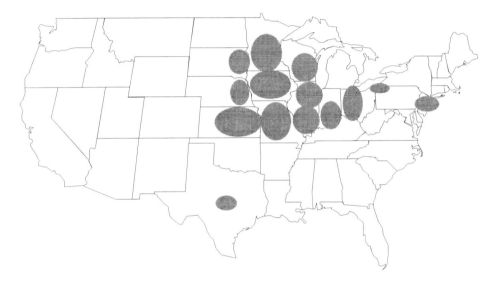

MAP A   LOW GERMANS IN MIDWESTERN UNITED STATES

This map shows the midwestern ten states in which many Low German speakers live today. Some are located around New York and Buffalo in the State of New York. Some also settled about halfway between Houston and Austin, in the State of Texas. If one counted the Low German speaking Mennonites, the distribution would be even broader, including a part of Canada. There are also Ost Frisians broadly spread out within the northwestern United States.

To varying degrees, there still exists some Low German speaking capability in each midwestern state. The situation here is similar to that in north Germany, being that only the older rural generations are still fluent in Low German. Also, similar to Germany, these American Low Germans and their descendants have, over the years, allowed some "loan" words to invade their dialect. Some of them have therefore avoided speaking it in public, because they feel they're not doing it right. Both past world wars caused a stigma to be attached to anything German, which indirectly generated prejudice against speaking Low German. During World War I, the term sauerkraut was changed to liberty cabbage. After World War II, the teaching of High German was discontinued in many schools. People who spoke either High German or Low German voluntarily muzzled themselves, to leave no doubt about their allegiance.

However, during the past 5 years, there has been a rejuvenation of interest in speaking Low German, througout the midwestern United States. Not as strong a trend as in Germany perhaps, where it has been going on slowly for about 100 years, but nonetheless a growing trend.

As some Americans have renewed their interest in Low German, especially their own inherited dialect, they feel some concern about how much "correctness" may have been lost over the decades. They realize that, after over 100 years, it is inevitable that some things have changed. Some Low German words known by the emigrant ancestor have, through lack of use, also been lost. There might even have been some words that never made it across the "big pond" in the first place, because the emigrant ancestors did not know them or had forgotten them. Some of the emigrants actively discouraged their children from speaking German of any kind, thinking that it would hinder their assimilation and succes in their new country. At the beginning of the 20th century, most Low German speakers could also speak High German. Thus they found both English and High German words as possible substitutes for Low German words. The churches were able to maintain some interest in High German, through their church services. This too became increasingly rare after the second world war.

Part of the problem in knowing whether a word was "correct" or a "loan" word is the fact that English and Low German are so similar. Most felt there must be some kind of relationship between the two languages, but they weren't sure what it was. Most didn't realize that their Low German (more specifically its ancestor Old Saxon) was the mother language of English. They only knew that if a Low German word sounded close to an English word, it was suspect of being "incorrect". They would wonder if a particular word was a true Low German word or was an English or High German word that had been given a Low German sounding pronunciation. They would use such words, but it affected the ease and frequency with which they spoke the language. This will be discussed in more detail in the Introduction Chapter.

In collecting information for this book, the author was aided by a number of people who offered thoughts about their own dialects and about Low German in general. There are too many to name, but each one is gratefully acknowledged. Fortunately some reference books were available in local book stores and libraries. From each reference perhaps only one or two points were extracted, so naming all such books is prohibitive. Those books which provided large amounts of helpful data are noted in the text.

Errors of fact or technical validity in this book are the responsibility of the author alone, and are sincerely regretted.

CHAPTER ONE   INTRODUCTION

To tell the history of the Low German people one must also delve into the history also of their cousins, the Scandinavians, the Dutch and the remainder of the Germans. These people have been interconnected for thousands of years. Over those years the individual languages and traditions have diverged somewhat, but their history cannot be changed. They all speak a version of an ancient Germanic or Teutonic language. In addition to the history of the German people, this book is interested in the whole German language family, but most specifically Low German branch.

In Chapter Two the historical path of the German people and language is followed, from the beginning of man and the inception of language, to the time that Low German and other Germanic languages first evolved in Europe.

Low German is one of two languages now spoken in northern Germany. The other is Standard German, which some call New High German. You will not find Low German spoken in southern Germany. In central Germany you may find a few Low German words interspersed with Standard German. The Low German language is today often referred to as Platt Düütsch (or Platt Dütsk). In Germany, Low German is referred to as Platt Deutsch in the Standard German language. Low German speakers are content to just call it *Platt*.

For centuries the Low German language was known by the name 'nieder deutsch' in the German languages. This is a direct translation of the words 'low' and 'german' in High German. The word 'low' is presumed to reflect the lowlying areas of north Germany, which have become the distinctive mark of the Low German language and people.

Low German is currently spoken by those German people who live in the rural areas of northern Germany. In farming areas, you'll very likely find some people both able and proud to speak *Platt*. In the villages, you may also find a few of the older people able to understand *Platt* The other language, Standard German, is spoken by all the people in Germany, because that's what they learn in school.

One can say this about the current language situation in Germany ... "It wasn't always thus". Several hundred years ago, it was not uncommon for a significant number of north German citizens, urban *and* rural, to speak Low German very fluently and even frequently. In rural areas it's possible that many spoke *only* Low German fluently, and Standard German not at all or perhaps haltingly. In addition to northern Germany and the northerly sections of central Germany, this was the case also in northern Poland, especially along the Baltic coastline. It also applied to the eastern edge of the Netherlands and around Cologne. Low German was used by people as they worked and socialized and also when transacting formal business. Then came a period, in the 16th century, when Low German was no longer used in business transactions. In the 17th century it was no longer used for much of anything in urban areas. In the 18th century, it was discontinued even in most rural church services It had by then become a necessity for everyone to know and use Standard High German.

The Low German spoken in the smallest villages and rural areas reflects a *dialect* appropriate usually to a fairly small local area, rather than a comprehensive language. There is no one version of Low German that is known and used throughout northern Germany. There are a number of dialects, each with their own idiosyncracies and histories. A Low German vocabulary for one dialect is contained in Chapter Three and Chapter Five. The glossary in Chapter Three shows the English word, then a phrase to help put it in its proper context, and then the corresponding Low German word or words. In Chapter Five, the glossary shows the Low German word, the corresponding Standard German word and then the English word or words.   There are also hints given as to, in addition to spelling, a preferred syllable emphasis and pronunciation.

In earlier times there was little interest in the correct spelling of Low German words, since it was 99% a spoken language. When a word was used verbally, then it was up to the person's own pronunciation and syntax to properly convey the meaning. Spelling had nothing to do with it. The spoken word was then the only means of personal communication. Literature was the domain of the church, and the church's language was Latin, not German. The spelling used was whatever the writer, usually a Monk, was used to using. Outside of a few exceptions, average people could neither read nor write, including nobility. When reading or writing was necessary, the nobility would hire it done. The noble would request that largely epic poems be written, to extol the strengths and virtues of a particular influential person; usually themselves. Or a requested poem might be liturgical, the content being based on some portion of the bible.

During this pre-literature period, there wasn't any need for anyone to learn to read because there wasn't much to read. If one wanted to tell a story, they did it verbally. This is how many otherwise boring evenings were endured by a family, sitting altogether in one room, in front of a large fireplace. In the winter time, they'd sit there with several layers of clothing. The eldest person was often the official story teller, but other family members would join in, if they knew a story they'd just heard elsewhere. Normally the story would be humorous in nature, or have lies judiciously interspersed to make it humorous. And the stories would be simple in concept, so both young and old would be equally entertained.

The humor aspect in those stories was not like one would expect to hear today. They were not "jokes" or "funny" stories whose primary (sometimes only) humor is contained within the "punch line". Instead, the story meandered around in a long tale that described a series of images, each meant to bring forth a smile, rather than one hard laugh. A story would engender periodic grins throughout and the ending would contain some kind of moral lesson. At the end everone would smile, and the older people nod their head while smiling, remembering similar funny things that had happened to them in their lives. This technique is carried on in the many Döntje, Märchen and humorous stories which exist throughout North Germany. These stories would be laced with words that create their own humorous image. For instance, there are at least 20 words that a storyteller could apply to a person in the story whose intelligence, veracity or character might be of less than "sterling" quality.

lümmel	slüngel	hansworst
knieps	hanswackel	tövel
üüz	orsewöddel	piependeckel
sleef	leegmichel	stinkefritz
döskopp	nixnutz	shietorse
propp	suurnees	snickelfritz
shelm	and the ever popular	dummkopp

A German literary period came along about the 8th Century A.D. More books were printed when block printing was invented. A variety of books were written, but the spelling was erratic. The language used was erratic, based on the author's own preference. The reader had to often guess at the meaning of many words. Nonetheless, those that made the effort to learn to read now had a much wider world of knowledge open up for them. There was no standard language then, much less a standard way of spelling. As books became more readily available, the need for establishing such standards became obvious. Appropriate spelling became of interest to, and a necessity for, the average person who could read. Until that time, it just did not matter.

There are some German words, of ancient Germanic origin, that have been remained nearly unaltered for the past 4,000 years. They were used by the ancient Germanic tribes and are still used by Low German speakers, and sometimes High German speakers, even today. Some of them are even familiar in English, such as 'land', 'arm', 'man', 'me', and 'you'. Perhaps a vowel has changed here or there, but they've basically survived almost intact. For instance, we have English words like 'mouse', 'was' and 'nose', which vary from German by merely a vowel or consonant.

In the Preface chapter it was mentioned that Low German speakers are sometimes confronted by words which they suspect may not be true Low German words. One example of such a possibly suspect word is the English word 'room'. It's Low German cognate is spelled 'ruum', with a trilled 'r', but yet the word is pronounced about the same in both languages. Hearing someone from Germany speaking the Low German word will sound just like it would sound if said by an American Low German speaker. But is it really Low German? This question can possibly be answered if one looks at how Low German words are spelled or research the history of the word. As it happens, 3,000 or more years ago, this word already looked very familiar ... 'rumo'. Over the years, many words with the letters 'u' have undergone a spelling change to 'uu' or 'oo' (the sound didn't change, just the spelling). So the way it is used by the American Low German speaker today is likely a perfectly valid Low German word, in spite of how close it sounds to the English word.

Other similar words can present less obvious conclusions. The words 'sure' and 'sugar' are suspect words. It is peculiar that these are also the only two words in English which begin with 's' but are pronounced as if they began with 'sh'. These are certainly unique words. If you listen to an American Low German using 'sure' or 'sugar' in Low German, their pronunciations may be just 'Low German-ized' pronunciations of the cognate English words. In Low German the words are pronounced something like "shoo-a" and "suk'ka". Of these two words, High German has something sounding similar only for the word 'sugar', that being 'Zucker'. This broad similarity might suggest that 'suker' is a proper Low German word. According to the dictionary, both English 'sure' and 'sugar' have a Middle English and Old French historical derivation. So the jury is out on the word sugar.

What about the other word 'sure'? Latin has a word 'cura', which roughly means 'certainty' and would have been pronounced "sura". Since Latin derives from the same mother language as Low German and High German, this suggests that it was a word in some ancient language. People in many Low German settlements in the midwestern U.S., without contact with each other, have been using the 'shoo-a' term when meaning 'sure'. Why did they all use the term, if the term was not a part of Low German? Why didn't they use the other word 'seker'? The evidence is tantalizing, but inconclusive.

The Low German word which Americans use for yard, which is 'jard' (pronounced jah't) in Low German, may be another suspect. In Low German the 'j' letter has a hard 'g' sound, as the first letter in the word 'joke'. The 'r' is silent. In Germany they more often use the word 'hof' to describe a large yard. Shifting between 'j' and 'y' is common in quite a few languages, so here again we have an English and possibly Low German word sounding almost alike. Is 'jard' merely a Low Germanized version of 'yard'? In Old English, or Anglo Saxon, the cognate word is 'geard'. If you recognize that the initial letter 'g' sounded like a 'j', it might sound exactly like the Low German 'jard'. We know that Old English derived from Low Saxon. We also know that Low German derived from Low Saxon. So the evidence here suggests that 'jard' is a proper Low German word, even though it sounds almost like the English word.

Another possible suspect is the English word farm, which is in Low and High German. In English it is spelled and pronounced (almost) the same as the Low German word. Is the way it is used by Low or High Germans just a corruption of the English word? About 4,000 years ago, in the ancient ancestor of both German and French, the closest word to farm was 'dhermo' (the language had no 'f' letter then). In medieval Latin a similar word was 'firma'. In Old French it was Ferme, meaning an "establishment that supports" or a piece of ground that is "rented". Both could be descriptions of famed land. Middle English therefore had a term that looked very much like 'farm'. Given, as we've said before, that vowels change over time, one can grasp enough comparative significance here to suggest that 'farm' could very likely be a word that has existed a long time, and has become part of both English, Low German and even Standard German.

Then there's the case of "lost" words. If you ask the average American Low German speaker to tell you the Low German word for elbow in their dialect, they'll either say they don't know or give you the English or High German equivalent. Has the Low German for 'elbow' been lost? It's antecedent in the ancient mother language is based on a 4,000 year old word 'el'. Combine 'el' with the word for 'bend' or 'bow', and in English you create the word el-bow. Where you bend your arm is your elbow and when bent, your arm approximates an "L" (el) shape. Such a physical analogy often becomes the original basis for coining a word. The ancient word for bend was bheurgh, which looks very similar to 'börg' or böög'; the Low German word for bend. So one could generate from this analysis a possible Low German word for elbow, such as 'elbörg' or maybe 'elboog'. Something like either of these words may have been used by Low Germans several hundred years ago. Over time, it may have lost out in Germany to the very similar High German word (Ellbogen) and in America to the English word (elbow).

We have been speaking primarily of the 'verbal' language. Reading Low German is, unfortunately, a rare thing for people to do   Although there are books available that are written in some dialect of Low German, they are normally written in a dialect that is foreign to *most* of the Low German speaking areas. It's just too much trouble for readers to distinguish between their own local dialect and the unfamiliar terms and spelling conventions used the dialect as written. And people who write such books suffer from a penchant to use 'loan' words to substitute for "hard to remember" Low German words. Or they succomb to actually 'manufacturing' Low German words by modifying the Standard German word. Those German nationals who speak Low German fairly well tend to incorporate, and understandably so, High German 'loan' words into their own dialect. While speaking or writing, they usually don't even realize that it happened. The High German word comes to mind before they can think of the proper Low German word. The similarity between Standard High German and Low German makes such word substitution just that much easier. And Low German authors tend to confuse matters by being inconsistent in their spelling of words used in the same identical context (sometimes on the same page).

In Chapter Four some of the grammar aspects of Low German are discussed, which deals with the way words are used in writing Low German. The mechanism that history has produced for using a language is referred to its grammar. Rules for the spelling and usage of a language, the *rules,* can be referred to an an orthography. The analysis in this chapter includes a look at the grammatical relationship between Low German, Standard German and English. Vowels and consonants, verbs and nouns, all have evolved in the three languages. As language vocabularies increased, there appeared a need to make a word express other conditions and periods in time. One of the earliest such needs was the need to differentiate between past, present and future. Another was the need to differentiate between yourself and others (creating the need for pronouns) and also the distinction as to number (singular and plural). Over time, the grammar of a language became quite extensive, adding such things as noun declension and verb conjugation. Even the very earliest language were quite complex, often more so than the languages of today. Languages tend to become simpler with time, which is discussed in Chapter Six.

As languages develop, the people who speak them interact with people who speak other languages. If this contact is prolonged they tend to begin borrowing from one another. The manner of pronunciation, as well as spelling, will often come along with any 'borrowed' word. These present to us peculiar anamolies, which don't follow the normally prescribed rules of pronunciation and spelling. This further complicates the grammatical rules for a language, which usually are already complicated enough. This is what makes a language difficult. Low German has remained fairly simple, more so than either English or Standard German.

There are places and events in Germany where Low German is still alive and well. Many rural families used it daily. In spite of all the hindrances and drawbacks, there are areas in Germany where Low German is actually making a comeback, on special occasions. The following map shows, in a broad sense, 3 sections of the area encompassed by Holland, Germany and Poland where Low German is fairly commonly spoken. The map takes some liberties with the boundaries of some of the dialects. If one were to attempt to draw a map that drew lines around each and every dialect and subdialect, one might as well take a picture of a plate of spaghetti. So, for overview purposes, we've narrowed the distinctions between all the dialects down to just three dialect families; the North Saxon, a combination of West and East Phalian, and a combination of East Low German dialects.

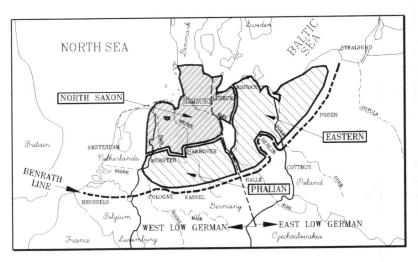

MAP B   THREE FAMILIES OF DIALECTS

The North Saxon dialect, which was mentioned in the Preface, is that family of dialects spoken in central northern Germany. This area is shown with a darker crosshatch. The Phalian family is a term invented here to refer to a combination of the major

Westphalian and Ostphalian dialects. The East German family lies basically in former East Germany and northern Poland, and includes the various East Low German dialects. The cross hatch pattern for the second and third families is the same, because the Phalian and Eastern dialects contain quite a few similar characteristics. There is a blank area in the middle of the map, in which there is still an enclave of a Wendish (Sorbic) dialect. It is of Slavic origin, rather than German.

Chapter Six will look at quite a few dialects, as well as the Standard and Low German languages. These dialects have been handed down to succeeding generations through largely verbal means. Only Standard German has been handed down in written form. The way succeeding generations learn a dialect depends on how their parents spoke it. Each parent, during their lifetime, developed their own way of expressing themselves. They were exposed, by marriage or travel to other languages and dialects, causing their own to undergo changes. In addition, some significant dialectical changes appeared on a community-wide basis. In pre-literature days, the way some locally influential person desired to pronounce words could become the *lingua franca* of that community. And if books and literature came along, people would adopt the manner of speaking contained in them. Since most of the original books were religious in nature, the church had a great influence on language development. And as local officials and royal offices began to keep records in writing, this too influenced the choice of language used in the community.

After a time, all these factors and influences coalesced into a number of different languages and dialects. With regard to dialects, sometimes only a few miles separate significantly different dialects.

Chapter Seven contains a summary of the findings found in the previously mentioned discussion and analysis.

In Chapter Eight the results of the discussion and analysis are discussed in connection with conclusions that can be drawn therefrom.

Indo-Europeans is the name given to an ancient people who are the ancestors of much of the European world. In Germany, scholars use the term Indogermanisch instead of Indo-European. This is because the area over which these ancient people wielded influence, over later years, was primarily the region that later became known as Germany. This includes the Low German people. The Indo-European history is the history of nearly every people and language we find in Europe today. The name Indo-European was chosen by historians because the influence of these people actually reaches all the way from India to western Europe. Its the history of the British, the Greeks, the French, the Poles, the Indians, the Persians, the Norwegian, etc. Each of these many European and near eastern peoples began as a separate group of tribes that split off from the original Indo-Europeans; 4, 000 to 8,000 years ago. And, indirectly, it is the history of a good share of the North Americans.

The settling of Europe will be discussed first, and then the focus will jump back millions of years to pre-history. Then the path will be followed into the future again, through the Indo-Europeans and finally back to Europe.

EUROPEAN HISTORY

The principal movement that brought civilization to most of Europe was the migration of the "barbarians" that descended from the Indo-Europeans. These were, for the most part, the Germanic tribes that lived in the Vistula River delta around the time of Christ. These various illiterate pagan Germanic tribes, as they migrated through central Europe, were almost constantly battling indigenous peoples or the Romans. The battles were bloody, to be sure, and that's how these troublesome people gained their name "barbarians".

Various other tribes were already spread around Europe when the Germanic barbarians came along. Some had been living there for thousands of years before the German tribes moved in; even thousands of years before the last Ice Age. These tribes comprise, all together, the fabric of the European canvas upon which the Indo-Europeans painted their history.

Who were they and where did they come from; these ancestors of ours? And who were *their* ancestors? The Indo-Europeans had ancestors, to be sure, but history gets pretty murky that far back. At some point, far enough back into this dim past, there weren't any people at all. When and where did these people step out of the mist? To tell the story in total, one has to start millions of years ago, although the most relevant part of the story occurs after the last Ice Age.

Before discussing the last Ice Age, the last of which was at its zenith about 50,000 years ago, let's look at the pre-mankind history of Europe. The various aspects of the story, as described, will be covered in very general terms. Each of the many aspects of this story could be, and most have been, the content of entire books.

DINOSAURS

Pre-history is such a large expanse of time that we have to refer to it in terms of million year chunks of geologic time. The Mesozoic *era* contained three *periods* of geologic time, which are referred to as the Triassic Period (245 million to 208 million years ago), the Jurassic Period (208 million to 145 million years ago) and the Cretaceous Period (145 million to 65 million years ago). This is the *era* in which the dinosaur (which means terrible lizard) reigned over the entire earth. At this time, the continents were all still connected, so ambulatory and winged creatures were able to roam far and wide across the globe; even from Europe into the Americas. For example, the "badlands" of Alberta (a province in Canada) and Montana (in the United States) encompass a terrain that is known to be at least as old as the dinosaur itself. In fact, so many dinosaur fossils have been found there that this part of the United States is considered to be the world's most prolific dinosaur fossil hunting ground.

It wasn't until toward the end of this *era* that the tectonic plates which make up the earth's surface began to move apart, thus creating separate continents.

When we think of dinosaurs we have in mind certain huge animals. Actually, their average size was about the size of a pony. Some of them were even the size, and general shape, of chickens. Quite a few had short front legs, looking something like a kangaroo. Only a few were of them were of the ferocious 100 foot long or 30 foot tall variety that interest Hollywood and comic books. Most were gentle plant eating animals, which means the big ones had to consume huge quantities of vegetation each day. This fact may have caused their downfall, about 65 million years ago.

There is some evidence of a huge natural disaster occuring about 65 million years ago. Perhaps, as some suspect, it was a huge meteor impact. Such an impact would, it is thought, create what has been termed a 'nuclear winter'. The ensuing dust from the impact would block out the sun for many months or even a year or two, all across the globe. This could cause much of the vegetation of the world to wither or die.

A small version of such a calamity really did occur as late as 1814; the year without a summer. It seems that a volcano eruption in Indonesia in the previous year produced enough dust in the lower atmosphere to block out most of the sun's rays for over a year.

But the disaster to which we allude here was many times worse. A meteor is said to have hit the earth, and the dust clouds in the atmosphere caused a loss of most of the vegetation. The dust from the crater impact blocked out the sun. Scientists suggest thus was bad enough, and lasted long enough, to cause the dinosair to die off. Scientists have actually found some corroborating evidence of such a calamity. There is a 120 mile wide crater in the waters off the Yucatan in southern Mexico, which dates back the requisite 65 million years. Most experts agree that this impact could have produced a sufficently terrible event Whether it actually caused the dinosaur to disappear is less than certain. This event's timing is right, and its power was adequate. However, some experts say that the dinosaur was already well along the road to extinction by that time. At best, such an impact might merely have finished off the remainder of the dinosaurs.

We do know that, 65 million years ago, the dinosaurs did become extinct. Other animals (especially mammals) and plants still thrived and evolved. Evolution also produced some very early forms of homonid (humanoid - humanlike creatures) in Africa. Between 16 and 17 million years ago, the land masses of Africa and Arabia moved northeast, closing off a large body of water that connected the Mediterranean and the Indian Ocean. This made it possible for creatures to pass from Africa to Europe and Asia. It is this bridge that may have been the path taken by early man into Europe.

EARLY MANKIND

An ancestor of mankind may possibility have appeared many years prior. Almost 4 million years ago, some *possible* ancestors of modern man appeared in Africa. Around 2.3 million years ago, a more advanced homonid creature known as *Homo Habilis* also evolved in Africa. They were very very primitive, certainly not having the brains necessary to discover the usefulness of fire or manufacture tools. Their brain was about half the size of modern man. Of course, if brain size was all that mattered, we'd be saying "sir" to every whale we meet. They were less than 5' tall, weighing under 100 lbs. and just smart enough to make only very rough stone tools. Their communication consisted of very short grunt sounds, whose *pattern* (rather than individual sounds or words) conveyed particular meanings. This is, in fact, how many animals and birds communicate today. The larynx of these creatures was situated too high in the throat for them to develop vowel sounds. Thus, their grunts might have approximated a few consonant type sounds.

About 2 million years ago, the creature we know as *Homo Habilis* evolved into *Homo Erectus*. Although their brain was about the size of a present day 4 year old, they were the first creature to actually use fire. They were about 5½' tall. They had the ability to fashion more advanced stone tools. They migrated out of Africa when one of the Ice Ages came along and dropped the temperature about 20 degrees. This changed lush woodlands into dry savannahs, sending the inhabitants in search of habitable land.

ICE AGES

The Pleistocene geologic period began about a 1 million years ago. It is also known as the Glacial Period, because of the many periodic ice ages that took place. Ice ages played an important part in this part of the story. It is certain that man could not evolve in Europe while sitting under hundreds of feet of ice. They had to wait until an ice age was over. During the past 2 million years, there occurred a number of separate ice ages, or glacial periods. These ice ages vary greatly as to length of time and intensity. The *more* intense glacial periods seem to have occurred about every 500,000 years. At such times the glaciation could last as long as 90,0000 years. During the *least* severe glaciation periods, the glaciation may have lasted only 10,000 years.

In spite of the ice ages coming and going, the world was seeing a civilization just beginning to take shape. During this time, horses and cattle appeared in North America, while elephants and camels appeared in Eurasia and Africa. At this stage in time, the area we now know as Europe was beginning to be settled by creatures that, although not yet humans, were smart enough to form social colonies.

This period of the Stone Age, known as the Mesolithic Period, saw new areas of the world now become suitable for human settlement. It is also known as the Neanderthal Ice Age, because during that period the creatures known as Neanderthals spread throughout much of Europe. He was probably evolved from *Homo Erectus*, but along a path different from *Homo Sapiens*. He was therefore not an ancestor of man, but was an example of evolution in that general direction.

The Neanderthal lived in northern Europe, during the Pleistocene Age. The ice ages had forced this species to spread widely in Asia and Europe. They returned home after each ice age receded. Fire finally became something to use as a tool, rather than merely fear and avoid. It was a gift from lightning and volcano eruptions. They learned to keep some embers alive for a week or so, but they didn't yet know how to ignite their own fire. This species had massive bones, but extremely short limbs. Remains of this Neanderthal man have been unearthed in Spain, France and Belgium.

In 1856-7, a Neanderthal skeletal was discovered in a cave near Düsseldorf, Germany. It was discovered on the banks of the Düssel River, in the Neander Valley ('thal' is the word for valley in Old German). Usually a valley is named for the river that flows through it, which in this case would have resulted in the remains being named Düsselthal man. Instead, the valley had a different name; given it by a late 17th century resident preacher named Neuman. The preacher was a scholar, and preferred to use the Greek translation of his own name, which thus becomes Neander. This is the name given to the valley; and thus the term Neanderthal is forever awarded to the skull remains of an ancient skeleton.

In 1997, DNA testing was done on one of the bones discovered at Düsseldorf. It was determined from this that Neanderthal was a separate branch and not the ancestor of Homo Sapiens. It's possible, however, that both Neanderthal and *Homo Sapiens* share a common ancestor.

So between 500,000 and 250,000 years ago, *Homo Sapiens* evolved from *Homo Erectus* in Africa. Coming from out of southwest Asia and northern Africa, they began moving into Europe, about 100,000 years ago. Homo Sapiens kept evolving and were fully developed as human beings soon after 20,000 B.C

The *Homo Sapien* brain was larger than that of previous homonids, but still a bit smaller than that of today's man. The brain is, after all, just another organ of the body, and is thus capable of growing and changing. The outer cortex portion of the brain of land dwelling animals, including man, has the ability to grow and gain additional intelligence. This includes the portion that coordinates the nerves that move the muscles of the mouth and tongue. The larynx of Homo Sapiens was dropped lower in the throat than before, enabling the chest cavity to become a sounding chamber. This afforded the ability to create a wider variety of sounds, including vowels, than it's ancestors could produce. Now we have the possibility of *language*. However, it wasn't until about 35,000 years ago that a human creature had the ability to actually create communicative speech, as we know it today.

The last Ice Age began happening in Europe about 70,000 years ago. The next ice age, by the way, is due in about 60,000 years, if you want to mark your calendars. The last ice age was relatively severe, covering all of northern Europe with hundreds of feet of ice and snow. The forests in its path disappeared. Animals either died or migrated to warmer climates. It lasted until about 45,000 years ago, when there was a short 10,000 year warming. And then, about 30,000 years ago, the ice began advancing again. About 15,000 years ago, it finally began receding in earnest. In most of Europe, it was finally over about 11,000 years ago.

The Ice and snow that covered much of northern Europe is sometimes referred to as the Scandinavian Ice Sheet, because it spread from and then retreated to Scandinavia. The Ice there had been as tall as a 30 story building, all over this part of Europe, which included Russia and western Siberia. It buried Ireland, most of England, and northern Europe south as far as Berlin, Warsaw and Moscow.

As the last Ice Age receded, many of the creatures who had survived by moving into southern Europe and Asia began to move back into northern Europe. This included the Neanderthals and Homo Sapiens, who co-existed for thousands of years. Here we pick up the trail again of those Indo-European peoples, as their ancestors move back into a Europe that had just squeezed out from under hundreds of feet of ice.

The melting of this huge frozen ice reservoir caused sea levels to rise hundreds of feet. This immediately flooded lowlying areas, especially around the North Sea and the Baltic Sea (which was then just a lake). The water that had been in the ice had earlier been part of the oceans, and now returned to the oceans. To provide the water that turned into the ice, the Ocean water levels had dropped as much as 300 feet. This lower sea level created the previously mentioned land bridges. These land bridges made it possible, in those days, to have walked from the southern tip of South America all the way to England; even to the southern tip of Africa. The return of the water closed off some of the land bridges.

There were land bridges in areas that might surprise us if we saw them today. Between 20,000 to 30,000 years ago, there was a land bridge at the Bering Straits, between

Siberia and Alaska. Even today there's only a 50 mile wide water gap between Siberia and Alaska, which once were connected by land. A lot of European creatures found their way to the Americas across this small gap.

The additional water from melting ice also significantly raised sub-surface water levels, which created the bogs and heaths of northern Europe. When man first re-entered this area, not all the ice was melted yet. However, they say that conditions were not yet, even after all the ice had melted, quite as wet as it is today. It has gotten wetter since then, and areas which are now under water were then still dry land.

All this climate change means that conditons then were much different from conditions today. About 15,000 years ago the western part of America was similar to the plains of Africa. There were elephants and lions roaming the plains. The natives were hunter-gatherers, just as they were elsewhere in the world. These people may have initially come out of Siberia, which could explain the Mongolian features among Alaskan Inuits and Native Americans. Development in eastern America lagged far behind development in Eurasia. Farming didn't get a foothold here until about 500 B.C, much later than in Europe. About 200 B.C. there was Hopewell Culture development in Ohio, but this was still 8,000 years behind what was happening in Eurasia.

About 8,000 years ago, the English Channel area between Europe and England re-flooded and England became an island again. Denmark, Sweden and Germany were, up until then, directly connected by land. This is how the Indo-Europeans got into lower Scandinavia, which will be discussed in the next section.

So now we've traced the geologic evolution of the land and of appearance of mankind in Europe, from pre-history to a mere 8,000 years ago. And we've established that language among these humanoids is now possible. We come now to the appearance of those ancient people which we've called the Indo-Europeans. We will describe them briefly, determine the location of their homeland in eastern Europe, and finally examine their common language.

INDO-EUROPEANS

When the last ice age had fully retreated, every human creature in the world was developmentally equal with all other humans creatures. All were then simple hunter-gatherers. Agriculture was hardly yet invented. They had learned about the taste of cooked meat after finding and eating animals that had been caught in a brush fire. Fire gave them a source of light, to prolong the daylight hours. They used this time to sit around the fire and *socialize* to a much higher degree than before. Sitting in these close groups, they probably soon got tired of simple sign language. Their evolved larynx and expanded sound making capability allowed them to converse more effectively - to create a language. With language, they could plan the next day's hunting in detail. When hunting and food gathering became sparse, they could plan for moving the whole clan on to new hunting grounds. Until they could learn to grow their own food, hunting and gathering continued to be the prime source of food. This kept their population from expanding, since hunting and gathering produces about only one tenth the amount of calories per acre that farming and cattle herding can generate.

About 8,000 years ago (6,000 B.C.) there was a particular grouping of Indo-European tribes that historians say were located somewhere in eastern Europe. In this location, which we'll call their homeland, various tribes had formed loose associations. Historians and Archeologists have long debated as to the exact location of this ancient *homeland*. More about this homeland in the next section.

Some of these Indo-European tribes began to migrate throughout much of Europe; but not yet in significant numbers. Most stayed in this one location, for several thousand years. This was how the settlement of Europe began.

About this same time there began to emerge some intensive agricultural activity, somewhere around Turkey and Syria. This part of Turkey, often called the Fertile Crescent, is where people began to learn how to make land fertile. Here existed a variety of micro-climates, each of which produced a particular local natural crop. These crops could intentionally planted; annually. Up until now, the various tribes had just cleared some land and cultivated whatever grew naturally. These initial farming efforts involved primarily wheat, barley, lentil, pea and flax. Flax and barley grew in the wild. Flax was soon recognized as a valuable source of fiber and oil (linseed).

Farming slowly spread throughout much of eastern Europe. In time it reached the Indo-Europeans who had settled north of Turkey and Syria. About the same time, copper became a useful material for creating tools, utensils and weapons. Some of these tools assisted in farming and thus proved useful in increasing the amount and value of foodstuffs. The agricultural activity was still based largely on sheep herding. The cultivation of wheat and barley was still secondary, because these particular crops were not native to that part of Europe. They had been brought in from the more advanced Fertile Crescent. It is interesting to note that the general culture in Asia, at this time, was still far superior to what was only now developing in Europe.

Agricultural activity permitted existing nomadic tribes to begin settling in larger groups, and staying in one place for a longer time. Stronger associations could develop between tribes, as they now became concerned about their *mutual* support and protection. The density of population could keep increasing, as food soon became more plentiful. This density of people brought with it an increased need for social and economic interaction among peoples and between tribes. Civilization was growing, but a long way from mature.

Between 6,000 B.C. and 3,000 B.C., the Indo-Europeans migrated short distances, in search of new land to farm or hunt. They usually moved as a large group of tribal clusters, but sometimes spun off small clusters into other farflung areas. As they roamed and these splinter groups moved away, they began to spread their Indo-European culture throughout Europe and east Asia. This migration happened over a period of several eons. As to what drove them to begin splintering off is open to speculation. There were probably lots of reasons. It is logical to assume that one large tribe, or subgroup of tribes, would at some point decide to move on to a new location. Not everyone may have agreed. They then would decide to leave the bulk of the other Indo-Europeans tribes behind. But why would *certain* tribes decide to move off into unknown territory. It is reasonable to suspect that some of the tribes were more adventurous. The clans, and small tribes, were the strongest units of social interaction. So entire clans would strike out together. Survival was still the strongest bonding element, so only the stronger ones would be brave enough to split off.

More specifically, some tribes would have, or acquire, certain characteristics which differed from the larger group's norm. These certain tribes recognize this and would begin keeping somewhat to themselves, although still part of the overall group. This smaller group might actually begin to develop their own 'dialect' of this Indo-European language, which would give them another distinct different characteristic. Subgroups might form because they had to jointly face a particular dilemma. Perhaps they were the first to run out of available food. Or perhaps they made some powerful personal enemies. After some time, they might decide that their problems or their different-ness was sufficient cause for seeking their own destiny. Then they would begin to geographically disconnect themselves from the main group.

INDO-EUROPEAN HOMELAND

The Indo-European people are known to have been located somewhere around the Black Sea. This might be considered a pecular location. Paradoxically, the Black Sea is the largest body of lifeless anoxic water in the world. However, the area is a broad plain of temperate climate, and at the time was relatively devoid of other settlement.

Some good hints as to the geographical location of the homeland comes from examining their language. This ancient language was not written, so there are no records of it to be read and studied. The words and their meanings, as used in their language, had to be derived backwards from cognate words found in those daughter languages which survived and later evolved into languages that we do know about. This has kept experts busy for a couple of hundred years. They have backward-constructed a prototypical version of what that ancient language most likely contained; even what it sounded like. For instance, if the older of such daughter languages had a word for beech trees, then one could assume that their homeland had contained beech trees. If other daughter languages also used this word, then one can expect their ancestors lived among beech trees. Other aspects of history then inform us as to which areas, in those ancient times, had contained beech trees. As it turned out, the Indo-Europeans actually did have words for beech, birch and willow trees, all of which grow in various parts of Northern Europe. They did not have words for olive, cyprus or palm trees, which grow in the Mediterranean. There were no beech trees in Asia. These two facts narrows the focus

16

somewhat. In those days beech trees were common from the Ukraine west toward the Black Sea. This narrowed it to north of the Black Sea.

This led many experts to believe that they lived in the Danube Valley (more directly, the Hungarian Plains), just northwest of the Black Sea. Others feel that the Indo-European homeland may have been, at one time, located further east, in the Steppes region of southern Russia. Another possible alternative for the earliest location is a point midway between the Black and Caspian Seas. And also in the northwest corner of China there has been discovered the remains of what is called the 'mummy' people. Their graves have been opened and artifacts found there suggest they were related to the Tocharians, which are said to have been some of the original Indo-Europeans. They may have been in *all* of these places, at one time or another.

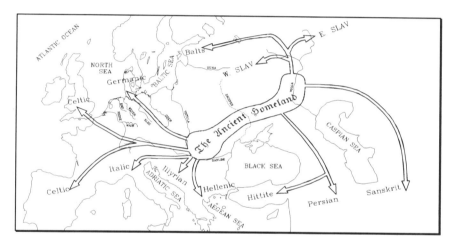

MAP C   THE ANCIENT HOMELAND

With all of these educated guesses, the various possible Indo-European homeland locations become rather widely spaced when placed on a map, as shown by the long polygon in the middle of the map. During the 6,000 B.C. era, they were probably located in the easterly end of this polygon, which we've referred to as the Russian Steppes. During the next 2,000 years, they may have slowly migrated westward. They may have detoured south and spent some time located between the Caspian and Black Seas. By 4,000 B.C. or perhaps 3,500 B.C., they had arrived in the Danube River basin. So somewhere in this polygon they like existed for almost 3,000 years, between 6,000 B.C. and 3,000 B.C.. This was near the end of the Stone Age. They were still a comparatively primitive people. Back in Africa, Egypt had already contained a complex society. China too was much further advanced.

These tribes were not nomadic, in the strictest sense of the word. However, over long periods of time they did move on to new areas. In fact, it may have been a necessity that they move some distance every few decades, to find new farming and hunting ground.

In the case of more warrior oriented tribes, they would also roam far and wide in order to find other tribes to plunder. When they came to a new area, they would usually find it already occupied by someone. They would drive off the less numerous locals or subjugate them as serfs.

This still doesn't respond to the question of where the Indo-Europeans come from originally, and when did they arrive in this general area? One school of thought says they were here all along, since early man came here from Africa. There are some who suggest that man developed in Asia at the same time that another branch was developing in Africa. This school of thought suggests that Europeans came from out of Asia or the Far East, as did the Huns in later years. When one tries to factor in the Tocharians found in northwest China, this option begins to sound worth investigating. However, there remains a gap in our historical journey, between the time Home Sapiens arrived from Africa 35,000 years ago, and the Indo-Europeans were noticed around 6,000 B.C. One can go into a bit more detail of what they were like while living in their ancient homeland.

Russian Steppes

The time period around 6,000 is associated with their likely being in the Russian Steppes region. There is strong historical evidence of a Kurgan culture in the Russian Steppes, along about 4,500 B.C., who may have been the Indo-Europeans.

While in the Russian Steppes area they began improving their farming. They were brought information about better farming practices by people migrating north out of the Fertile Crescent. This increased the food supply, enabling the population to increase. At some point theor increase could outpace the resources available in the area.

Perhaps that is because, while here, the splitting off process began. Some Slavic tribes may have moved northward, covering much of western Russia. Later on, another splinter group may have moved a bit further west and became the Prussians (who were of Baltic origin, not Slavic). Another group may have moved to the East Baltic, becoming the tribe known as the Balts. There they would have encountered an indigent people known as Finns and Ugrians (non Indo-Europeans). It is remarkable that, in the area now known as Lithuania, the people speak a language not much changed since the B.C. era. Their language has retained many original Indo-European language features that other languages have lost.

Danube Valley

They reached the Danube Valley perhaps around 4,000 B.C. to 3,500 B.C. Other people had already been living there since 6,000 B.C., and these became merged in with Indo-Europeans. Their agriculture continued to improve. They raised wheat, barley, pears, beans, etc. They herded cattle, sheep, goats, and swine. They harvested wild apples, cherries, grapes, honey (which they fermented into mead). Most of Europe was, in fact, lightly settled by many small farming cultures. The Indo-European word for 'pigs' is *sui*. Does that sound familiar?

The splitting off process continued From this more recent Danubian homeland location some Celt tribes soon moved westward over the mountains. It is pretty certain that they spread widely throughout Europe much before the German tribes did. In fact, the Celts soon populated most of western Europe and the British Isles, especially Scotland. As they roamed in Spain and France, some decided to stay in an area, which explains why their influence has remained in such a wide geographical range. In Spain, they ran into the indigent Basque people (who are not Indo-European). The Basques speak a language even older than Indo-European. Their words for the first five numbers are bat, bi, hirur, laur, and bortz. As shown later in this chapter, this is much different from any Indo-European language.

Some tribes moved southward and some northward. A few large ones are believed to have moved into Greece, which was already settled by Minoans and Hatti Tribes. Other tribes likely moved into Asia Minor, becoming the language groups that were later called Indo-Iranian and Hittite. Some also moved into southern Europe, becoming the people known as Illyrians and Thracean Phrygian

INDO-EUROPEAN LANGUAGE

The tribes in the ancient homeland had a common language, but that doesn't mean they all spoke exactly the same language. Their vocabulary was about the same, but clans probably varied as to how words were used or pronounced. As they migrated, during these thousands of years the language became complex, largely because verbal communication was the only kind available. There was no written language then, beyond a few symbols scratched onto wood. There are Sanskrit inscriptions from around 1,500 B.C. and Mycenean Greek inscriptions dating from 1,400 B.C. The earliest inscriptions were found in the Hittite area, about 1,700 B.C. The very earliest symbols were mostly for wielding some magic power, rather than general communication.

A powerful verbal language became increasingly important. Their stories and fables, told over the campfires, were important to their society. Such stories comprised their history journal. It's interesting that the German word for history, which is Geschichte, also contains within it the word 'Schicht', which means 'layer'. In the same way, the English word 'history' also contains the word 'story'. A history is thus a verbalization of layers of time, related as a story. In addition to helping keep their history, their verbal communications were needed to fulfill an ever widening range of inter-social requirements, such as coordinating hunts, planning harvests, meting out penalties, describing laws, etc As their society became more complex, their language had to keep pace.

As each tribe or group of tribes split off and roamed into a new area, a variation of the language would likely ensue. This process is how the languages Greek, Latin, Baltic, etc. began. The existing local people they would meet would already have some kind of language, which merged with the Indo-European language, thus generating a new language. Some of them were recorded and have survived until today. It was by studying these languages, especially the roots (central important parts) of their words, that the prototypical Indo-European language we mentioned previously was extrapolated.

Here are some examples of the content and complexity of Indo-European.

It had eight cases for its nouns, adjectives and pronouns (Nominative, Genitive, Accusative, Dative, Vocative, Ablative, Locative and Instrumente).

It had the 3 normal genders and 4 moods. It also had 3 voices (Active, Passive and Middle).

It had 6 tenses, along with 5 long and 5 short vowels. In terms of numbers, it had a single, plural and a dual. It had 10 monophthongs, 6 short diphthongs and 6 long diphthongs (ei, oi, ai, eu, ou, au).

It's 18 consonants were the familiar - b, d, g, j, p, l, m, n, r, plus the more unfamilar - bh, dh, gh, kh, ph, g^w, k^w, þ and ð. The letters 'w' and 'y' could be, depending on usage, either consonants or vowels. The Indo-European language did not have the f and v sounds.

Beginning with a narrow basic vocabulary, by today's standards, they developed a splendid technique for expanding their vocabulary. They took 'root' words, and modified or *flexed* them to represent various conditions, such as past, present and future tenses. Most often, the endings of words would also be modified to represent gender and tense. This technique of *inflection* allowed then to greatly expand a basic vocabulary.

It so happens that all Indo-European major languages, as well as their daughter languages, have this *inflectional* characteristic. Prefixes, suffixes and vowels of *root* words become altered to reflect not only tense, but also gender, case, or number. For example, in English many words are altered to reflect the past tense by just adding an "ed" on the end. This negates the need to create a new word. Those who have studied Greek, German or Latin are familiar with the elaborate conjugation of verbs and declension of nouns, which is thankfully less evident in English, French or Spanish.

Indo-European found its way to other parts of Europe, there spawning other languages. These can be referred to as daughters of the original Indo-European language.

DAUGHTER LANGUAGES

There is a group of daughter languages that came from Indo-European. This group of languages can be divided into two major groupings. The one group is referred to as the *Centum* languages, while the other group is referred to as the *Satem* languages. These two major groups arise from the way the languages within the two groups eventually differed in their pronunciation of what was the first letter of the Indo-European word for "hundred", namely *kmtóm*. The people that used the *Centum* group of languages pronounced the first letter of this word with a strong "k" sound. The *Satem* group pronounced the first letter with an "s" sound. Even today the 'c' letter is sometimes pronounced with an 's' sound and sometimes with a 'k' sound. However, when 'c' is the first letter of a word, it is pronounced with a 'k' sound. English and German speaking people would feel at home with the "k" sound, because their languages belong to this *Centum* group. In the Indo-European era, it was a more significant difference, because it was applied to the letter 'c' as used anywhere in a word.

This leaves the question as to why this overall group of tribes would cleave themselves into these two camps. One might suspect that they might early on have started dividing themselves into two groups, by virtue of having been separated into two living areas. The tribes that spun off while in the Steppes homeland are, for the most part, in the *Satem* group. Those that may have spun off while later living in the Danubian homeland largely fall into the *Centum* group. So it was natural that they would develop some differences. In this case, it was how they pronounced the word *kmtóm*.

The *Cambridge Encyclopedia of Language* by David Crystal gives the following translations for the biblical phrase "Our Father who art in heaven". These languages are daughter languages of Indo-European.

Celtic:

Welsh:	Ein Tad, yr hwn wyt yn y nefoedd.
Irish Gaelic:	Ar n-atheir, ata ar neamh.
Scottish Gaelic:	Ar n-athair a tha air neamh.
Manx:	Ayr ain, t' ayns niau
Cornish:	Agan tas ny, us yn nef.

Germanic:

Standard German:	Unser Vater, der Du bist im Himmel.
Yiddish:	Undzer voter, vos bist im himl.
Dutch:	Onze vader, die in de hemelen zijt.
Norwegian:	Fader vår, du som er i himmelen.
Low German:	Uus Voder, kehr du bis in heven.
Swedish:	Fader vår, som är i himmelen.
Danish:	Vor Fader, du som er i himlene.

21

Italic:

Latin:	Pater noster, qui es in caelis.
French:	notre père, qui es aux cieux.
Spanish:	Padre nuestro, que estas en los cielos.
Portuguese:	Pai nosso, que estas nos cèus.

Balto/Slavic:

Lithuanian:	Teve müsu, kurs esi danquje.
Russian:	Otce nas, suscij na nebesach.
Ukrainian:	Otce nas, sco na nebi.
Polish:	Ojcze nas, ktorys jest w niebiesiech.
Czech:	Otce nas, kteryz jsi v nebesich.

Indo-Iranian

Persian:	Ei pedar-e-mä, ke dar äsmän ast.
Sanskrit:	Bho asmäkham svargastha pitah.
Hindi:	He hamäre svargbasi pita

Other:

Albanian:	Ati ynë që je në qiell
Greek:	Pater 'emön, 'o en tois ouranois.

The 'European' langauges are very similar. However, the further one goes away from Europe, the more differences there are between languages. One reason is that the latter were among the first to break off from Indo-European. This means they are an older people and thus have gone through language evolutionary changes over a much longer time; thus more differences.

The following three charts take a look at all the Indo-European languages. The charts show which languages fit into which daugher language group.

A time frame is attached to the second chart, which provides some indication as to when a certain language developed. However, much of this is based on the historical date when some written evidence of a language was first discovered. We've said previously that a people, and their language, obviously existed quite a while before evidence of their writings were preserved. It took a while just to develop any literary ability. The time frame is thus questionable, but does indicate a possible sequence of relative language development in Europe. Chart One gives an overall picture of the Indo-European langauges, especially with regard to *centum* and *satem* groupings. Chart Two shows the non-Germanic languages, and the general time frames of the various daughter languages.

INDO-EUROPEAN LANGUAGES

HITTITE (3500 B.C.)

CENTUM				SATEM				
HELLENIC	ITALIC	CELTIC	PRIMITIVE GERMANIC	BALTO/ SLAVIC	TOKHARIAN	ALBANIAN	ARMENIAN (2500 B.C.)	INDO-IRANIAN

DAUGHTER LANGUAGES

		(Extinct)	Gothic (Extinct)		(Extinct)			
Greek	Latin*	Old Irish*	High German	Russian		Albanian	Armenian	Sanskrit*
	Italian	Gaelic	Low German	Polish				Iranian
	French	Welsh	Dutch	Lithuanian				Persian
	Spanish	Cornish*	Flemish	Old Prussian*				Kurdish
	Rumanian	Manx*	Frisian	Latvian				Farsi
	Portuguese	Breton	Afrikaans	Sorbian				Hindi
	Catalan	Erse	Yiddish	Slovenia				Punjabi
	Provencal	Scots	Swedish	Czech				Urdu
			Danish	Serbo-Croat				Sindhi
			Norwegian	Macedonian				Singhalese
			Icelandic	Bulgarian				Bengali
			Faeroese	Ukranian				
			English					

(Extinct)

* No longer spoken. Old Prussian died out in 7th Century.

CHART ONE

23

APPROXIMATE TIME OF DEVELOPMENT

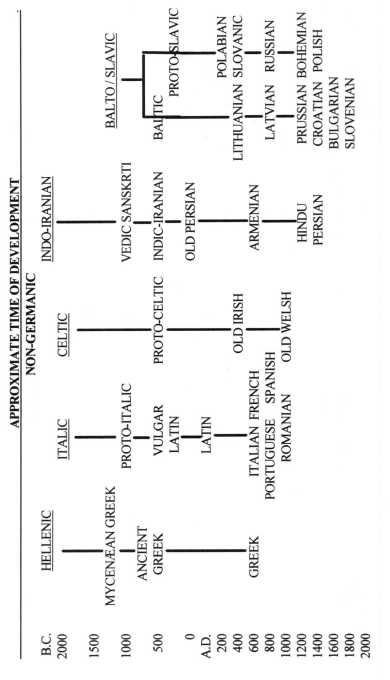

CHART TWO

24

PRIMITIVE GERMANS

Having described the Indo-European people and language, and followed their history as far as their Danubian homeland, we now come to the point in time when they become the Germanic people. After so many eons, the Indo-European tribes that were left happened to be those that later became the Germanic tribes. While in the Danubian homeland, they had developed an efficient ability to roam, using their domesticated horses to drag sleds; possibly even wheeled vehicles. All their goods could easily be moved over the tundra and plains with large sleds. They could now move a long ways, without having to replenish all their goods in the new location. By now they would have many metal tools to help them.

These pre-christian people were obviously pagan, but that doesn't mean they had no gods. They were a polytheistic people, having a variety of gods, including gods of the sky, earth, sun, etc. They sacrificed animals to the gods Thor and Tiwaz. It is from the war god Tiwaz's name that we get the day name Tuesday (Tiwaz-dag). Thor was, among other things, the god to which the farmers prayed for protection against giants. It is from his name that we get the day name Thursday (Thors-dag). They also had a god called Tuisto, whose name later evolved into the designation Teutons.

These early societies were much more organized than one might think. As regards leadership, the original Indo-European language evidently didn't have a word for "king". Their leaders were often elected, usually from among their male nobles or best male warriors. Their society was fairly democratic. Major decisions were made only after input of all tribe members. Perhaps these elected leaders came from one family line, but succession to power was never assured. This eventually developed into what we today would call king type leaders. From time to time they might elect an overall sort of a king, but it appears that not that many people wanted to be a king. They didn't want to have ultimate responsibility over so many free thinking and unruly separate tribes. Whoever was king had to follow some general rules as well. He would have to seek the advice of a Council of Nobles and a General Assembly of Warriors. The king was, however, very much honored by his people. The worst that could happen to a warrior was to survive a battle in which the king had been killed. Such a person was shunned forever, even by his own family. A warrior who died in gallant battle and didn't disgrace himself was thought to go to Valhalla and live for eternity in the company of the war god Wodan. From him we get the day name for Wednesday (Wodans-dag).

To the outsider this land and the people living there were mysterious. When Ceasar was challenged about why the Romans had not conquered these people, his excuse was that the lands of these Primitive Germans contained huge animals that had *special* magic powers. They had Shamans and Priests, to interpret omens and force the public to make the necessary sacrifices to the gods. Though their society was complex, their culture was still quite primitive. They did not create works of art. Their agriculture was improved, but not yet advanced. They would acquire new plowed land each year, requiring additional trees to be felled or annually changing location. Their dead were buried in hollowed out logs, and later cremated. The ashes were buried in urns. And in later times their grave sites (megalithic tombs) were made up of huge boulders walls, with one great boulder across the top. Their society was very patriarchal and certainly politically incorrect. Only the male and the male's relatives had names. They had a word for "in-laws", which referred only to the wife's parents. The wife became such a part of the husband's family that his parents became her parents. Her parents became the "in-laws" to both of them. Wives were not important enough to have names; they were considered as chattel. A widow might be thrown into the grave, alongside the husband, if the husband died in battle. She wasn't expected to want to go on with her life. Murdering a leader or nobleman was considered the worst crime imaginable, while murdering a woman was but a minor infraction.

PRIMITIVE GERMANIC HOMELAND

By about 3,000 B. C. a major portion of the main body of the Indo-Europeans group had begun moving out of the Danube Valley. They struck out northwards, because that was the path of least resistance. There's a chain of small mountains that traverses diagonally in a northwesterly direction from the Danube Valley. The Celts, who left much earlier, had gone through them, heading directly west. It was perhaps too cumbersome for the whole Indo-European group to traverse even these small mountains. They skirted along the north edge of these mountains, temporarily moving into what today we would call southern Poland. They may have encountered Slavs there and decided to move on. A major portion of the group of the Germanic tribes, or the entire group, headed even further north, toward the Baltic. When they reached the Baltic, a few may have stayed behind on the south edge of the Baltic.

We know that the area south of the Baltic soon became populated by Slavic tribes, who were slowly moving westward out of Russia. Historians speak of a Lusatian (Slavic) Culture in Poland and northern Czechoslovakia. This culture is said to have included farming peoples who moved from the Danubian area About 2,500 B.C.

The Indo-European tribes were now far from their ancient homeland. It is at this time that they became what is better termed Germanic tribes. This doesn't mean just "Germans", but rather those who spoke on of the Germanic languages (Swedish, Gothic, etc.) The Germanic tribes were encouraged to continue moving northerly around the western end of the Baltic Sea, into what is now Denmark and Sweden. This is what would later be called southern Scandinavia.

This Scandinavian area is largely a peninsula, which makes it an attractive place to settle, since it can be easily defended. It's soil is usually good farmland and water is readily available. The area just to the north may have been too cold yet, since the Ice Age had been thickest in northern Sweden. Even if not too hospitable yet, this area was at the end of the mountain chain they had skirted, and north of them was either water or a prohibitively cold climate. They had to stop here or turn around and go ... where?.

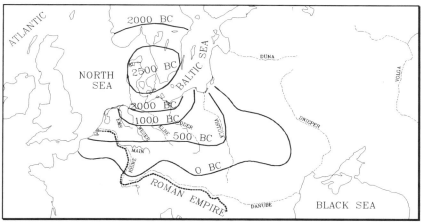

MAP D   THE GERMANIC HOMELAND

The area within the 2,000 B.C. zone on the map is considered to be the homeland of the Germanic tribes in southern Scandinavia. At that time, even this northerly area was not empty. Archaeologists have found traces of human habitiation here as long ago as 10,000 B.C. It seems that artifacts (and human bodies) are well preserved when buried in the bog-land prevalent in this area.

Historians have discovered that, since even as far back as 3,500 B.C., three waves of wandering people had found their way into this part of Scandinavia. The first two probably were not Indo-Europeans, and therefore not Germanic. They likely were nomadic herders and fishermen. As they developed some farming in this wooded area, they learned to create farmland by clearing the trees. They did this by stripping the bark off the trunk, letting the tree die, and then burning them.

The third and last wave of outside people may have been the people we have been tracking. Historians have also referred to them as the 'battle-ax' people. These are believed to have been members of the Germanic branch of our Indo-Europeans. Very likely most of them were members of the tribe later known as the Saxons.

They went on to spend many centuries here, which reaches into and beyond the christian era. In the first few years of the christian era, the Germanic tribes were distributed even beyond this area. They moved southward and eventually ran into the Romans, who were waiting behind a frontier line of defense, called the Roman *Limes*.

This Primitive Germanic branch also developed its own family of daughter languages. These are shown in the chart on the next page.

27

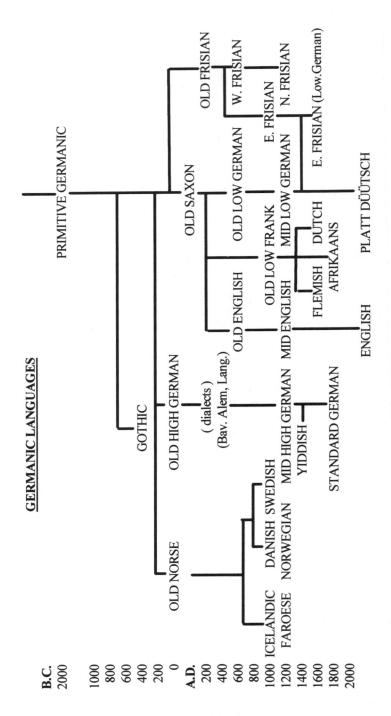

GERMANIC LANGUAGES

B.C.		
2000		PRIMITIVE GERMANIC
1000		
800		
600		
400		GOTHIC
200		
0		OLD HIGH GERMAN · OLD NORSE · OLD SAXON · OLD FRISIAN

A.D.

200
400
600 · ICELANDIC
800 · FAROESE · DANISH · SWEDISH · NORWEGIAN
1000
1200 · MID HIGH GERMAN · (dialects) (Bav. Alem, Lang.) · OLD ENGLISH · OLD LOW GERMAN · OLD LOW FRANK · W. FRISIAN · E. FRISIAN · N. FRISIAN
1400 · YIDDISH · MID ENGLISH · MID LOW GERMAN · FLEMISH · DUTCH · E. FRISIAN (Low.German)
1600 · AFRIKAANS
1800 · STANDARD GERMAN · ENGLISH · PLATT DÜÜTSCH
2000

CHART THREE

28

PRIMITIVE GERMANIC LANGUAGE

While this group of Germanic tribes lived in their Scandinavian homeland, they spoke a Primitive Germanic version of the Indo-European language. This was the result of the First Sound Shift, as explained later. They may well have developed the beginnings of this Primitive Germanic language already while they were in the Danube Valley. This difference may have been somewhat responsible for banding together and moving on.

The daughter languages on the preceding page are broken into rough groups. Basically, these groups are the Norse, the German, the Low German and the Frisian. There are significant differences in these languages when the groups are compared against each other. However, there are also differences within each group. However, here the similarities far outweigh the dissimilarities According to the time line on the left, the chart further suggests that Old Norse, Old Saxon and Old German existed about the same time. This would also support the contention that these languages were, initially, very similar. Normally, Old Saxon is considered to be the same as Old Low German. A differentiation has been made in the chart, to reflect the thought that there might have been an early version and a later version (Old Low German) of the Old Saxon language. Old Frisian was similar to the early version and it was the one carried by the Angles and Saxons into England, where it developed into English.

Now let's look closer at how the various languages shown on the preceding three charts compare, word for word. The first series of 'numeral' words is for the Primitive Germanic language, which spun off from Indo-European, which is shown first.

TABLE ONE
COMPARISON OF NUMERAL WORDS

Primitive Germanic Language

oinos   dwo   treies   kwer   penk

Indo-European Centum Daughter Languages

Germanic:

English	one	two	three	four	five
Std. German	eins	zwei	drei	vier	fünf
Dutch	een	twee	drie	vier	fiiw
Old High.Germ.	ains	twai	Þrija	fidwor	fimf
Gothic	ains	twans	Þreis	fidwôr	fimf
Low German	een	twee	**dree**	veer	fiev
Danish	en	to	tre	fire	fem
Swedish	en	två	tre	fyra	fem
Nord Friis	iin	tweer	träi	fjover	fiiw

When comparing Primitive Germanic with other Germanic languages, one notices the "f" vs. "p" first letter difference in the "five" column. There are some other differences to be noted, but the words for "one", "two" and "five" seem more consistent. When compared to the following non-Germanic languages, we see additional differences.

Non-Germanic:

Latin	unus	duo	tres	quattuor	quinque
French	un	deux	trois	quatre	cinque
Celtic	un	dau	tri	pedwar	pump
Old Irish	aon	dhá	tri	ceithre	cúig
Greek	oine	dyo	treis	tettares	pente

In the "three" column of Table One, the Germanic d or Þ can be compared to the Non-Germanic t. The Þ (th sound) in Gothic later became d in Standard German. The comparison holds fairly well for the following *satem* Non-Germanic languages. Again we show the words for the first five numbers.

Indo European Satem Daughter Languages

Slovak	jeden	dva	tri	styri	pät
Russian	odin	dva	tri	chetyre	pyat
Lithuanian	vienas	dvi	trys	keturi	penki
Persian	yek	do	se	cahar	panj
Hindustani	ek	do	tin	char	panch
Sanskrit	eka	dva	trayas	catvaras	panca

When you compare them to non-Indo European languages, such as the four listed below, you quickly see major differences.

Non Indo European Example

Hungarian	egy	kettö	három	négy	öt
Finnish	yksi	kaksi	kohna	neljä	viisi
Japanese	ichi	ni	san	shi	go
Basque	bat	bi	hirur	laur	bortz

Notice there is no similarity here with any of the Indo-European language. But also notice how similar Finnish is to Hungarian. That's because both are part of the Uralic language family, which also includes other languages of eastern Europe and the northwest Soviet Union. Finnish is the Uralic language of the Magyars.

In the above examples of Indo-European in Table One, the pronunciation and spelling vary, but there are many more similarities than one would expect by happenstance. There are other words in these languages that would represent the same amount of similarity. Compare the English word "foot" with the fairly similar Greek word for foot; "podos". The major difference is the first letter; the ending has been dropped in English. Compare the German word "nacht" with it's Sanskrit equivalent "naktam". Here there is a difference inside the word; "ch" in one, versus "k" in the other. These particular letters represent a very common differentiation amongst languages and dialects.

The following two lists contain quite a few examples of daughter languages, and were taken from Kenneth Katzner's *The Language of the World*. The first list is made up of 4 non-Indo-European languages. Notice how the words for 'mother' all start with 'a'.

Language	month	mother	new	night	nose	three
Basque	hilabethe	ama	berri	gai	südür	hirur
Finnish	kuukausi	aitl	uusi	yò	nenä	kolme
Hungarian	hònap	anya	új	èjszaka	orr	három
Turkish	ay	anne	yeni	gece	burun	üc

The next list contains examples of 22 Indo-European languages. All the words for 'mother' start with 'm'.

Language	month	mother	new	night	nose	three
Welsh	mis	mam	newydd	nos	trwyn	tri
Gaelic	mi	máthair	nua	oiche	sron	tri
French	mois	mere	nouveau	nuit	nez	trois
Spanish	mes	madre	nuevo	noche	nariz	tres
Portuguese	mês	mæ	novo	noite	nariz	tres
Italian	mese	madre	nuovo	notte	naso	tre
Latin	mensis	mater	novus	nox	nasus	tres
Std German	Monat	Mutter	neu	Nacht	Nase	drei
Low German	maand	moder	neet	nacht	nees	dree
Dutch	maand	moeder	nieuw	nacht	neus	drie
Icelandic	mánuður	moðir	nyr	nott	nef	þrir
Swedish	månad	moder	ny	natt	näsa	tre
Polish	miesiac	matka	nowy	noc	nos	trzy
Czech	mesic	matka	novy	noc	nos	tri
Rumania	luna	mama	nou	noapte	nas	trei
Albanian	muaj	nënë	iri	natë	hundë	tri
Greek	men	meter	neos	nux	rhis	treis
Russian	mesyats	mat'	novy	noch'	nos	tri
Lithuanian	menuo	motina	naujas	naktis	nosis	trys
Armenia	amis	mayr	nor	kisher	kit	yerek
Persian	mah	madar	nau	shah	bini	se
Sanskrit	mas	matar	nava	nakt	nas	trayas

A few features stand out. Standard German is the only world language that capitalizes all nouns. There is a strong similarity between Low German, Dutch, Icelandic and Swedish.

FIRST SOUND SHIFT

The Primitive Germanic language developed during 1,500 B.C. and 500 B.C., while the Germanic tribes were enroute to or more likely already living in lower Scandinavia.

The process of change, whereby the Primitive Germanic language became different from the other Indo-European languages, has come to be known as the First Sound Shift. It probably did not occur uniformly amongst, or even within, the individual tribes. This diversity may be what reinforced the many dialects of German. The result of the shift, the creation of a Germanic family of languages, was shown on Chart Three.

Germanic Languages, even when compared against Hellenic and Italic languages, show many similarities within their group. The "f" vs. "p" first letter is an obvious exception, and is the most visible of the differences created by the First Sound Shift. This is how the Germanic family of languages was born. The other Indo-European peoples (and their languages) did not undergo this shift This structural change, a shifting of certain vowels and consonants, happened over a period of several centuries. The nearby Finns did not undergo this shift either. The nearby Finns did take some Germanic loan words into their language. However, these words did not show the affect of the sound shift. Therefore, the transfer of words from Germanic to Finnish must have happened prior to the sound shift.

Primitive Germanic was not a written language, and therefore no remnant of this shifted language can be examined directly today. As with the original Indo-European language, the experts had to work backwards from surviving 'daughter' Germanic languages, to determine the words that made up Primitive German. In this way the probable root words and inflectional endings in the original Primitive Germanic were estimated to a reasonable certainty. Primitive Germanic appears to be less complex than its mother language; Indo-European. It retained only four of the eight cases in Indo-European. It lost the dual number, the middle and passive voice, and the number of tenses also was reduced.

In this sound shift we're talking mainly about changes occurring in the sounds of letters, as opposed to changing the symbol used to denote a sound or letter. If we say that a "p" shifted to an "f", this means that words that had a "p" sound were later pronounced with what we today consider the sound associated with an "f". Changing a symbol or letter of the alphabet doesn't affect pronunciation, and therefore doesn't change how the language is spoken. The Indo European word for fish was "peisk". In Latin it is "piscis" and in Gothic is was "fisks". The sound of the first letter "p" was later weakened to something sounding more like an "f", and subsequently the spelling was changed to conform to this shift in sound. The pronunciation changed first and then later the spelling changed to conform.

At this point let's review a few technical terms, which will be used in succeeding paragraphs. The casual reader may choose to ignore them.

The most dramatic structural change occurred in those consonants which are labeled *stops*. Your breath has to *stop* when these consonants are voiced (spoken). These are sometimes called explosives. This includes the 'plosive' letters b, p, d, t, g, and k. These changes are termed phonemic changes, meaning that they affected a category or class of sound

Additional classes of sound need to be defined. The *spirants* result from pronunciations involving a forced blowing of air through a restricted passage; as when pronouncing 'f' or 's'. This is sometimes also called a *fricative*. These letters include v, f, z, s, ð, w, and Θ.

A *voiced* sound occurs when, during pronunciation, you feel a 'buzz' feeling in the throat. It is called *voiceless* when this feeling is not involved, such as when pronouncing the letter 'p'.

A *dental* letter is one where the tongue has to touch the teeth or just behind the teeth, such as the letter 't'.

A *velar* letter is one where the back of the tongue is placed near or onto the upper palate, such as the letter 'g' in the word good.

A *bilabial* -b- letter is pronounced almost like a 'v'. The lips are, however, held almost together, from which comes the term bilabial (two lips). This particular relationship between 'b' and 'v' is present also when one distinguishes between Low German and Standard German. For example, consider the Low German leev (live) versus the Standard German lebe (live).

In the table on the next page, the process by which consonants were changed is explained. However, they may not be listed in a correct chronological order. The experts do not agree on the exact order of events.

Some tribes that were Indo-European at one point, shifted to speaking Primitive Germanic, while other Indo European tribes did not participate in this shift. However, several of the other tribal languages did go through some similar changes. It is presumed, though not proved, that this shift occurred after the Germanic tribes split off from the other Indo-Europeans. We have not assumed this in the book. In any event, this is generally how the Germanic branch of languages was born.

TABLE TWO
FIRST SOUND SHIFT
INDO EUROPEAN TO PROTO GERMANIC
1500 B.C. to   500 B.C.

Type		From Indo European			To Proto Germanic .	
dental:	*(voice-*	**t** tres (three)	became	*(voice-*	**Þ** (th)	threi
labial:	*less*	**p** pecu (cattle)	became	*less*	**f**	faihu
velar:	*stops)*	**k** canine (dog)	became	*spirants)*	**ch,h**	hund

and then later...

dental:	*(voiced*	**d** decem (ten)	became	*(voiceless*	**t**	taihun
labial:	*unaspirated*	**b** (1) (2)	became	*unaspirated)*	**p**	(3)
velar:	*stops)*	**g** genu (knee)	became	*(stops)*	**k,c, qu** kniu	

and then, much later (4) ...

dental:	*(voiced*	**dh** dhygater (daughter)	became	*(voiced*	**ð, d**	ðachter
labial:	*aspirated*	**bh** bharami (carry)	became	*spirants*	**b, v**	bairan
velar:	*stops)*	**gh** ghostis (guest)	became	*stops)*	**g**	gasts

(1) In the above table there is no example given for the change from *b* to *p*
   because the use of an initial *b* was rare in Indo-European.
(2) The *b* and *g* shift occured mostly in the most southern German area.
   Also , it apears the dentals shifted most widely, the labials less so, and
   the velars perhaps least frequently.
(3) The p, t, and k shift occured more often after vowels than in initial
   position.
(4) In words that were already using d, b and g, they sounds shifted
     instead to p, t and k.

Note that the above largely pertains to the use of letters at the beginning of words.

The table explains why the word *tres* in Latin (beginning with a "t") becomes *three* in English (beginning with a "th"). Why it becomes the word *drei* in German (beginning with a "d") is explained in a subsequent Second Sound Shift discussion.

Such a table can be very confusing, partly because you find the letters t, p, and k in both the "from" column and the "to" column. One has to remember, as mentioned before, these changes did not all happen all at the same time. Certain changes preceded others, although some of it was probably overlapping as well.

34

The original Indo-European didn't have the sounds we now associate with the letters 'f' and 'v'. The ᵬ- letter was, however, very close to the 'v' sound.

Some of the more important vowel shifts were as follows.

initial short o	became	short a,	and
medial short o	became	short u,	and
long o, long a	became	long o,	and
diphthong ei	became	long e, ai	

In all Germanic languages except Gothic, other vowel shifts took place.

long e	became	long a, æ	and
short e	became	i,	and
u	became	o.	and
oi	became	ai	
ou	became	au.	

These shifts may have taken almost a millenium to complete. Some of these shifts appeared on a more widespread basis than others, which once again contributed to the variety within daughter languages.

Primitive Germanic also developed a new verb form, which are verbs ending in a dental (d or t). They are called 'weak' verbs, as opposed to 'strong' verbs where the internal vowel changes but the ending does not. This distinction was discovered by Jakob Grimm, as described below. And in Primitive Germanic there was also lost one of the two ways Indo-Europeans applied stress to a word; loudness and pitch. The pitch, similar to the way the Chinese change tone to reflect meaning, was not carried over into Primitive Germanic.

How were these things discovered? In 1767 a French Jesuit named Coeurdoux pointed out certain resemblances between the European languages and Sanskrit (the ancient language of the Hindus). The fact that there ever was such an Indo-European language was determined by a series of subsequent individual efforts.

The contributions of a series of other researchers will be described.

Sir William Jones

In 1780, Sir William Jones, was a British judge stationed in India. On his own, he strived to learn an ancient and, by then, extinct language called Sanskrit. He wanted to learn Sanskrit because he felt a need to peruse the ancient legal codes written in that language. He soon puzzled over the similarity between Sanskrit and other European languages. He was familiar with quite a few, since he had studied both Greek and Latin in college. He noticed that the Sanskrit word for three, *tri*, was similar to Latin *tres* and Greek *trias* and to English *three*. In an address he gave to the Bengal Asiatic Society in 1786, he reported on his preliminary findings, which caused quite a stir. Jones expanded his comparison to include Celtic, where the word for three is *tri*, and the Germanic tongue, where it is *drei*. Even in an exotic language like Persian, the word for three is *thri*. He was certain that all these languages were related, and he opined further that they probably all came from one original "source" language. He felt that he was studying 'daughter' languages of some 'common' tongue.

Franz Bopp

In 1816 a German, Franz Bopp, did some additional comparative philology and published his own report. It drew further attention to the similarity between Sanskrit, Persian, Greek, Latin and German

Rasmus Rask

In 1818 this whole phenomenon was further studied by a Dane, Rasmus Rask, who concentrated on the similarity between German, Greek, Latin and the Baltic languages. There was, he noted, also an obvious similarity amongst the Romance languages. He proclaimed that German was different; exhibiting some kind of *shift* away from the original Indo European. Looking at the oldest known German, which was Gothic, he find that some similarity still exists between these languages and Gothic, especially between the basic structure of words, but there is a significant 'difference' in the *spelling* of these words. Greek and Latin are old Indo-European languages. There seems to more difference between Gothic and Greek than between Gothic and Latin. This might be because Greek is an older language.

English	Greek	Latin	Gothic
is	estì	est	ist
seven	heptà	septum	sibun
middle	mèsos	mediùs	midjis
senile	hènos	senex	sineigs

Jacob Grimm

Four years later, in 1822, the theories that Rask offered were expanded upon by another German, Jacob Grimm, and to some extent, his brother Wilhelm Grimm. These are the same brothers, by the way, who wrote or popularized the Grimm Fairy Tales. They postulated that the languages in question all derived from one original language, namely Indo European. Prior to this, most people thought that the major languages probably came from Hebrew,

their only proof being that it was the language of the Bible. The follow list
shows similarities among certain languages, which again presents glaring
proof of some connection. The Latin is shown here, to represent the old Indo-
European, as compared against several contemporary Germanic languages.
Notice that the Latin for father and brother, in the last column, differs only in
its first letter from all the other Germanic words for father and brother.

English	German	Dutch	Swedish	Danish	Latin
one	ein	een	en	een	unus
father	Vater	vader	fader	fader	pater
mother	Mutter	moeder	moder	moder	mater
brother	Bruder	broeder	broder	broder	frater
sister	Schwester	zuster	syster	soster	soror

Here we see quite a bit of difference between Latin and the Germanic
languages. He assumed that the differences between Germanic and other
descendant languages was due to some *shift* in the use of certain letters.
Something had to explain the use of 'f' in Germanic and the corresponding use
of 'p' in the other Indo-European languages. The theory surrounding this shift
has also become known as Grimm's Law. For some reason, the name of the
person who first postulated about this shift theory, Rasmus Rask, has been lost
to history.

Karl Verner

In 1875, another Dane, Karl Verner, delved further into several exceptions or
inconsistencies in Grimm's theories and found a probable explanation. This
inconsistency is reflected in the previous First Sound Shift table, in which the
first of the 3 sections (p,t,k changing to f, þ-th,ch,h) did *sometimes* instead
change to b,d-ð,g. Verner showed when and why. He showed that when the
stress was not on a consonant's preceding vowel, then a voiceless spirant
became voiced in Primitive Germanic. This explained why the 'th' sound
sometimes changed to 'Þ' (voiceless) and sometimes to 'ð' (voiced). This
revision to Grimm's Law, concerning a *stress shift*, is known as Verner's Law.
Later on, in some West Germanic languages, the 'ð' changed to 'd', but not in
Old English or Old Saxon. For example, the word for "become" was weorðan
in Old English but was 'werden' in High German. In Low German, it often
became a silent letter (đ) or it kept the 'th' sound.

In the old Indo-European language, words could have the stress put on any
syllable. There was no consistency at all. But the Germanic languages have
their stress on the first syllable, except for words with prefixes. Verner showed
that this *Stress Shift* took place some time <u>after</u> the First Sound Shift.. The
stress shift finding may not sound like much, but it was about as important as
all the findings of Grimm. This shift had more affect on how words were

pronounced in the Germanic languages than did the First Sound Shift. For instance, the word lovable has the stress on the first syllable. The root word is love. With a prefix, such as in the word beloved, the stress is not on the first syllable, but on the first syllable of the root portion.

Verner also determined that, in some cases, 's' later shifted to a 'z'. The letter 'z' subsequently went on to become an 'r' medially in West Germanic. And 'th' evolved into 'd'. Some of this depended on whether the letter appeared first in the word, or in a subsequent syllable.

During the pre-christian era, the tribes that spoke this Primitive Germanic language still comprised a fairly tight grouping southern Scandinavia. After the christian era, they spread out into more diverse tribes, each with it own dialect of the Primitive Germanic language. Over time, as each tribe wandered and expanded into new territories, they encountered neighboring tribes, such as the Celts, Gauls and Finns. They also spread their own version of this Primitive Germanic language over a large part of Northern Europe.

The next section briefly describes some of the characteristics of these wandering tribes, who were on the verge of settling throughout Europe.

TRIBAL GERMANS

At the end of the 1st century A.D., Tacitus described a land lying somewhere in the north, by the name *Germania*. It was populated by *Germans*. He said the were located in the area between the Danube, Rhine and Vistula Rivers. 150 years previously Julius Caesar had described these tribes as *barbarians*. In his chronicle "The Gallic Wars", Caesar further described them as a primitive semi-nomadic people living off of their livestock; doing little hunting or fishing. According to him, the people understood agriculture, but didn't have much enthusiasm for it. They lived in round shacks. In time their very primitive housing initially gave way to rectangular houses, which combined the hearth, sleeping area, and livestock holding area - all under one gable roof. This housing has become a trademark of German rural farmhouses.

These tribes settled in groups, but remained somewhat separated clan by clan. A clan might be made up of a large extended family or family group, tied together by a common ancestry. Socially, the well-being and honor of each member was the collective responsibility of the clan, not just the individual member.

Beginning in about the 5th century B.C., the first of these primitive Germanic tribes began expanding southward from their Low Scandinavian homes. The Goths were probably the first to move. The complete migration of these tribes took centuries; up to perhaps the 8th century A.D. The reasons for this migration probably came from overpopulation and the aggressive influx of Slavs from the east.

The geographical distribution of these tribes is shown on the following map.

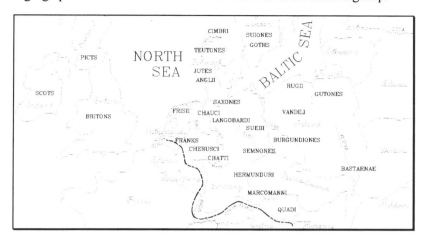

MAP E   PRE-CHRISTIAN ERA TRIBES

The map shows the Roman *Limes*, the heavy dashed line which was the Roman defensive frontier along the Rhine and Danube. Now the history of the Holy Roman Empire becomes entwined with the history of Germany. As they clashed over the centuries, it is quite likely that neither the Germans or the Romans knew that their respective languages stemmed from the same source.

During this tribal migration period, Rome ruled much of the known world. They had already founded a great republic by 510 B.C. The Romans began expanding in all directions, one of them being north toward the Germans; about 250 B.C. As the Germanic tribes moved south and eastward, they encountered and pushed out some Celt tribes. To their East were Baltic tribes, with whom they had little contact.

There was, in the succeeding centuries, a good deal of bloodshed between the Germans and the Romans. The basic weaponry of the Germans was poor, although the Romans admitted that the Germans fought fiercely and courageously. The Germans wore neither helmets or breastplates; often fighting naked from the waist up. Their wooden shield splintered easily, when struck by heavy Romans swords. However, the battle tactics of the Germans was superior to that of the Romans. They fought on foot, using a lance, although it sometimes proved unwieldy in close combat. They would rush at the enemy in a triangular flying wedge. The front row of troops would yell and carry huge spears, mostly to scare the enemy. It didn't take long for them to open up a hole in the Roman front line. The Romans later adopted some of these 'barbaric' fighting tactics.

The relationship between Romans and Germans was complex. One time they'd be fighting and the next time the Romans were paying some of them to fight other

39

Germans. From the 3rd century on, many soldiers from German tribes actually enlisted in the Roman army, some ascending to very high rank.

And all the while they engaged in active trading. Roman traders from the Mediterranean area traveled throughout the Germanic area, conducting profitable business with these *barbarians*. The Germans traded amber and furs for Roman olive oil and wine. The Germans had learned to make a fermented drink they called 'aluth'. This word has the same root as the English word 'hallucination', for obvious reasons. When the Roman traders were in German territory and wished to partake of this German drink, they would yell for ' biber', which became their favorite word for drink (thus the basis for the English word 'imbibe'). The Germans subsequently adopted a variation of this Roman word, which later became our word 'beer'.

Amongst the earliest migrating tribes were the Frisians. The Frisians moved slowly south and west, along the edge of the North Sea. Their long association with Norse tribes, up to this time, accounts for the similarities between Frisian (a West Germanic language) and Old Norse (a North Germanic language). However, Old Saxon speakers lived in the same area, and can be said to have about the same amount of similarity to Old Norse as Frisian does.

As they began expanding, the Germanic tribes now formed linguistically and geographically into roughtly three different major groups. We can refer to them as North Germanic, East Germanic and West Germanic. The West Germanic tribes include those that later contributed to the evolution of the Old Saxon, and therefore the Low German language. The others produced the High German and Norse languages.

Each tribe that made up each of the three major group areas will be described, along with a brief description of when and where they migrated before and after the beginning of the christian era.

NORTH GERMANIC

These tribes originated in, and largely remained in, lower Scandinavia. This language subgroup was located where the original Germanic tribes spent many centuries. They shared a common Nordic language in the beginning, known as Old Norse.

> Norse: The Norse tribe, appearing in about the 4th century B.C., remained in what is now known as Denmark and Norway. This area had been vacated by the Anglii and other tribes as they moved south. Inscriptions in Runic in the Old Norse language date back to the 4th and 5th centuries A.D. The term Rune, in the Euro-European language (runo), meant 'mystery' or 'secret'. Runes were used primarily in Scandinavia. In the Germanic and Celtic languages, it meant 'magic'. Common people then thought that just being able to *write* with symbols was some form of magic. In the 8th century, Danes and Norwegians became known as Vikings, basically pirates and explorers. The

Norwegian Vikings roamed the North Atlantic and at one point discovered Iceland and Danish Vikings discovered the Faroese Islands

The Faeroe Islands (a self-governing part of Denmark) are located in the North Atlantic about 250 miles north of Scotland. Faroese is closely related to Danish. The Faeroese and Icelandic languages are both examples of archaic German, and are more similar to each other than to the rest of the North Germanic subgroup. Faeroese uses the ð letter, but not the þ letter.

Icelandic still uses both of these old letters. Iceland was colonized by settlers from Norway about 874 A.D. Icelandic and Norwegian were similar until the 13th century. At this time Danish had already broken off from Old Norse. The former included Old Norwegian, Old Icelandic and Faeroese. The latter included Old Swedish and Old Danish. A modern Scandinavian can often understand both Danish and Norwegian (since they were united for several centuries).

The Norse Vikings made repeated invasions into Britain, Ireland and Scotland. In the 9th century the Vikings attacked the Frisians and plundered as far east as Hamburg, which they looted and all but destroyed. In the 10th century they attacked and settled the French coast, becoming what we know as the Normans. King Canute, a Dane, led the Norman Invasion of 1066 and became the ruler of England.

The daughter languages that came out of this northern area included Swedish, Danish, Norwegian, Faeroese and Icelandic. The following list makes a comparison of the North Germanic languages (Danish and Swedish) today, with the West Germanic English, Standard German and Low German. The first letters in these words are almost all the same. Even the vowels are often the same. These are sister languages for sure.

ENGLISH	DANISH	SWEDISH	STD GERMAN	LOW GERMAN
earth	jord	jord	Erde	eer
field	mark	fält	Feld	feld
frost	frost	frost	Frost	frost
grass	graes	gräs	Gras	gras
hail	hagl	hagel	Hagel	hagel
heath	hede	hed	Heide	heide
moon	maane	måne	Mond	maand
sand	sand	sand	Sand	sand
summer	sommer	sommar	Sommer	sommer
star	stjerne	stärna	Stern	steern
water	vand	vatten	Wasser	woter
world	verden	värld	Welt	werlt
wind	vind	vind	Wind	wind
winter	vinter	vinter	Winter	winter

EAST GERMANIC

The East Germanic tribes were originally located close to the North Germanic tribes, which probably explains many similarities between Old Norse and Gothic. Then the Goths began to migrate. The only East Germanic language about which very much is known today is Gothic, which is considered the oldest Germanic language. It contains many archaic Germanic features, such as certain word endings and the letter þ, not found in today's Standard German; as illustrated below.

ENGLISH	STANDARD GERMAN	GOTHIC
lift	heben	hafjan
hell	Hölle	halja
herdsman	Hirt	haideis
to call	heißen	haitan
hard	hart	hardus
heath	Heide	heiþi

Gothic was not a written language until Bishop Wulfilas created a Bible translation in about 350 A.D. In order to do that, he first had to invent an alphabet. It was based on the Greek uncial alphabet, to which he added some Latin and runic letters (eth and thorn). This is why both Gothic and Greek had that unusual way of using the 'v' letter in place of the 'u' letter (as seen in the lettering on many old building facades up until the 17th century).

There is so much similarity between the Gothic and Old Norse, that some experts suggest they should not be differentiated. However, after the Goths began migrating, crossing over the Baltic beginning about 500 B.C., these two languages did develop more differences. The following table shows some remaining similarities. It seems that Old Norse has a strong similarity to Low German as well.

ENGLISH	OLD NORSE	GOTHIC	LOW GERMAN
eye	auga	augo	oog
other	annarr	anþar	anner
out	ût	ût	ut
good	goðr	gôda	good
I	ek	ik	ik
no	nei	ni	ne

After they had crossed the Baltic the Goths became widely spread out. They joined up with the Burgundians and their cousins, the Vandals. Their joint migrations, in the years just before the christian era, are shown on the following map.

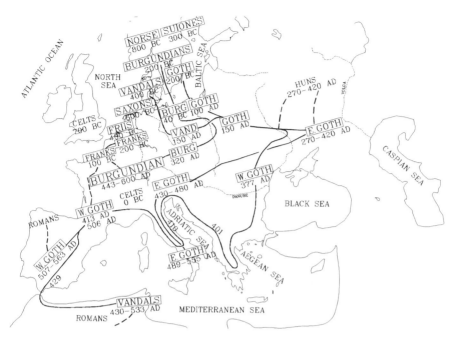

MAP F   PRE-CHRISTIAN ERA TRIBAL MIGRATION

The migration of the Goths had the greatest influence on the history of the Germans.
The paths shown on the map are also described in the following text.

> Goths: The Goths had first settled in the south central area of what is now
> known as Sweden and the island of Gotland. In the 1st century A.D. they
> moved south, to the south shore of the Baltic. By the early 2nd century they
> were noted by Greek and Roman historians near the mouth of the Vistula.
> Here they pushed out the local tribe, the Vandals, who later joined them again..
>
> The people left behind in Sweden were known as Suiones; considered the
> forbearers of the Swedes. Those that stayed behind in Sweden developed a
> Nordic tongue. The Swedes developed extensive trade along the Baltic, and
> under the tribal name Rus, they moved eastward to the far end of the Baltic
> Sea. Ruric, their pirate chief, there established the Republic of Novgorod in
> 862, which proved to be the founding of the Russian Empire.
>
> By the end of the 2nd century the Goths moved from the lower Vistula into
> southern Russia. They seemed to be heading back toward the ancient
> homeland of the Indo-Europeans, their ancestors. As they entered the
> Balkans, they were exposed to christianity for the first time. Bishop Wulfilas
> (311-383) converted the Visigoths to his form of Catholicism, called Aryanism
> (Orthodox Christianity). It differed from Roman Catholicism in the following

43

manner. Bishop Arius believed in the eastern orthodox view that Jesus was *like* God, but was *not* God. The Council of Nicea, in 325, was supposed to rectify this difference, but it didn't. Aryanism spread among the German tribes, except for the Franks, who had already met the Romans and tied themselved to Roman Catholicism.

The Goths (both the pagan and christian Goths) encountered the Huns in 375, and were defeated by them. In 370 the Huns had moved westward out of Tartari, on their first invasion trek into western Europe. They had been driven out of northern China. Although the Huns defeated the Goths, they were so impressed by the Goths that the leader of the Huns took a Gothic name; Attila.

About this time the Goths split into the Visigoths (western Goths), and some of them broke off as the Ostrogoths (eastern Goths). Both names have become common in European history.

In 378 the Visigoths moved south into the Roman Empire. The Emporor Valens didn't take them seriously, simply ordering the Goths to disarm. In the meantime, however, the Visigoths decided to fight instead and defeated the Romans at Adrianople; killing Valens. In 402 the Roman General Stilicho (who himself was a Vandal) was now worried and recalled troops from the Roman frontier to help defend Italy against the Visigoths. Stilicho was one of those barbarians who had joined the Roman army, and rose to the rank of general.

The Visigoths then invaded Greece, and following that they sacked Rome, in 410 B.C. This caused Rome to worry even more and decide to withdraw its legions from Britain. This laid the British Isles open to the Anglo Saxon invasion, which had a huge affect on history. In 507 the Franks under Clovis defeated the Visigoths, and drove them into Spain (southern Gaul). In 563 the Romans smashed the remainder of the Visigoths, bringing all Italy under the rule of the eastern Roman Emporer Justinian. These Goths then either disappeared or they eventually became either Italian or Spanish.

By the early 5th century, the other Goths (Ostrogoths) had moved into the Crimea and Ukraine, where they were defeated again by the Huns. Soon after, when Attila the Hun died, his son Irnak took the Huns and marched them back to Asia.

In 489, Theodoric, the king of the Ostrogoths, invaded Italy (with the backing of the Emporer of the easterly Roman Empire). In 493 he slayed Odoacer and assumed power in Italy. The Ostrogoths were initially victorious but were eventually defeated by the Romans. However, they resisted the Romans valiantly enough to be given the privilege of ruling their own area. But in time the Gothic language was lost to history, having been supplanted by Latin. The last known trace of a Gothic tongue was recorded in the Crimea in the 16th century.

Vandals: About 400 B.C. this tribe moved from Norway, through Jutland (Denmark), to near the Oder River. By the 1st century B.C., the Vandals were located between the Vistula and the Oder. By the 3rd century they occupied what would later be called Prussia. Beginning in 409, they accompanied the Goths as they moved south to engage the Romans. On the way there they invaded Gaul and formed an empire on the ruins of Carthage in 435. The Franks attacked and pushed them into Spain, and they settled down in Andalusia. In 429 some of them crossed the Strait of Gibralter from Spain into Roman North Africa. After creating a strong Vandal empire there, they attacked and sacked Rome (455) but were eventually defeated by the Romans in 534 B.C. Here they accepted Roman suzerainty.

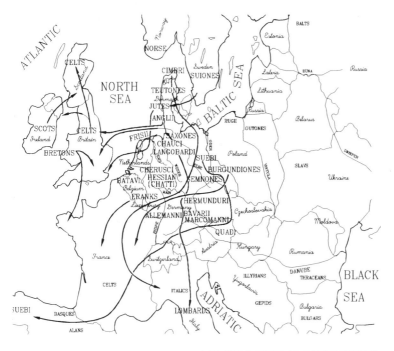

MAP G   A.D. ERA TRIBAL MIGRATION

WEST GERMANIC

This map doesn't show the movement of the Goths, Burgundians and Vandals, because that was covered earlier. This map shows some of the subsequent movement of the other tribes. There was some overlap in the movement of these tribes and the earlier

45

tribes, but that introduces an inordinate amount of complexity in the telling. With regard to Low German history, the tribes to watch are those that remain in the north German area.

The West Germanic tribes also expanded southward from the original Scandinavian homeland, as had the Goths and Vandals.. They too were forced to migrate by climate change and by increased population. The latter reason also required them to become more warlike, so as to conquer new lands.

The West Germanic tribes can be divided into the Weser-Rhine group, the Elbe group and the North Sea group. Some of the more important tribes involved in these groupings are the Cheruscans, Batavians, Chatti, Franks, Chauci, Basternae, Skiri, Frisians, Saxons, Suevi, Semnoni, Hermunduri, Langobardi (Long Beards, who became the Lombards), Marcomanni, Quadi, etc. Each tribe will be discussed, within the three groups mentioned. First is the Rhine-Weser group.

Rhine-Weser

Tacitus and Pliny made mention of a group of tribes in the Weser River and Rhine River area, along about 100 A.D. Among them were the Franks, Hessians, Suebi, Burgundians, Cherusci and Semnones. The Franks went on to develop a huge empire. They essentially later on became the French and indirectly became the Dutch and Flemish. The Hessians later became absorbed into the Frankish Empire. The geographically close grouping of these tribes may go a long way toward explaining the close relationship between the Old Franconian, Westphalian and Ostphalian dialects.

Their migration pattern is described now in more detail.

Franks: Ancestors of this tribe had been encountered by the Romans as early as 55 B.C. The Romans were then allied with a German tribe called the Batavians (in Belgium), who lived just south of the Frisians. In 9 A.D., the Roman General Varus and three of his Legions were defeated by an alliance of Germanic tribes (including Franks) in the Teutoburg Forest (near Detmold). This enabled the Germans, under Arminius, a chief of the Cherusci, to keep the Romans from taking control of this area. Historians have given Arminus the name "Herman the German".

The Franks now had a base, from which to expand throughout Gaul and most of Germany. In the 3rd century a number of small tribes on the lower Rhine formed a loose sort of confederation, under the collective name of the Franks (the free ones). The Romans permitted these Frankish tribes to also settle in Belgium. The Frankish tribes included the Salians (by the sea), Ripaurians (by the river) and also the Hessians. By the 4th century the Salians took control of the Brabant area in lower Holland. The Ripaurians controlled the Cologne area. The other Franks proceeded to build the empire, first by invading Gaul (France).

The Roman Empire was just beginning to weaken in France and the Franks moved in to fill the vacuum. Under King Chlodwig, they became a strong political entity in the 5th century A.D. They conquered the Burgundians, Thuringians and Bavarians. The Frankish King Merovich built a powerful Merovingian Empire in the 5th century. His grandson was the famous Clovis, who became king of the Franks in 481. He succeeded his father Childeric I. Clovis defeated the Alemanni and drove the Romans completely out of France in 486. Clovis, a pagan, took an Aryan catholic wife (a Burgundian princess named Clotilde) and became a christian in 496. Clovis, to spite the Burgundians, adopted Roman Catholicism and required that everyone in his kingdom be baptized in the same faith.

Clovis, grandson of King Merovich, died in 511. His four sons were able to defeat the Burgundians but mostly they.fought amongst themselves This greatly weakened the empire, for a long time. Charles Martel (illegitimate son of Peppin II) became king in 714, and achieved a few victories. His son, Charlemagne (Charles the Great), became king of the Lombards in 774. He brought back the empire to its earlier greatness, and beyond. He had a profound influence on Western Europe in the 8th century. In 784 Charlemagne subdued the Frisians on the North Sea coast. In 779 he completed his control over the Saxons on his east flank. He was crowned by Pope Leo III as Holy Roman Emporer on Christmas day 800 A.D. He ordered a mass baptism of *all* his nobility. When he died in 814, his son Louis the Pious crowned himself Emporer. When Louis died, in 840, the Carolingian Empire was divided among his three sons - Lothar, Charles the Bald and Louis the German. The Treaty of Verdun, in 843, re-divided the empire among his three sons. The Franks would, for many centuries, controll much of Germany.

The westerly Franks spoke a French that was influenced by Low Franconian. The westerly Franks gave us the Old Low Franconian language, which later became the basis of Old Dutch. Meanwhile, the central Franks spoke a dialect that was influenced by High German. And the easterly Franks provided the Middle German dialects which later became the basis for Standard German.

Hessians: They were located between the Elbe and the Rhine Rivers. The Chatti tribe descended from them and played an important role in the war against the Romans. Domitian campaigned against them in 83 and eventually the Hessians too were swallowed up by the Franks.

Cherusci: This tribe became extinct by the 2nd century, probably absorbed by the Franks or possibly the Alemannians.

Semnone: This small tribe became extinct by the 2nd century. They were probably absorbed by the Suebi.

Suebi: In the early 2nd century B.C. this tribe, along with the Marcomanni and Quadi, migrated southwest. They encountered the Romans in southern Germany, and were defeated by them. They were then forced to retreat into Bohemia. In about the 3rd century A.D. they regrouped (with the Alemanni) and made peace with the Romans. The Romans allowed them to move into the Neckar Valley. In the 4th century, they moved further west, into the Alsace, as well as north to Trier and south into Switzerland. In the 6th century they settled in northern Portugal and northwest Spain, where they settled alongside the Visigoths.

Burgundian: They followed the path of the Goths, migrating from the Swedish island of Bornholm, to south of the Baltic Sea (between the Vistula and the Oder) in about 100 B.C. In the 3rd century they were forced westward from the Vistula River to what is now known as Brandenburg. Then they moved along the Main River to Thuringia, on their way to Gaul. They encountered the Alemanni on the left bank of the Rhine, from whom they retreated into the French region of Burgundy. In 443 they reached Lake Geneva and established the Kingdom of Burgundy, on the Saône and the Rhône Rivers. In 534 they encountered, and were conquered by, the Franks.

Elbe

This name refers to a group of tribes along the Elbe River, which - according to the Roman Tacitus - included the tribes named Langobardi, Semnones, Suebi, Hermunduri, Quadi and later the Alemanni and Bavarians (earlier known as Marcomanni).

In various ways and at various times, they migrated south into southern Germany and northern Italy. Of course, here they ran into the Roman defences. Caesar Augustus (63 B.C. - 14 A.D) had established defensive positions all along the frontier. Caesar Domitian (51 A.D. - 96 A.D.) had a wall built to keep the barbarians out, which was earlier referred to as the Roman *Limes*.

The *Limes* was a fortified 9 foot high Roman defense wall of forts and towers stretching over 300 miles, between Koblenz and Regensburg. It ran roughly parallel to the east bank of the Rhine and along the Danube. It stood for about 2 centuries, until the Alemanni overran it. The Romans abandoned the wall in the 3rd century and retreated back to the south. After stopping to resolve local conflicts back home in Rome, the Romans returned to the north frontier in 357 A.D. Here they met up with and drove the barbarians back across the *Limes*.

Quadi:. In the 8th century, historians found evidence of this tribe in Hungary, but soon it became extinct or absorbed

Langobardi: This tribe had migrated from their original home in southern Sweden. By the 1st century A.D. they were noted by Roman and Greek reports to be located along the lower Elbe, in the general vicinity of the Saxons and other North Sea tribes. They moved through Brandenburg and over to between the Elbe and the Weser. Then on to Austria, Bohemia, Hungary and northern Italy, where they became neighbors of the Bavarians and Allemanians. There they were converted to christianity by the Goths.

In 568 they crossed the Alps, and in concert with 20,000 Saxons, they invaded north and central Italy. They defeated the Gepidae and established a kingdom. Their name then changed in the history books to the Lombards. Between 568 and 572, they drove the Romans out of northern Italy. In 774 the Lombards were conquered by Charlemagne, who made himself their king. Eventually they were taken over by the Franks, leaving only their name, in the Lombardy province of Italy.

Hermunduri: They lived on the east side of the Elbe, mixed in with other Elbe German tribes. For awhile they moved into Bohemia, where they competed with the Marcomanni for control. They were almost defeated, but more reinforcements came from the north. In the process they survived and, in the 5th century, changed their name to the Thuringians. Subsequently they expanded north to the Harz Mountains. In the 6th century northern Thuringia fell to the Saxons and Franks, and the survivors were integrated with the Franks.

Bavarii: They originally came from between the Elbe and the Oder. This 5th Century group of tribes was initially known as Marcomanni. Or some say they were descended from the Marcomanni. It is also said they were a subgroup of the Suebi. Whoever they were, they migrated into Bohemia. In the 4th century their name changed to Bavarii, which means "the men from Bohemia". While they did battle with the Romans, they were also under attack by Slavs, Alemanni and Franks. They were forced to retreat into present day Bavaria and Austria. By the 8th century they were fully assimilated by the Frankish Empire.

Alemanni: This tribe's area of influence was located along the Upper Rhine and in the Alsace. It was first noticed there in about the 3rd century A.D., south of the Main River. The Frankish King Clovis conquered them in 456 and pushed them out of the Alsace. By the 8th century they too were totally assimilated by the Franks.

The northern Alemanni became the Alsatians. Some of the Alemanni moved into the Alsace, where they were repulsed by the Franks, and then they moved south into present day Switzerland. Some of the southern Bavarians expanded into Austria. Those members of this Elbe group that remained in the north moved into the Thuringia area, and subsequently became absorbed by the Franks.

North Sea

This name refers to the tribes that settled near the North Sea. They were so named by the Roman historian Tacitus, who also referred to them as the people "of the God Ingwaz". He said they existed here about 100 A.D., worshiping Nerthus (Mother Earth). The individual tribes usually assigned to this area include what we have come to call the Saxons, Anglii, Cimbri, Jutes, Chauci, Teutoni and Frisii. It is basically the dialects of these tribes, most directly the language of the Saxon, that developed later into the English and Low German languages.

Cimbri and Teutones: The Teutones and Cimbri left the northern Jutland area about 110 B.C. Following the ancient amber route to Bohemia, they were defeated by the Celts. They headed for the Danube (about 114 B.C.), near to the ancient homeland of the Indo-Europeans. Later in the 2nd century B.C. they swept southward to the northern frontier of the Roman world, where they were defeated and soon disappeared.

Saxons: This was a distinct tribe even before the christian era. It was mentioned as early as the 1st century A.D. The Greek geographer Ptolemy originally located them near the North Sea, from just south of the Elbe north to just below the base of the Jutland peninsula. Later their location was associated with the lower Weser and Elbe valleys and the adjacent coastlands. They later spread out from their home (approximately today's Holstein) to the south as far as Hannover and west to Oldenburg. They became land hungry and warlike, because of continued harassment by the Slavs on their east border. This forced them to expand westward.

Perhaps due to their warlike nature, they were named after their favorite short sword, called a Sahs (or Seax). This also became the basis of the German word for knife (Messer) - which literally means "my sahs". This actually makes sense, if you consider a knife as just a short sword. For comparison, we note that the Franks, on the other hand, used a hand axe as their favorite weapon. The Franks sometimes threw their axe at their opponent, but actually the small Saxon knife was more useful for close-in fighting.

The Saxons continued moving west, crossing the Elbe by 350 A.D., conquering other tribes (such as the Chauci) along the way. They also began moving into the area of the Rhine, but opposition by the Franks convinced them to shift their interest instead to Gaul and Britain. They battled against the Romans in Gaul, as early as the 3rd century, but were not too successful. They soon decided to return to along the North Sea.

They then moved along the North Sea coast, invading the Frisii. At that point, in the middle 5th century, they partook in the Anglo Saxon Invasion against southern Britain. Along with the Anglii and Jutes and some Frisii, they invaded northern and eastern Britain. It is not well known that, prior to the invasion's beginning, the Saxons had been invited to Britain to come over and help the Celts control marauding Picts and Scots. Once there, the Saxons and Angles decided to stay, and soon the warlike Saxons were more of a threat than the Picts or Scots had been. This started the 'invasion', which took over a century to achieve domination of the island.

Back on the main continent, in 531 A.D., the Saxons joined with the Franks to conquer the Thuringians. This added north Thuringia to the Saxon empire. Later the Franks and Saxons became bitter enemies again. The western Saxons wanted to displace the Franks from the Rhine area, and fought many battles with them in the 6th century. In the 7th century they reunited with the Franks, just long enough to drive off the Slavic Wends.

The Saxons remained a dominant force in their area until about 772 A.D., when the central Saxons were invaded by and came under the strict control of the Franks (under Charlemagne). After the final battle in 782, in which the Saxon King Widukind was defeated, 4500 Saxons were beheaded by the victors. King Widukind surrendered and the Franks demanded that he be baptized. Charlemagne required, in fact, that all the enemy battle survivors be converted to christianity. The Franks also required the Saxons to accept the Frankish form of direct administrative rule by nobles, but they allowed the Saxons to keep their own version of common law. From then on the Saxons were closely linked to the Holy Roman Empire. The wide ranging and long lasting power of the Frank's Carolingian Empire accounts for the influence of the Old Franconian version of German on Old High German, Old Saxon, Old Frisian, Old Dutch, and even Old French.

In the 9th century, the lower part of the Saxon area was loosely divided into three parts; *Westphalia* on the west, *Angria* (or Engern, as it was known along the Weser) in the middle, and *Eastphalia* on the east. This is one reason for today's similarity between Westphalian and Ostphalian. The term Angria, which is no longer familiar today, came from a small German tribe called Angrivari. They were defeated by the Saxons at the end of the 4th century. These subdivided areas were further divided into Gaue, each of which had a Fürst - the beginning of the noble aristocracy.

Anglii: This tribe was situated in what is today northern Holstein and southern Schleswig. It joined with the Jutes and Saxons in the invasion of Britain in the 5th century. From the 5th or 6th century on they are no longer cited in history.

Jutes: The Jutes tribe is believed to have lived in the Jutland Peninsula, which is now known as southern Denmark. Some Jutes were also thought to have lived along the Rhine, before they became absorbed by the Franks. They may have co-mingled with the Frisians as well. Some have speculated that it was not the Jutland Jutes but rather these Rhineland Jutes that accompanied the Saxons and Anglii on the invasion of Britain.

Chauci: This tribe was located just south of the Saxons. They were defeated and absorbed by the Saxons in the 3rd century A.D.

Frisii: As early as the 5th century B.C. the Frisii occupied an area along the North Sea coast, west of the Ems River. Because of the lowland marshes there, they had to build huts on artificial mounds that were raised slightly above the tides. This tribe spoke a language similar to that of the early Franks and early Saxons. Their language also had points in common with Norwegian, Swedish and Danish. It does differ in significant ways from Dutch, which also was strongly influenced by the Franks. In fact, at the time of Christ, there was probably not a great deal of difference in the language of the various West Germanic tribes.

The Frisii first appeared in the Roman chronicles in the 1st century A.D. They were conquered by the Franks and remained under their control for the next 300 years. The Frisii became a sea power, rivals to the Vikings, but Charlemagne destroyed their naval power. In the 5th century the naval capability of the Frisians proved helpful in the invasion of Britain.

In 784 Charlemagne again subdued the Frisians. In the 8th century they spread out and occupied the area between the Ems and the Weser (which later became known as Ost Friesland). In 810 they were attacked by the Vikings, but were able to drive them off. In the 9th century, by virture of the insistence of the Franks and the influence of Irish priests, they were christianized. By the 13th century they had spread along the North Sea coast into what is now known as Nord Friesland.

Over time the West Germanic languages of the various tribes expanded to include several High German dialects, Low German (Platt Düütsch), Frisian, English, Low Franconian, Dutch and Flemish. These are usually divided into Low and High German, which is differentiated in the following list. Of these, Old Saxon and Old English and Low Franconian are no longer existing, having evolved into more modern versions. It can be said that Old Saxon became Low German and Low Franconian became Dutch.

Low German: Old Saxon, Low German, Frisian, Dutch,
              Old English, Dutch, Flemish, Afrikaans, Frisian,
              and Old Low Franconian.

High German: Old High German, Bavarian, Langobardian,
              Alemannic (Swabisch), Middle High German
              and Standard (High) German.

Of these, all but Standard German are dialects which are seldom heard, but do certainly exist. The southern German dialects are held very dear today, and they are fond of putting pressure on radio and television to include their dialects when possible.

Other Tribes

In northern Europe there were tribes that were not Germanic tribes, but played an important part in the history of the area later known as Germany. The Celts and Slavs were members of the Indo-European peoples, but split off before the Germanic tribes reached their homeland in lower Scandinavia.

Celts: About 1,200 B.C. there were Celts in the Danube Basin, along with all the other Indo-Europeans. They were the first Indo-European people to spread across Europe. Some of them migrated to the Alps, France and Germany. About 600 B.C. some settled in Spain and Portugal. By 300 B.C. they had found their way to British Isles In effect, they were all over Europe, long before the Germanic tribes began migrating through Europe. However, the Celts retreated before these Germanic tribes when they finally encountered them, for reasons unknown. Latin displaced their language. The Celts did wield an influence on German metalwork, especially weaponry. They were pioneers in iron working.

The Celts became the Welsh and Cornish in Britain. Latin did not displace the Celtic dialects in Britain, as it had in Gaul. Cornish died out in the about 1777, when the last speaker is said to have died, but there have been recent efforts to revive it. Welsh is still alive, but shifting slowly to English. Welsh was carried by emigrants to Argentina in 1865, and is still visible there. The Bretons in northwest France speak a Celtic tongue. The most visible Celtic language today is Gaelic, which is the Celtic that survives today in the Irish tongue and in Scotch Gaelic (found only in the Scottish Highlands).

The Manx dialect just recently died out on the Ilse of Man.

Slavs: These people were encountered in the Vistula-Dnieper area as early as 700 B.C., even before the German tribes migrated south. They had broken off from the Indo-Europeans even before the Celts. About 100 B.C. the Slavs, the original settlers of eastern Poland and the Ukraine, had begun to move in a westerly direction. They encountered the Goths at the Dnieper river and stopped. They remained on their side of the Vistula, along the Dnieper, until about 200 A.D. Then they expanded in all directions. In 559 they joined with the Huns to attack Constantinope, but they were driven off. The Slavs were finally defeated defeated by Constantine V. A large number of Slavs then settled in Asia.

Those that expanded toward the west became the Poles, Czechs and Slovaks. The Germans initially referred to all the Slavs as 'Wenden'. They however prefer the term 'Sorbs'. Their language was based on an earlier Macedonian dialect. They adopted Roman Catholicism.

Those that expanded toward the east became the Russians and Ukranians, and adopted the Greek Orthodox religion. The western Slavic people included the ancient tribes known as the Abodrites, Sorbs, Wends and Pomerani. The Abrodites were once found in the Hamburg area.

Some Slavs settled east of the Elbe River, when the area was vacated by Germanic tribes. This lasted for about 650 years, until the Germans pushed most of them out. They adopted the Roman Catholic religion

The Slavs had almost constant battles with Germans over territory. In 1147, under Henry the Lion, the Germans initiated a crusade against the Slavs. The Slavs had other enemies as well. In 1241 the Hun Invasion devastated the Slav area that lay east of the Elbe-Saar frontier. At this time German settlers were invited by independent Slav nobility to enter and settle Mecklenburg and Brandenburg, in order to help rehabilitate it. Many villages and towns were established by these German immigrants. German occupation became like the nose of the camel under the tent wall. The Germans spread into Behomia and Poland. The German language became the local common language in a very wide area that was formerly Slav.

The Germans even spread into Latvia, Estonia and Hungary. This German expansion and dominance of German culture began to wane in the 14th century. The Teutonic Order was finally defeated by the Poles in the early 15th century/ The power of the Hanseatic League also began fading at about the same time. The nationalistic spirit of the indigenous local populations began to reveal itself again. However, the law of the Slavic nobility deprived the peasants of being able to own their own land, which greatly hindered development and social progress there for many years.

The Germanic tribes had, since 1,500 B.C., been speaking Primitive German in lower Scandinavia. A few hundred years earlier they had been speaking Indo-European. By about the christian era, maybe even as early as 500 B.C., the Primitive Germanic language had begun changing into a number of regional Germanic tribal dialects. And now, a thousand years later (about 500 A.D.), along came another sound shift, affecting only *some* of the Germanic tribes.

It began in southern Germany, somewhere near the Alps, and slowly moved north. It was probably was completed as it reached central Germany by the 8th century B.C. This was still a pre-literary period, when verbal speech pronunciation was vulnerable to change. This shift affected only words which were then in the vocabulary. It didn't necessarily affect words which appeared later, or loan words, which is one way of guaging the age of various words. The word for pepper (peper) underwent the change (pfeffer - with the "f" sound), but the later word for paper (papier) did not alter its initial "p" sound. The next table shows some of the changes that occurred during the full history of the language. The differences between the 2nd and 3rd columns are the result of this second shift.

TABLE THREE
SECOND SOUND SHIFT
HIGH GERMAN CONSONANT SHIFT
(500 A.D. to 800 A.D.)

IE	From Prim. Germanic	To Old H. German	Unaffected Low German
t	Þ (th),d		
p	f		
k	ch (later h)		
d	t, tt initial	ss, ts, z	t
	t medial	zz	t
b	p, pp initial	pf	p
	p medial & final	ff, f	p
g	kk, k initial	k, ch, kh	k
	k medial & final	hh, kk	k
dh	medial ð	t	d
	initial d	t	d, ð
bh	b,v	b,p	b, v, f
gh	g	g, k	g
	Þ	d	d
h	followed by l,n,r,w	dropped	dropped

The table shows a number of consonant changes. This shift is sometimes called the Great Consonant Shift. The *b* and *v* sounds varied, under control of their location in a word. The *b* is pronounced as a *v* when it falls between two vowels. This is how he<u>b</u>en becomes he<u>v</u>en (heaven). The p, t and k sounds remained as 'plosives' in Low German, which is why the word 'village' is dor<u>p</u> in Low German and dor<u>f</u> in Standard German. It's also why the English word 'that' is da<u>t</u> in Low German and da<u>s</u> in Standard German. The same goes for i<u>k</u> in Low German and i<u>ch</u> in Standard German.

The column for Low German represents where the shift did not take affect. The *z* at the beginning of a High German word was still spelled with a *t* in Low German, as it had for eons. In this way Low German retained the use of consonants that had evolved during the first shift that created Primitive Germanic centuries before. That is also why Low German is a much older language than High German.

As mentioned, this Second Sound Shift started in or near the northern Alps in about 500 A.D. The change may have been induced by contact with the Celts, Illyrians or Rhaetians. The latter were not Indo-Europeans, and may have been using a radically different language. This area had been infiltrated by Bavarians and Alemanni, who came from the Bohemian area and were exposed to other languages. These people spent several centuries in a mixed environment with indigenous people (aforementioned Celts, Illyrians, Rhaetians, etc.). They had also been, for perhaps 3 centuries, under Roman rule and would have been influenced by the *vulgar* Latin of the Romans. The term *vulgar* Latin refers to the spoken Latin. The *classical* Latin was not spoken; only written. So the term Vulgar refers to "people'", not to anything bad or base.

In any event, in southern Germany they began speaking somewhat differently. The change slowly moved north. As it reached the Franks in central Germany, it slowed down drastically, in both scope and intensity. In central Germany there were already a group of Middle High German dialects (mostly Middle and East Franconian). The speakers of the latter did accept some of the change in consonant usage, but they kept most of their own dialect. In addition, they also embraced small parts of the Low German dialects to their north. The Franks had not yet conquered the Saxons, so the Frankish ability to influence the north was insufficient to require the Saxons to adopt any language change. The Saxons were subsequently conquered, in 804, but by this time language was no longer so open to outside influence. The shift's influence did move into the Rhineland area, but only to a partial extent.

Part of the reason this second shift was accepted at all was the existence of a perceived need for a *standard* language. This thought had begun amongst the elite, but the people felt such pressure from several other sources. This included various political, economic and cultural factors. The political reason came down from heads of state, who said the people were asking them to devise a more *german* way of keeping records. Everyone did wantt to be less tied to the Latin of the Holy Roman Empire, even in their everyday lives. The economic reason was that the leaders of the industrial and commercial interests needed a more standardized language in which conduct their growing business. The cultural reason came along later, to reinforce and shape the direction of this movement. This involved primarily the Protestant Reformation. These reasons didn't start the change in the south, but they did help to keep the transition going as it moved north.

It was in central Germany that the shift caused the greatest result. The easterly part of central Germany area produced the dialect (Old East Franconian) which formed the basis for the Standard German used today. The westerly part provided the Low Franconian dialect, which became the main language of Belgium and the Netherlands.

This Second Shift period represents the point at which High German and Low German departed in different directions. Old High German shifted significantly away from the previous Primitive German. Old Saxon (Old Low German) kept many of the features of Primitive German, although it too underwent other changes. Thus today Low German is a bit softer sounding than High German, as represented by the consonant sounds reflected in the following list. The first letter is the High German 'plosive' sound, while the second is the corresponding Low German 'fricative' sound.

$$p \Leftrightarrow b \qquad z \Leftrightarrow s \qquad t \Leftrightarrow d$$
$$k \Leftrightarrow g \qquad g \Leftrightarrow ch \qquad d \Leftrightarrow th$$

Old High German language had not been too much different from Old Saxon. However, as it evolved into regular High German and later Standard German, the sounds of certain consonants greatly altered. The story of how a standard High German came into being is quite involved.

STANDARD GERMAN

During the 14th and 15th century the Court at Dresden spoke what's called a Kanzleisprache (court language) version of German. This court language became very influential on the speech of the surrounding people in central Germany. When Thuringia was captured, the court was moved to Meissen, where it underwent further maturation. Meissen is nearby to where Martin Luther made his decision on the appropriate lauguage for his interpretation of the Bible. Luther grew up in this Low German speaking area in Saxony, but chose to use a compromise version of East Middle German dialects (from Frankfurt to Leipzig) for his bible translations (1522-32). He referred to it as the official Kanzleisprache of the Saxon Chancellery.

Meanwhile, In the northern Low German area, Low German remained the principal language until the 15th century. Then the Saxony area High German became increasingly predominant. Low German speaking people did not accept the change very quickly, largely because many of them could not speak High German very well

This went on until the 17th and 18th century, when pressure to create a really *standard* language started to take root. The term Standard German is used, instead of High German, to describe the new standardized form of High German.. This Standard German is that which is spoken today throughout most of Germany, Austria, and

Switzerland. This term is used to differentiate the standard High German from the Old High German language. They belong to two separate times in history. Speakers of old dialects of High German consider Standard German to be somewhat artificial. They view it as something found in newspapers and TV news reports, but is not for the everyday life. The term High German has historical significance quite apart from the German language spoken and taught today, and this distinction should not be disregarded.

One might even argue that there never was a 'High German' language as such. The ancestor of Standard German was, one might say, primarily a collection of southern Germany dialects. Even as it moved from Old High German through Middle High German, the bulk of it consisted of a loose conglomeration of dialects (in spite of the Second Sound Shift). This is somewhat different from Low German. It can be said that the ancestor of Low German was a *language*, whose name was Old Saxon, rather than a collection of dialects. However, dialects were then so pervasive that one cannot say for sure.

A new standard High German helped re-establish in Germany a new literary German period. The German culture had been lagging behind other civilizations, who already had a long and quite continuous history of culture and literature. While the Germanic tribes were migrating around northern Europe, other parts of the world had been busy developing new ways of writing and even printing their particular language.

Paper

About the time of Christ the Chinese were already making paper from vegetable fiber. This was an improvement on papyrus, which goes back to 4,000 B.C. There were no books then, just scrolls. The earliest use of ink was around 2700 B.C. Until papyrus came along, scrolls had been made from bark or animal skin, which were actually more durable than papyrus. Vegetable fiber paper spread to Europe in about the 11th century. A primitive form of what we think of as a book was now possible, to replace scrolls. The word *book* comes from the Primitive German word 'boc', which means bark or beech.

Writing

Writing actually dates all the way back to around 15,000 B.C., as stick drawings on cave walls, bone or wood pieces. These "ideographs" contained symbols, each of which expressed a word or described an action. The Chinese still write this way; with symbols. The Sumerians invented real writing about 5,000 years ago. About 3,000 B.C. the ancient Greeks used symbols to represent syllables, rather than words, creating thereby a kind of 'phonetic' alphabet By 1,500 B.C. this had graduated to a symbol representing every letter, which was then more of a normal alphabet. But it had only consonants, no vowels. The 24 letter Runic Alphabet appeared about the 2nd century.. The Hebrew alphabet didn't have vowels until the 7th century. The Phoenicians and Greeks added some vowels, and incorporated a few Runic letters. Italic speakers added 'y' and 'z', to complete the alphabet in today's terms. They rounded the shape of the letters, so they write more quickly. Their Latin Alphabet then became the standard in western Europe.

When 8th and 9th century clerics wanted to write in the German language, they chose the Latin alphabet. The Pagan Runes had already vanished by about 700 A.D. Two runic characters that survived in subsequent alphabets were Þ (called thorn - with the 'th' sound of the word *th*in) and ð (called eth - with the 'th' sound in the word *th*en). The distinction between these two pronunciations of '*th*' is slim, but nevertheless there.

Around the 11th century, they began writing the letters taller, and could therefore squeeze them closer together. This created the Gothic script. Gothic script appeared about the 13th century, replacing the Latin alphabet. Its way of connecting letters closer together resulted in some of the elaborately hand drawn 14th century manuscripts. Some of this got too fancy, with all the curlicues that broke up words. So the Germans adopted a Fraktur form of letters. It also created the Alte Schrift in German, which looked so beautiful when done right, but if done sloppily could quickly disintegrate into illegibility. The Alte Schrift, was popular until the middle 20th century. Hand writing continued to improve, using letters that were more 'curved' than the Fraktur script or the Alte Schrift.

Printing

In the ancient times, we are told that monks in the basement copied books by hand. The first actual printing device was developed in China in the 7th century. The movable blocks form of printing were invented in the 11th century. The first book that was block printed was *The Diamond Sutra* in 868. The Psalter was the first book printed by a press, in 1457. An early Latin bible, printed in 1460, was the real beginning of the print age. Bronze metallic type sets were developed in Korea earlier in the 15th century.

Gutenberg and metallic movable type came along, although its doubtful he invented movable type. At first Gutenberg used the Gothic script called Fraktur. He started printing Luther's Bible, but due to economic troubles, it was completed by Johann Fust and his partner Peter Schiffer. Luther's Reformation caused an increase in the number of books written in German. Latin had been the language of choice until then, which could only be read by clerics and academics - not the ordinary person. In north Germany, the ordinary person could only understand Low German.

Luther had the New Testament printed in 1522 and the whole Bible in 1534. Luther was not the first to translate and print the Bible in German. There were 19 High German and 5 Low German translations already in existence. The High German versions were in the dialects from around Munich and Vienna.

He made a lot of changes to the language between these two dates, attempting to create a more acceptable "standard" German. Even the initial Kanzlersprach wasn't the best model, because the preferred language of royalty was more often French than German; Italian in Vienna. He needed to convert the royalty and elite, if he ever hoped to convert that average person to his way of thinking. Another problem was that Roman Catholicism and Calvinist Switzerland accused him of heretical distortion of the ancient Greek text and they fought his every move. Luther thought it better that the language of the more powerful people, those in royal courts, should become the standard for High German.

Luther's version of German, on its way to becoming the Standard German, spread rapidly along with the spread of the Reformation. It took immediate hold in Protestant north German. By the 17th century it was adopted by the German literati and grammarians. In the 18th century it was chosen as the language for classical literature. However, in the area where the second shift started, such as Bavaria, it was still not totally accepted. They resisted, for instance, the '-e' ending on a word like 'leute'; preferring leut. Eventually they, and the Austrians, yielded to pressure.

The following list affords a glance into the heritage of High German and Standard German. It shows the original Indo-European language, from which came Primitive German. Gothic is about the only known language that might represent something close to this Primitive German. Then Old High German split off, as a result of the second sound shift. Standard German, as we've just discussed, came along in the 18th century.

When perusing the following list, one could look for similarities between Indo-European and Gothic. And one should note the differences between Gothic and Old High German. Both Old High German and Standard German should reflect the Second Sound Shift, but Standard German has undergone subsequent changes, due to the effort to create a standard for the language.

ENGLISH	INDO-EUR	GOTHIC	OLD H. G.	STD GER
believe	leubh	gilaubjan	gilouban	glauben
brother	bhrater	brôÞar	bruoder	Bruder
call	gal	haitan	ruofan	rufen
daughter	dhughter	daûhtar	tohter	Tochter
day	daghos	dags	tag	Tag
dog	k^{w}on	hunds	hond	Hund
earth	er	airÞa	erda	Erde
eat	ed	fraitan	ezzan	essen
eye	ok^w	augo	ouga	Augen
father	phter	fadar	fater	Vater
five	penk^{w}e	fimf	fimf	Fünf
give	ghabho	giban	geban	geben
go	ghe	gaggan	gangan	gehen
good	ghedh	gôda	guot	Gut
he	ko	is	her	Er

hear	kleu	hausjan	hôren	höre
house	tkei	gardi	hûse	Haus
I	eg	ik	ih	Ich
let	le	lêtan	lâzzan	lassen
mine	meno	meina	min	meine
moon	menon	mêna	mâno	Mond
more	me	maiza	mêro	mehr
no	ne	ni	ni	nich
old	al	alþiza	alt	Alt
other	an	anÞar	andar	ander
our	nes	unsara	unser	unser
out	ud	ût	ûz	aus
set	sed	satjan	setzan	setzen
seven	septm	sibun	sibun	sieben
ship	skipam	skip	skef	schiff
six	sweks	saihs	sëhs	sechs
sleep	slep	slêpan	slâffan	schlaf
speak	spreg	qiþan	sprehhan	sprechen
stone	stei	stains	stein	stein
tree	deru	bagms	boum	baum
two	dʷo	twai	zwei	zwei
under	ndher	undar	untar	unter
us	nes	uns	uns	uns
were	wes	wêsun	uuârun	werden
will	wel	wilja	uuili	will
with	wi	miÞ	mit	mit
word	wer	waurd	wortu	wort
year	yer	jêr	jâr	jahr
you	tu	Þu	dû	du

The Indo-European words used in the preceding list were obtained from several sources, including Robert Claiborne's *The Roots of English* and the Indo-European section of the *American Heritage Dictionary of the English Language*, prepared by Calvert Watkins.

In this final section, the evolutionary transitions in both the High German and Low German languages.will be described briefly, which took place over many centuries,

EVOLUTIONARY TRANSITIONS

Here we're not looking at the changes in the first or second sound shift, but rather the subsequent normal changes that come to every language.

The First Sound Shift did create Primitive Germanic. The Second Sound Shift put Old High German and the various High German dialects on their own course.

Eventually Old High German evolved in Middle High German and then New High German, which acquired an orthography and then became what we here refer to as Standard High German.

Meanwhile, on the other branch, Primitive German evolved into Old Saxon. It eventually changed into Middle Low German and finally into Platt Düütsch.

In both branches, the languages became simpler, but the Low German branch is definitely the simpler of the two branches. This greater simplicity was also passed on to English.

Why should one expect languages to become simpler. Let's take the pseudo words "apa" and "aba". The first one is more difficult to pronounce than the second one. The "aba" is easier to say, because at the beginning of the word, you have to 'turn on' the vocal chords and then just pronounce the whole word. In the case of "apa", you 'turn on' your vocal chords at the beginning, shut them 'off' to pronounce the 'p' and then 'on' again to finish the word. For example, the Low German word for apple (appel) is easier to pronounce that the Standard German cognate (apfel). In Low German one pronounces the 'p' letter in appel (apple) using the easier 'b' sound, while Standard German pronounces the 'p' letter in Apfel with a 'p' sound. To a large degree Low German has remained a 'verbal' language and thus experienced a longer period of 'simplification' than did Standard German.

PRIMITIVE GERMANIC TO OLD HIGH GERMAN (770-1050)

This change is a consequence of the Second Sound Shift, but it sets the stage for the subseqent evolutions. Quite a bit of this shift change occurred in the endings of words. For instance, the primitive 'dagaz' became 'tag', and 'Pfaffe' became pfaffo. The word 'bruodar' became 'bruoder'. And 'leuhtjan' became 'luihten'. We also have 'gastiz' becoming 'gast'. Some endings had already changed when Old Norse and Gothic broke off from the Primitive Germanic stem.

Some spelling changes were ...

ai becomes ei (bain becomes bein or stains becomes stein)	and
h becomes ch (hoh becomes hoch).	and
e becomes ie (her becomes hier)	and
o becomes uo (god becomes guot)	

Some changes depended on which letters followed the change, such as ...

au before 'h', 'd', 't', 'l', 'n','r' becomes long 'o' (hauhs to hoh)	and
ai before 'h', 'w', 'r' becomes long 'e' (air to er)	

The initial 'h' letter was dropped from a word like 'her', becoming 'er'. This seems to agree with the theory that the musculine pronoun 'er' in German derives from the word 'herr' (her in Primitive German) for "mister". Additional changes were ...

initial 's'	becomes	schneid	(sneit to cut)	and
'þ'	becomes	'd' (in the 9th century)		and
medial 't'	becomes	'zz'	(ĕtan to ezzan)	and
'ai'	becomes	'e', 'ei'	(stains to stein)	and
'eu'	becomes	'iu', 'io'	(leuhtjan to liuhten)	and
'au'	becomes	'o', 'ou'	(augo to ouga).	

OLD HIGH GERM. (770-1050) TO MIDDLE HIGH GERM. (1050-1350)

Old High German consisted primarily of the Allemani, Lombardi, East Franconian, South Rhenish Franconian, Rhenish Franconian and Central Franconian dialects. The following list describes how widely these dialects varied, although this is largely a matter of spelling differences, rather than sound differences.

English	Alemanni	Bavarian	E. Franc.	Rh. Franc.	Cen. Franc.	Old Saxon
to have	haben	hapen	haben	haben	havan	hebbian
deep	tiuf	tiuf	teuf	diuf	dief	diup
gave	gab	kap	gab	gab	gaf	gaf
belief	kilauba	calaupa	gilouba	cjilouba	gilouba	giloba

In the second line of the list, the southern dialects use 't' while the northerly ones use 'd'. In the last line, there seems to less of a rigid pattern.

During the Middle Ages (500 A.D. to 1500 A.D.) the term 'ir' was beginning to be used by the upper class, instead of 'du'. Possibly it was a corruption of a word like 'ehrte', meaning something like *honored one*. In succeeding centuries, this grew into the extra polite 'Sie' and 'Ihr' form of address used in Standard German.

The beginning of the Middle High German period was also the beginning of the German literary period. The Middle High German (basically the East Old Franconian dialect) became the vehicle for prose and poetry. During this particular evolution we find the beginnings of the common umlauted vowels, such as ö and ä and ü. The spread of the umlaut began in Franconia, around 1200. We also find the following additional changes.

hh	becomes	ch (mahhon becomes machen)
k	becomes	ch (skif becomes schif)
a	becomes	ä (mahti becomes mähte
o	becomes	ö (lohhir to löcher and mohte becomes möhte)
on	becomes	en (zungôno becomes zungen)
io	becomes	ie (bietan becomes bieten)

ou	becomes	oü (louber to loüber) or üe (fuoren to füehren)
u	becomes	ü (dunni becomes dünne)
i	becomes	e (gilouben becomes gelouben)
û (long u)	becomes	iu (hûsir becomes hiuser)
â (long a)	becomes	æ (swârî becomes swære)
ô (long o)	becomes	oe (sconi becomes shoene)

With regard to word endings ...

a becomes e (herza becomes herze and singan becomes singen), and

o becomes e (zungôn becomes zungen)

In pluralization, the Old High German 'gast' (guest) becomes 'geste' (guests); the 'a' umlauts to 'e' instead of to 'ä', as it does today. In the same fashion, 'hand' (hand) becomes 'hende' (hands), not 'hände'. However, late in the period it does change to the more familiar 'ä'. This reminds one of the common Low German problem of deciding whether to use 'e' or 'ä' in many words. For instance, should one write 'et' or 'ät' for "eat". In nearly all cases, the 'e' seems preferable, but there are a few words that are more understandable when using 'ä' (when the sound seems to call for 'ae' rather than 'aa').

MIDDLE HIGH GERM (1050-1350) TO NEW HIGH GERM. (1350-1650)

The term New High German is somewhat similar to Standard German. The New High German period includes the era of Luther's bible, and thus reflects some of the changes brought about by Martin Luther. As we've noted, some of the evolutionary changes during this period did not equally affect all the High German dialects. Among the changes, we find that a consonant following a short vowel becomes doubled. The Middle High German 'veter' becomes 'Vetter' in New High German, as well as the Middle High German 'hamer' becoming 'Hammer' in New High German.

With regard to initial letters, the initial 'v' becomes 'f' (vart becomes fahrt) and (varwe becomes Farbe). The latter also shows the change or 'rw' to 'rb'. There was also a change in an inital 's' or 'sh', becoming 'sch'.

Within words, the vowels change ...

e becomes ä	(hende becomes Hände and geste becomes Gäste)	and
e becomes ö	(leffel becomes Löffel and zwelf becomes Zwölf)	and
æ becomes ä	(wære becomes wäre)	and
oe becomes ö	(hoeren becomes hören and hoehe becomes Höhe)	and
æ becomes ee	(lesære becomes Leser)	and
ou becomes au	(boum becomes Baum and mous becomes Maus)	and
u becomes o	(sun to sohn, sunne to Sonne and kunnen to konnen)	and
ü becomes o	(sümer becomes Sommer)	and

uo becomes u (muoter to Mutter, ruofen to rufen, buoch to Buch)	and
u becomes ie (siben becomes Sieben)	and
iu becomes eu (diutsch becomes Deutsch)	and
ie becomes a monophthong ie	

Within words, some consonants change ...

mb or mp is changed to mm (tumber becomes Dumm)	and
nl changes to ll or l (einlif becomes Elf)	and
d becomes t (hinder becomes hinter)	and
sk becomes sch (skriben becomes schreiben)	and
s becomes sch (slange becomes Schlange)	

Some vowel lengths are changed ...

short a	becomes long â (ta-ge becomes Tâg)	and
short e	becomes long ê (ge-ben becomes gêben)	and
short o	becomes long ô (bo-te becomes Bôte)	and
long â	becomes short a (strâze becomes Strasse)	and
long î	becomes ei (mîn becomes mein)	and
long û	becomes au (hûs becomes Haus)	

With regard to word endings ...

m following unaccented vowel, changes to n (buosem to busen)	and
a to e (pforta becomes pforte)	and
e is dropped (herze becomes Herz and frende becomes fremd)	

And finally, w becomes pronounced as a v, but is still written as a w.

At this point our interest is shifted to the other branch - Low German. Again we start with Primitive Germanic. From an evolutionary standpoint, Primitive Germanic evolved into Old Saxon, which some refer to as Old Low German. Old Saxon (or Old Low German) then evolved into Middle Low German and then finally into Platt Düütsch.

PRIMITIVE GERMANIC TO OLD SAXON (200-1,000)

The Old Saxon language is often said to have begun around the 8th century, the date of the oldest written record, but we know it was spoken long before that, perhaps as early as 500 B.C. It was also certainly written much earlier than the 8th century, but such writings have just not survived.

The transition from Primitive Germanic to Old Saxon is a fairly direct route. It did not branch off from the main stem as drastically as did Gothic, Old Norse, and Old High

German. Low German and Old Norse seem to contain more remnants of Primitive Germanic sounds than do the others. However, all of them shared in showing a weakening of word endings.

Among the changes during this evolution were ...

þ	became d	and
ai and â (long a)	became long ê	and
au	became long ô (not before 'w') or ou	and
um, un	became om, on	and
a	became u or o	and
o	became u or uo	and
or	became ar	and
al	became ol	and
ai	became long ê (not before 'j')	and
ai	became ei before 'j'	and
eu (before a, e, o)	became eo	and
eu (before i, j, u)	became iu.	

OLD SAXON (200-1,000) TO MIDDLE LOW GERMAN (1,000-1,500)

The changes to Middle Low German are not as well documented as are changes in the evolution from Old to Middle High German. Changes during this period include the weaking of word endings, such as 'bindan' becoming 'binden' or 'mugan' becoming 'mogen'. The 'm' ending becomes 'n' (bium becomes biun). More examples are found in the following list.

Some addition changes were ...

~~b~~	becomes v (medial) or b (initial)	and
ð	becomes d	and
i	becomes long ê	and
ê (long e)	becomes â (long a) (geban becomes ga~~b~~un)	and
u	becomes long ô	and
k^w	becomes qu	and
kk	becomes ck	and
h	becomes ch (dohtar becomes dochter)	and
sh, sk	becomes sch	and
au	becomes long o, ou or u (baum becomes bôm)	and
a	becomes e (sandjan becomes sendian)	and
a	becomes o (ald becomes old).	

The diminutive endings became '-ken' and '-lin'. Also during this period, certain letters changed position. The word for "horse" was 'hros', and then it became 'hors'.

These are some of the changes that helped form the current Low German, which can be called Platt Düütsch. Here again, the literature is not very forthcoming, partly because most experts have focused on High German.

ch	became	g (mannich becomes mannig)
i	became	ie (sin became sien)
i	became	ee (vil became veel)
e	became	i (ek became ik)
ei	became	ee (ein became een)
a	became	o (vader became voder)
y	became	ie (myn became mien)
m ending	became	n ending (godem became gooden)
v	became	f (vrou became frou or fru or fro)
o	became	u (von became vun, geboren became geburen)
e	became	a (hert becames hart)
long o	became	monophthong ôô

COMPARING LOW GERMAN AND HIGH GERMAN

The Old Saxon language existed about the same time as Old High German. The Middle Low German language existed about the same time as Middle High German. The question is whether they resembled each other very much. They appear to, as can be seen from the following comparison of these contemporaneous languages.

OLD SAXON (200-1,000) *VERSUS* OLD HIGH GERMAN

Since Old Saxon is Old Low German, we're actually comparing Old Low German and Old High German. Some of the differences between these older languages reflect the same differences that exist today between Standard German and Platt Düütsch. For instance, with regard to long vowels in Low German, they became doubled in Platt Düütsch.

Old Saxon	Platt Düütsch	Old High German
bên	been (leg)	bein
bôm	boom (tree)	baum
stên	steen (stone)	stein
hûs	huus (house)	hus

Old Saxon is very close to Platt Düütsch, as we might expect. However, there is also a clear resemblance to Old High German (hus vs. huus vs. hûs).

The following list contains additional examples of both languages. Except for the differences brought about by the Second Sound Shift, the similarities are greater than one might expect. The English is shown to provide word meaning, and the Indo-European is shown just for historical reference.

ENGLISH	INDO-EUR	OLD SAXON	OLD HIGH GERMAN
and	en	endi	inti
are	er	sind	sint
bird	awi	fugal	fugal
brother	bhrater	broþer	bruoder
by	mbhi	bi	bi
come	g^{w}em	cuman	queman
daughter	dhughter	dohter	tohter
dead	dheu	dod	tot
earth	er	erÞa	erde
eat	ed	etan	ezzan
eye	ok^w	augo	ouga
father	phater	fadar	fater
five	penk^{w}e	fîf	fimf
give	ghabho	gevan	geban
good	ghedh	gôd	guot
have	kap	hebbian	habe
help	kelp	helpan	helfan
I	eg	ik	ih
land	lendh	land	lant
let	lîta	lât	lâzzan
make	mag	makôn	mahhôn
many	menegh	manag	manag
me	me	mî	mih
mine	meno	mîne	min
more	me	mêrr	mêro
offer	bher	biodan	biotan
open	upo	opan	offan
other	an	ôÞar	andar
ship	skipam	skip	skef
there	to	Þar	dar
water	akwa	uuater	aha
we	we	uue	wir
will	wel	uuileo	uuili
with	mithi	mid	mit
word	wer	uuord	uuortu
world	wiro	uuerold *	uuerol
year	jêr	jêr	jâr
you	Þu	Þi	dû

* the letter 'w' didn't exist, so it was represented by 'uu'.

68

The Middle High German language was surprisingly similar to its contemporary Middle Low German. Therefore, many of the factors in the preceding list which pertain to 16th century Middle High German also may pertain to current Middle Low German. Martin Luther was a Thuringian, and therefore was familiar with both Middle High German (East Franconian dialect) and Middle Low German.

The resemblance between the 'middle' versions of these two languages is not as obvious as it was when the 'old' versions were compared. They had begun drifting further apart. The vowels had changed in each language, but they changed in different ways. However, the resemblance is still greater than exists today between Standard German and Platt Düütsch. And even today, the two languages are as close as sister languages may be expected to be.

The following is a simple comparison of the corresponding vowels used in these two languages. Cognate words that used a certain vowel in Middle High German would instead use the other vowel in Middle Low German.

Middle High German	Middle Low German
ä	e
ie	e
uo	o
ei	e
ou	o
o,u	a
iu	ü
long i	short i
long u	short u
long a	short a, short e
short u	o
short i	e, ee
z, zz	t
f, pf, ff	p
ch	k
t	d
b (medial and final)	v
g (medial and final)	ch
y	i

It could be instructive to compare Old Saxon against the more modern Low German. The list on the following page includes quite a few comparisons. The English is included to convey word meaning. Indo-European is included merely for historical reference.

69

ENGLISH	INDO-EUROPEAN	OLD SAXON	PLATT DÜÜTSCH LOW GERMAN
acre	agro	akar	aker
also	allaz	ok	ok
and	en	endi	un
any	oino	ênig	ennig
are	er	sind	sünd
be	bheu	biun	bün
believe	leubh	gilouba	glöv
bird	awi	fugal	vagel
brother	bhrater	broþer	broder
by	mbhi	bi	bi
come	g^{w}em	cuman	kumm
daughter	dhughter	dohter	dochter
day	agh	dag	dag
dead	dheu	dôd	doot
dog	k^{w}on	hond	hund
door	dh^{w}ero	dura	döör
earth	er	erþa	eerd
eat	ed	etan	eten
eye	ok^w	augo	oog
father	phter	fadar	voder
fish	peisk	fisk	fisch
five	penk^{w}e	fîf	fiev
foot	ped	fôt	foot
from	per	fan	vun
give	ghabho	geban	geev
go	ghe	gangan	goh
good	ghedh	gôd	good
guest	ghosti	gast	gast
had	kap	habde	harr
hard	kar	hard	hart
have	kap	hebbian	hebben
he	ko	hê	he
hear	kleu	hausjan	hôren
heart	kerd	herta	hart
help	kelb	helpan	hölp
here	ko	hêr	hier
his	ko	is	sien
holy	kailo	hêlag	hillig
horse	kers	hross	peerd
house	tkei	hus	huus
how	k^{w}o	huô	wo
hundred	dekmtom	hund	hunnert
I	eg	ik	ik

70

ENGLISH	INDO-EUROPEAN	OLD SAXON	PLATT DÜÜTSCH LOW GERMAN
if	i	of	ob
inquire	prok	biddian	fraag
is	es	ist	i
lamb	lambh	lamb	lamb
land	lendh	land	land
let	le	lât	lat
make	mag	makôn	mok
man	mano	erl	kirl
many	menegh	manag	mannig
me	me	mî	mi
mine	meno	mine	mien
more	me	mêr	meehr
mother	mater	moðar	moder
much	meg	filu	veel
my	me	mîne	mien
name	nomen	namo	naam
neck	mon	hals	nacken
no	ne	ne	ne
now	nu	nû	nu
offer	bher	biodan	beden
old	al	ald	olt
one	oino	ên	een
open	upo	opan	open
other	an	ôÞar	ander
our	nes	ûsa	uus
out	ud	ût	uut
she	so	siu	se
ship	skipam	skip	schipp
sister	swesor	swestar	swester
sleep	slep	slâp	slaap
speak	spreg	queÞan	snacken
stone	stei	stên	steen
street	ster	strâta	straat
teach	deik	lêrian	leehrn
ten	dekm	tehan	teihn
that	to	thê	dat
the	to	thê	de
then	to	thô	do
there	to	thar	dor
to	de	te	to
thorn	tern	thorn	doorn
tongue	dnghu	tunga	tung
tree	deru	bom	boom

ENGLISH	INDO-EUROPEAN	OLD SAXON	PLATT DÜÜTSCH LOW GERMAN
true	deru	triuwi	truu
two	dʷo	twêne	twee
under	ndher	under	ünner
up	upo	up	up
us	nes	ûs	us
value	wal	wairÞ	weert
wake	weg	wekkian	waak
warm	kelh	warm	warm
water	akwa	uuatar	woter
way	wegh	uueg	weg
we	we	uue	wi
will	wel	uuileo	will
winter	wed	wintrus	winter
with	wi	mid	mit
word	wer	uuord	woort
world	wiro	uuerold	werlt
year	yer	jêr	johr
you	tu	Þi	du
you (plural)	yu	jus	ji

Here we can see a strong resemblance across the board, from the ancient to the modern versions of Low German. The letter combinations in Indo-European, such as 'bh' and 'dh' have been lost, as a result of the First Sound Shift. They are replaced respectively by 'b' and 'd'. This also has caused some of the 't' or 'th' changes to 'd' in the Low German.

The cognate words for the English word 'believe' are quite interesting.

English	Indo-European	Old Saxon	Low German
believe	leubh	gilouba	glöv

The oldest version 'leubh' comes through in the 'louba' part of the Old Saxon. But a prefix 'gi-' has been added for grammatical reasons. In Low German such prefixes were eliminated, but here it was somewhat preserved in the 'g' beginning. And in English the prefix and root word are evident (be-lieve), which attests again to the historical relationship between Old Saxon and English.

The 'th' sounding letters in Old Saxon have either remained in Low German (although the letter has changed) or that part of the word now has a silent letter.

The letters 'l', 'r', 'm' and 'n' have remained very constant. With a little effort, the Old Saxon and parts of Indo-European can be recognized by today's Low German speaker.

72

The first column on each page contains the English word. The middle column contains a phrase (sometimes silly) which puts the word into some context, in order to show how the word is used.

Sometimes a word can be used and stressed differently, even though it is spelled alike in each case. Therefore, the syllable in a word that is pronounced as stressed is shown as underlined. This can help in determining how the Low German word should be pronounced. Such stress is shown for the English words as well, so one can determine the appropriate context for whic the Low German word is applicable.

The third column contains one or more Low German words that correspond to the English word. This column, while focusing on words from the North Saxon area also contains words that are more directly applicable to the Phalian and Eastern areas.

The Low German words represent primarily a North Saxon dialect (basically northcentral Low German). They relate very well to those dialects found throughout central northern Germany; basically those surrounding Hamburg. It is somewhat less representative of those dialects much further south, east, west of this general area. However, the differences are largely a matter of spelling, rather than usage or even pronunciation. The following map shows the North Saxon dialect area.

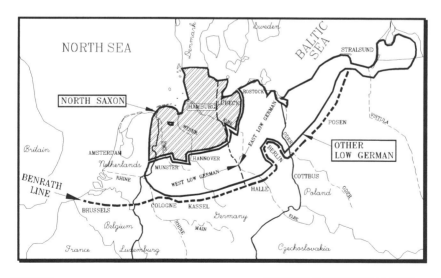

MAP H   NORTH SAXON DIALECT

The North Saxon dialect area generally covers the area where the dialects of Heide, Ost Frisian, Oldenburg, Schleswig, Holstein, Emsland, Bremen, Hamburg and west Mecklenburg are spoken. The other dialects are different but closely related.

English	Phrase	Low German
a	one of something	een
abide	endure	utstohn or verdregen
abominable	horrible	abscharlig
about	concerning	öwer or um or vun
about that	specifically that	doröwer or dor öwer
above	overhead	boben or boven
absent minded	forgetful	vergeterig
absolute	for sure, certain	obsluut or absluut
accept	consider	benehm (past: benohmen)
accessory	added part	tobehör
accident	whoops	malör or unfall or unglück
accidental	just by chance	tofellig
according to	accordingly	dorno or dor no
accordion	music instrument	buukörgel, trekörgel, trekfidel
account book	keep the record	rekenbook
accurate	very correct	akroot or akraat or genau
accuse	make accusation	anklogen or vörsmieten
accustomed	comfortable with	gewinnt or gewinnt mit
ace	top card	ass (pl: assen)
achieve	attain	dörhalen (past: dörhalt)
acorn	just a nut	eckel (pl: eckeln)
acquaintance	you know him	bekannte (pl: bekannten)
acre	0.4 hectare	acker
across	to other side	röwer
act	as in law, a statute	gesett
act	way you behave	anstellen (past: anstellt)
act	in a play	törn
action	lights, camera,	akschoon
active	playful, spry, lively	lustig
actually	really	sogor or woll or egentlig
added to	on top of	todeelt or togeben
additional	extra, contribution	togeev or extro
address	speak to	ansnacken or anküren
add up	find the total	uptellen or tohopentellen
admission	cost to get in	rinlott or rinlaat
admonish	scold	schimpen or afkanzeln
adore	like a lot	heff geern (past: harr geern)
adore that	something particular	heff dat geern
adored that	liked it a lot	harr dat geern
adroit	agile, clever	adrett
advantage	one up on	vördeel (pl: vördeelen)
advantage	has leverage	öwerhand
adventure	scary fun	belevnis
adult	full grown	vullwussen
advocat	representative	afkat
advice	keep it to yourself	raad or rod
afraid	scared of	bang
afraid of	fearful of	groot or bang vun

after	following	no	or	achter
after a while	some time went by	tiedlangs hen		
after that	when it's over	nodem or nodat	or achter dat	
afternoon	after dinner	nomiddags or	s'nomiddags	
afterward	when it's over	nachher	or	nodem
again	to repeat	weller	or	wedder
against	not agree with	gegens		
against	lean against	ran	or	blangto
against that	not for that	dorgegens		
age	of that age	öller		
agent	middle man	middelsmann		
agitated	kind of mad	füünsch		
agitation bother		gewöhl		
agree	in agreement	inverstoh,	instimm,	mitstimm
agreed	done deal	afmokt	or	eenigt
agreement	decision	afkommen	or	afmokung
agrees	concurs	stimmt		
agrees with	concurs with	bestimmt	or	stimmt mit
agriculture	farm business	buuree		
ahead	in front of	vorut		
ahead of	out in front	invorut		
aim	draw a bead	teel		(past: teelt)
air	breathe it	luft		
air mattress	camp necessity	luftmatratz		
air rifle	pellet gun	puuster		
airplane	flying vehicle	avion		
aisle	narrow path	gang	or	gangweg
alarm clock	hear the rooster	wekker		
alcohol	hic	alkohol		
alder	type of tree	eller	or	ellerboom
alike	equal, parity	egol		
alive	not dead	lebennig		
all	everything	all		
all around	everyplace	rumdum		
all arranged	completely discussed	afsnackt		
all the time	won't quit	alltied		
allow	permit, give permisson	lott	or	latt
almond	nut	mannel		
almost	nearly	binoh	or	meist
alone	by yourself	alleen	or	bi misülms
along	along a line	henlang	or	hendohl
alongside	next to	blangs		
already	now	al		
also	in addition	ok	or	ook
alter	revise	änner		
although except		blots or bloss	or ower	
always	all the time	jümmer or jümmeto	or ümmer	
am	'I' am	bün		
a moment ago	just now	eben		
American	yankee	Amerikoner		

75

among	between	mang	or	mank
amuse	keep happy	amusieren		
amuses	happy about	hög	or	höög
ancestor	forbearer	vorföhrner		
anchor	what a drag	anker		
ancient	really old	uroolt		
and	also, as well	un		
anecdote	amusing little story	döntje	or	vertellsel
angel	in heaven	ingel		(pl: ingeln)
anger	rage	raasch	or	ärger
angry	frustrated, gruff	bös	or	vertöönt
animal	four legged thing	deet		(pl: deeter)
ankle	foot bone connection	knokel		
announce	report in	anmellen	or	anseggen
announcement	notice	ankünnigen		
annoys	angers a little	verärgert	or	verdrütt
annual	once a year	johrlig		
answer	retort	anwoort		(pl: anwörte)
answers	responds	antert		
ant	little bug	ampel	or	migent
anthill	ant apartment house	ampelhumpel		
anticipated	saw it coming	invorrutsehn		
anxiety	aggravation	bammel		
anxious	nervous like	angstig		
anyhow	anyway	sowiso	or	doch
anyway	in spite of	anhhin	or	liekers
apart	separated	uteenanner		
ape	monkey's uncle	aap	or	app
apothecary	drug store	apteke	or	aptek
apparently	seems to be	wohrshienlig		
appearance	how they look	utseht		
appears	seems to be	shient	or	lett so as
appears	looks to be	utsüht	or	süht as wenn
appears to be	pretends to look like	biert		
appendix	in back of a book	anhäng		
appetite	I'm hungry	aptiet		
applause	appreciative with hands	bifall		
apple	nice red one	appel		(pl: appeln)
apple sauce	smashed up	appelmoos		
apple orchard	all in one place	appelgoorn	or	appelhof
appoint	place into office	insetten		
apprentice	learner	gesell		(pl: gesellen)
approval	OK by me	tostimmen		
April	4TH month	Aprill	or	Ostermaand
apron	dishes time	shörten		
ardor	passion	gloot		
are	'you' are	büst		
are	'we' or 'they' are	sünd		
area	region	gegend	or	bereek
argue	to disagree	strien	or strieden or	vertüren

arise	to stand up	upstohn
arm	appendage	arm (pl: arms)
armchair	so relaxing	lehnstohl (pl: lehnstöhl)
around	circle about	rüm
around back	behind	achterrüm
around here	in this area	hierrüm
around outside	on the rim	butenrüm or utsiedrüm
arrange	put in order	ornen or ansetten
arrested	taken in custody	fastnommen
arrival	appearance	ankomm
arrive	finally show up	ankommen
arrogant	stuck up	grodsporig
arrow	feathered bullet	piel
arse	butt	orse or morse
arsonist	fire starter	füürböter
art	pretty drawing	maleree or maaleree
article	a thing	deel (pl: deelen)
artist	drawer	maler or maaler
as	as if	as or aswenn
ash	type of tree	esch or eschenboom
ashamed	want to hide	verschämt
ashes	fire leftovers	ashen
ash tray	put your butt here	ashenbeker
ask	question	froog (past: frogt)
ask about	take interest in	bekümmern
ask around	check it out	rümfrogen
asks	act of asking	froogt
asphalt	black road	eerdpik or teer
assert	claim, declare	behaup or behoop
assign	pass out	utdeelen
association	formal group	gesellschop
as soon as	right then	so drod as
assure	make safe	verseker
asylum	quiet place	dullhuus
at	by	bi
at first	right up front	toeerst
at home	in the house	tohuus or bihuus
at least	not any less	wenigstens or tominnst
at the time	when	damols or denntied
attach	fasten to	anmoken or fastmoken
attack	let's get him	öwerfall (past: öwerfalln)
attempt	try to do	versök (past:versocht), probeer
attend to	pay attention to	kiehr or ankiehren
attorney	lawyer	afkat
attractive	nice looking	smuck
August	8th month	August
aunt	parent's sibling	tante (pl: tantes)
author	writer	shriewersmann
authorization	permission	verlöv
autumn	the fall	harvst or harvst tied

available	you can have it	free		
avenue	broad street	allee		
average	down the middle	dörschnittlig		
avoid	take guard against	wohren	or	bargen
awake	quit yawning	wook	or	waak
aware	know about it	bescheed		
awareness	inkling of	ohnung		
away	off from	af		
away	put it away	weg		
awful	terrible	gräsig	or	schrecklig
awhile	small time	tiedlang		
axe	chopper	hex	or	biel

baby	junior person	kind	or blagen	or gör
babysit	watch kids	kinnerwohren		
bachelor	lucky dog	gesell		
back	rearward	trüg	or	trüch
back	rear of upper body	puckel	or	pukkel
back and forth	this way-that way	hin un her		
back and forth	to there-back again	hin un trüg		
back door	deliveries only	achterdöör	or ächterstendöör	
backpack	carry along behind	knappsack		
backside	the far side	hinnern		
backwards	turned around	trügwards	or	trüchwards
bacon	pig fat	speck		
bad	poor or rotten	slecht	or	slimm
bad luck	problems	pech	or	unglück
bad weather	stormy	unwedder	or	unweer
badge	identifier	aftecken	or	schild
bag	paper bag	tuten		
bag	doctor's leather kit	kuffer		
baggage	luggage	packelausch	or	gepack
bailiff	get out of jail	panner		
bake	prepare in the oven	bak	(past: bakt)	
bake	to bake	baken		
bake house	bread making place	bakhuus	(pl: bakhüs)	
bake oven	lovin in the oven	bakoben	or	bakoven
baker	makes bread	baker	or beker	or bäker
baking flour	white dust	bakmehl		
baking powder	secret ingredient	bakpulwer		
bald	hairless	kahl	or	kahlkopp
ball	round object	ball		
bang	to hit noisily	baller		
bang	explosion sound	knall		
bank	money house	sporkass	or	bank
bankbook	keep track of loot	sporbook		
bankrupt	out of money	bankrott		
baptism dress	wear it once	dööpkleed		
baptize	christening	dööp		
baptized	christened	döft		

barber	cuts hair	putzbüdel
barefoot	oozes between toes	barft or barfoot
barely	hardly at all	kuum or knapp
bark	tree skin	bork
barley	grain	garsen or garst or gruben
barn	place for hay	scheurn or shüün
barn floor	place to dance	deel
baromenter	weather indicator	weerglas
barrel	beer holder	tuun or bardel or bärdel
barrel band	can be used as a toy	tüdelband
barrel organ	hung around the neck	dudelsack or dudelkassen
basement	lowest room	keller
basis	foundation	ünnersatz or grund
basket	container	korv (pl: körv) or korb or korf
bass	fish	gadder
bat	hangs upside down	fleddermuus
bats	nest of them	fleddermüüs
batchelor	single man	eenspanner
bathtub	bubble time	balje
battled	struggled	beddelt
be	must be so	wesen
beach	sandy walk	strand
beak	nose on bird	snobel
beaker	container	beker
beam	wood support	bill
beans	ammunition	bohnen
bear	big and fuzzy	baar or bär (pl: bären)
bear it	endure something	utholen
beard	whiskers	bort
beast	zoo resident	beest
beat	beat up on	prügel
beat	timing, as in music	tack
became	has become	woren or worden
became aware	took notice	androgen or wiesworrn
because	that's why	dorüm or worüm or wiel
because	that's the issue	wegen or wegens
because of that	reason for	wieldat
become	will be	weerst
become	will become	weern
become aware	take notice	andregen or wies kommen
become aware	finally get it	spitz kommen
become habit	need to do it	anwinnen
bed	to sleep on	bedd or bett or puuk
bedeviled	pestered	verdübelt
bedsheets	bed linen	bettüch, bettlaken, bettloken
bedstead	holds the springs	bettstell
bedtime	ho-hum	betttied or tobeddgohntied
beef	where is it	rindfleesch
beef cattle	on the hoof	rinder or rindveh
beehive	bee's home	immenkorv

been	was or has been	ween or wesen or west
beer	the good stuff	beer
bees	honey makers	immen
beet	sugery plant	suckerrööv
beetle	little bug	kaver (pl: käver)
before	already happened	eher or vör or vörher
before noon	a little early to eat	vörmiddag
before yesterday	2 days ago	vörgistern
beg	plead	snurren
beggar	can you spare a dime	snurrer
begin	make a start	anfangen (past: anfungen)
beginning	at the outset	anfang
behind	not in front	achter or hinner
belch	unpolite comment	upstöten
believe	to have faith	glööv
believe	think it's true	lööv
bell	small ringer	bimmel
bell ring	very small ringer	pingel
bellow	holler	brüllen
belly	stomach	buuk
bellyache	groan	buukweh or buukkniepen
belly button	inny or outy	buukknop
belong	owned	hüürt or gehüret
belong to	member of	tohüren
beloved	loved	beleevt or gelövet
below	down there	nerden
below	under there	ünner
belt	take in a notch	gördel
bench	to sit on	bank
bend	lean your body over	bück
bend	make not straight	börg (past: börgt)
bent	curvy	krumm
berry	on the vine	beern
beside	along the side	blangs
best	better than all	besten or aller besten
bet	wager	wett
better	nicer	beter or bäter or biäter
better mood	friendlier	beter stellt
between	surrounded	twüschen or tüsken
between times	meanwhile	twüschentied
bible	the good book	bibel (pl: bibeln)
bicker	wrangle, argue	kritt
bicycle	transportation	rad or fohrrad
bid	make a bid	beeden
bid	the bid, as in cards	bott
big	large	groot or grod
biggest	no bigger	grötste
billion	with a 'b'	biljoon
binder	makes bundles	binder or binner
binder twine	wraps bundles	bindertweern

binoculars	snooperscope	wietkieker	
bird	winged one	vagel	(pl: vagels)
bird house	tweety's place	vagelhuus	
bird nest	tweety's birthplace	vagelnest	
birthday	special annual day	geburtsdag	
biscuit	baked twice	tweeback	
bit	in horse's mouth	tuum	
bit in two	chomp	dörbeten	or dörbäten
bitch	female dog	tev	
bite	take a chunk out	biet	(past: bäten)
bite off	bite in two	afbieten	
bitter	acidic	bidder	
bitterly	with rancor	bidderlig	
black	color	swatt	
black ice	very slippery spot	glatties	
blackberry	a fruit	brummelbeern	
blacksmith	horseshoe maker	smied	
blame	have some fault	shuld	
blanket	covers	bedddecken	
bleat	like a lamb	blarr	or blarren
bleed	lose blood	blööt	(past: blöör)
bleeding	losing blood	blöded	
bleeds	can bleed	blöd	
blend	mix together	mengeleern	
blessing	benefit	segen	
blind	can't see	blind	
blink	wink	pliern	
block	to hinder	blocken	or blockieren
block	of wood	pluck	
block and tackle	hoist 'er up	talje	
blockhead	wood for brains	klotz	or holthopp
blood	don't faint	bloot	
blood pressure	danger sign	blootdrück	
bloom	to flower	blöör	
blooms	in full flower	blööt	or bleiht
blouse	summer wear	bluus	
blow	on a candle	bloos	or puus or weih
blow away	get rid of	wegblosen	
blow down	knock her over	dahlblosen	
blow off	dislodge	afblosen	
blow out	extinguish	utblosen	or utpusten
blow through	strong wind	dörweihen	or dörblosen
blow up	kaboom	upblosen	
blow your nose	use a hanky	utsnuben	
blows	puff of wind	puust	or weiht
blue	color	blau	
blunt	not sharp	stump	
board	plank	brett or bredd (pl: brede)	
boardinghouse	place to stay	kösthuus	
body	your container	liev or lief or lieb	

bog	kind of swampy	moor		
boil	a hot one	brölen	or	kook
boil over	boil too much	utkoken		
bold	not afraid	driest		
bolster	front of wagon	dreihshimmel		
bone	chew on this	knoken		
book	with pages	book	(pl: böke)	
boot	made for walking	stebel	or	stevel
bootjack	fixes boots	stebelknecht		
border	edge of area	rebeet	or	kant
borderland	on the periphery	mark		
borderstone	like a curb	kantsteen		
bore	talks too much	dröhnbuddel		
boring	wake when over	dröhnig		
born	see the light of day	geburen		
borrow	have just for a while	bören	or	lehnen
bosom	pretty chest	bosem		
boss	top dog	baas or boos or buur or buer		
both	two together	beide		
bother	but in	stöör		
bothers	regret it a bit	stört	or	verdrütt
bottle	glass container	buddel	(pl: buddels)	
bought	all paid for	kofft	or	inkoft
bound	tied	bunnen	or	upbunnen
bouquet	bunch of flowers	bloomenstruss		
bourgois	common people	pahlbörger		
bow	of a boat	boog		
bowl	container	gropen	or	kump
bowlegged	knees apart	scheevbeenig	or scheefbeenig	
bowling	kegling	pudel smieten	or	kegeln
box	container	doos or kist or kasten		
boy	young male	jung	(pl: jungs)	
brag	I am great	prohl	or	prool
braid	cord	snoor		
brain	smart box	bregen	or	brägen
bran	grain	schroot	or	missing
branch	twig	telgen	or	telling
brand	identifier	mark		
brandy	schnaps	kööm	or	brennen
brash	in your face	snodderig		
brass	keep shining	messelig		
brat	little wise guy	göör	(pl: gören)	
brave	not scared, much	tapper	or	modig
brazen	a hussy	pampig	or	driest
bread	staff of life	brot	or	broot
bread & butter	just butter on it	bodderbrot		
bread end	1st and last slice	knoos	(pl: knös)	
bread knife	slices easy	brotmest		
break apart	knock in two	uteenannerbreken		
break away	lose a part	wegbreken		

break down	goes kaputt	dahlbreken		
break in	be a burglar	inbreken		
break into	forced entry	rinbreken		
break loose	get away	losbreken		
break off	snap off	afbreken		
break open	crack open	openbreken		
break out	escape	utbreken		
break through	make a hole in it	dörbreken		
break up	wreck	upbreken	or	opbreken
breakfast	first meal of the day	fröhstück		
breath	suck it in	oten	or	ooten
breathless	can't run anymore	utpuust	or	otenlos
breed	instill variety	tucht		
breedhorse	stud	tuchtpeerd		
breese	nice wind	bries		
brew	witch's tonic	bröer		
brewery	place is 'hop'ing	broeree	or	bröree
bribe	help persuade	beköpen		
brick	block	baksteen	or	tegel
brick yard	where they're made	tegelee		
bricklayer	mason	müerker	or	muurman
bride	wife to be	bruut		
bridegroom	Mr. Lucky	brögam		
bridge	path over river	brüch	(pl: brüchen)	
bridle	front reins	toom	or	togel
bright	shiny	hell		
bring	carry along	bring	(past: brocht)	
bring in	carry inside	rinbringen		
bring over	carry over	röwerbringen		
bring to order	settle down	ordnen		
brittle	breakable	sprööd	or	krümmelig
broadaxe	ungentle persuader	breedbiel		
broil	barbecue	braden		
broken	needs fixing	broken or twei	or	kaputt
brood	grumble	klamüstern		
broom	sweep's clean	bessen		
broomstick	witch's taxi	bessenstehl		
broth	kind of soup	bröh		
brother	male sibling	broder	or	broer
brother-in-law	wife's brother	swieger		
brought in	dragged in	rinbrocht		
brown	a dark color	bruun		
bruise	owch spot	brummsen		
brush	your teeth	bööst		
brush off	tidy up	afbösten		
buck	male deer	bock	(pl: böck)	
buckel	for the belt	snall		
bucket	carry water	ammel		
buckwheat pancakes	yum for sure	bookweeten pannkoken		
bud	beginning of flower	knoppe		

83

buddy	mate, good friend	maaker or macker
bug	crawly thing	bock
bug out	head for the hills	utknippen
build	construct	bohn or baun
building	structure	geböt or gebööt (pl: geböde)
built	already up	boht or baut or boot
builtup	additional construction	upboht or upboot
bull	mr. bovine	stier
bullet	fired from gun	kugel
bumble bee	big stinger	hummung
bump	little knob	knubben
bump	knock	stött
bump over	to topple it over	öwerstötten
bumped against	touched	anstött
bumped over	toppled	öwerstött
bundle	tied up stuff	bünnel (pl: bünneln)
bung	plug in a barrel	tappen
bung hole	hole in barrel	spundlock
bunkbed	double decker	sloopkist or alkoon oder kabuz
burglar	wears a mask	inbreker
buried	put under ground	begroben
burn	make very hot	brinn (past: verbrinnt)
burn off	clear brush	afbrinnen
burn through	make a hole	dörbrinnen
burning nettle	really stings	brinn nettle
burrow	dig in	wöhl
burst	stick the balloon	bost
bury	first dig a hole	ingroben
bush	clumpy plant	busch
bushy	looks like a bush	buschig
busy	busy time	hill or hillig or flietig
busy	in a hurry	in a iel or ielig
busy work	just looking busy	ketelflicken
but	except, however	ower or awer or over or apatt
but, so	but, see this?	süh
butcher	slaughter	slachter
butcher knife	carver	slachtenmest
butt	always behind you	orse or morse
butter	not margarine	bodder or boddern
butterfly	so pretty	bodderlicker or bodderflegen
buttock cheeks	sitter cushion	orsebacken
button	fastener	knoop (pl: knööp)
button up	ready for cold	toknöpen
buy	make a purchase	kööp (past: kofft)
buy back	retrieve again	trügköpen
buy from	purchase from	afköpen
buy on credit	put it on the books	anshrieben loten
buyer	takes the goods	köopman or inköper
by	near, around	bi
by foot	walk all the way	tofoot

84

bypassed	went by in front	vörbigohn		
by heart	just from memory	utenkopp		
by which	by what	wonehmbi		
cabbage	from the garden	kohl	or	kabuus
cabin	in the woods	kabine		
cabinet	space in the kitchen	schapp		
cabinet maker	handy in the kitchen	discher		
cabinet shop	where they're made	discheree		
cackle	funny laugh	snatern	or	kackle
cake	baked goody	koken		
calculate	do the figures	reken		
calculator	magic adder	rekner		
calendar	lists all the days	kalenner	(pl:kalinner)	
calf	baby cow	kalf	(pl: kalwe)	
calf of leg	cramps here	waad		
call	summon	roop	(past: roppt)	
call	assign a name	heet		
call away	summoned	wegropen		
call off	terminate	afropen		
call on	speak to	anropen		
called	is named	heeten		
calls	is calling	roppt		
calm	quiet	pomadig	or	rohig
came	arrived	kömm		
can	able to	kann		
can	container	kannen	(pl: kannen)	
can	'you' can	kanns		
can	'they' can	könnt		
canal	watery road	kanol		
candid	free speaking	freemödig		
candidate	up for office	kannedat		
candle	light source	karse	or	lücht
candles	light makers	karsen		
candy	sweet stuff	kinnig	or	naschkroom
candy maker	a 'sweet' person	kanditer		
cane	to help you walk	handstock	or	godendagstock
cane chair	porch seat	rohrstohl		
cannon	shoots big bullets	kanon		
canny	deviously clever	plietsch		
cap	little hat	mütz	or	kappen
cape	overcoat	mantel		
capitalize	big letters	grootschrieben		
capsize	tip over	ümkippen		
captain	boss of the ship	käppan		
car	automobile	koor	or	koar
caraway	seeds on a bun	kümmel		
card	ace high	korden		
cardboard	heavy paper	papp		
cardigan	sweater	strickjack		

85

care	give help	plege		
careful	watch out	vernünftig	or	sorgsom
carp	kind of fish	karp		
carpenter	wood worker	timmerman	or	schreiner
carpenter shop	wood work shop	timmeree		
carpentry	do the work	timmern		
carpet	floor cover	tappet		
carriage	usually horse drawn	kutsch	or	kutschwogen
carries	does the carrying	driggt		
carrots	rabbit food	wöddel	or	wörtel
carry	drag	dreeg	(past: drogen)	
carry	act of carrying	dreeg		
carry over	till next time	öwerdregen		
cart	pulled vehicle	koor	or	koar
cartload	unit of measure	foder		
carve	cut woodcash	shnitzeln		
cast iron	make a good stove	geetiesen		
cashbox	safe place	geldkasten		
castle	nice place	börg		
cat	puss type	katt	(pl: katten)	
catechism	study time	katechissen		
catholic	religion	kathoolsch		
cattle	farm animals	veh		
cause	reason for	ursaak		
cautious	mindful, careful	sinnig		
cavalry	organized riders	riederee		
celebrate	have a party	fier		
cellar	room underneath	keller		
cement	the hard stuff	sement		
cemetery	last stop	kerkhof or karkhof or doodenhof		
century	100 years in time	johrhunnert		
ceramic	made in an oven	püttjerkunst		
certain	for sure	gewiss		
certainly	obviously true	gewiss		
chaff	winnowed stuff	kaff		
chain	iron rope	keeden	or	kedden
chair	sitting apparatue	stohl		
chairman	runs the meeting	övermann	or	vörsittter
chalk	for the blackboard	kried	or	kalk
chamber	big official room	komer	or	kamer
champaign	the bubbly	schuumwien		
change	apply difference	wesseln	or	ännerung
changeable	flexible, flowing	flussig		
change mind	female prerogative	besinnen	(past: besunnen)	
chaotic	confusing	döreenanner		
characteristic	birthmark	kinnmark		
charcoal	barbecue	holtkohl		
charge	hand a bill	reken		
charm	sweet talk	scharm	or	riez
charming	well behaved	orrig		

86

chastity	purity	küüschheit		
chase	go after	achternolopen		
chat	casual conversation	klönen		
chatter	idle talk	gedibber	or	babbeln
chatter box	mouthy type	rappelsnuten		
cheap	not expensive	billig		
cheat	take advantage of	beshieten	(past: besheten)	
cheats	doesn't play fair	fuget		
checks out	looks alright	stimmt		
cheek	one on each side	backen		
cheerful	happy go lucky	höglig		
cheese	made from milk	kees	or	käs
cheese spread	out of the bottle	smeerkees		
chemisty	test tubes	sheedkunst		
cherry	red fruit	kirschen	or	kassbeern
cherrytree	for climbing in	kassbeernboom		
chest	hairy spot (men only)	bost		
chest	like a trunk	laad	or	kuffer
chest pocket	for pencils	bost taschen		
chew	eating gum	kau (past: kaut)	or	gnaag
chew cud	cow loves it	ederkaun		
chew out	give em hell	utschellen		
chewing tobacco	splat!	kautabak		
chewy	hard to bite	tau		
chicken	egg layer	hehn	(pl: höhner)	
chicken coop	egg-zact place	höhnerstahl		
chicks	baby chickens	küken		
child	baby person	kind	(pl: kinner)	
childhood	the good times	kinnertied		
chill	in the air	küll		
chimes	bells	gelött		
chimney	tall smoker	schorsteen		
chin	bottom of face	kinn		
chisel	shape wood	betel		
chocolate	yummy	schokolad	or	kakao
choir	of angels	chor		
choke	gag	wörgen		
choleric	sick	gallsüchtig		
choose	pick out	utsöken	(past: utsocht)	
chop	lop off	afhauen		
chores	feed the chickens	toshick moken		
christening	baptism	kinnelbeer	or	dööpen,
christian	saintly	christlig		
Christmas	time to open it yet?	Wiehnachten	or	Julklapp
Christmas eve	can't wait for morning	Juulklappsobend		
Christmas wish list	live in hopes	wünschzeddel		
chubby cheeked	little darlin	puusbacken		
church	for religious services	kerk	or	kark
churchtower	bell home	kerktoorn		
churn	keep cranking	boddermöhl		

cigar	stinks so good	zigar		(pl: zigarren)
cigarette	coffin nail	zigarette		
cinnamon	spicy	kaneel		
citizen	owns and votes	borger		(pl: börger)
citizenry	populace	börgerschop		
city	big town	stadt		
city council	elected officials	stadtrot		
city hall	main building	rothuus		
city people	slickers	stadtlüüd	or	stadtlüer
civil war	states fight	börgerkrieg		
civilized	well behaved	maneerlig		
claim	so sue me	klogen		
clamp	to hold together	klempen		
clap	hands together	klap		
clarify	make clearer	upkloren		
class	one grade	klass		
clean	no dirt	rein		
clean	to make clean, polish	putzen		
cleaning woman	like a maid	putzfro	or	putzfru
clear	can see through	klor	or	kloar
clear away	make room for	rümen	or	rümmen
clear up	better weather	upkloren		
clever	crafty	klövtig		
climb	go up the ladder	klatter	or	upstiegen
climb on	get onto	rupstiegen		
climb out	get out	rutstiegen		
clip	a cut out	utsnitt		
clip	snap off	knipp		
clique	special community	sippschop		
clock	time piece	klock		(pl: klocken)
clock hand	pointer	wieser		
clod	clump of dirt	kluuten		(pl: klüten)
cloister	retreat	klooster		
close	near	dicht		
close by	near abouts	dichtbi	or	neegbi
close friend	very special	dicke fründ	or	anbroder
closed	made shut	to	or tomokt	or sloten
cloth	useful rag	dook		
clothes	or cloth material	tüüch		
clothes pin	hang to dry	washknieper	or	klimmer
clouds	in the sky	wulken		
clove	stinky but good	negelken		
clover	feed the horse	klever	or	kleehau
clover leaf	four of them	kleverblatt		
clown	funny person	hansworst		
club	head knocker	knüppel	or	küül
club	organized group	vereen		
clump	small pile	klump		
clumsy	stumbler	tapsig		
cluster	pile	kluster		

88

coal	black fuel	kohl		
coarse	rough	groff		
coast	big water's edge	küst		
coat	jacket	jack	or	rock
coat	work jacket	kittel		
coat of paint	could use one	anstrek		
cobblestone	rough road	koppelsteen		
cobweb	spider's home	spinnweev	or	spinnwark
cock	mr. chicken	hohn	or	hahn
coffee	hot and black	kaffe	or	koffi
coffeebean	aromatic	kaffebohnen		
coffeecake	scrumptious	kaffekoken		
coffee cup	keep it full	kump		
coffeepot	holds coffee	kaffepott	or	kaffeputt
coffeetime	any time	kaffetied		
coffin	a place to stay	sarg		
coin	small bucks	klingelgeld	or	klöttergeld
coincidental	just happened	tofellig	or	tofällig
cold	below zero	kold	or	koolt
cold feet	don't touch me	koldeföten		
collapsed	knocked in	instött	or	dahlbroken
collar	around the neck	kraagem	or	kragen
collect	go and get it	afholen	or	rinnehmen
collection bag	church offering	klingelbüddel		
cologne	stinkky water	kölnwoter		
color	it's got a hue	klüür	or	farv
colorful	very lively bright	bunt		
colorless	no brightness	ahnfarv	or	grieshaftig
comb	pull through hair	kamm	(pl: kämmen)	
comb	to use a comb	kimmen		
combine	grain harvester	meihdösher		
come	to arrive	kumm	(past: kömm)	
come in	enter in	rinkommen	or	kommrin
come up	come to your notice	vörkommen		
comes	is coming	kummt	or	kommt
comes on	presents themself	kummt an	or	kommt an
comes to mind	just remembered it	infallen		
comfortable	really cozy	kommodig		
command	says behave yourself	gebott		
committee	working group	utshütt		
common	usual	gemeensam		
common sense	a rarity	verstand		
commotion	unruly noise	bestakel		
communion	wine and bread	obendmohl		
company	a going concern	sellschop	or	bedriev
compare	match up	verglieken		
compartment	section	afdeel		
compassionate	sympathetic	mitleedig		
competent	can do it	tostännig		
complain	whine	sabben or	grübeln or	quäsen

89

complain	whine, part II	jammer	or	sörge
complete	over and done with	vullstännig	or	heel
complaint	can't be pleased	sorge	or	grübel
completely	entirely	ganze	or	gans un gor
compliant	easy pickins	nogevig		
complicated	hard to understand	komplizeert		
comprehend	get it	begriepen		
computer	smart machine	rekner		
comrade	buddy	kumpan	or	kumpel
conceited	puffed up	hochnäs	or	hoch inbild
concern	be concerned	kümme	or	kümmer
concerns	be your business	sheret or sheert or		vergeiht
conclusion	how it came out	utkommen	or	afsluut
condition	state of being	tostand		
confession	fess up officially	bicht		
confirmed	made sure of	kumfermiert		
confiscated	took away	beslagnohmen		
confused	mixed up	verdattert or tumpig or verbiestert		
congregation	the flock	gemeen		
congratulate	good job	gratulieren		
connector	snap on	ansluut		
conscience	part of mind	geweten		
consequence	comes from it	achterklapp		
considered	gave thought to	bedacht		
constant	continuous	beständig		
construct	make, to build	mok		(past: mokt)
consume	use up	upbruken		
consumed	used up	upbrocht		
contemplate	consider	nodenken		
contemptuous	look down on	minnächtig		
contend	claims	behoop		
content	satisfied	begnögt		
content	what it holds	inholt		
contract	legal deal	verdrag		
contra dance	old style line dance	kunterdans		
contrary	against something	gegendeel		
contribute	fork it over	röwergeben		
contribution	share	togeev	or	bidrag
control	keep in line	kontroll	or	överhand
convenient	acceptable to you	topass		
conversation	neighborly discussion	klönsnak		
convince	talk into	insnaken		
coo	like a dove	gurren		
cook	make food	kook (past: kookt) or		kok
cooked	done	goar	or	goor
cooking	make the meal	koken		
cool	low temperature	köhlig	or	kölig
cool off	summer breeze	afköhlen		(past: afköhlt)
cooperation	work together	scharwarken		
cooperative	joint organization	maatschop		

90

copper	metal	kopper
copy	make an image, xerox	afbild or kopie
copy	by hand , writing	afschrift
copy	by hand, drawing	nomalen
cordial	pleasant manner	hartlig
cork	stopper in bottle	propp
corn	silky crop	korn or koorn or mais
corn	on the big toe	liekdoorn
corner	wall meeting point	eck (pl: ecken)
cornflower	bachelor buttons	kornbloomen
corpulant	full figured	dickliev
correct	factually accurate	richtig
cost	what you pay	kost
costs	this is the price	köst
cosy	comfy	mackelig
coterminous	all at same time	gliekentied
cottage	little house	kott
cottager	owns a cottage	kotter
cotton	wad of the wooley	wadden
cough	bark out	hussen
could	maybe could	könn
council	government body	rot
count	take a number	tellen
Count	royal male	Grof
count off	take a count	aftellen
Countess	royal female	Grofin
country	offical area of people	land
counts	is counted	tellt or gellt
county	political district	kring
county chairman	major local official	kringbaas
courage	bravery	mood
course	stay on it, study	kür or leehrgang
courteous	polite	höflig
cousin	male relative	vedder or kusin
cover	put something over it	todecken
cow	milk animal	koh (pl: keih)
cow hold still	don't kick the bucket	wo bass
cow pasture	walk and chew	kohkamp
cow pie	watch your step	kohshiet
coward	he splits	haasenfoot
cowhide	a bit leathery	kohfell
cozy	very comfy	mackelig
crabby	ill-tempered	kotterig
crack	a sharp sound	knack
crackle	sounds like static	kneder
cradle	rock-a-by	weege
crafty	clever	plietsch
cranberry	good juice	prieselbeeren
cranky	temperamental	kortanbunnen
crash land	plop onto the ground	bomms

crash into	metal bender	rinjogen	or	rindäbeln
crawl	walking low	kreepen	or	krabbeln
crayons	coloring sticks	kriede		
craziness	wierdness	splienigkeit		
crazy	pretty nuts	verrückt or dwatsch or mal		
crazy	not thinking	up'n kopp fallen		
cream	from a cow	rohm	or	flött
crease	unwanted seam	krimp		
creep	slide along floor	kreep	(past: krüpt)	
creeps	is creeping	kröpt		
crest	family emblem	segel		
crib	baby jail	kinnerbett	or	krüff
cricket	noisy buggers	singhöhnken		
criminal	crook	inbreker		
cripple	handicapped	krüppel		
crisp	fresh	krosch	or	knusperig
crochet	make a doily	hekeln		
crooked	unaligned	sheev		
crop	in the field	kropp		
cross	sign of the	krüüz		
cross beam	hold up roof	dweerholt	or	dwarsholt
cross bow	handy shooter	armbost	or	flitzbog
cross road	four corners	krüüzweg	or	veereck
cross street	going the other way	dweerstraat		
crossways	diagonally	dwars	or	dweers
crouch	hide behind	hucken	or	huken
crow	like a rooster	kreihen		
crown	king me	kroon	(pl: kröön)	
crows	is crowing	kreiht		
cruel	mean	grusam		
crumb	leftover	krümmel		
crushed grain	left overs	shrot	or	schrott
crutch	helper	krüken		
cry	baby's refrain	blarren or shreen or weenen		
cry out	scream, end crying	utshreen		
cuckoo	little birdie	kukuk		
cucumber	big pickle	gurk		
cultivator	dig weeds, not corn	shüffelploog		
culture	civilized manners	kulture		
cup	of tea	tass		
cup	of wine	beker		
cup	of coffee	köppen	or	kump
cupboard	where dishes are kept	schap	or	schapp
curdle	milk goes sour	kesen		
cure	to make well	heelen		
curfew hour	get off the street	sperrstunn		
curious	nosy	neeshierig		
curl	wavy part	krüll		
curls	gets kinky	krüllt		
curly	wrinkly	krüllig	or	kruus

curly head	not very bald	kruuskopp		
currant	red berry	kakelbeern		
currently	in these times	upsteed	or	upstunns
curtain	front of stage	vörhang		
curved	full of bends	krumm		
cushion	pillow	küssen		
cuss	colorful language fluch			
custom	regular way	mode		
customer	maybe a buyer	kunne	(pl: kunnen)	
cut	take a slice	snie	(past: sneen)	
cut	act of cutting	snieden or snien or sheeren		
cut	a cut out of	snitt		
cut off	lopped off	afsneen		
cut through	sliced	dörsneen		
cute	sweet like	nüdlig		
cute	in an odd way	putzig		
daily	every day	däglig	or	dääglig
daisy	flower	goos bloomen or mardel bloom		
damage	been hurt	shoden		
damn	very mad at it	verdamte		
damp	muggy	klumm		
dance	do a jitterbug	dans	or	danz
dance	the event itself	ball	(pl: dänz)	
dance floor	stomp on it	sool	or	saal
dandelion	all over the yard	hunnenbloom		
danger	possible harm	gefähr	or	lebensgefähr
dangerous	could hurt	gefährlig		
dank	cold and wet	beklumm		
daredevil	takes chances	waaghalsig		
dark	night time	düster	or	düüster
darn	almost damn	verdreihte	or	verdullte
darn	fix the sock	stopp		
dash	go by quickly	suus		
daughter	female offspring	dochter		
day	part of week	dag	(pl: daag)	
day after tomorrow	2 days away	öwermorgen		
day dream	be half awake	dosen		
day laborer	hard worker	daglohner		
day time	during daylight	bidagstied		
daylight	sunshine	daagslicht		
dead	as a door nail	doot	or	dood
dead ones	not lively	doden		
deaf	can't hear	dief	or	duuf
deal	distribute	deel		
deal out	like in cards	utdeelen		
dear	favorite	lewe	or	leve
dear	hold in close regared	leew	or	leev
dearest	most special one	leevste		
dear lady	get on her good side	beste fro	or	beste fru

debt	what you owe	shuld (pl: shulden)
deceive	cheat	bedregen or biesterföhren
deceived	has been cheated	bedrogen
December	last month of year	Dezember
decided	mind made up	besloten
decision	agree on it	besluut
deck	shelf	deck
declare	mean it	meen
decorate	make nice	fien moken
dedicate	celebrate the start of	inweihen
deduction	part off	aftog
deep	way down under	deep
defeat	overcome	ünnerdrieben
defend	back them up	tostohn or bistohn
defer	put off	upschuuv
delay	do it later	upshuben or upshuven
deliberate	with fore thought	sinnig or saakmodig or wetenlig
delicacy	special treat	fienkost
demolish	really smash up	tonichts moken
dent	smashed in place	buul
dentist	tooth puller person	tähnknieper or tehndokter
deny	say no with head	shüttkopp
department store	what size you need	kööphuus
depend on	rely on	verloten
depends on	based on	hängt an
depot	train station	bohnhof
depressed	down	benaut
depressing	a downer	sluukoorig
derisive	down on	spietsch
derive	come from	stamm
descendants	come after	nofohrnen
descended	heirs	afstammt
describe	tell about	beschriev or utmaalen
desire	wanting to do it	lust
dessert	best part of meal	nodisch
detailed	all the facts	utföhrlig
detour	taka another route	ümtog or ümweg or ümdriev
devil	ol pointy tail	dübel or düvel
devilish	act like him	dübelig
devout	strongly believe	froom
dew	moist grass	dau
dew drop	sparkle in the sun	daudroppen
diameter	dimension	dörmet
diamond	card suit	ruden
diamonds	jewels	brillianten
diaper	wet pants	winnel or kinnerdook
dictionary	glossary, wordbook	wörtebook or wöörbook
did	he once did	dä (pl: dään)
die	keel over	storb or storv or dootgohn
died	was killed	ümkommen

94

died	went dead	doot gohn	or	doot bleben
difference	what's not the same	ünnersheed		
different	not the same	anners	or	anders
differentiate	make distinction	ünnersheed moken		
difficult	hard to do	swoor		
difficulty	problematical	swoorheit		
dig	start a hole	groov	or	groob
digest	consume	verknusen		
dike	hold water back	diek		
diminish	make less of	tominnen	or	minnern
dimple	hole in cheek	kühlken		
dinner	eat at noon	meddageten		
dinner service	all the plates, etc.	etengeshirr		
dinner table	where you eat	etdisch		
dip into	makes a donut good	rinstippen		
diptheria	ickness	kruup		
direction	a certain way	direkschoon		
director	of a play	speelbaas		
dirt	small piece of earth	dreck		
dirty	unclean	smuddelig	or	shieterig
disadvantage	goes against you	nodeel		
disc	in the field	disken		
discharge	make gun go off	afsheten		
discharged	went off	afschoten		
discipline	in control	tucht		
discipline	to chew 'em out	utoosen		
discover	find out	utfinnen		
discuss	talk over	öwersnacken		
discussion	conversation	gesprek		
disgrace	demean	schännen		
disgrace	belittle	blamieren		
disgraceful	shame on you	schimplig		
dish	small plate	schöttel or disch or schaal		
disheveled	not looking good	habbelig		
dishonor	desecrate	schännen	or	unehrn
dishrag	dishwasher	schötteldook		
dismount	get off the easy way	afstiegen		
distance	far to go	wiet	or	afstand
distillery	good place to work	brenneree		
distinct	clear	düütlich		
distinct	very clear	klor	or	kloar
distress	tension	drang		
district	official area	krink		
disturb	bother	stöör		(past: stört)
disturbing	bothersome	ärgerlig		
ditch	roadside pit	grab	or	kuul
divert	different path	aflieden	or	verföhren
divide	separate shares	sheeden		
divide up	pieces for everybody	updeelen		
divisible	can be cut up	deelbor		

divorce	split up	sheeden	or düsig
dizzy	spinning feeling	swinnelig	or düsig
do	'I' do	doh	(past: dohn)
do	'they' do	(se) doot	
doctor	say 'aaaah'	dokter	(pl: dokters)
doe	female deer, goat	seeg	
does	'it' does	deiht	
dog	best friend	hund	or rüe
doghouse	fido's domocile	hundenhuus	
doll	toy person	poppen	
dollar	a buck	doler	or dolar
dominate	rule, master	meestern	
donate	give to	spennen	
done	finished cooking	goar	
done	completed	ferdig	
done eating	burp	satt	
donkey	beast of burden	esel	
donut	hole'ly food	fettcakes	
door	entranceway	döör	
door bell	ping ping	döörpingel	
door handle	made of iron	klink	
doorsill	step over and in	süll	
doorway	opening to go through	döörlock	
dose	amount of medicine	geev	or gaav
dotted	spotted	punktlig	
double	twice as good	duppel	or dubbel
double tree	to hitch up with	tau	
doubly	two kinds	tweerlie	
doubt	suspicion	twiefel	
doubtful	might not	twiefelig	
dough	for baking	deeg	
dove	he coo'ing bird	duuv	
down	pointing south	dahl	
downhill	down the slope	bargdahl	
dozen	12	dutz	
drag	carry along ground	slep	or shlepp
drag	use the farm implement	shierwark	
drag along	walk and carry	mitdregen	or mitdrägen
dragon	monster	draak	
drain	place to flow away	gütt	
drank	all gone	drunken	
draw	make a picture	maol	or maal
drawer	for socks	schuuvlood	
dream	think in your sleep	droom	(past: drömt)
dreams	is dreaming	drömen	
dress	woman's clothing	kleed	(pl: klede)
dress	put clothes on	antehn	or antrecken
dresser	clothes holder	buro	
dribble	let leak out slowly	drüppel	
dried	not wet anymore	drögt	

dried off	not behind the ears	afdrögt		
drink	imbibe	drink		
drink	just take a sip	suup		
drive	take the car	föhr	or	jaag
drive apart	divide in two	uteenannerdrieben		
drive away	leave in a car	wegjogen		
drive back	return	trügföhren		
drive into	proceed into	rindrieben	or	rindrieven
drive in	drive into	infohren		
drive off	take off in car	afjogen	or	afföhren
drive over	run him over	öwerjogen		
drive over	run him down	dohljogen		
drive through	down the middle	dörföhren	or	dörjogen
driver	does the driving	föhrmann	or	stüürman)
drivers license	ok - pull over	föhrshien	or	föhrteken
driveway	car entrance	drievweg		
driving lane	stay on the left	föhrbohn		
drizzle	light rain	snudderegen		
drop	piece of rain	droppen	or	druppen
drop it	let it drop	lat't fallen		
drowned	down for 3rd time	versopen		
druggist	mixes potions	apteker		
drugstore	apothecary	aptek		
drum	noise maker	trummel		
drunk	3 sheets to wind	duum or duun or besopen		
drunkard	professional drinker	suupmickel		
dry	no moisture	drög	or	dröög
dry out	get dry	utdrögen		
dry up	shrivel up	updrögen		
duck	water bird	aant	(pl: aanten)	
duck	bend or kneel down	duken		
duckweed	green scum	aantenkruut	or	poggenslick
Duke	royal	Hertog		
dull	not sharp	stump	or	stumm
dull	not colorful	duff		
dumb	ignorant	dumm		
dumbness	acting stupidly	dummheit		
dummy	a nut case	döskopp		
dumpling	from potatoes	klüten		
dumptruck	unloads quickly	kippkoor	or	kippkoar
dune	pile of sand	düün	(pl: dünen)	
dunk	put into coffee	rinstippen		
durable	it'll last	deftig		
during the day	work time	bidags	or	bidaags
dusk	late in the day	shummern		
during the day	daylight	bidaags		
dust	cloudy dirt	stoff		
dusty	air is full of it	stövig		
dwarf	little person	ünnereerdsch	or	dwargen

each	every one	jeder				
each one	individually	jedereen				
eager	let's go	iewrig				
ear	hear with	uhr		(pl: uhren)		
ear of corn	good crop	koornuhren				
earlier	happened before	fröher	or	eder		
early	ahead of time	fröh				
early times	the good ones	oolentieden				
earn	get paid	verdeen				
earnest	very serious	ernst	or	eernst		
earnestly	trying hard	truhartig				
earth	home sweet home	eerd				
earthquake	rumble	eerdbäben	or	eerdbeven		
earthworm	let's fish	maddick	or	merken		
east	one direction	oost				
Easter	egg hunt	Osten				
Easter rabbit	egg hider	Osterhaas				
easy	not hard	liecht				
easy chair	big and comfy	lehnstohl				
eat	by animal	fret				
eat	by person	et	or	ät	or	eet
eats	something to eat	eten			or	eeten
eat your fill	all you can	satt eten				
eaten up	gobbled up	upfreten				
eaten up	consumed	upeten				
eavesdrop	listen	lüsten				
echo	say again?	ecko				
edge	rim	kant				
editor	checks the text	sniemester				
educate	make smart	utbilden				
eel	electrifying	aal				
egg	cackle berry	ei		(pl: eier)		
egghead	over-educated	eierkopp				
egg timer	2 minute egg	eierklock				
egg whites	healthy part	eierwitt				
egg whites	when whipped	eiershuum				
egg yellow	not as healthy	eiergeel				
eight	8	acht				
eighteen	18	achteihn				
eighth	1/8	achtel				
eighty	80	achtsig				
either	this or that	entweder				
elbow	arm joint	ellentipp				
electric	hot stuff	elektrisch	or	elektrik		
elegance	trim and fit	schick				
elevator car	get a lift	föhrstohl		(pl:föhrstohl)		
eleven	11	ölven	or	ölben		
eliminate	remove	siedmoken	or	besiedigen		
elsewhere	some other place	annerwegens				
embarrass	make feel small	schänneren				

embarrasing	I didn't do it	peenlig or schenerlig or pienlig
emblem	sign	wohrteken
embroidery	fancy stitching	stickelree
emergency	trouble	noot
emergency exit	head for it	notutgoh
emigrant	look for new home	utwanner
emigrate	leave the country	utwannern
emphasize	strengthen	nodrücken
employee	wage earner	bedeente, anstellte, arbeider
empty	nothing in it	leddig or ledig
empty	clean it out	utledigen
enclosed	sent along with	bileggt
encounter	meet, hit	andrepen
end	last of it	enn
ended	no more	vorbi
endure	take it some more	verdregen or utholen
endured	held out	mit dörhalt or mit dörholt
enemy	bad guy	feend
energetic	full of life	lustig
engaged	almost hitched	verlobt
engaged	busy with	mit togang
english	amerikanski	inglisch
enjoyment	pleasurable	vergnögen
enormous	really huge	beestig groot
enough	all you need	noog or genoog
enroll	sign on	anmellen
enter	go in	ingohn
enter into	go into	ringohn
enthused	excited	happig
enthusiasm	get excited about	ievrig
entire	all of it	ganze or gans or heel
entirely	the whole thing	ganslig or ganzlig
entitled	it's your right	berechtig
entrance door	where to go in	ringoh or ringah
entryway	step into	rintritt
envious	jealous	afgünstlig
envy	be jealous of	benieden
equal	very similar	liekdeel or egol
equalize	make even	utglieken
equally	same proportions	liekedeels or liekedeelig
equipment	trappings	geschirr
erect	establish, put up	oprichten
ermine	nice coat	hermel
escalator	the easy way	rolltreppen ot rulltreppen
essay	textual thought	upsatz
even	no bumps	eben or schier
even	anyway	sogor
even	same pace	glieck
evening	early night time	obend or aobend or ovend
evening meal	some call it supper	obendbrot or ovendbrot

99

evenly	consistently	egolweg		
ever	for all time	ewig		
ever	did you ever	jemols		
every	each one	jeder		
every place	all over	allerwegens		
everyone	all of them	jedereen	or	elkeen
everything	all of it	alls	or	allens
everywhere	all over	allerwegens		
evidence	proof	bewies	or	nowies
evidently	looks like it	ogenshienlig		
exact	right on	genau		
exactly	just the same	süss so	or	genau so
exaggerate	over do it	öwerdrieven		
examine	look over	öwerkieken	or	bekieken
example	as an example	bispill	or	bispeel
exasperating	just too much	to dull		
excellent	pretty darn good	uttekend		
except	but for	blots	or	bloss
exceptional	important	besonners	or	utnehmlig
exchange	trade	tuusch	or	vertuusch
excited	flustered	hiddelig or fuchtig or orrig		
excuse	wasn't me	vörwand	or	inwand
exert	extra force	anstringen		
exerted	used extra force	anstrengt		
exhibit	set on display	utstellen		
exit	way to go	utgoh or utgah or uttritt		
exit	place to go out	utgang		
expand	add a room	utbaun	or	utboon
expenditure	gave at the office	utgeev	or	utgäv
expensive	too many bucks	düür	or	düer
experience	lived thru it	beleven	or	beleben
expert	smarty	fakminsch	(pl: faklüüd)	
explain	clear it all up	upkloren		
explore	snoop around	nospören		
export	sell abroad	utföhr		
expose	show the faults	blamiern		
expression	facial look	gesicht		
extendable	stretchable	uttrekbor		
extra	even some more	extro		
eye	singular peeper	oog	(pl: ogen)	
eyebrow	hair line	oogbrau		
eyeglasses	always lose them	brill	(pl: brille)	
eyelash	flap them	ooghoor		
eyelid	cover	oogendeckel		
eyepatch	pirate look	oogklappen		
eyewash	ake you out	oogenwasch		
face	your mug	gesicht	(pl: gesichten)	
face off	settle the matter	uthebben		
fact	item	ümstand	or	item

fail	not successful	dahlfallen				
failed	business goes broke	ünnergohn				
failed	fell through	dörfallen				
faint	swoonish	flau				
fair	a county show	messe				
fair	just	recht				
fairly	sort of	seemlig				
fairy tale	fancy story	märken				
faithful	to the end	trulig	or	truulig		
fall	harvest time	harvst				
fall	go down	fall	(past: fallen)			
fall back	get pushed	trügfallen				
fall down	not true	falsch				
fall shut	closes itself	dicht fallen				
familiar	known to you	bekannt				
family	relatives	familie	or	familje		
family name	last name	tonohm				
family tree	ancestors	stammboom				
famous	well known	famos				
fancy meal	holiday table	köst				
fantasy	make believe	fantasie				
far	long way off	wiet				
far away	way way off	wietaf				
farce	funngy goings on	spijöök				
farewell	take my leave	afscheed				
far from	not close to	wietvun				
far off	far away	wietaf				
farm equipment	plows and stuff	ackergeshirr				
farmer	he's the boss	buur	(pl: buurn)			
farmer's wife	the real boss	buurfro				
farmhand	hired male help	knecht				
farmhouse	the old place	buurhuus				
farmland	under cultivation	ackerland				
farmyard	just the yard area	hof	or	hoff		
fart	let one rip	een gohn loten				
farther	more distance off	wieder				
fashion	what's current	mode	or	mood		
fast	quick	dull	or	gau		
fasten	attach to	fastmoken	or	anknöppen		
fat	lots of calories	speck	or	spek	or	fett
fathead	real dummy	döskopp				
father	the old man	voder	or vader	or	voer	
faucet	emits water	hönken				
favor	do something nice	gefallen	or	günn		
favorable	useful to someone	günsdig				
favorite	most dear	leewste or leevste or allerleevste				
favor with	wish them good	günn				
fear	boogy man	angst				
feasible	possible	utföhrbor				
feather	tickler	fedder	or	feller		

featherbed	comfy and warm	federbett	or	fellerbett
featherhat	what a sight	fedderhoot	or	fellerhoot
February	second month	Februor	or	Hornung
fee	something extra	geböör	or	geböhr
feeble	weak	fipsig	or	duff
feeble minded	weak headed	koppswaak		
feed	give food to animals	fudder		
feeding time	finally	fuddertied		
feel	in touch w/ yourself	föhl		
feelings	feel something	föhlen	or	geföhlen
feet	both of them	fööt		
fell	dropped down	fallen		
fell away	slipped away	wegfallen		
fell down	hit the ground	dahlfallen		
fell out	popped out	rutfallen		
fellow	guy or chap	kirl (pl: kirls)	or	keerl
felt	animal skin	pelz	or	pelt
fence	picket	tuun	or	rickel
fence post	holds it up	tuunpahl		
ferment	slowly rot	geren		
fertilizer	natural stuff	mess	or	dungen
fertilizer	manmade	kunstdungen		
fetch	to go and get it	haal	or	hal
fever	102 plus	fevers	or	fewers
few	only a couple	wenig		
fewer	not even that many	weniger		
fiance	victim to be	brögam		
fib	medium lie	flunken		
fickle	make up you mind	fludderig		
fidget	struggle, mess around	ampel		
field	one field	feld (pl: felln)	or	kamp
field work	on the back 40	plackerwark	or	plackerarbeid
fifteen	15	föffteihn		
fifth	1/5	föfftel		
fifty	50	föfftig		
fig	fruit	fieg		
fig tree	where they come from	fiegboom		
figure it out	detective work	utklooken	or	utkeesen
figures	small statues	figuren		
file	rough scraper	fiel		
fill it up	top her off	vullmoken	or	uptankern
filled	made full	vüllig		
finally	at last	ennlig	or	endlich
finance	economics	finanz		
find	to discover again	finnen		
find out	discover	utfinnen		
find the way	figure the route	hinfinnen		
fine	pretty O.K.	fein		
fine	delicate, smooth	fien		
finery	fancy puffery	flitterkraam		

finger	on the hand	finger	(pl: fingern)
finished	complete	ferdig	
fir tree	stays green	dann	or dannboom
fire	hot stuff	füür	or füer
fire chief	hot boss	füürbaas	(pl: füürbaasen)
fire extinguisher	very handy	patschen	
fire place	cozy spot	füürsteed	or füerplatz
firm	holding solidly	fast	
first	number one	eerst	
first name	familiar greeting	vörnohm	
first one	be first in line	toerst	
first time	never happened before	erstenmol	
fish	likes worms	fisch	
fishing	angling	fischen gohn	
fist	knuckle sandwich	fuus	or füüs
fit	in shape	fuchtig	
fits	be the right size	passt	
five	5	fiev	or fiiv or fiev
flag	old glory	fahn	or flagg
flail by hand	thresh grain	flegeldösch	
flake	piece of snow	flock	
flame	piece of fire	flammen	
flap	hinged lid	klappen	
flat	broad and even	platt	
flatterer	honey mouth	glattsnacker	
flattery	flowery words	smuseree	
flax	for making linen	flass	
flea	little bug	flüh	
flee	bug out	fleehan	
flesh	meat	fleesch	
flew	has flown	floogen	or flogen
flew	did fly	flöög	
flies	is flying	flööt	or flücht
flight	flying trip	fluug	
flirt	tease a bit	fründjen	
flock	of chickens	koppel	
flood	too much water	flott	or floot
floor	keep it swept	fluur	or deck
flounder	flat fish	buttfisch	
flour	ground up grain	mehl	
flour sack	for carrying it	mehlsack	
flower	one posy	bloom	(pl: blömen)
flowerpot	keep watering	bloomputt	or bloompott
flute	instrument	flohtpiepen	
fly	in air	fleeg	(past: floogen)
fly	the bug	fleegen	or flegen
fly around	buzz around	rümflegen	
fly off	up and awaaaay	affleegen	
fly out	get away	rutflegen	(past: rutflogen)
flyswatter	smash em	flegenklopper	

foal	baby horse	fohl
foam	head on a beer	schuum
fog	cloudy	nebel or daak or dauk
foggy	can't see much	daakig or daukig
fold	together	kniff or fool
folding table	space saver	klappdisch
follow	let them precede	notreken, nokommen, nopedden
food	for animal	fudder
food	for people	eten or eeten or spies
foolish	peculiar, odd	dwatsch, appeldwatsch, töfelig
foot	below ankle	foot (pl: fööt)
footpath	stroll on it	footpadd
footprint	something to track	footspur
footstool	rest your dogs	footstohl (pl: footstöhl)
for	not against	för
forbid	don't do it	verbeden
fork	eating utensil	gobel or gabel
for nothing	in vain	umsunst
for sure	certain	gewiss
for what	what's it for	woneem för
forbid	just say no	verbeden
foreign	strange	frömd
foreign trade	between countries	butenhannel
foreign word	unfamiliar	frömdwoort
foreigner	from other country	utlanner
foreman	middle boss	öwerste or stootsgesell
forenoon	in the morning	vörmeddag or vörmeddags
forest	woods	holt
forever	all the time left	ewig
forfeited	given up, lost	verschüttgohn
forge	hot spot	schmiede
forget	disremember	verget (past: vergeten)
forgetful	can't remember	vergeterig
forgive	never mind	vergeben
forhead	top of face	vörkopp
fork	to eat with	gabel or gobel
fork	for loading hay	haufork
fork in the road	which way?	tweeweg or tweeler
former	previous	vöriger
forth	take off	foorts or forts
fortune teller	can see the future	spökenkieker
forty	40	veerdig
forward	go ahead	vörwarts
foster parents	guardians	plegöllern
found	looky here	funnen
found	to establish	gründen
foundation	holds it up	grundsteen
four	4	veer
fourleaf clover	lucky week	klewerveer
fourteen	14	veerteihn

fourth	¼	vertel		
fourth finger	indicates hitched	ringfinger		
fox	crafty animal	voss		
fox squirrel	small squirrel	vosgetekel		
fraidy cat	timid, shall we say	bangbüx		
frame	picture border	rohmen		
framework	skeletal structure	gestell		
fraud	act of fraud	bedrug		
fraud	act will be done	bedregen		
fraud	has happened	bedrogen		
freckles	sun dots	sünnsprütten	or	sünnenplacken
free	costs nothing	free		
free of charge	for nothing	umsüss		
freedom	no barriers	freden	or	freeden
freeze	brrr	freer	(past: froren)	
frequent	often	foken		
fresh	nice and bright	frisch		
fresh water	pure and sweet	söötwater	or	frischwoter
friday	day of week	freedag	or	fredag
friend	a buddy	fründ	(pl: frünnen)	
friendly	be friendly	fründlig		
friendship	buddy-ness	fründschop		
fright	a scare	shreck		
frightening	act of scaring	shrecklig		
frisky	gay and jolly	poppenlustig		
frivolous	not so important	lichtfardig		
frock coat	tail in back	steertrock		
frog	prince in disguise	pogg		
from	come from, of	vun		
from behind	sneak around back	vunachtern		
from memory	by heart	ut'n kopp		
from there	from a place	dorvun		
from what	what's the cause	woneem vun		
front	out in front	vörn		
front steps	up to the door	tritt		
frost	icy	frost		
frozen	totally hard	verfroren		
frozen stiff	like a board	stievfroren	or	stieffroren
fruit	off the limb	frucht		
fruitful	gains something	fruchtbor		
full	got it all	vull		
full	even over the top	hubben vull		
full	enough to eat	satt		
fully	all of it	vüllig		
fun	enjoyment	spoos	or	spaas
function	work	funkschoon		
funeral	burial ceremony	begräbnis		
funerals	several ceremonies	begräbnissen		
funny	peculiar	sposig	or	spasig
furnish	get all the furniture	inrichten		

furrow	plow path	forrow
further	farther along	wieder
furthermore	use additional words	wollerwöör or wellerwöör
fussy	picky	nierig or pütscherig
future	the future	tokommt or tokunft
future	in the future	tokünftig
gable	roof peak	geebel or geevel
gape	stare wide-eyed	jaapen
garbage	ugh!	quasch or qualsten
garden	full of flowers	goorn or gorn
garden	dedicated small plot	shrewegoorn
gargle	clear throat	görgel
garlic	stinky stuff	knuublok
gas lamp	smoky light	lüchen or lüchten
gasoline	makes it go	benzin
gate	doorway in fence	port
gather	collect in a place	sammeln or opsammeln
gave	has given	geben or geven
general	average	generol
generation	next in line	generatschoon
generous	gives with a smile	freegävig or freegewig
gentleman	a person	minsch
german	teutonic	düütsch or dütsk
get	come by	krieg (past: kregen)
get	to actually get it	kriegen
get along	can handle it	langskommen
get away with	scott free	mitwegkommen
get off, get on	change trains	ümstiegen
get rid of	want to lose it	loswiern
get started	let er rip	geiht los (past: losgohn)
get up	arise	steiht up (past: upstohn)
get used to	used to something	anwinn (past: anwunnen)
gets	gets it	kriggt
ghost	spirit	spökel
giant	awfully big	hüün
gift	present	geshink
giggle	half a laugh	huchel or lächel
gigolo	may I cut in	rindanser or rindanzer
gill	breathing hole	kiem
gin	martini mix	jannever
giraffe	long necked one	giraap
girdle	waist belt	gördel
girl	young woman	deern or mäke or wicht or dirn
girls	young women	deerns or wichten
girl chaser	a leg man	shörtenjaager
girl crazy	doll crazy	poppenlustig
give	hand it to someone	geev
give away	don't need it	weggeben or weggeven
give back	return	trüggeben or trüggeven
give in	give up	nogeben or nogeven

give up	quit	upgeben or upgeven
give up	quit	upgeben or upgeven
given	handed over	geben or gebem
gives	is giving	gifft
glad	happy about	froh
gladly	with pleasure	geern
gland	part of body	drüs
glass	breakable	glas
glass cupboard	keep it safe	glas schapp
glasses	for drinking	gläs or glääs
glasses	optical kind	brillen
gleam	sparkle	schemer or schummer
glide	slide along	glieden
gloomy	down in the dumps	munkelig
glove	warm the hands	fingerhandshen
gloves	a couple of them	fingerhändshen
glow	shine bright	glötern or glösen or glimmen
glowing	shining	glinnig or glöhnig
glue	it binds together	klebe or liem
glue on	attach it to	anbacken or ankleben
glue together	make as one	tohopenbacken
glutton	very big eater	fretsack
gnat	teensy bug	gnitt or üzz or üüz
go	to move on	goh or gah (past: gohn)
go after	pursue	nogohn
go ahead	do it already	man to
go around	on the edge	rümgohn
goat	can get yours	zegen or seegen
go away from	leave	vunafgohn
godfather	stand up for	voderstohn or volerstohn
goes	travels	geiht
goes on	is happening	angeiht (past: angohn)
go home	that sweet place	nohuusgohn
going	is going	geihs
go out	socialize	utföhren
go over	looked at	öwergohn
goblet	large glass	kelk
goes	takes off	geiht
gold	shiny stuff	gold
golden	made of shiny stuff	golden
gone	just slipped away	futsch
gone	departed	weeg or weg
good	really o.k.	good
good day	howjado	goden dag
good evening	top of the evening	goden obend or goden ovend
Good Friday	go to church	Karfreedag
good morning	top of the morning	goden moren
good one	a good something	gode
goodbye	like wiedersehn	tschüss
good for nothing	worthless person	nixnutz
goose	mean bird	goos

gooseberry	hard to find	stikbeern or stickelbeern
gossip	the dirt	lüüdsnak or klönsnak
gossip	the dirt	snackaree or snöterwark
gourmet	particular taste	leckertähn
govern	officially in charge	regeern
government	final authority	regeerung
governor	state official	vaagt
grab	reach out and get	griep
grab	take hold of	fotkriegen or fatkriegen
grab onto	get a grip	tofoten or tofaten or angriepen
granary	keep grain in it	spieker
grandchildren	perfect children	grüsskinner or kinnerskinner
grandchildren	more perfect children	enkelkinner
granddaughter	apple of the eye	enkeldochter
grandfather	granpaw	grussvoder or Opa or bestvoder
grandmother	granma	grussmodder or Oma or bestmoder
granular	grainy	küürnig or kümmelig
grape	wine kernel	druuv
grasp	finally understand	begriepen
grasp	take hold of	griep
grasped	held on to	fot or fat
grass	needs cutting	gras
grasshopper	good jumper	springer or graspringer
grater	rub-er	riebiesen
grave	6' hole	grab or grav or kuul
grave stone	granite marker	grabsteen
gravedigger	hole digger	kulengräber
graveyard	spooky place	freedhof
gravy	for on potatoes	stipp
gray	dull color	gries
graze	chomp grass	grasen
grease	black and sticky	smeer
grease gun	fix the squeeks	smeerpistol
grease up	good and gooey	insmeern or infetten
great aunt	grand sibling	omaswester or opaswester
great luck	really hit it big	swiensglück
greatly	immensely	gräsig
great uncle	grand sibling	omasbroder or opasbroder
greedy	gimme more	giezig or happig or gabberig
green	bright color	grön
greenhorn	wet behind the ears	grönsnobel
green wood	let it dry first	sappholt
greet	say hello	grööt
greeting	felicitation	gröten
greyhound	fastest dog	windhund
gr-grandfather	grandpaw's pa	urgrussvoder
grgr-grandfather	two back	ururgrussvoder
grieve	be sorry about	grömen or bedröven
grilled	cooked outside	brüllt or braadet
grillwork	set of bars	gadderwark

grin	sneaky smile	grien	
grind	to make flour	möhlen	
grind	your teeth	gnaaster	
grip	to get a grip	tofoten or tofaten or anpacken	
groan	kind of a moan	grünsen or janken or anken	
groom	condemned man	brögam	
ground	terra firma	grund	
ground floor	where entrance is	grundstock	
ground hog	nasty beast	grundswien	
grouse	bird, not attitude	moorhohn	
grow	like a weed	wass	(past: wussen)
growl	dog's muttering	gnuur	or grummel
grown onto	grown against	anwussen	
growth	act of growing	towass	
gruesome	not pretty	grieselig	
grumble	brood	grübel	or brummel
guaranteed	backed up	wohrt	
guess	try to solve	roen	
guest	invited one	gast	(pl: gasten)
guild	production group	gild	or gill
guilty	hang em	shuldig	or shullig
guitar	stringed instrument	plückfidel	
gum	make a bubble	kaugummi	
gums	holds the teeth	tähnfleesch	or gumen
gun	pistol, rifle	flint	
gutter	edge of roof	rünnen	or dackrünn
gyroscope	keep on the path	krüsel	
had	once possessed	harr	(pl: harrn)
haggle	discuss details	akkediern	
hail	raining icecubes	hagel	or hogel
hair	fuzzy on top	hoor	
hair part	comb other way	sheedel	
half	½	halv	
half portion	even share	hälvsheed	
half the time	doesn't always work	hälvstetied	
hall	place to dance	saal	
ham	and eggs	schinken	or swiensmors
hammer	bang that nail	homer	or hamer
hamper	container	korv	or korf
hand	end of arm	hand	(pl: hännen)
handcloth	dry your face	handdook	
handfull	all you want	handvull	
handkerchief	blow your nose	tashendook	
handkerchiefs	several	tashendöke	
handle	grab by	swengel	
handle	take care of something	hannel	
handwriting	illegible	handschrift	
handy	nice to have around	hännig	
hang	hook onto	hing	(past: hüng)

109

hangs	sag down	hengt		
happen	to occur	passeer		
happens	is occuring	passeert	or	angohn
happy	be happy	froh	or	vergnögt
happy	makes me happy	freiht mi		
harbor	ship haven	hoben	or	hoven
hard	can't dent it	hatt		
hard bread	crumble in milk	knabbel		
hard of hearing	...eh?	hatthören		
hardly	almost not at all	kuum		
hard bread	dried beef	knabbel		
hardworking	very busy	flietig		
harm	does damage	shoden	or	shaden
harmonica	play a tune	mundörgel		
harmonize	in a barber shop	öwereenstimmen		
harmony	in tune	wollklang		
harms	is damaging	shodet	or	shadet
harness	horse holder	geshirr		
harp	instrument	harp		
harrow	farm implement	iggen	or	ingen
harvest	get the crops in	arnten	or	ahren
harvest hay	wagonloads to the barn	hau inföhren		
harvest time	get crops in	harvstied		
has	to possess	hett		(past: harr)
hat	keep flees warm	hoot	or	haut
hatchet	hand axe	heetje or bül	or	biel
hate	dislike a lot	hass		
haul	transfer a load	treck	or	haal
haul manure	spread it around	messföhren		
have	to possess	heff		(pl: hebbt)
have on	wear	anhebben	or	antrecken
hawk	dark bird	klemmvogel	or	hauk
hay	stack in the barn	hau	or	hai
hay fork	stick it with	hau fork		
hay rake	pushes into rows	hauraaker		
haze	mirky	dunst		
he	male pronoun	he	or	hei
head	top part of body	kopp		(pl: köpp)
head cold	sniffle	koppkäält		
headache	excedrin number 12	koppweg		
headlight	see the road	shiensmieter		
headscarf	head covering	koppdook		
headstone	grave stone	koppsteen		
heal	get well	heel moken		
healthy	of sound body	gesund or heel	or	fuchtig
heap	big pile	dutt or		barg
heaping	over full	huupen		
hear	listen	hör or höör		(pl: höret)
hear	be able to hear	hören		
hears	is listening	hört		

110

heart	blood pumper	hart
heart	in cards	harten
heart attack	ticker stopper	hartpuckern or hartslag
heart beat	thump thump	hartklopp
heartily	with great regard	hartlig
heart's desire	love the most	hartenlust
heat	hot-ness	hitt
heating oil	keeps furnace going	hittöl
heating stove	uncool place	kacheloben
heath	meadow	heide
heaven	up there somewhere	heben or heven
heavy	lots of weight	swoor
hectic	very busy at the time	hill or hild
hedgehog	nasty bugger	swienegel
hedges	small bushes	hecken
heel	back of foot	hacken
heel	end of bread loaf	knoos
height	tallness	höh
held	keep up in the air	höld
hell	that other place	höll
helmet	steel pot	iesenhoot
helmsman	steers the ship	stüermann or stüürmann
help	aid, assistance	hölp
help out	come to the aid	uthelpen
help up	raise him up	uphelpen
hemp	for ropes, not smoking	hemmet
hen	mrs. chicken	hehn
henceforth	from now on	vun nu af or vun nu avant
her	the lady's	ehr
herd	watch cattle	höden or höjen
herding	keep them together	hödd or höjed
here	in this location	hier
here piggy	feeding time	sui sui
hers	belongs to her	ehr
herself	herself alone	ehr sülbens or ehr sülms
hesitate	take a minute	fackel
hidden	not visible	versteken or verstekt
hide	can't find it	verstek
high	way up there	hoh
high german	standard german	hoh düütsch or hoch düütsk
high german person	foreigner	quiddje
higher	even further up	höhger
highest	man in charge	böverste
highway	wide road	bohn
hiking	tromp in the woods	wannern
hill	bump in ground	barg (pl: bargen) or bült
hilly	small mountains	bargig
him	to him	üm
him	himself	em
himself	himself alone	sik sülbens or sik sülms

hinder	to hold it back	hinnern		
hinge	squeeky plate	hingen		
hip	where fat grows	hüft		
hire	rent his time	hüür		
his	belonging to him	sien		
hit	to strike	hau		
hit	hit the target	drep	(past: dropen)	
hitch up	tie on horses	spann		
hoarfrost	cold mornings	ruhriep		
hoe	work in the garden	hak		
hoe	used to do it	haken		
hold	maintain grasp	fot an	or	fat an
hold	take a hold	anfoten	or	anfaten
hold	take it a while	hol	(past: holt)	
hold back	woa	trügholen		
hold in	flattens the stomach	inholen		
hold out	endure	utholen		
hold together	squeeze tight	tohopenholen or tosomenholen		
hold up	detain	upholen		
hold up	to exhibit, show	upwiesen	or	afwiesen
hold fast	don't let go	wissholen	or	fastholen
hold tight	don't let go	holwiss	or	holfast
hole	opening	lock or lok	(pl: löker)	
holiday	time off	festdag	(pl: festdaag)	
holy	like a saint	hillig		
home	home area	heem	or	heimot
home	be at home	tohuus	or	bihuus
homework	ugh	schoolleehren or schoolarbeid		
honest	above board	ehrlig		
honey	bees make it	hunnig		
honey bee	sweet biter	iim		
honor	revere	ehr		
honorable	with pride	ehrbor		
hood	cover up head	huuv	or	huben
hoof	horse's foot	hoof	or	hoov
hook	to hang it up on	hook (past: hookt) or	haak	
hook in	snap to	inhoken		
hook up	attach the wagon	uphoken	or	ophoken
hoot	make a noise	jaulen		
hop around	hot foot	rümhüppen	or	rümspringen
hope	wish	hopp or huppen or	hopen	
hops	for brewing	hopps	or	hoppen
horizon	edge of the world	kimm		
horizontal	even with the world	flack		
horn	trumpet	hoorn	(pl: höörn)	
horrible	pretty bad	beestig		
horse	old dobbin	peerd	(pl: peer)	
horse	white horse	schimmel		
horse harness	all that leather	peergeshirr		
horseshoe	iron shoe	hooviesen		

horsestall	dobbin's room	peerstall		
hospital	medical place	krankenhuus		
hostile	not friendly	feendlig	or	opsternaatsch
hot	extra warm	heet		
hothead	easily aroused	hittkopp		
hot tempered	ready to fight	hitzig	or	kortanbunnen
hound	certain dog	rüe		
hour	1/24th part of day	stunn		
hourglass	tell time	sanduhr		
house	domicile	huus	(pl: hüüs)	
household	family business	huushold	or	huusstaub
household goods	mostly furniture	huusrot		
housekeeper	sleeps all day	huusfro	or	huusfru
how	in what way?	wo or woans or		wegenweg
how come	what's the reason	wiso		
how else	what's the choice	woans		
how far	how many miles	wowiet		
how many	what's the number	woveel		
however	but	ower or allerdings or		apatt
howl	ooooooooo	huul		
hub	of a wheel	hobe		
hug	embrace	ümfotten		
human	member of the race	minsch		
human	act like one	minschlig		
human rights	basic rights	minschrechte		
humble	aw shucks	pulterig		
hundred	100	hunnert		
hung up	held high for a while	uphung		
hunger	crave food	schmacht	or	hunger
hungry	where's the icebox	schmachtig	or	hungrig
hunt	go shoot game	jagt		
hunter	shooter	joger		
hunting	go on hunt	jogen		
hurdle	jump over	höörd		
hurricane	big wind	orkan		
hurry	be in a hurry	in'a iel	or	in'a büx stöven
hurry	get moving	rögen		
hurt	is pained	wehdoon	or	wehdohn
husband	legitimate	ehemann		
husband	"my" husband	mann	or	mien mann
hut	small house	hütt		
I	me, myself	ik	or	ick
ice	keep it cold	ies		
ice cold	brrr	ieskold	or	ieskoold
icicle	cold stick	iestappen		
idea	a new thought	ahnung	or	idee
idiot	real nut	döskopp		
if	whether	wenn	or	ob
illegal	illegitimate	unehrlig		

113

imitate	monkey see, etc.	nomoken	
immerse	dip into	instippen	
import	incoming trade	infohr	
important	worthwhile	wichtig	or notwendig
impossible	can't do it	unmöchlig	
impression	how it's taken	indruck	or indrück
impudent	pugnacious	butt	
in	inside	in	
in addition	on top of	bobento	or bovento
inch	twelfth of a foot	toll	
in front	front of line	vörn	or vörn an
ingratiate	kow tow to	anköteln	
inside	within	insied	
install	put into place	insetten	
in the morning	A.M.	vörmeddags	or s'morrns
in the past	old times	fröher tieden	
in there	in the midst of it	dorin	or hinin
in time	all in good time	betieds	
incense	smelly stuff	weihrook	
inch	one dozenth of a foot	toll	
incidental	marginally important	bilöpig	
incision	where's that appendix	insnitt	
incline	rising ground	bargup	
include	keep in	insloten	or mit insloten
income	revenue	innehm	or inkommen
incomparable	no comparison	ahnglieklig	or unvergliekbor
increase	something added to	anwuss	
increase	add to the amount	vermeehren	
incurable	can't fix	unheelbor	
index finger	next to thumb	wiesfinger	
indicate	point out	andüden	or anwiesen
indication	seems to show	anwies	
indifferent	all the same to me	shietegol	or pottegol
indignant	huffy	heemsch	
indulgence	patient	nasicht	or nosicht
industrious	very busy	flietig	
inertia	reducing motion	duddigkeit	
infirm	not too stable	krüpelig	or krükelig
inflate	make it round	uppustern	
inflow	coming this way	inflott	
influence	can affect	beinflott	
ingratiate	feed em bull	anköteln	
inform	give the news	bescheed seggen	or norichten
ingredient	belongs in there	todo	or todoh
ingenious	terrific ideas	sinnriek	
ingratiate	kiss butt	anköteln	
ingrown	sore toenail	inwussen	
inhabitant	lives there	inwohner	
in heat	where's the bull	brüllsch	
inherit	from the will	arv	

114

inheritance	what you got	arvdeel	
inherited	money the easy way	arvt	
initially	right up front	toeerst	
inject	take a shot	inspritt	(past: insprütt)
injustice	raw deal	unrecht	
ink	to write with	dinte	
inn	motel	weertshuus	or harbarg
innermost	furthest inside	innerste	
innkeeper	tavern owner	kröger	
innocent	not guilty	unshuldig, unshullig, ahnshuld	
inquire	interrogate	affrogen	
inquire	ask about	bekümmern	
inscription	written on	opschrift	
insert	place into	inleggen	or rinleggen
inside	within it	insied or innen or binnen	
insignificant	don't mean much	unbedüdend or nich wichtig	
insofar as	as far as	sowiet as	
insolent	bratty	pampig	
insomnia	a long night	slooplos	or slaaplos
inspect	examine, look into	nosehn	or nokieken
inspire	get excited about	tosnacken	
instance	in this case	deel	
instead	in the place of	staats	
instruction	teach something	ünnerricht	
insult	nasty words	spott	
intake	process of getting	innehm	
intend	expect to	vertohl	or vörhebben
intent	desire to do	afsicht	
intention	deliberate move	insinn or afsichten or inwill	
intermission	a pause in the action	pause	
intervene	get involved	ringriepen	
intestines	long string of guts	darm	
into	place inside	rin	
introduce	how-ja-do	vörstellen	
introduction	front part of talk	vörreed	or vörred
investigate	do some looking into	ünnersöken	
invitation	please come and visit	nödig	
invite	ask in	nöding	or nödigen
inviter	come to a wedding	hochtiedbitter, hochtiednödiger	
iron	to iron clothes	plätten	or strieken
iron	a hard metal	iesen	
iron	used to iron with	plättiesen	
irrigate	add water	trietsen	
irritate	bugs you	verdrütt	
irritated	bugged	vergrellt	or füünsch
is	just is...	is	or iss
island	patch of land	ieland	
itch	a little lower	jark	
itself	or himself	sik	or sik sülms
ivy	vine	iloov	or ieloof

jacket	small coat	jack or rock
jail	temporary hotel	knast
jam	spread on bread	marmelood or fruchtmoos
January	first month	Januor, Hardemaand, Sneemaand
jealous	envy	niedisch
jelly	shaky food	wackelpeter
jewelry	bobbles and beads	gereide or smuck or smieg
job	an ugly word	arbeid
joke	funny remark	witz or döntje
journey	trip	tuur or reis
joy	cheer	hög or freiht
joyful	playful	högelig or kanditel
judge	court boss	gerichtsholter
jug	if you like likker	steenkruug
jug	6 liter stone jug	bullenkopp
juice	breakfast drink	saft or soft or sapp
July	seventh month	Juli or Haumaand
jump	to jump	jump or spring
jump out	bail out	rutspringen
jumped at	attacked	ansprungen
June	sixth month	Juni or Braakmaand
juniper	type of bush	machandel
junk	waste	schrott or rumpelkraam
just	just in time, only	jüst or süss
keep	retain	behol
keep house	not under the rug	huusholen
keep open	don't shut	openholen
kernel	of corn	küüren
kettle	pot	ketel or kettel
kettle fixer	goes door to door	ketelklopper
kettle repair	fix holes	ketelflicken
key	unlock with	slotel
kid	brat	gör
kill	deep six 'em	ümbringen or afmorken
killed	caused death	ümbrocht or doot mokt
kind	type or species	sorde
kind	be very nice to	gödig or goodhartig
kindergarden	play and learn	kinnergoorn
King	big royal boss	Künig
kingdom	his playground	riekdum
kiss	a juicy one	söten updrücken or küss
kitchen	baking room	köken or kök or bakstuuv
kitchen utensils	pots and pans	kökengeschirr
kite	dragon kite	dracken or draaken
knapsack	carry on your back	turnüster
knead	punch bread	kneden
knee	leg joint	knie
kneel	on the ground	knien

116

knife	utensil	mest		
knit	needlework	knütten		
knitted	like a sweater	knütt	or	strick
knitting needle	knit one,etc.	stricknodel	or stricknadel	
knitwear	sweater	stricktüüg	or	stricktüch
knob	lump	knob		
knobby	kind of lumpy	knubberig		
knock	on the door	klopp		
knock off	tip off	stöttaf	or	vun stöten
knock out	punch a hole	utkloppen		
knock over	all the way	öwerstöten		
knot	lump in a string	knutt	or	knütt
knothole	hole in tree	knast	or	knass
knots	all tied up	knudden		
know	recognize	kenn	or	kinn
know	have knowledge of	weet	(past: wüss)	
know about	be informed of	besheed		
knowledge	scientific knowledge	wetenschop		
knuckle	finger joint	knökel		
know	to be aware of	weet	(past: wüss)	
lace	fine edging	lotz	or	schnur
ladle	big spoon	kell		
ladder	get to the top	leller	or	ledder
lady	proper female	daame or mamsell	or beste fro	
ladybug	helpful in the garden	sünnenküken	or	sünnenkind
lamb	mutton chops	lamb	(pl: lamber)	
lame	prone to limping	lohm		
lamp	light fixture	lampen	or	licht
land	ground, earth	land		
landlord	owner	weertsmann		
landscape	nice view	landschop		
language	formal words	sproch	or sprok	or spruch
lantern	carry a light	latern	or tinkel	or lüchen
lap	don't stand up	schoot		
lard	for cooking	fett	or	smalt
large	big	groot		
larger	even bigger	gröter		
largest	biggest	grötste		
lark	bird	lauerk		
last	last one	letz		
last	last in line	toletzt	or	letzte
lasts	stays a long time	weret	or	weret nich ut
late	past the time	laat		
later	after more time	laater	or later	or loter
later on	after a while	later hin	or	loter hin
lateral	to the side	scheel		
laugh	giggle pretty good	lach		
laughing	got the joke	lacht		
laugh at	make fun of	utlachen		

117

laughable	very funny	lächerlig		
laughter	sound of laughing	lachen		
laundry	the washing	wasch	or	wäsch
law	enacted rule	gesett		
lawyer	attorney	afkat	or	avkaat
lay	to put down	legg		
lay down	go to sleep	lingen gohn	or	liggen gohn
lay off	stop work	afleggen		
lay over	cover up	öwerleggen		
layer	on top of another	shik		
lays	puts it down	liggt		
lazy	no gumption	fuul	or	nuddelig
laziness	no work ethic	fuulheit		
lead	metal, in a pencil	blee		
lead	go out in front	anföhren		
lead off	first to drive off	afdrieven	or	afdrieben
lead pencil	keep it sharp	bleestick		
leader	out in front	lieder		
leaf	on a tree	blatt		
leak	always dripping	lek	or	leken
lean	over to the side	lehnen	or	kanten
learn	absorb knowledge	leehrn		
least	littlelest	wenigste		
leather	animal hide	leder	or	leler
leave	go away	weggohn	or	weggahn
leave	stays behind	trügloten	or	trüglaten
leave	in a big hurry	sheden		
leave off	deliver somewhere	afleevern		
leave out	don't include	rutloten	or	rutlaten
lecture	give a boring speech	leksen	or	lekture
ledge	edge of a hill	sims		
left	direction	links		
left	already gone	verloten	or	verlaten
lefthanded	southpaw	linkpoot		
leftover	over supply	öwrig	or	pottschrapels
leg	one of two	been		
legible	can read it	leesbor		
lemon	sour fruit	zitron		
length	how long	länge	or	lengd
lengthwise	long way	langenweg	or	längswies
lenient	easy going	glemlig	or	nosichtig
less	smaller amount	weniger		
let	allow	latt		
let go	release	los loten	or	free loten
lets go	get going	man to		
let in	allow within	rinloten		
letter	mail	breef		(pl: breev)
letter	of the alphabet	bookstov	or	bookstob
level	class or distinction	shik		
lever	pry with	hevel		

118

lice	little nasties	lüüs		
license plate	car code number	nummerschild		
lick	tongue wiping	lick		
lick off	clean good	aflicken		
lick out	last of the chocolate	utlicken		
lid	put a top on it	deckel	or	klappen
lie	telling a fib	leegen	or	flunket
lieing	is doing it again	lügt		
liesure	take it easy	freetied		
lied to	was told a lielife	vörlogen		
lier	does the lieing	lüggbuddel		
life	beats the option	leben	or	leven
lifelong	during lifetime	lebenlang	or	levenlang
lifetime	all the years	lebens tied	or	levens tied
lift	raise up	böör		
light	not heavy	liecht		
light	pale in color	hell		
light	not much weight	licht		
light	start a fire	ansteken		
light a stove	get it warm	inböten		
lightning	scary sight	blitz		
like	want to do something	mög or much	or	müch
like	admire	mag or gliek or	mag lieden	
lilac	smells good	fleder		
limp	walking problem	hinken		
linden	tree	linn		
line	straight mark	lien		
linen	nice cloth	linnen	or	lienen
lingerie	shhh: unmentionable	ünnertüch		
link	connector	lenk	or	koppel
lip	area around mouth	lipp	(pl: lippen)	
listen	to hear	hör or höör	or	lüstern
listen to	pay attention	anhören	or	tohören
little	small	lütt	or	kleen
little bit	just a bit	beten or betken	or	bisken
little by little	incrementally	bilüttens		
little guy	a rascally runt	knieps		
little one	tiny one	lüttje	or	lütting
live	resides	wohn		
lived	has resided	wohnt		
lively	having fun	lustig	or	kriegel
liver	part of body	leber	or	lever
liverwurst	good to eat	leberworst		
lives	is alive	leevt		
lives	people's existences	leeben		
lives	resides	wohnt		
living room	main room	wohnstuuv		
lizard	creepy snake	eerkröppel		
load	to put on board	loden		
loaded	piled on board	uplodet	or	lodet

119

load off	take it off	afloden
loads	is loading	lodet
load up	pile it on	uploden
loaf	unbaked bread	loov
loaf	baked bread	stuten
lobster	clawy delight	hummer
local	in the area, homegrown	eenheemig or heemlig
lock	where key goes	slott
lock away	box up and hide	wegsluten
locked	can't get in	sloten
lock up	close up	tosluten (past: tosloten)
locked in	lemme out	insloten
locked out	don't come back	rutsloten
log cabin	Lincoln's home	blokhuus
logical	makes sense	logisch
loiter	hang around	nödeln
lonely	by your lonesome	eensom
long	in length or time	lang or lank
long for	wish for	verlengen
look	take a see	kiek (past: keken)
look after	watch over, inspect	nokieken
look around	survey the area	rümkieken
look at	observe	ankieken (past: ankeken)
look back	over the shoulder	ümkieken
look into	inspect or search	nosehn or bekieken
look out	watch out for	pass up or kiekut
look through	peruse	dörkieken
look up	do research	upkieken
looks like	appears as	sühtut or kiekt so or lett so
loop	like a noose	slinge
loose	darn, got away	los
loosen	cut loose	los moken
lose	will lose	verleren
lose	is losing	verlütt
lost	gone	verloren, verschwunn , verlopen
lots	bunch of things	allerhand
loud	noisy	luut
loudmouth	noisemaker	grodmuul
louse	bug	luss
louse	a bug	sössbeente
lout	sort of a bum	lausbub or lümmel
love	in love	verleewt or verleevt
lovely	nice, pretty	schön
low	not high	nedder or siet
Low Danish	language	pulterdänsch or kartuffeldänsch
Low German	language	platt düütsch or platt dütsch
Low German	old name for it	nedderdüütsch or nedderdütsk
lowlands	a little moist	marsch
Low Saxon	ancient name	neddersaxsich
loyal	stick by it	tru

120

luck	cross your fingers	glück		
lucky	not for the rabbit	glücklig		
luggage	trunks	gepäck	or	bagasch
luke warm	heat is almost gone	lauwarm		
lumber	wood	holt		
lunch	midday meal	meddageten		
lungs	air pumps	lungen		
machine	equipment	mashien	or	maschin
mad	very angry	bös		
mad	a little crazy	mal	or	mall
made up	from imagination	upmokt		
madness	wierdness	tühnkraam	or	tüünkraam
magazine	periodical	tiedshrift		
maggot	mealy bug	maad		
magic	special powers	hokus pokus		
magnificent	great person	staatsch		
magpie	bird	heister	or	keekster
maid	female helper	deenstdeern	or	maag
mailbox	letter holder	breefkassen	or	breefkasten
mailman	letter carrier	breefdreger		
main	the most important	haupt	or	hoopt
main reason	prime cause	hauptsaak		
main thing	prime aspect	hauptdings		
maintain	preserve	plegen		
majority	most	meehrheit	or	miehrdeel
make	construct	mok	(past: mokt)	
make a face	petulant frown	snut upsetten		
make up	make it alright again	trechtmoken		
malleable	spreadable	smeerdig		
mallet	wood pounder	holthomer	or	bürker
malt	used in brewing	molt		
man	somebody male	mann or kirl or keerl		
man	of mankind	minsch		
mane	horse neck hair	mähne		
manger	animal eating area	krüft	or	krüff
mankind	all of us	minschheit		
manner	by his account	oort	or	maneer
manners	good behavior	manieren		
manufacture	make it	anferdigen		
manure	lots of vitamins	mess		
manure fork	tasty (?) bite	mess fork		
manure pile	walk around it	mess barg		
manure spreader	spread it around	mess smieter		
many	quite a few, much	veel		
many	many a person	mannigeen		
maple	kind of tree	ahoorn		
marble	little ball	knicker		
marble	has a swirly pattern	knippelsteen	or	marmeln
march	tramp in unison	marschen	or	rümtrampen

121

March	third month	März, Lenzmaand, Märtmaand
mare	she horse	stoot
mariner	big ship sailer	Jan Moot
mark	note, imprint	mark or tecken
mark down	take note of	dohlmarken
marketplace	place to sell	markt
marriage	a real institution	ehe
marriage	the ceremony	trauung
married couple	him and her, the pair	ehepoor or ehepaar
married people	all of them	ehelüüd
marry	to tie the knot	freen (past: freed) or heiroden
mason	brick layer	muurmann
master	fancy for boss	meester
match	got a light	striekholzer or rietsticken
mate	buddy	maat or maaker
material	cloth	tüüch or tüüg
mattress	to lie down on	matratz
may	with permission	dröv or dröf
May	fifth month	Mai
maybe	possibly	villicht
mayfly	trout food	gnitt
mayor	city boss	börgermeester
me	just myself	mi or mik
meadow	full of flowers	wisch or weise or moor
meager	small amount	knapp
meal	something to eat	eten or mahl or mohl
mealtime	time to eat	mohltied or mahltied
mean	essence of the words	meen
meaning	opinion	meenung
meaningful	lot's of relevance	sinnvull
means	translates to	meent or bedüdet
meanwhile	after some time	tiedlangs hin
meanwhile	during the time	twüschentied or middewiel
measure	get a ruler	met
measure off	do the measuring	afmeten
measure out	determine dimension	utmeten
measured	got the distance	afmett
meat	chew it well	fleesch
medicine	makes you well	medizin
meet	come together	tomööt kommen
meet	get together	drepen (past: dropen)
meet in passing	cross paths	begegen
meeting	group gets together	sittung or samlung
melody	main song part	melodie
melt	to soften up	smöln (past: smölt or upsmölt)
member	participant	bisitter or mitsitter
men	all men	mannslüüd
mend	darn the sock	flick
menu	what's for dinner	etenkorden or spieskorden
mercy	benevolence	gnaad

merely	only	blots	or	bloss
merry	happy, joyful	kanditel	or	lustig
messy	being cluttered	klotterig		
metal	usually tin	bleck		
midafternoon	about 3 P.M.	halvignammidag		
middle	smack dab	midde		
middle ages	way way back	middeöller		
midnight	middle of night	middenacht		
midwife	helps birth	wiesemoder or Moder Griepsch		
might	strength	macht		
might	could happen	mach	(past: müch)	
migrate	one place to another	utwannern		
mile	certain length	miel		
milk	cow juice	melk		
milkcan	keep it cold	melkkann		
milkhouse	a cool place	melkhuus		
milkman	he comes early	melkkirl		
milkpail	milk container	melkammel		
milkstool	sit and squirt	melkbock	or	dreebeen
mill	grind flour	möhl		
miller	runs a mill	möhler		
million	1,000,000	miljon		
mind	all in your head	sinn		
mindless	willy nilly	sinnlos	or	kopplos
mine	just my own	mien		
minority	smaller part	minnheit	or	minnedeel
minus	less than zero	minus	or	wenig
minute	part of hour	minuten		
miracle	pretty wonderful	wunner		
mirror	see your face	spegel		
mischief	up to no good	leegheit		
mischievous	hard to handle	eisch	or	fiegeliensch
miser	tightwad type	giezhals		
miserable	its the pits	elennig		
miserly	has first nickle	giezig		
misfortune	bad thing happens	malör		
miss	don't hit	miss		
missing	come up short	fehlt	or	vermisst
misting	a very slight sprinkle	miesst or de müngen de pisst		
mistrust	can't count on	mistruu	or	mistroo
mitten	has no fingers	fuushanschen		
mix	shove together	mengeln	or	mischeln
mocking	deride, be critical	spöttsch		
modern	up to date	mode	or	moderne
molars	back teeth	kuusen	or	backentähn
mold	green growth	shimmel	or	spaak
moldy	spoiled already	vershimmelt		
mole	subway maker	wimmworm		
moment	just a moment	ogenblick	or	tiedpunkt
moment ago	just a minute ago	eben		

monday	2nd day, moon day	maandag or moondag
money	paper kind	popiergeld
money	moolah	geld
monotonous	ho hum	eenerlei
month	30 day period	munat or maand
monument	statue	denkmol
mood	feelings	luun or loon
moody	grumpy	nücksch
moon	evening light	maand
moor	meadow	heide
more	additional	meehr or miehr
morning	first part of day	moren or morrn or vörmeddag
most	nearly all	meehrst or meehrsten
mostly	most of the time	meehrstens or meehrstied
moth	light freak	mott (pl: motten)
mother	the saint	moder or modder
motherinlaw	yup, that's her	swiegermoder
motionless	don't move	still
motto	words to live by	sinnspruk
mountain	big hill	barg (pl: bargen)
mouse	junior rat	muus (pl: müüs)
mousetrap	wham!	muusfall
mouth	opening	mundt or muul or muulwark
move	make a motion	röög
moved	slightly	rögt
move into	occupy a place	töög
mow	cut wheat or grass	meih
mow	to do mowing	meihen
mower	equipment used	meihmashien
much	amount	masse or veel or gehörig or dull
muddle head	twirpy	himphamp
muddled	confused	döreenannern
muffler	end of tailpipe	utpuuser or utsuuser
mulberry	blue and wrinkly	muulbeeren
mule	jackass	mool
multiple	many faceted	meehrfak
muscle	strong part	knöf
mushroom	pick the right one	mushrosen
mushy	spongy	pampig
music	melodious	musik
musician	music maker	musikant (pl: musikanten)
must	have to	mutt (pl: mött)
mustard	for the hot dog	simp
mute	speechless	dumm
mutton	lamb chop	motten or matten
myrtle	plant, not lady	myrtel
myrtle wreath	festive display	myrtel kranz
my sake	on my regard	mienhalben or mienwegens
myself	you yourself	misölbens, misölvens, misülms

124

nag	be a pest	quarken
nagging	bitching	quesig
nail	hang a picture	nogel or nagel
nail on	fasten with nails	annogeln
naked	birthday suit	naakt or splitternaakt or bloot
name	moniker	naam or noom
named	is called	heet
nap	snooze after lunch	rohstunn or meddagspause
narrator	long winded speaker	dröhnbüdel
narrow	tight squeeze	ing
narrow opening	hole in the fence	knick
nasty	very distasteful	igitt
nation	Nation	natschoon
native	local born	heemgeburen
naturally	obviously	noturlig
nature	all around us	notur
naughty	bad	eisch or unnaasch
navy	the fleet	flott
near	close	dicht
nearby	close by	dichtbi or stievbi or neegbi
nearer	closer	nöger or neger or dichter
nearest	closest	nögste or neegste
nearness	closeness	neeg
necessary	have to	nödig or notwendig
necessity	needed	nood or not
neck	pain in the	gnick or nacken
necklace	beads	halskeden or halskedden
necktie	not too tight	hals strick
need for	can utilize	gebruuk för
needle	pointy	nodel or nadel
neighbor	next door people	nober, nohber, naober, nawer
neighborhood	the surrounding area	noberschop or nawerschop
neighborpeople	the whole bunch	noberslüüd or noberslüer
neighbors	all of them	nobers or naobers or nabers
nerves	the shakes	nerven or närven
nervous	ant-sy	nervös or hiddelig
nest	bird's home	nest or neest
net	made of string	nett
never	not any time	nie or niemols
nevertheless	well, anyway	liekers or doch or ebengliek
new	not old	neet or neiet or nejet
new	a new one	neen or neien or neje
new year	hear them horns	nee johr or nei johr
new years eve	mistletoe time	oolt johrs obend
news	latest bulletin	noricht
newspaper	daily paper	blatt or popier or zeidung
next	next in line	nexte or nächts
next to	beside	blangs or nextto or nächtsto
nibble	gnaw at	gnibble
nice	good, pretty	schön or nüüdlich or fix or fein

125

nickname	alias	binaam	or binoom
niece	brother's daughter	nichde	or nichte
night	late evening	nacht	or obendstied
nightcap	so flees can sleep	sloopmütz	or slaapmütz
night owl	a hooter	nachtuul	
nightingale	bird	nachtigall	
nine	9	negen	
nineteen	19	negenteihn	
ninety	90	negentig	
nipple	milky way	titt	
no	negative	nee	
nobody	not any person	nüms	
no one	not anybody	keeneen	or keene
noble	extra good	vörnehm	
nobleman	aristocracy	eddelmann	
nobody	no person	nüms	
nod	move head up & down	nickkopp	
noise	hard on ears	lärmt	
none	not a one	keen	
none	not any	gorkeen	
nonsense	craziness	blöödsinn, tüünkraam, quatsch	
noon	12 o'clock	meddag	or meddagstunn
normal	quite O.K.	normol	
north	direction	noord	
nose	honker	näs or nääs or niäs or snuut	
nosy	curious	näschierig	
not	negative	nich	
note	list of things	zeddel	
notes	on music sheet	noden	
nothing	not a thing	nix or nams or nichs	
notice	bulletin, call, inform	kunnig	(past: künnigt)
November	eleventh month	November	or Nevelmaand
now	at the current time	nu	
now a days	these times	upsteed	
noway	just won't work	narms de weg	
nowhere	nothing here or there	narms	or keenwegens
number	counter	nummer	
nuts	to you	naart	or nöört
oak	tree	eeken	
oar	steer in water	roder	
oat grits	warm meal	hoovegrütt	
oath	pledge, swear	swor	
oats	grain	hooven	or hovern
obedienct	toes the mark	gehoorsom	
obey	listen to parents	tohören	
objection	don't agree	gegenspruk	
obligation	owe something	plicht	
observed	noticed	bemarkt	
obviously	to be sure	doch	or openbor

126

occasionally	once in a while	wecke tiedens or biweglanglig
occupant	lives there	inwohner or insitter
occur	is happening	geiht an or passeer
occurred	has happened	angohn or gescheht or passeert
October	tenth month	October or Saatmaand
odd	peculiar	afsunnerlig
off	not on	aff or af
off and on	sometimes	afunan
offer	make the offer	anbeden or beden
offer	the offer itself	anbott
offspring	little offshoots	sprüttling
often	many times	öfters or mannigmol or foken
oftener	not just once	meehrmol
oil	used in a lamp	ööl or öl
oil lamp	warm shiner	öl lampen
old	not new	olt or oolt
old car	junkmobile	klapperkassen
old man	dirty old guy	knass
old nag	swayback	kracker
old stuff	goes way back	olendeel
older	over 30	öller
oldest	greyest	öllste
oldfashioned	not new	oltmodisch
on	on top of	op or up
on the way	on the trip	ünnerwegens
one	1	een
one of	particular one	eene or een vun
one another	comparative	eenanner
one time	once is enough	eenmol
onion	smells	zipollen or zibbel
only one	just one	eensige or eensigste
onto	climb on	ropp or rupp
on what	on which hook?	woneem an
open	not closed	open
open it	break into	anbreken or openmoken
operate	make work	schaff
operate	like a doctor	operien
opinion	by his account	oort
opponent	player against	gegenspeeler
oppose	against	gegenswesen
opposite	not the same	gegendeel or gegensiedig
oppressed	picked on	benaut
or	choice	oder
orchard	apple trees	boomgoorn or appelhof
orchestra	brass band	blooskapell
order	like from a catalog	bestellen
order	proper activity	ornung
orderly	properly neat	ornlig
organ	instrument	örgel
origin	starting point	herkommt

ostrich	big bird	struus		
other	not the same	anner	(pl: annerde)	
other kind	not that one	anner sorde		
other time	some other day	anner tied		
otherwise	without it	süss		
our	belongs to us	uus		
our	belongs to all	uusen		
out	not in	ut		
out of	from out of	rut		
out of the way	no problem	utenweg		
out the back	skip out	achterrut		
outcome	as it turned out	utkomm		
outlook	looks like	utkiek	or	utseht
outloud	very noisy	utluud	or	luuthals
outside	outdoors	buten		
outside	outer surface	utsied	or	butensied
outside door	where to go out	butendöör		
oval	sort of round	eierrund		
oven	cook stove	oben	or	oven
over	its all over	öwer	or	röver
overall	in every place	allerwegens		
overboard	throw a line	butenbord		
overcoat	big coat	öwerrock	or	mantel
overflow	over the bank	öwerflott		
overlay	lay on top of	öwerleggen		
overnight	Federal Express	öwernacht		
over there	look there	dorhen		
overturned	on its head	koppöwer		
owe	should give to	eeg		
owed	should have given to	mi shullig	or	mi shuldig
owl	night bird	kattuul	or	uul
own	belongs to you	eegen		
owner	has the bill of sale	besitter		
oxen	pull wagons	ossen		
pack	arrange	pack		
pack up	fill the bags	inpacken		
package	bundle	pakeet		
page	in a book	blatt	or	sied
pail	bucket	eimel		
pain	hurts a lot	wehdaag	or pien or	peen
paint	act of painting	anstrieken		
painter	sign painter	schiller	or	schilder
painter	portrait	maaler		
painting	oil picture	bild	(pl: biller)	
pair	two of a kind	poor	or	paar
pair	two horses, team	spann		
pale	bleached	blass	or	bleek
palm	tree	palm		
pan	metal plate	pann		

128

pancake	baked in a pan	pankoken
pane	part of window	shiev
panel	part of wall	paneel
pantry	keep food	spieskomer or bodderköken
pants	trousers	büx (pl: büxen) or hosen
paper	to write on	popier
papercup	not styrofoam	pappbeker
paper sack	for candy	tuten
paragraph	sentence bunch	afsatz
parallel	equidistant	lieklopen
parents	older people	öllern
parents house	old place	öllernhuus
parish	church area	kerkspell or karkspell
parlor	front room	goodstuuv or vörstenruum
parsley	green sprigs	petersill
part	a slice	afsnitt
part in play	actor	andeel
partial	just a part	deelwies
partially	partly	deelbor
participate	join in	mitmoken or mitsnacken
particularly	especially	sunnerlig
parting	say goodbye	afscheed
partition	in hair	schedel
partridge	wild bird	raphohn or feldhohn
pass the time	while away hours	tiedverdrieben or tietverdrieven
passed	has gone by	vörbi
passed by	went past	vörbi gohn or vörbigahn
passenger	comes along	fohrgast
passport	travel papers	utwies
past	in the past	fröher or verleden
paste	glue	kliester
pastor	of the church	pastoor or pastor or paster
pastry cook	make tortes	fienbeker or fienbäker
pasture	hay field	weid or haufeld
patch	hide the hole	flicken
path	trail	padd
patience	take it easy	geduur or geduld
patient	is easy going	gedüllig
patrol	keep watch	patroon
patron	favored one	günner
pattern	to make dress	muster or vörbild
paunch	beerbelly	fettbuuk
pavement	paved surface	ploster
paw	animal foot	poot (pl: padden)
pawnshop	under three balls	pandhuus
pay	take care of bill	betohl
pay	earnings you get	lohn or daglohn
pay attention	take notice	kümmer or ankiehen
pay back	repay loan	trügbetohln
pay extra	added charge	nobetohln

pay in	contribute	rinbetohln
payment	item payed	toll
pays	worth it	lohnt sik
pea	vegetable	arfen or arven
peace	left alone	freeden or freden
peach	the keen kind	pirsch (pl: pirshen)
peacock	show off bird	pageluun
peasantry	our kind of folks	buurschop
peat	soil used for heat	torv or torf
peat harvesting	dig it up with a spade	torvsteken
peat spade	for digging up	sniespaden
peculiar	bit funny	gediegen or sposig
peddler	wanders w/ sack on back	kiepenkirl
pedestrian	walker	footganger
peek	sneek a look	piek
peel	make a naked apple	shell
peep	a chick's song	piep
pencil	lead pencil	bleestick
penitentiary	big jail	tuchhuus
pension	extra bucks	pankschoon
Pentecost	Whitsunday	Pingsten
Pentecost Fox	fairy tale animal	Pingstvoss
people	folks	lüüd or lüer or lüür
people	folks in general	lüüde
pepper	not salt	peper
peppernuts	special one	pepernäärt
perceive	take to be true	wohrnehmen or afsehn
perceptive	can notice things	föhlbor
perfume	aroma	rükwoter or rükwater
perhaps	possibly, maybe	aminn
periphery	outside border	butenkant or ümkant
permission	give OK	verlööf or verlööv
perpetrated	committed it	utfreten
persist	doggedly	anduuren
persuade	talk into	insnacken
petroleum	gas	eerdöl or steenöl
petticoat	don't let it show	ünnerrock
pharmacy	drug store	aptek or apteek
pheasant	not a turkey	fason
piano	music instrument	klaveer
pick	get cherries from tree	plück
pick out	select	utsöken (past: utsocht)
pickpocket	sticky fingers	langenfinger
pick up	elevate	upsöken (past: upsocht)
picked	selected, picked out	utsocht or utplückt
picked up	went and got it	afhalt or afhaalt
pickel	gerken	gurke
pickled	in brine	gepökelt
pickled pig feet	supposed to be good	poten
pickled pig nose	it smells	snuten

picky eater	hard to please	leckersnuut		
picnic	ants not welcome	piknik		
picture	on the wall	bild		(pl: biller)
piece	one part	stück		(pl: stücke)
pierced	stuck through	dörsteken		
piglets	suckling oinkers	farken	or	pugge
pigs	oinkers	swien		
pigs knuckles	wierd dish	eisbeen		
pike	type of fish	heek		
pile	lot in one place	huupen	or	humpel
pill	tablet	pill		(pl: pillen)
pillar	narrow post	pieler		
pillow	head holder	küssen		
pincers	pinching pliers	knieptang		
pinch	ouch	kniep		
pine	evergreen	dann		
pine tree	christmas tree	dannboom		
pipe	for smoking	piepen	or	piep
pirate	peg-leg	eeröber		
pissing	emptying bladder	strütchen	or	miegen
pitch dark	can't see a thing	stickendüster		
pitiful	sorry sight	beduurlig	or erbärmlig	
pity	feel sorry for	beduur		
place	a location	platz (pl:plätz) or stell or steed		
plague	sickness	plaag		
plain	simple	eenfach	or	slicht
plan	idea	plaan		
plane	wood plane, scraper	högel		
plane	with wings	luftshipp		
plant	in ground	plant		(pl: planten)
planted ground	seeds in place	saatland		
plaque	formal message	plakeet		
plaster	on the wall	pläster		
plate	for food	teller		(pl: töller)
play	fun or stage show	speel		
play along	join the game	mitspeelen		
play clothes	informal	speeltüch		
play director	in charge of show	speelbaas		
play together	make a team	tohopenspeeln		
play trick on	do him dirty	anshieten		
play trump	play highest card	trumpen		
playground	play ball	schoolgrund	or	schoolhof
playlet	short play	speeldeel		
playroom	boxes of toys	speelruum	or	speelstuuv
plead	whine like a pest	puug	or	pug
pleasant	nice	genehm		
pleased	made happy	vergnögt	or	froh
pleasure	happy time	vergnögen or pläsier or moi		
pledge	give support	pand		
pledge	of allegiance	truupand		

131

pliers	grippers	tang
plop	fall in a clump	plumpsen
plow	turn ground over	plögen
plow	equipment	ploog (pl: plöög)
plow share	does the digging	ploogiesen or ploogschar
plowed land	been plowed	ackerland
pluck	remove feathers	plück
pluck off	make a nude chicken	afplücken or vunplücken
plug	hole in barrel	tapp
plum	fruit	plumm
poacher	woodsy thief	wilddeev
pocket	in your pants	taschen or tashen or tasken
pocketwatch	flip the cover	tashenklock
poem	like a sonnet	dichtel or gedicht
poetry	bunch of poems	poesie
point to	look there	hinwiesen (past: hinwiest)
pointed	sharp	spitz
poison	never take seconds	gifft
poke	stir, punch	prökeln
pole	rod	pahl
pole	steel	stang
policeman	flat foot	kunstabler or schandarm
polish	make shiny	putzen
police	peace keeper	schandarm
polite	courteous	höflig
pond	small lake	diek
ponder	give it more thought	besinnen
poor	maybe even rotten	slecht or leeg
poor	got no bucks	arm
poorly	hurts a little	leeg
poplar	tree	pappel
porcelain	shiny surface	porzellan
pork	other white meat	swienfleesch
porous	full of holes	lockerig
portion	part of it	portschoon or deel
portray	play the part	schillern
possible	could be	möglig
possibly	if at all possible	jichens or jichtens
post	holds a fence up	posten
postal stage	pulled by horses	postwogen
post office	stamp place	postamt
postman	mail carrier	postkirl or postkeerl
postpone	until another day	vershuuben
postscript	note at the bottom	nowoort or noschrift
postwar	after the shooting	nokriegs tied
pot	holds a plant	pott (pl: pött) or putt (pl:pütt)
pot	large iron pot w/ legs	gropen or grapen
potato	not fried	kartüffel, kantüffel , eerdappel
potato	mashed	kartüffelbrie, moosdekartüffel
potsmith	ixes holes in pots	blecksmied or ketelklopper

potter	makes pots	pöttjer	or	püttjer
pouch	bag	büdel		
poultry	chickens	höhner	or	fellenveeh
pound	16 ounces	pund		
pound	to hit	hau	or	slag
pour	from a bottle	geet		(past: goten)
pouring	is pouring	gött		
powder	dust-like	pulwer		
power	might	macht		
powerful	mighty	deftig		
powerless	without might	ahnmachtig	or	swiemelig
practical	commonsensical	praktische		
practical joker	prankster	uulenspegel		
practice	learn to do better	ööv	or	öwen
praise	compliment	löv		
prank	trick	shelmstück		
prattle	idle chatter	praatschen		
pray	for help	beden		
preach	long hour	predig		
precious	costly	kostbor		
precocious	a little ahead	fröhriep		
predict	prophesy	vörherseggen		
pregnant	with kid	sworfoot or een unner de schöten		
prepared	ready to go	parat	or	praat
prescribe	give medicine	vörshriev		
present	gift	geshenk	(pl: geshenke)	
present	set up, offer up	vörstellen		
presented	presented itself	vörkommen		
presently	current time	upstunns		
preserve	make jam	inkoken		
press	place pressure	druck	(past: drückt)	
pressure	push on	drück		
pretty	nice to look at	glatt or hübsch or smuck or schön		
prevent	stop from happening	twüschenkommen or vörkommen		
previous	one just before	vörige		
price	costs *how* much?	pries	(pl: priesen)	
priest	catholic father	preester		
primarily	mainly	hauptsechtlig	or	haaptsechtlig
prince	royalty	först		
primary	most important	höchstens		
print	make a book	drück		
printer	publisher	bookdrücker		
prize	the winnaaaah	pries		
prizewinner	he beat em all	priesdreger		
problem	to be solved	problem	or	pech
procession	parade around	ümtog	or	wannelbohn
proclaim	announce	künnigmoken		
profession	position	profeschoon		
profit	nice surprise	öwergeld		
prohibited	not allowed	verbeden		

133

project	something to do	project	or	vörhebbt
promise	to promise	toseggen		
pronoun	in place of noun	förwoort		
pronto	right away	proot	or	praat
pronunciation	how you say it	utspruk		
proof	evidence	nowies		
proper	quite presentable in	schick	or	schicklig
proper	behaved	örnig		
properly	nicely	örnig		
proposal	suggested action	vörschutt		
proud	done good	stolt		
prune	wrinkled food	swetschen		
psalmbook	song book	salmbook		
public	out in the open	openbor		
public spirit	charity minded	börgersinn		
puddle	pile of water	pool		
puke	upchuck	kotzen		
pull	move toward you	tehn	(past: töög)	
pull off	take it off	aftehn	(past: aftogen)	
pull through	needle hole	dörtehn		
pulled in	drawn in	intogen		
pulled out	got unstuck	ruttogen		
pulls	is pulling	tüht		
pulp	wet paper	pamp		
pump	water source	pumpen		
pump handle	water flows from well	sootswang		
pumpernickel	good bread	swattbrot		
pumpkin	in a patch	flaschappel		
punch	awl	preen		
punishment	just desserts	straaf	or	stroff
pupil	learner	schoolkind	(pl:schoolkinner)	
pup	junior dog	welp		
purchase	buy	kööp	(past: kofft)	
purse	holds everything	geldknipp		
purse	small one	knieptasch		
put	place	legg		
put aside	for a rainy day	wegleggen	or	wegsetten
put in place	put it there	hinstellen		
put on	clothe	antehn	(past: antogen)	
put on	put on just the hat	upsett		
quarrel	spat-man vs wife	ehekrach		
quarrel	spat with anyone	strien	or	quälen
quarter	one fourth of a buck	vertel	or	veddel
queen	big boss's wife	künigen		
queen, clubs	in game of Solo	spandelje		
queen, spades	in game of Solo	baschaan		
questionnaire	nosy letter	ümfraag		
quibble	disagree noisily	vertörn	or	strien
quick	fast, agile	flink	or gau or dull	

quickly	hastily	düchtig
quiet	to be quiet	swieg or still
quiet	soft noise	lies
quiet	restful	roh
quilt	fancy stitching	öwerbett
quiet hour	nap after lunch	rohstunn
rabbit	hare-y animal	haas or kanink
race	compete for speed	rennen or rasen
race	running competition	wettlopen
raced after	took out after	tÖÖg achter
racehorse	Man of War	rennpeerd
radish	rabbit food	rettich
rag	to wash with	lappen
rag	to clean with	plünnen
rage	terrible temper	raasch
railing	keep from falling	glind
rain	the wet stuff	regen or rägen
raining	getting wet	regent
raise	lift	böör
raise up	elevate	upbörn (past: upbört)
raisin	tired grape	rosien
rake	rake leaves	raaken (past: raakt)
rake	what you rake with	haark
ram	wild he-animal	bock
ram	plow into	knall dorrin
rancid	foul liquid	galsterig
rankel	vines intertwine	rankel
rapid	speedy	flink or gau
rare	like a steak	raar or nich oft
rare	hard to find	sporsom
rascal	tricky person	slüngel or bingel
rascal	cute and tricky	shelm
rascal	mischievous kid	snickelfritz or piependeckel
rascal	nasty trickster	swienegel or orsewöddel
rasp	metal scraper	fiel or riebiesen
raspberry	gets in your teeth	himbeeren
rat	mouse on steroids	rott
rather	prefer	lewer or lever
rather	seemingly	simmlig or tämlig
rattle	noise	rötern or klappern
raven	black bird	raav
ravine	big swale	slucht
ray	beam of light	strahl (pl: strahlen)
reach	stretch for	reck (past: reken) or lang
reach for	gimme that	henlangen or hinrecken
reach through	through the hole	dörrecken
read	peruse the paper	lees (past: lesen)
read off	say what's on paper	aflesen
read to	tell a nursery story	vörlesen

135

ready	available	praat	or	parat
really	actually	würklig		
rear	bring up	upbringen	(past: upbrocht)	
reason	that's why	sach	or saak	or grund
reasoned	figured it out	utdacht		
rebel	fight against	upmucken		
rebellious	like a brat	upsässig	or	wrevelig
receipt	proof of purchase	bewies		
recently	very short time ago	eben	or	nülig
recipe	cooking instructions	rezept		
recite	say your piece	vörseggen		
reckless	get out of the way	drieversch		
recluse	almost a hermit	kluusner		
recognizable	can be distinguished	kennbor		
recognize	able to identify	kenn	or	kinn
recognize	recognize features	afsehn		
recommend	advise about	anroden	or	vörslaan
reconsider	should I?	nodenken	or	öwerleggen
reconsider	think awhile	upbesinn		
red	bull's favorite color	rood	or	root
red cross	aid society	rotkrüüz		
red one	a red one	ruden	or	roden
reduction	take some off	nolat	or	nolot
redundant	unnecessary	öwerleidig		
reference	points to	hinwies		
reflect	make an image	spegel		
reflection	second image	afglans		
refuse or deny	just say no	afseggen		
refuse	garbage	shietkraam		
regrew	like a weed	wellerwussen or wedderwussen		
regulate	make rules for	regeln		
rein	horse strap	tögel		
rejoice	go crazy	juchen		
related	blood or marriage	verwand		
relatives	all of them	verwandschop		
relax	sit a while	hinsetten		
rely on	bank on it	up af gohn		
remaining	leftover	öwrig	or	öwerbleben
remarkable	worth a look	afsunnerlich		
remember	where did I park?	beholen	or	besinnen
remember	all of a sudden	infallen		
remembering	to remember	upinnern	or	beholen
remote	far off	wietaf		
remove	be rid off	los moken	or	rutnehmen
renounce	take it back	unseggen		
rent	get & own temporarily	hüüren or packten or vermeden		
repair	fix machinery	repareeren		
repair	small patch	flicken		
repeat	say again	noseggen	or	wiederseggen
repeatedly	more than once	miehrmol	or	meehrmol

replace	in place of	versetten		
report	answer the call	mellen	or	anmellen
represent	presents oneself as	vörstellen		
reputation	how you're seen	ansehn		
request	seek an answer	affrogen		
rescue	save somebody	redden		
research	look up, examine	ünnersöken		
resembles	looks familiar	kiekt ähnlig		
reserve	hold back	freeholen	or	besett
reserved	kept for you	trügloten	or	trügsett
resharpen	make sharp again	nosliepen		
reside	live there	wohn		
residence	place of living	wohnplatz	(past: wohnplätz)	
resign	beg off	afdanken		
resist	work against	gegenstohn		
rest	take a nap	roh	or	rauh
rest	take time off	utrohn	or	rast
rest	the remainder	rest		
restless	squirmy	wunderlig		
rest time	take a nap after lunch	rohstunn		
restaurant	place to eat	weertschap		
restless	uneasy	kabbelig		
rethink	go over it again	besinnen		
retrieve	go and get it	hool		
return	come again	vertrüg kommen	or	retuur
returned	came again	wollerwesen	or	wedderwest
revenge	get back	vergellung		
reversed	ass ackwards	vertwiert		
revise	make changes	anners moken	or	ümdoon
revised	changed	ümarbeidet	or	ümdohn
reward	dead or alive	koppgeld		
rhyme	like poetry	riemel		
ribs	finger lickin good	rippen		
rice	instead of spuds	ries		
rich	lotsa bucks	riek		
rickety	about falling apart	lapperig		
rid of	get rid of habit	afwinnen	(past: afwunnen)	
riddle	tricky question	radel		
ride	travel on back of	rieden		
rider	doing the riding	rieder		
riding boots	special shoes	riedstebel	or	riedstevel
right	direction	recht		
right away	immediately	bautz	or	batz
rigid	very stiff	stiev	or	stief
ring	bell noise	klingel		
ring	circle	ring		
rinse	wash off	spöhl		
rinse away	down the drain	wegspöhln		
ripe	good time to eat it	riep		
risk	take a chance	riskiern	or	riskeern

river	stream	strom	or	flott
roam around	wander here and there	rangeern		
roar	bellow	rorr	or	bullern
roast pork	white meat	swienbroden		
rob	to rob	röben		
robber	"stick em up" crook	röber		
rock	move back and forth	weegen		
rocking chair	to and fro	weevstohl	or	weegenstohl
rocking horse	giddy ap	schaakelpeerd		
rod	stick	rod oder rod oder stock		
roll	spining move	rull		
roll up	put the hose away	uprullen		
rood	stick, switch	rood		
roof	top of house	dack		
room	part of a house	ruum or stuuv or kamer		
rooster	crower	hohn	or	hahn
root	ground end of plant	wörtel	or	wöttel
rope	thick strong string	reep	or	strick
rose	smell's the same	roos		
rotation	all the way around	rundlop		
rotted out	too far gone	utrotten	or	utverrott
rotten	too old	verrott		
rough	tough talk	groff		
round	like a circle	rund		
round dance	schottisch	ringeldans		
roundtrip ticket	both ways	trügfohrkorden		
row	all in a line	reeg		
rub	scour	shüür	or	shüer
rub off	erase	afshüren	(past: afshürt)	
rubber	elastic	robber		
rubber boots	keep dogs dry	robberstebel	or	robberstevel
rubbish	junk	krimskraam		
rubble	all broken up	schutt		
rudder	to steer with	roder		
rule	reign	regeeren		
ruler	measuring stick	metstock		
rumor	hear the latest?	gesegge	or	snacksch
rump	hind quarter	stüüts		
run	go pretty fast	loop	(past: lööp)	
run after	chase, follow	nolopen		
run around	here and there	rümlopen		
run away	abscond	weglopen		
run by	zooom	vörbilopen		
run into	enter in a hurry	rinlopen		
run out	end of a rope	aflopen	or	rutlopen
run out	no more left	utlopen		
run out	sneak off	utknippen		
run under	sneak under	ünnerlopen		
rung	step on ladder	rang		
runs	act of running	lopt		

rural	country like	dörplig
rush around	helter skelter	rüm suusen
rust	oxidized iron	rust
rusty	full of rust	rustig
rustle	sound leaves make	rassel
rutabaga	funny plant	stickrööv or kohlrööv
rye	grain	roggen
sabre	long sword	sabel
sack	bag	sack
sack	paper sack	tuten
sad	down	trurig or bedripst
saddler	makes saddles	saadler
said	talked	sä (pl: sään)
said	to have said	seggt
sail	a boat	segel
sailmaker	able to sew	büdelneiher
sailor	uses a boat	seemann (pl:seelüüd), mariner
salad	oil and vinegar	solaat or salat
salt	not pepper	solt
salve	for the hurt	salv
same	no diff	sülvig or övereen
same one	identical	sülvige
sample	just to taste	tosmeck
sand	on the beach	sand
sand castle	don't kick it down	sandborg
sank	went down	dohlsackt
sap	maple syrup	sapp
sarcastic	meany mouth	spietsch
sat	took a seat	seet
satisfied	enough to eat	satt
satisfied	content	tofree
saturday	last day of week	sünnobend or saterdag
sauerkraut	and hot dogs	suurkohl
sausage	a wiener	mettwust or wurst or wusst
save	put in the bank	heeg or heeg up or sporren
save	rescue	redden
savings bank	low interest	sporkass
savior	saves your bacon	redder
saw	to cut wood with	saag
saw buck	holds it steady	saagenbock
saw off	don't sit on it	afsaagen
sawdust	saw leftover	saagmehl
sawmill	cut into boards	saagmöhl
say	to mention	segg (past: seggt)
saying	adage	seggwoort or sprickwoort
scab	it's healing	schorv
scales	weighing machine	waag
scale bowl	put in, to be weighed	waagschaal
scamp	no good bum	lümmel

139

scandal	bad news	schandal
scar	produces a scab	narv
scarce	not many of	knapp
scare	make afraid	schrecken or bangmoken
scarf	head cover	koppdook
scarlet	sort of red	hellrot
scat	get away, cat	kitze
scatter	sow wild oats	strei or streih
scatterbrain	dizzy type	himphamp
school	place of learning	school (pl: schoolen)
school board	in charge	schoolrot
school desk	hole for inkwell	schoolbank
school year	will it never end?	leehrjohr or schooljohr
science	book learnin'	wetenschop
scissors	to cut with	shier
scold	give em the devil	schimp or utschellen or utoosen
scolding	got a scolding	schimpas
scram	get rid of a cat	kittsa
scrambled eggs	no sunny side	röhreier
scrap	leftover cuttings	snippel
scrap of paper	note	zeddel
scrape	rub and remove	schraapen
scratch	on your new car	schramm
scratch	cat leaves a mark	klei or kratz
scratch off	win the lottery	afkratzen
scream	screetch	shrieg
screw	fastener	shruuv (pl: shrüüv)
screwed up	kinda crazy	verdreiht
screw in	make fast	rinschruben
scribble	doctor's writing	kratzeln
scum	top layer	afshuum
scurry	hurry around	rümflitzen
scythe	to cut grass	seesel
sea	big pond	see
seagull	water bird	mööv
seal	water animal	saalhund
seam	stitched together	soom
search	to look for	sök (past: socht)
searching	act of looking	söken
searchlight	light up the sky	shiensmieter
seasoning	salt and pepper	krüderee
seat	place to sit	sitz or sitzplatz
second	tick on the clocks	sekund (pl: sekunde)
second one	not first one	tweete
secret	hush	stillken
section	compartment	afschnitt or afdeel
security	safeness	sekerheit
see	observe	seh (past: sehn)
see	see there!	süh
seed	to plant	saat

140

seemingly	evidently	shienbor	
seems	appears to be	süht ut as	
seems as if	appears like	shientso	
seems like	appears like, resembles	bedüdet	
seems to be	appears so	lett so	or künn weren
seen	was viewed	sehn	
seldom	hardly ever	selten	
self	himself or herself	sik	
self important	big shot	groodsporig	or groodorig
self interest	what's in it for you	egennutt	
sell	to get rid of	verköp	
send	put in the mail	schick	
sense	not too common	sinn	or verstand
senseless	not wise	sinnlos	
sensible	should do it	sinnig	or insichtig
sensual	with feeling	sinnlig	
sentence	part of paragraph	satz	
sentence	life without parole	strof	
separate	pull in two	uteenannertehn	
separate	make a distinction	sheeden	
separated	keep apart	uteenannern	
September	month of year	Harvstmaand,	Micheelismaand
serene	peaceful	liekmodig	
serious	in ernest	ernst	
sermon	long hour	predig	
servant	hired hand	knecht	
serve	wait on	deenen	
set	place down	sett	
set fire to	light it up	anstiken	
settle	into place	dahl laten	or versetten
seven	7	söben	
7 of clubs	in card game Zolo	spitz	
seventeen	17	söbenteihn	
seventh	after sixth	söbente	
seventy	70	söbentig	
sew	with a needle	neih	
sewing basket	grandma's favorite	neihkorv	
sexton	in the church	küster	
shabby	run-down	spökig	or pukkelig
shade	out of the sun	schadden	
shaft	hole in ground	schacht	
shaft	long metal pipe	schaft	
shake	trembling	beven	or beben
shake	like dice	shüttel	
shake out	roll the dice	utshütteln	
shaky	unsteady	wackelig	
shall	intend to	schall	
shallot	smalll onion	schallott	
shallow	not deep	flak	or flaak
shame	embarassing feeling	schäm	

English	Definition	Low German
shame on you	you did it	schäm di
shameless	not ashamed	schämlos or unverschämt
shape	condition	schick
share	portion	andeel or schaar
sharp	have a keen edge	scharp
sharpen	give it a sharp edge	scharpen
sharpening stone	needs a little spit	sliepsteen
shave	trim close	putzen or rasiern
shaving brush	apply cream	putz börst
shawl	warm the shoulders	slingdook
she	that female	se
shears	that's cut it	sheer
shed	where to park it	shedd
sheep	big lambs	schaap
sheep raisins	nonedible raisins	schaapsködel
sheep shearing	make a naked sheep	schaapsheeren
sheeps wool	warm	schaapswull
sheet iron	metal	iesenbleck
shell	nut covering	shell
shell	cut skin off apples	shell
shelter	in the dry	ünnerdack
shepherd	sheep's boss	sheper
sheriff	of Nottingham	panner
shield	sign, protector	shild
shine	like the sun	shien
shiny	bright	blank or hellig
ship	boat	shipp
shirt	off your back	himd
shirt sleeve	use to wipe with	himdelmel
shiver	shake	beev or beben
shock	of wheat, or scare	chok
shoe	foot cover	schoh
shoebrush	make em shine	schohbörst
shoehorn	ake it fit	chohlepel
shoelaces	keep them tied	snürbinnen or schohbinnen
shoemaker	cobbler	shohster
shoo away	scram	wegsheen or wegsheren
shoot	fire a gun	sheet (past: schoten)
shoot	act of shooting	sheeten
shooting match	competition	shützenfest
shopkeeper	small one	krömer
shopping	o and stock up	inköpen
shore	lake's border	woterkant or küst
short	not long	kort or koart or kuort
shortly	pretty soon	körtens
short pants	like knee britches	kinnerbüx
shotgun	boomer	büssenflint or shrottflint
shotgun pellets	in your behind	shrott
should	ought to	schull
should	you should, must	schass or schalls

142

shoulder	spot for chips	schullern	or	schullen
shove	push along	schuuv	(past: schoben)	
shovel	can you dig it	schüffel		
show	bring into view	wies	(past: wiest)	
show	act of showing	wiesen		
show how	how to do it	wiesmoken		
show off	ut on airs	dickdoon	or	afwiesen
shred	rag remnant	snippel		
shrink	get smaller	shrunk	or	shrump
Shrove Tuesday	church holiday	Fastelobend		
shuffle	amble along	humpel		
shut	closed	to	or	tomokt
shut off	turn off	afmoken	or	afdreihn
shut down	stop the presses	dohlsluten		
shutters	when it blows	finsterklappen		
shy	timid	shu	or	shuu
sick	feel bad	krank	or	leeg
side	laterally	sied		
side door	another way in	sieddöör	or	blangdöör
sidewalk	easier to walk on	plosterweg		
sieve	drain thru holes	seev	or	seef
sign	signal	teken		
sign, directional	way to San Jose	wegwieser		
signpost	shows the way	wiespohl	or	wiespahl
silent	be quiet	still		
silliness	acting up	fuulheit		
silly	kind of funny	mall or	alvern or	dwallerig
silly stories	anecdotes	döntjes	or	dösen
silver	precious metal	sülve		
similar	about the same	ähnlig		
simple	absolutely	eenfach		
simply	clearly	düütlig		
simultaneously	at exact same time	togliek		
sin	naughty	sünn		
since	from a time on	vundenntied	or	siet
sing	go la-de-da	sing	(past: sungen)	
sink	edge lower	sack		
sink down	to your knees	sack dahl		
sip	take a small drink	sippen	or	nippen
sister	female sibling	süster	or	swester
sit	sit down	sitt	(past: seten)	
six	6	söss		
sixteen	16	sössteihn		
sixty	60	sösstig		
size	how big	grött		
skating rink	sailing along	iesbohn		
skeleton	bunch of bones	knokengestell		
skeleton key	fits anywhere	didrik		
sketch	make a drawing	sketts		
skiff	small boat	schunt		

143

skimmer	remove top layer	shümer			
skin	people's hide	huut			
skin	animal's hide	fell			
skin	to take hide off	shinnen			
skirt	hide those legs	rock			
sky	way up there	luft	or	in a'luft	
slack	room to move	slapp			
slam into	crash into	rinknallen			
slat	small board	latten			
slate	roof material	lie			
slaughter	butcher	slacht			
slave	owned by someone	slaav			
sled	slide down hill	sleden			
sleep	snore time	sloop	or	slaap	
sleepy	tired	möör	or	möer	
sleepy head	can't keep eyes open	slaapmütz			
sleeve	coat's arm	elmel			
slender	thin	slank			
slice	cut potatoes	dörsnien	or	upsnien	
slide	on your pants	rutsch			
slight	just a little	minnhaftig			
slime	runny stuff	sliem			
sling	broken arm holder	sleng			
slingshot	aim for the cat	flitzbogen			
slip	don't let it show	ünnerkleed			
slip	whoops	glipp	or	rütsch	
slippers	kee toes warm	huusschoh	or	pantuffel	
slippery	woops	rütschig			
sliver or splinter	ouch	splidder	or	splitter	
slobber	need a napkin	slabber			
slope	down a hillside	barg			
sloppy	spills a lot	slakkerbüx			
slouch	hunker down	runksen	or	duuken	
slow	not fast	langsom			
small	little	lütt	or	kleen	or small
small change	a few coins	klottergeld			
smallest	littlest one	lüttste	or	ringste	
smart	brainy	klook			
smart	very artsy or classy	plietsch			
smarter	brainier	klöker			
smarty pants	wise guy or guyess	klookshett			
smear	smudge it up	smeer			
smell	a smell	rüük	or	gerucht	
smells	do the act of smelling	rüken			
smells	is smelling	rükt			
smile	grin for real	smiel			
smirk	half smile	smüstern	or	smuustern	
smoke	to smoke a pipe	smöken			
smoke	from a chimney	smok	or	damp	
smoke house	cure sausage	smokhuus			

144

smoked eel	delicacy	speckaal
smooth	very even	shier — or — glatt
smoulder	fire almost out	sengeln
snail	escargot	snick
snake	with fangs	slang
snatch	grab up quickly	upgriepen — or — begriepen
sneak	do it hidden	sliek
sneak away	crawl and hide	wegslieken
sneeze	gesundheit	pruusch
sniff	take a whif	snuuv — (past: snoben)
sniffed	took a whif	snööv
sniffle	bad cold	snüffel
snipe	let's go hunting	moorbock
snoop around	be nozy	rümsnuben
snore	ZZZZZ-beep	snork
snort	breath thru nose	snuuv
snot	drainage	snappen
snotty	being a pest	snodderig
snout	pig's nose	snuut
snow	very flakey	snee
snow white	dwarf's guardian	sneewittshc
snowball	look out	sneeball — or — sneeklüten
snowfall	snowman time	sneefall
snowsuit	nice and warm	sneeantog — or — sneebüx
snuff	gets you happy	snuuvtabak
snuggle up	get cozy	ansmusen
so long as	while	solang as
so much	a certain amount	so un soveel
so to say	something like that	so to seggen
soap	to clean with	seep — or — seepen
social	companioniable	liedsom
society	people in general	sellschop — or — gesellschop
sock	one of them	sock — (pl: socken)
soft	spongy	week — or — möör — or — saft
softdrink	cola	saftwoder — or — saftwater
solder	weld	löden — or — klempen
soldier	military man	suldat — (pl: suldaten)
sole	type of fish	seetung
sole	on your shoe	sool
solid	heavy weight	massiv
solo	card game	solo — or — zolo
some	a few	wecke — or — welk
some	a small amount	etwas
some	a small number	eenige — or — welke
some	a row of	een reeg vun
some time ago	recent past	letzthinn
somersault	go head over heals	stolterboltern
something	better than nothing	wat
something new	a surprise	wat nees — or — wat nejes
sometimes	not often	mitünner — or — wecketiedens

145

somewhere else	not here	annerwegens	or	woanners	
son	it's a boy	sohn	or	jung	
song	music	leed			
soon	almost now	glieks			
soon	in the near future	bald			
soon as	when it happens	sogrode as	or	sobald as	
sores	blisters	swielen			
sorrow	grief	leed			
sorrowful	too bad	trorig			
soul	food	seel			
sound	noise	ton	or	klang	
sounds like	make noise like	klingt so			
soup	in a bowl	suppen			
soup spoon	little bigger	suppenlepel			
sour	not sweet	suur			
sourpuss	grumpy one	suurmuul			
south	to mexico	süüd			
southeast	florida	südoost			
southwest	new mexico	südwest			
souvenir	trip remembrance	andenken			
sow	momma pig	sög			
sow	planting seeds	sei	or	seien	
sow	young one	gilt			
space	room	ruum			
space	area	ruum			
spacious	have room	rümig			
spade	in cards	schippen			
spade	you dig it?	spaden			
span	of time or space	spann			
spanking	bend over	klapps	(past: klapps kregen)		
sparkle	shines	plinkern			
sparrow	little bird	spatz	or lüün	or	lüning
spatula	I wanna lick it	spadel			
speech	talk to group	anspruk			
speed	go fast	karjolen			
speak	to speak	snack	or küer	or	proten
speaks	act of speaking	snackt		or	snackt
spear	sharp stick	speer			
special	important	besonners			
specifically	that's the one	nehmlig			
spectacle	a show	spektokel	or	spetackel	
spectator	looker on	tokieker	or	ankieker	
speeds	go by fast	suust			
spelling	get letters right	shrievwies	or	rechtshriev	
spend	shell out	verkloppen	or	verspenn	
spent	bucks are gone	verspend			
spice	seasoning	krüderee			
spider	weaving bug	spinnbock			
spiderweb	don't get stuck	spinnwark			
spigot	water comes out	hönken			

146

spill	bump over	slakker	or	slaker
spin	round and round	küsel		
spinning wheel	thread maker	spinrad		
spinster	old maid	juffer		
spirit	ghostly	geest		
spit	expectorate	spee	or	spae
spiteful	nasty	tüksch		
spit out	flying tobacco	utspeen		
spit up	barf	upspeenf		
splash	puddle sound	platschen	or	palschen
splendid	excellent	grotoorig		
split	separate	klöben or klöven or splieten		
sponsor	stand up for	paat, voderstohn, volerstohn		
spook	ghost	spöök		
spool	roll of twine	spool		
spoon	utensil	lepel (pl: löpel) or liäpel		
spot	small blemish	plack		
spray	to spray	spritt		
spray	is spraying	sprütt		
spread	butter on bread	smeer		
spread word	get the message out	rümsnacken		
spring	jump	spring (past: sprungen)		
spring	early in the year	fröhjohr		
spring fountain	cool drink	born		
sprinkle	slight rain	miessen		
spry	lively	lebennig		
squabble	have a spat	sik vertören		
squalling	noisy complaining	kattenjammer		
square	carpenter's tool	winkel		
square	same length each side	veereckig		
square dance	4 couple dance	bunte	or	veereckig dans
squat	kneebend	huuken	or	dahlhuuken
squeamish	uncomforatable	pimperlig		
squeek	needs oil	jiep		
squint	look at the sun	plieren	or	scheel
squirrel	literaly - oak cat	eekkat	or	katekel
squirt	spray	sprütt		
stab	stick into	stek		
stack	of wheat	schok	or	bult
stagger	fumble step	rümstebeln		
stairs	steps	treppen		
stalk	shaft of wheat	stalk	or	spier
stall	shed partition	stall		
stallion	horse for stud	hings	or	tuchpeerd
stamp	for mailing	stempel		
stand	be vertical	stoh	(past: stohn)	
stands	is doing it	steiht		
standard	to measure by	metstock		
stare	just look	spreegen		
stark naked	just a smile	splitternaakt	or	splitternokt

147

starling	black bird	spree		
stars	in the sky	steern		
start	beginning point	anfang	(past: anfungen)	
start a fire	light it up	anböten	or	inböten
started	and now its going	ingang		
starts	gets going	losgeiht		
starve	no food	verhungern		
state	unit of government	staat	or	staot
statement	retort	angeev	or	utsegg
station	all aboard	statschoon		
stay	remain here	bliev		
stay away	and don't come back	wegblieben		
stay out	remain out	utblieben		
stay out of	don't go in	rutblieben		
stay overnight	bring toothbrush	öwernachten		
stay there	remain there	dorblieben		
stays	remains	blifft		
steak	red meat	ossenfleesch		
steal	swipe	stehl		
steam	from a kettle	damp		
steel	hard stuff	stahl		
steer	on the hoof	oss	or	stier
steer	guide direction	stüür	or	stüer
steering wheel	to aim with	stüürrad		
stem	plant part	stengel		
stems from	derives from	stammt vun		
stench	whew!	gestank		
step	one at a time	shredd	or	pedd
step back	back off	trügpedden		
stepbrother	not same parents	stievbroder		
stepchild	not by marriage	stievkind		
stepmother	ain't she great	stievmoder		
step out	get going	peddut		
stepping	is walking	peddt		
step out	get out of	utstiegen		
steps	lead to front door	tritt		
stewed fruit	liquid mess	moos		
stich	tied together	stig	or	stich
stick	poke	stek		
stick	short pole	stok	or	stock
stick out	protrude	rutstohn		
stick to	become stuck on	ankleben		
stiff	rigid	stief		
stimulate	prod	uppietschen		
stinger	bee's revenge	stingel		
stir	move around	röhr	(past:röhrt)	or röhg
stirrup	foot holder	bögel		
stocking	socks	strümp		
stolen	swiped	stohlen		
stomach	belly	maag	or	maagen

148

stomach ache	bad food	buukweh	or	lievkniepen
stone	small rock	steen		
stone age	full of neanderthals	steentied		
stone jug	keeps wine	kruuken		
stood there	checking things out	stühn dor		
stoop	duck down	duuk	or	duken
stop	desist	stopp		
stop sign	don't coast by	stoppschild		
store	place to buy	loden	or	stuur
storm	rough weather	stuurm	or	gewidder
stormwater	rain runoff	bruuswoter	or	bruuswater
story	tale	geshichte		
story telling	over the back fence	klönsnak		
stove	heating element	oben		
straight	not a curve	grod		
straight one	no bend in this one	grode		
straight out	go in straight line	liekut	or grodeut	or richtut
strain	try extra heard	anstringen		
strainer	pour through it	dörslag		
strange	odd	snaaksch	or	sünnerbor
stranger	unknown one	frömde		
strangle	grab the throat	wörgen		
strap	sharpen razor	stropp		
straw	wheat stalks	stroh		
strawberry	with shortcake	eerdbeern		
stream	meanderer	bek		
street	urban road	stroot	or	straat
strength	muscle-ness	macht		
stretch	reach	streck		
stretch out	really relax	lang moken		
strike	to hit	slag	(past: slagen)	
strikes	makes the hit	sleiht		
string	make a ball	band	or tweern	or twirn
stripe	line on the wall	striep		
strütchen	it spells relief	piss		
striped	lots of lines	striepelt		
stroll	walk around	twalen	or	spazeern
strong	mighty	stark		
struck	has been hit	slaan	or	slagen
stub	short cigar	stummel		
stubble	cut corn stalks	stobble		
stubborn	mule-ly	stievnacken	or	stievkopp
stubborn	mule-ly, part II	eegensinning	or	muulsch
study	hit the books	studiern	or	studeeren
stuff	dust	stoff		
stuff	to push into	stopp		
stuff	things, junk	kroom	or	kraam
stuff into	push inside	rinstoppen		
stuff like that	whatever	so wat as dat		
stuffy	dusty	stövig		

stumble	maybe he's drunk	starkel		
stump	leftover tree	stump		
stupid	idiotic	blöd		
stupidity	terminal dumbness	dummheit		
sturdy	strong	steevig		
stutter	jerky talk	stotter		
stutterer	easy for you to say	stötterbüx		
subject	item of discussion	fack	or	faak
submarine	dive	ünnerseeboot		
subsidy	kick in extra	tobaat	or	tobott
subtitle	second name	ünnertidel		
succeed	gain from	glücken		
such a	such a one	so'n		
such as that	stuff like that	sowatts	or	sowatt as dat
suck	draw on pipe	sugen	or	suchten
suddenly	at one time	upeenmol	or miteens	or batz
suds	on top of beer	schuum		
sue	take to court	verklogen		
sugar	sweet and low	sucker	or	sukker
sugar beets	sweet and red	suckerrööv		
suggested	recommended	vörslagen	or	vörslaan
suitcase	or small trunk	kuffer		
sulk	moon around	mulen	or	schüüt moken
sulphur	chemical	swewel		
sultry	hot and muggy	beklumm	or	bruddig
summer	sunny time of year	sommer		
summer sausage	good on rye	mettworst		
summertime	go barefoot	sommertied		
summit	top of the hill	spitz		
sun	the big hot eye	sünn		
sunday	first day of week	sünndag		
sundown	end of day	sünnfall		
sunglasses	shades	sünnbrill		
sunk	down	dohlsackt		
sunshine	welcome	sünnshien		
superstition	black cats	höhnergloben	or öwergloben	
supervisor	always watching you	opseher		
supper	evening meal	sopper	or	vesperbrot
supplement	added item	bislap		
supplies	goods	noshuuv		
supply	deliver goods	toföhren		
support	be a buddy	bistohn		
support	keep it standing	upholen		
support	speak up for	förwoort		
sure	certain	seker	or	gewiss
surely	certainly	sekerlig		
surprise	sneak up on him	verjog	or	verjoog
surprised	out of my socks	verjogt		
suspenders	keep 'em up	büxendregers	or büxendrägers	
suspicion	looks funny	gehüür		

swaddling	birthing clothes	winneln			
swale	very small ditch	göl			
swallow	down the hatch	sluuk			
swallow	bird	swalk			
swallow	to take a swallow	dohlsluken	or	öwersluken	
swamp	wet ground	sumpheid			
swan	big and white	swaan			
swarm	of bees	swaarm			
sway	back and forth	swalken	or	trüseln	
swear	oath	swören			
sweat	boy it's hot	sweet			
sweat	to sweat	sweeten			
sweep	with a broom	feeg			
sweep out	clean the place	utfegen			
sweet	not sour	sööt			
sweet girl	cute child	suckersnuut			
sweets	candy	naschkroom			
swim	cool off	swem			
swimming	back stroke	swemmen			
swindle	con out of	bedregen	(past: bedrogen)		
swine	pigs	swien			
swipe	steal an apple	klau	(past: klaun)		
swiped	permanently gone	knippt			
sword	en gard	swerd			
sycophant	always agrees	morslicker			
symbol	sign for	sinnbild	or	wohrteken	
symbolize	supposed to mean	bedüden			
synonimous	means the same	sinnverwand			
syrup	sweet and sticky	sirup			
table	with 4 legs	disch			
table cloth	covers the table	dischloken	or	dischlaken	
table rag	to clean it off	dischlappen			
tablespoon	bigger spoon	etlepel			
tablet	to write on	tabel			
tack	small nail	tachnogel			
tadpole	future frog	steertpogg			
tail	waggy ending	steert			
tailor	let out the waist	snieder			
take	take possession	nehm	(past: nohmen)		
take a bite	chomp	anbieten	or	tobieten	
take ahold	grab it	anfoten	or	anfaaten	
take away	remove	wegnehmen			
take back	gimme that back	trügnehmen			
take off	leave, take a picture	afnehmen			
take over	take the reins	öwernehmen			
take trick	in card game	steken			
take up	begin dealing with	upnehmen			
takes	grabs it	nimmt			
talk	speak	snack, snak, proten, küren			

talk out of	convince otherwise	afsnacken
talkative	always babbling	sabbelig
tall tales	funny stories	döntje
tallow	animal fat	tallig
tame	friendly	tamm
tan	treat leather	garv or gierven
tangible	touchable	föhlbor
tar	black and sticky	teer
tart	bitey	bidder
tassle	end of cord	troddle
taste	sample a taste	smeck
taste	the taste that it has	gesmack
tasteless	bland cooking	smecklos
tastes	is tasty	smeckt
taut	stretched tight	stramm or spannt
tavern	inn	kroog or weertshuus
tavern keeper	owner	kröger
tax	certain thing	afgeev
tea	not coffee	tee
teacher	instructor	schoolmeester
teacup	hold your pinky out	tass or teetass
team	a crew	mannschop
team	of horses	spann peer
tear	rip up	riet (past: reten)
tear down	demolish	dahlrieten
tear open	what's in there	openrieten
tear out	remove a page	rutrieten
tear up	into small pieces	uprieten
tears	salty ones	trannen or tränen
tease	just kidding	brüden
teaspoon	smaller spoon	teelepel or teeläpel
tedious	somewhat boring	stumpsinnig or langwielig
teeth	pearly whites	tehn or tähn
telephone	hello, vas you dere?	klönkassen or telefon
telescope	to watch the stars	steernkieker or stirnkieker
tell	tell a story	vertell
tempo	the beat	taak
ten	10	teihn
tenant	renter	hüürmann
tender	kind of soft	möör
tent	canvas cover	telt
tenth	1/10	teihntel
terrible	deplorable	gräsig or gehörig or schrecklig
terrible	done very poorly	abärmlig or abscharlig
terrible	ugly looking	hesslig
terrifically	tremendously much	vörpelig
test	try out	proov
testify	give witness	tügen
testy	easily mad	kortanbunnen
thank	you veddy much	dank

thankful	appreciative	dankbor		
thanks a lot	really appreciative	veel mals'n dank		
that	some thing	dat		
thatched roof	straw overhead	strohdack		
that way	over there	dorhin		
that way	in that direction	dennweg		
the	that one	de		
theater	play house	theoter		
their	belongs to them	ehr		
theirs	not ours	jümehr		
them	those folks	jüm	or	se
then	at that time	domals	or	denn
then	at a particular time	do		
there	over there	dor	or	doar
thereby	and that's how	dorbi		
therefor	the reason for	dorüm		
thereon	on which, on there	dorup		
thereto	in addition	dorto		
therewith	and with that	dormit		
these	ones in particular	düsse	or	disse
these days	nowadays	upsteed	or	düsse daag
thick	fat	dick		
thief	small time crook	deef		
thigh	upper leg	schinkel		
thimble	save the fingertip	fingerhoot		
thin	like a slice	fien		
thin	not fat	dünn	or	plörig
thing	portion of something	deel		
thing	that thing	dings		
think	to think	denk		
think about	reconsider	nodenken		
third	not best prize	drütte		
third	1/3	drüttel		
thirst	hot outside	döst		
thirsty	pour me one	döstig		
thirteen	13	dörteihn		
thirty	30	dörtig		
this	referring to some thing	dütt		
this afternoon	after the noon hour	vernommeddag		
this evening	tonight	vunobend	or	vanovend
this morning	today before noon	vermoren	or	vermorgen
this one	one in particular	düsse		
this time	right about now	düsstied		
this time	on this occasion	dütmol		
this year	about now	dütjohr		
this way	come over here	hierher		
thistle	sticky plant	dissel		
thong	strap	reem		
thorn	prickly	doorn		
thought	I thought so	dacht		

153

thought of	remembered	andacht		
thoughtful	thinking mode	sinnig	or	nodenklig
thoughts	what's in my mind	gedanken		
thousand	1000	dusend		
thousand times	pretty often	dusenmol		
thrasher	winnow wheat	döschmaschin		
thread	string it along	droht	or	droot
threaten	give a scare	dronken		
three	3	dree		
threshing	harvest grain	döschen		
thrifty	tight?	giezig	or	sporsom
thrive	earn good	gedeen		
throat	down the hatch	hals	or	görgel
through	down the middle	dör	or	dörch
throw	into orbit	smiet	(past: smeten)	
throw away	give it a heave	wegsmieten		
thrown out	kicked out	rutsmeten		
thrush	a bird	drossel		
thud	falling sound	bums		
thumb	fifth finger	dumen		
thunder	and lightning	dunner	or	dünder
thunderbolt	zig zag zap	dünnerslag		
thursday	day of week	dünnersdag		
thus	therefore	so		
ticket	take a trip	billjet	or	föhrkort
tickle	make 'em laugh	keddel		
tie	wear around throat	slips		
tie	make a knot	binn		
tie into bundle	make a bunch	bunneln		
tie shut	close sack at the top	tobinnen		
tie up	to hitching post	anbinnen		
tied together	joined	tohopenbunnen		
tight	hold tight	wiss	or	hol wiss
tight	fit very tight	pottdicht		
tightwad	has first nickel	giezhals		
tile stove	special stove	kacheloben	or	kacheloven
tiller	steer with	pinn		
tilt	put on an angle	kanten		
time	period of day	tied	or tied or tiit	
time interval	chunk of time	tiedsnitt		
timeless	lasts forever	tiedlos		
timely	good time	tiedlig		
tin	a metal	bleck	or	tinn
tinsmith	fixes metal	blecksmied		
tin snips	metal cutter	bleckshier		
tip	to tip over	kipp		
tip	knock over	ümkippen		
tip over	completely over	koppöwer		
tire	not too flat	rad		
tired	sleepy	möö	or	möer

154

tired	totally done in	kaputt
tires	5 per car	röör
title	main identifier	tidel
to	toward	to or no or tau
to	to that one	todenn
today	before tomorrow	vundaag or vondage
to home	presently at home nohuus	or bihuss
to one another	face to face	toeenannern
to where	where do we go	wohin
toad	jumper	krööt or üüz
toast	burnt bread	toost
toast	when raising glass	drinkspruk
tobacco	habitual weed	tobak or tabak
today	current day	vondag or hüüt or hüüttodags
toes	this littly piggy...	töhn
together	grouped	tohopen or tosamen
toilet	fresh air version	backhuus or shiethuus
toilet	inside version	tolette or Tante Marie
tolerant	easy going	duldsom
tolerate	put up with	dullen or utholen
tomcat	the alley romeo	bolz
tomorrow	next day	moren or morgen
ton	weight	tunn or tonn
tongue	don't bite it	tungen
tongue twister	word game	tungenknieper
too	like in 'too much'	to
too much	overwhelming	to dull
too much	more than enough	toveel
took	grabbed it	nöhm
took out	placed away from	utnohm
took out	took out of	rutnohm
top	upper end	topp
torch	blazing stick	taach
total	all of it	totall or heel
totality	in all	geheel
totally	covers everything	gans un gor
tough	hard to chew	tau
tour	trip	tuur
tow path	along the canal	treckpadd
toward	in that direction	no
tower	high building	toorn
town	urban area	stadt
toys	play things	speelsoken or speeldings
trace over	follow the line	nogohn or noföhlen
tracking dog	look for convicts	snüffelhund
tracks	trail	spuur or spoor
tractor	pulls plow	treckter or trecker
trade	tit for tat	tuusch
trade	business of trading	hannel
trader	dealer	höker

train	choo choo	tog	or	togg
tramp	vagabond	landstrieker		
translate	one to another	öwersetten		
transparent	see through-able	dörschienig		
transport	haul	anföhr		
trap	catch a bear	fall		
travel	wander around	wannern		
treacherous	a little dangerous	venien		
tread	walk on	tramp		
treacherous	not to be trusted	veniensch		
treadle	pumps spinningwheel	tred		
tree	woody plant	boom		
trellis	plant frame	gadder		
tremble	oh it's cold	beev		
trembles	is shaking	beevt		
tremendously	greatly	führpelig		
triangle	three corner	dree eck		
triangular	has three corners	dree eckig		
tricycle	beginner bike	dreerad		
trifle	teensy bit	puulkraam	or	puulkroom
trip	journey	reis	or	tuur
triple	three of them	dreefak		
troll	take a walk	spazeern	or	lustwannern
trouble	things not going right	trubel	or	pech
troublesome	burdensome	lastig		
trough	pig feeder	trog		
trousseau	goes with bride	utstüürn		
true	veritably so	wohr		
true	loyal	truu		
trump	best card	trump		
trumpet	instrument	trumpet		
trust	have confidence	truen	or	vertruun
truth	honestly	wohrheit		
truthful	never lies	wohrhaftig		
try	attempt	versök (past:versocht),		probeer
tub	bath	balje		
tuesday	day of week	dingsdah		
tulip	spring flower	tulp		(pl: tulpen)
tumble	head over head	stolterboltern		
tumult	crowd, throng	gewrögel		
turd	excrement	kötel		
turkey	Mr. gobbler	kuhnhahn		
turkey hen	girl gobbler	kuhnhehn		
turn	take the corner	dreih		
turn	turn around	ümwinnen	or	ümdreihn
turn away	chase away	afwiesen		
turn off	twist off	afdreihn)		
turn on	start it	andreihn		
turn shut	stop from flowing	todreihn		
turnip	or beet	rööv	or	grube

tv set	idiot box	kiekkassen
twelve	12	twölf
twelve	12 items	dutz
twenty	20	twintig or twentig
twice	two times	tweemol
twig	small branch	telling or telgen or twieg
twilight	dusk	shummerlicht
twin	double	twilling
twine	string	tweern or twiern
twisted	intertwined	verdreiht
two	2	twee
two thirds	2/3	tweedrüttel
type	a kind	sorde
typewriter	use both hands	shrievmaschin
udder	teats	jidder
ugh!	that's nasty	gittigitt
ugly	not cute	egelig or hesslig
umbrella	keep dry	schirm or perplüs
unashamed	not red faced	unverschämt
uncle	not Tom	ohm or unkle
uncomfortable	not soft enough	unkommodig
under	beneath	ünner
under here	below this	herünner
underneath	below something	rünner
under there	below this point	hinünner
under way	begun	ünnerwegens or ünnerweeg
underline	emphasize	ünnerstricken
underpants	time for a change	ünnerbüx
understand	know what's said	verstoh or begriep
understood	have comprehended	verstohn or bigrepen
undertaking	enterprise	ünnernehm
undressed	clothes taken off	uttohgen
unequal	not the same	ungliek
unequivocal	no doubt about it	eendütlig
uneven	kind of rought	uneben
unfamiliar	don't recognize	nich bekannt
unfriendly	nasty about it	schabbig
unharness	to de-pair horses	afspannen
unique	one of a kind	eenmolig
unintentional	didn't mean to	unachtsom or unbesichtlig
union	voluntary group	vereenigung
union	workers group	vereenschop
unite	bring together	vereenigen
unkind	not nice	ungood
unlearn	rid of habit	afleehrn
unnecessary	don't need to	nich nötig or överscherig
unruly	behave badly	unarsch
unsafe	dangerous	gefährlig
unskilled	inept	tapig

157

unsuspecting	unaware	unbewiss		
until	up to then	bet		
until now	up to this time	bet herto		
unusual	peculiar	egenortig	or	apaat
unwind	unwrap	afwickel		
unwrap	take off outside	utwickel		
up	on top	op	or	up
up above	overhead	bobenop	or	bovenup
up here	on top of this	herup		
up there	on top of that	dorup	or	hinup
uphill	puff puff	bargup		
upright	erect	piel	or	pielup
upside down	place upside down	stülp		
upside down	turned on head	koppöwer		
upstairs	next floor up	böhrn		
urge	feeling should do it	driev		
urine	bladdermilk	miege		
us ·	the group of us	us		
use	usage of	gebruuk		
use	to utilize	bruuk		
used to	accustomed to	gewint		
useful	worth having	nützlig		
use up	consume	upbruken		
usual	commonly	gewöhnlig	or	öftlig
vacation	time off	verlööv		
vaccinate	punch a hole	impen		
vacuum cleaner	not under the rug	stoffsuuger		
vague	unclear	dehnbor		
vain	must have a mirror	iedelig		
valid	it counts	gellt		
valley	between hills	dahl		
various	different ones	vershiedene		
varnish	nice finish	lienöl		
vegetable	the greens	gröön, grönkroom,		gemöös
vegetable trader	sells green stuff	grönhöker		
veil	hide behind	sleier		
venetian blind	keep sun out	rulladen		
venom	don't get bit	slanggift		
ventriloquist	C. McCarthy	buuksnacker		
verb	action word	tiedwoort		
verse	part of tune	vers		
very	quite a lot	bannig		
very loud	top of the lungs	luuthals		
very much	a goodly amount	gans beten	or	bannig veel
very tight	screwed on good	pottdicht		
vest	small coat	west		
veterinarian	animal doctor	vehdokter		
vice	bad habit	unaart		
vicinity	in the area of	neegde		

vicious	physically mad	bösortig			
victory	the winner	sieg			
view	what you look at	utsicht	or	utblick	
viewer	watcher	tokieker			
village	small town	dorp	(pl: dörp)		
village edge	suburb	brink			
vine	grape growing twig	rankel	or	reve	
vinegar	too old wine	essig			
vineyardist	grower of grapes	wien buur			
violet	color, flower	vigelett			
violin	instrument	vigelin			
viper	poisonous snake	krüüzadder			
virgin	chaste lady	jungfro	or	jungfru	
visit	a visit	besök	(past: besocht)		
visit	to drop by	besöken	or bi rinkieken		
visitor	droppers in	besöker			
voice	person's sound	stimm	(pl: stimmen)		
voluntary	of free will	freewillig			
vow	take an oath	gelööv			
vulgar	coarse	asig			
wad	bunched up	knuffel			
wagon	big 4 wheeled cart	wogen	or	wagen	
wagon	rubber tired one	gummiwogen			
wagon tongue	hook up to this	disselboom			
waist	growing middle	midde			
wait	hang around for	töv	or luur	or	luer
wait on	wait for	upluurn			
waiting	already waiting	töben	or töven	or	luuret
wake	time to get up?	wook	or	waak	
wakeup	rub your eyes	upwook	or	upwaak	
walk	go by foot	goh or gah	(past: gohn)		
walk	hike	trek			
wall	side of room	wand			
wall clock	little big ben	wandklock	or	hingklock	
wallow	pigs love to do it	wöhl			
wallpaper	one armed hanger	tapeet			
walnuts	cracking good	walnaart			
wander	go here and there	wanner			
want	*I* or *he* wants to do	will			
want to	*we* want to	(wi) wött			
want to	*they* want to	(se) wollen			
want to	*you* want to	(du) wolls			
war	armed conflict	krieg			
warbler	pretty song	tuunsinger			
ward	has a guardian	münnel			
wardrobe	enclosure	kleedschap			
warm	not cold	warm			
warmth	feels good	warms			
warm up	make hotter	uphitten, upheeten, upwarmen			
was	in the past	was			

was	has been	wersen or west or was
wash	get clean	wasch (past: wuschen)
wash	stuff to hang on line	wäsch
washer	drier's twin	waschmashien
wash cloth	wipe face, do dishes	waschlappen
wash line	hang em to dry	struk
wash maschine	beats by hand	washmashien
wash off	clean	afwischen
wash tub	clean clothes	washbalje
wash up	do the dishes	upwashen
wasp	stinging fly	wessen
wasted money	lottery tickets	wegsmeten geld
waste land	not much use	wildnis
watch	observe	oppassen or wohren
watch	time in your pocket	taschenuhr or tashenuhr
watch	on your arm	uhr
watch out	look out	kiekut or pass up
water	H$_2$O	woter or water
waterbed	don't smoke in it	woterbedd or waterbedd
watermill	for grinding	wotermöhl or watermöhl
wave	wiggle your arm	weih or wink
waves	in the water	bülgen
wax	shiny floor	wass
way	path	weg
way	have your way	willen
ways	means, opportunities	weeg
we	just us	wi
weak	not strong	week or swaak or swiemelig
wealth	rich-ness	gud
weather	think it'll rain?	weer or wedder or wäär
weave	make a rug	weev (past: weevt)
wedding	occasion of marriage	hochtied
wedding eve	traditional party then	pulterobend
wedge	splitter	kiel
wednesday	day of week	middeweken or gunsdag
weed	in the garden	kruut
week	7 day period	week
weekday	between weekends	alldag (pl: alldaags)
weep	cry	weenen or schreen
weigh	to measure weight	weeg or wääg
weight	heavy-ness	gewicht
welcome	come again	welkomm
welded	attached	anlöt
well	wet hole in ground	soot or pütte
well	assuredly	woll
well sweep	to pull up container	sootswingel
went	made the trip	güng
went on	was happening	angüng
were	they had been	weern or west or wesen
were looking	caught observing	keken

west	to California	west
wet	moist	natt
whale	biiiiiig fish	walfisch
what	huh?	wat
what time	sort of like when	wanneer or watvuntied
wheat	yellow grain	weeten
wheelbarrow	handy for hauling	schuuvkoor or schuuvkoar
wheelchair	rolling around	rollstohl
when	what time	wenn or woneer or wanneer
where	what location	wo or woneem or wonehm
whereby	by which	wobi
where from	come from	wonehmher
where to	where are we going	wohin , wonehmhin, wonehmto
whether	don't know if	ob
whetstone	for sharpening	sliepsteen
whey	along with curds	keeswei
which	which one	wokeen or watvun
which way	which direction	wegenweg
while	during	wiel
whimper	simper	wemern
whine	complain	jammer or jank
whip	stick and string	sweep or wipp or shecht
whirl	weeeee	küssel
whirlpool	round and round	warvel
whisper	in the ear	flister
whistle	pucker and blow	fleiche
whistle pipe	toy	fleichepiepen
white	colorless color	witt
white horse	smoky	shimmel
Whitsunday	7th Sunday after Easter	Pingsten
who	who was it?	kehr or wokehr or wo
whole	complete, whole thing	ganse or heel
whom	who	wokeen
whore	expensive lady	hor
whose	belong to you?	wokehr sien
why	what's the reason	worüm or wieso
wide	not narrow	breed
widen out	get wider	utbreden
widow	husband gone	witfro or witfru
widower	wife gone	witmann
width	breath	breede or breede vun
wierd	a little nuts	dull
wife	female spouse	fro or fru
wife	formal for wife	ehefro or ehefru
wife	derogatory	wief (pl: wiev)
wife	the old lady	olsche
wig	hair piece	prüük or hoormütz
wild	and crazy guy	wild
wild boar	nasty animal	eber
wilderness	wasteland	wildnis

161

will	your desire	will
willingly	glad to do it	geern
willow	weepy tree	wichel
win	take the prize	gewinn (past: gewonnen)
winch	crank and pull	blockdreiher
wind	breeze	wind
wind	make ball of string	wickel
window	hole in wall	finster (pl: finsters)
window pane	glass section	finstershiev
window sill	place for plants	finsterbank or finsterbrett
windpipe	breathing hole	otenpiep
windy	breezy	winnig or windig
wine	the good stuff	wien
wine grower	vineyardist	wienbuur
wine merchant	lucky person	wientapper
wing	bird arm	flunk (pl: flünken)
wink	blink once quickly	kniepogen
winter	ah-choo	winter
winter cap	wooly and warm	kapüttelmütz
wipe	wipe off	wisch
wire	metal string	wiern or iesendrood
wisdom	knowledge	wissheit
wish	look in catalog	wünsch
witch	broom driver	hex
with	accompanying	mit
with pleasure	happily	geern or mit vergnögen
with what	what did you use	wonehmmit
with who	accomplice	womit or wokehrmit
within	inside	binnen
without	don't have it	ahn or mitut
wobble	back and forth a bit	wackel or jackel
wobbly	shaky	wackelig
wolf	animal	wulf
woman	female person	frönsminsch or fröngsminsch
women	bunch of 'em	frönslüüd or früngslüer
wonder	think about	wunner or wunder
wonderful	terrific	wunnerbor
wood	cellulose being	holt
wooden	made of wood	hölten
wooden bowl	shallow	mölle
wooden leg	peg leg	hölten been
wooden shoes	clomp clomp	hölschen or hölsken
wooden slippers	klip klip	klippeken
woods	clump of trees	bush or holt
woodshaper	half circular blade	rundmest
woodshaver	small hatchet	deesel
wool	soft material	wull
woolen cap	roll over the ears	puddelmütz
word	informative sound	woort (pl: wöör or wörte)
work	god forbid	arbeid

162

work	make it work	schaff	
work at	be busy at	biarbeiden	
work clothes	a bit grubby	alldaagstüüch	
worked out	was successful	hett klappt	
worker	he does the job	arbeider	(pl: arbeiders)
working hours	watch the clock	deenstunnen	
workplace	job area	arbeidsteed	or warksteed
works	has a paying job	deent	
world	the whole thing	welt	
worldly	of the world	eerdsch	
worm	wiggly bait	worm	(pl: wörme)
worn	rubbed at	woren	
worn off	rubbed away	afworen	
worries	troubles	sorgen	
worry	problems	sorge	
worse	more than bad	leeger	
worth	it has value	weert	or wiert
worthless	no value	nichs weert	or weertlos
worth seeing	quite a sight	sehnweert	
worthy	has enough value	weertvull	or uprichtig
would be	or could be	wöör	
would like	wish to happen	woll	or müch
wound	hurt place	wund	
wounded	hurt people	verwunnen	or verwunden
wrap	like a package	inwickeln	
wrapped around	enclosed	rümwickelt	
wreck	make a mess of	wrack	
wren	small bird	tuunkrüper	
wrench	nut.t turner	shruuvslotel	
wrestle	romp around	wrangel	
wretch	destitute person	stackelsminsch	
wretched	pretty horrible	plöterig	
wrinkles	lines in the face	falten	
wrinkled	all messed up	kruus	
write	create a letter	shriev	
write up	put down on paper	upshrieben	
wrong	not right	verkeehrt	

yarn	for mending	gorn	
yeah	sure, you betcha	tja	
year	365 days	johr	
yeast	for baking	gest	
yell	really loud	bölk	
yelling	such a noise	bölken	
yellow	bright color	geel	or gäel
yes	affirmative	jo	or jup
yesterday	day before today	gistern	or güstern
yet	still	noch	
you	as in "hey you"	du	
you	as in "to you"	di	

163

you	as in "you-all"	ji		
young	not old	jung		
youngest	least old	jüngste		
youngsters	kids, young people	jungen		
your	referring to all	juun	or	jo'n
yours	belonging to you	dien		
yours	belonging to all	juun	or	jo'n
zebra	striped horse	striekpeerd		
zero	nothing	null		
zigzag	weavy route	sinksank		
zipper	garment closer	rietversluut		

CHAPTER FOUR   GRAMMAR

This chapter contains a review of some of the rules of analytical grammar, as applied tor English and Standard German and Low German. The dialect of Low German used is primarily North Saxon Low German. This discussion shows that there is a strong grammatical structure for Low German, in spite of the vagaries of the many dialects. It is not totally consistent, of course, but then inconsistencies can be found in other languages as well. From these findings a Low German orthography could be developed. With such guidelines a literary Low German language could be created.

ORTHOGRAPHY

The term *orthography* refers to an officially *preferred* set of guidelines (rules may be too strong a word) for spelling and pronouncing words in a given language. The *ortho-* part of the word comes from the Greek word orthos, meaning "correct". The *-graphy* part comes from the Greek word grapho, meaning "to write". So, in this instance, a Low German orthography would provide a prescribed or *preferred* manner of writing Low German. How Low German is spoken would still be dictated by the pronunciation and spelling habits inherent in each of the current dialects.

Creating such an orthography isn't the main objective here, at least not directly. Here and elsewhere in this book there will be comments regarding the benefits of such 'writing' guidelines. The vast majority of people who speak Low German do not write it. So many have never even seen it in writing. Most of them, including the author, believed for years that Low German was never a written language. Chances are that those people who did come across Low German in print, probably were looking at a dialect different from their own. The difficulty of reading an unfamiliar dialect could have the affect of reducing any desire to attempt further reading or writing their own dialect.

It is important for any language on the endangered special list to be written and preserved. It is contended here that if it isn't set down in writing, then it will not survive. Low German has survived these many centuries primarily by being handed down from generation to generation; as a strictly verbal language. That 'handing down' process has all but ceased to exist. One can pretty safely make the broad statement that younger children are no longer being taught Low German at home.

There are scattered efforts to teach some Low German in elementary schools, but their scope is inadequate. Such efforts should be encouraged and expanded, but the number of children involved is relatively small, and it is limited to only a few German schools.

To preserve the life of the language beyond the current generation, both adults and children need to begin *writing* the language. After that, people can be expected to make the effort to learn to *read* the langauge. The written language provides a physical means of handing it from generation to generation. What is written will be available for succeeding generations to read. However, the other part of this is that they must be able to read it. Without any standards for writing the language (as opposed to speaking the dialect), those future generations will not be able to read it. Their ability to even speak Low German will, at best, be minimal Therefore, the following discussion of the grammar of Low German reveals some of the effort it might take for the Low German people, regardless of dialect, to learn to read it, write it and speak it.

Of course, the subject of a literary Low German language is made doubly difficult by the question ... "what is the Low German language?". There is not 'a' Low German language. Instead, for each individual, there appears to be just their own dialect, which they understand is the Low German language. Therefore, where is the basis from which to start constructing a literary Low German?

The following discussion attempts also to describe how the grammar, spelling and word usage varies to other dialects, apart from North Saxon. When one considers the great variety among Low German dialects, this may be akin to climbing a linguistic Mount Everest. And what are, one wonders, the chances that these disparate dialect users will ever accept a particular orthography? Nonetheless, it is task that must be attempted and accomplished ... wat mutt, dat mutt!

It would difficult enough to encourage people who speak one dialect to learn how to write *that* dialect. The task at hand is even tougher; encouraging people to learn to read some overarching version of Low German. This would be a version that is not *exactly* like anyone dialect"language"; rather a composite version that people of all dialects could *read* and *write*.

Which of the many dialects should become the basis for developing a single written Low German? All the existing dialects suffer from some degree of internal non-uniformity. All the existing dialects have, over time, become tainted by "loaners" from other languages. In Germany, the Low German dialects have incorporated many Standard German words. In the United States, the dialects spoken throughout the Midwestern states have also absorbed some English words. The same has probably happened in South America and South Africa. It is suggested that loan words be avoided, wherever possible, when developing a uniform literary Low German.

In Chapter Two we've shown how languages, and dialects, change and evolve over time. How much change occurs often depends on three things; (1) the length of time that has transpired, (2) the degree to which its speakers are insulated from outside influences and (3) the degree to which the language has been set down in print. These changes should evaluated and a compromise developed through concensus. This would then create a standard version, as far as writing is concerned. One hesitates to call it a 'correct' version. It is rather a 'concensus' version.

The question of 'correctness' comes up once in a while. One might say that a language's *correctness* is very time oriented. It depends on *when* you ask the question.

If you had asked the question about a correct Low German during the 14th century, then one would have pointed to the Low German spoken by the Lübeck region and all the Hanseatic League participants. This was also the Low German spoken in much of the North Saxon dialect area.   So in those days there was one regional dialect considered to be Low German. But that is an oversimplification. Even in that Low German there was a mixture of several very "regional" dialects. Today we have many dialects to choose from, but none of them is now considered to be only or best way of speaking Low German. Perhaps, to each speaker, his or her own dialect will be the only acceptable dialect.

Correct Low German grammar, spelling and pronunciation are elusive goals. Those that are now attempting to create a Low German orthography are wrestling with whether it should be based on some older version of Low German, on some older dialect, on one of the current dialects, or perhaps on the present Standard German orthography. Most of the currently ongoing efforts appear to fail to adequately and/or accurately take into account the differences amongst the dialects.

HIGH GERMAN ORTHOGRAPHY

There has existed a standard High German since the 18th century, and a true High German orthography since early in the 20th century. But, there is still some debate going on about certain aspects of *correctness*.   High German began very diversely; as a collection of coarse dialects. Some of them were used by royalty. Latin was too elite; a province of the church. The commoner had his own dialect, but few knew how to write any language. Low German was then no longer in favor. People wanted to have official records set down in some offical German langauge. Businesses needed some standard language in which to conduct commerce. Governments could use French in official international discussions, but it couldn't be used for drafting national treaties and laws.

At some point, people took one or more dialects and collectively created from that a 'correct' one. With the intervention of many influential people, it became the High German *language*. After books like the Duden were printed, there was now a Standard German and an orthography. The dialects have continued right on living; right alongside the standard language. However, the standard language orthography was used thereafter in all literature, theater, business, governnment and communication. Actually, this orthography is probably not a "finished" standard. It is still being tinkered with, and one might say there is no *ultimately* correct High German.

On the local level in this process, there were Sprachgesellschafts created, to argue for and help develop some High German orthographic standards. A very prominent one, called the Fruchtbringende Gesellschaft was formed in 1617 by Prince Ludwig von Anhalt-Köthe, near Weimar. In addition to a standard, they also endeavored to promote literature and poety, in some kind of a standard language. And a third objective was to cleanse the German language from *foreign* words. The royalty especially used foreign words; preferred speaking French. Frederick the Great (1740-86) always wrote everything in French. When Voltaire visited the court, he said it was hard to believe he was in a foreign country. Even many of the middle class could speak some French.

The Gesellschafts disdained the use of certain foreign words; they preferred 'Bücherei' over Bibliothek and much preferred 'Anschrift' to adresse. Such efforts gained some ground with contemporary major literati, especially in the 18th and early 19th century. Johann Wolfgang von Goethe (1749-1832) and Johann Christoph Friedrich Schiller (1759-1805) were moved to support a literary German, although they opted to incorporate some Greek constructional influences. However, the Gesellschafts lost much of their effectiveness when they focused too much effort on getting rid of *foreign* words, rather than focusing on developing a standard language. When telephones were invented, they spent a lot of time pressuring people to use 'Fernsprecherbuch' rather than Telefonbuch. There were some members who loudly touted using the German 'Zwanggläubige' in place of Katholic and 'Freigläubige' for Protestant. One might say that this battle is still going on. Perhaps, after the advent of television, the battle is lost already. Today every German uses words like baby, job, manager, live show, lunch, strip-tease, mega-hit, feeling, O.K., know-how, girl and Coca-cola.

LOW GERMAN ORTHOGRAPHY

Currently the general population is unaware of any recognized need for a Low German orthography, which is different from the case of High German in the 17th century. In the case of Low German, most people would likely agree that there is not 'a' Low German language. But how many of them will agree that it is an issue to worry about, or a problem that needs solving.

Unfortunately, the fall of the Hanseatic League and the creation of a High German orthography have all but erased Low German as a literary language. As a result, the concept of one standard Low German language has dropped out of the picture and it lives only in the imagination of some speakers of the various dialects. Today there are perhaps 15 or more major dialects, along with hundreds of "local" variations. Some might argue that this collection of dialects constitutes a Low German language, but that accomplishes little. It is quite fortunate that people have not stopped speaking their own version of Low German.

The current lack of a *standard* Low German, one that is applicable and relevant to each major dialect, doesn't mean that people haven't tried to create one. The following is a rough overall view of some of the many individual efforts made during the last 100 years to develop a standard for Low German. They have also attempted to prescribe guidance for speaking Low German dialects, which may be carrying the effort too far. This discussion aims to highlight the variety of viewpoints involved, as well as the issues that arose when these viewpoints collided. None of the efforts to date can be considered to have been successful, although each one has made gains on the goal.

The language had almost died out in the 17th century. It was still spoken in some areas, but not on a wide scale. In the late 18th century, interest was revived, but the principal effort to rejuvenate Low German came in the 19th century. In most cases, it was not based on Standard High German. However, many felt it should be somewhat close to Standard German, in order to make it easier for the common north German national to understand it. Some felt that a Low German standard should be *etymologically* based on the spelling used in Middle Low German, basically the Low German of the Hansa period (13th to 16th century). Others felt that it should be based on *phonology*, meaning the letters should directly reflect the pronounced sounds. The obvious problem in such an approach is that each dialect has its own word pronunciation and spelling conventions.

An early exponent of a standard for Low German was Klaus Groth, who started a publishing group in 1851 called "Quickborn". One reason for starting a publishing capability was to promote Low German literature, and secondarily to foster a standardized Low German. He was in favor of using special accent marks on certain letters, to denote particular vowel usage.

There were Low German magazines published in the latter 19th century, each with their own idea as to proper spelling and grammar. They include "Plattdütschen Husfründ" (Schleswig, 1876), "Plattdütsche Vereens Blatt" (Leipzig, 1878) and the popular "Eekbom", published by the Allgemeinen Plattdeutschen Verbandes. The latter supported using the special characters suggested by Groth. They also leaned heavily on Standard High German orthography. The group was still active in the early 20th century.

There were some persons or groups who recommended using special but unfamilar letter symbolss to guide pronunciation and spelling. These special letters did not exist in Standard High German. This proposal was resisted, even by people as influential as the ever popular Mecklenburg author Fritz Reuter. He wanted to bring back the good old days when Low German was a true literary language, but was willing to accept a compromise solution. He originally supported the concept of the Quickborn approach, but he didn't agree with all of Groth's recommendations. His friend, Pastor Franz Boll (from Brandenburg) recommended using special characters, such as the Danish symbol å for the long vowel 'a'. Unfortunately, Fritz Reuter wasn't very consistent in his use of spelling in his books during the 1860's, and this confusion detracted from his influence on standardization.

A Mecklenburger contemporary of Fritz Reuter, John Brinckman, recommended that the use of diphthongs to designate long vowels be discontinued. This seemed to fly in the face of convention. He later changed his views, so as to almost completely support Reuter.

Interest in this matter virtually disappeared during the course of the World War I. It was quickly reawakened after the war. Interest in continuing use of Low German in church services served to lend some sense of urgency and awareness to the discussions.

The writings of author R. Kinau, in the 1920's, were influenced by his Hamburg area (Finkenwerder) Low German dialect. His works were popular, but did not appeal to all Low Germans. A contemporary of Kinau, Bremer, published his own rules for a new Low German orthography. Bremer recommended that spelling not be used to directly dictate pronunciation. He wanted to make Low German easier to read, rather than tell everyone how to pronounce every word.

There were several strong efforts on hand during the period between the two world wars. Although they didn't agree on all counts, there were three entities that banded together. They were the author C. Borchling, the Lübecker Richtlinien, and the Hamburger Richtlinien. They all recommended that a *single* Low German standard not be attempted, but rather set up rought *guidelines* to develop some writing consistency in Low German. They hoped that word spelling in the various dialects could be changed and made more similar to each other. In addition, they felt that the concept of phonology should preempt etymology. In other words, spelling should be more in harmony with *pronunciation* conventions, rather than be governed by 12th to 15th century Middle Low German *spelling* conventions. On the other hand, they felt that basing spelling on High German conventions should not be rejected out of hand. This general view, hoping to retain *some* of the characteristics of individual dialects, appealed to a broad audience.

Johannes Saß generally acceded to the Lübecker Richtlinien. He had a strong influence on Low German language publications that were aimed at school children. In some areas, pre-World War II school children were then still exposed to Low German reading in school. As had happened during the "Great War", discussion of a Low German orothography for school chldren all but disappeared during the Second World War.

In the 1954-56 years, a series of 4 conferences was convened by Pastor Boeck, chairman of the Fehrs Guild, to achieve a compromise between various existing forms of standardization. They leaned heavily on the previously mentioned Lübecker Richtlinien. With the help of people like Johann Saß, they agreed on a simplistic compromise. However, as an orthography, it appears to be incomplete. It does not speak adequately to the idiosyncracies of individual dialects. The participants remained divided on several important matters, one being the use of special characters to represent some monophthongs. Today there is some support for the Fehrs Guild rules. They recommend use of an apostrophe at the *end* of those word where überlange is concerned Many people have stated general support of the Fehrs Guild compromise, but they seem to do it selectively, accepting what they like and rejecting what they don't like.

As regards individual dialects, there do exist dictionaries for most every major dialect. Allowing for particular instances of uniqueness, many of the "basic" words in the various Low German dictionaries do provide some degree of commonality. They also could yield to some general grammatical rules, if you accept that each dialect will differ from the standard to some degree. A standard should avoid discarding the many unique and interesting aspects of each separate dialect. Each and every dialect of Low German has an interesting and, to its practicioner, very dear background. This is part of the simple beauty for which Low German is well known.

We've mentioned before that some argue for adopting much of the already existing Standard German orthography. A complete adoption of Standard German orthography would probably be both impossible and undesirable. Low German already has its own grammatical framework, which varies from Standard German in some significant ways. However, one aspect of Standard German that could be, and largely has been, adopted is the alphabet and the alphabet letter designations. As to adopting other aspects of the Standard German orthography, the prospect is highly debatable.

The remaining portion of this chapter will discuss analytical grammatical rules, as applied to the English, Standard German and Low German languages.

GRAMMATICAL ANALYSIS

The following discussion covers only the more commonly used grammatical features. Some technical terms have been used, because they necessary for pointing out similarities in the three languages. This may help English and Standard German speakers to better understand how the rules affect Low German.

A number of the High German grammar references were excerpted from George Curme's fine book entitled *A Grammar of the German Language.*

As each grammatical item is discussed, the way Standard German operates is discussed first. Sometimes this will agree with English or Low German grammar. The English grammar is then discussed. The average reader will probably be familiar with one or both.

Some references will be made to Old Saxon, which predates Low German, because it is interesting to see how Low German compares with its almost 2,000 year old ancestor. Sometimes reference is made to Gothic, for the same reason.

FORMALITY

In Standard German, the term *du* is used only for family, close friends, poetry, children and animals. The term *Sie* is used otherwise. In practical use, the formal address is beginning to lose adherents in Standard German, but it is still considered "manners" in most of Germany.

It is hard to imagine Low German with a formal (Sie) pronoun. There is no prescribed formal address in Low German or English.

CAPITALIZATION

In Standard German the concept of capital letters first appeared in the 16th century and expanded slowly. They were expanded in the 17th century for 'important' words. By the 18th century they were used for all nouns. Every noun and words used a nouns must be begun with a capital letter, and Standard German is the only language with this broad requirement.. An adjective used as a noun must also be capitalized.

In English and Low German, only titles and proper nouns (specific persons, place or thing) need to be capitalized.

CONJUNCTION

A conjuction is a word used to connect words or sentence parts.

In Standard German there are two type of conjunctions. One is called 'coordinating', e.g. aber, allein, denn, oder, sondern, und, etc. They don't affect word order. The other is 'subordinating', e.g. bevor, auf, damit, da, etc. These are always followed by a transposed word order.

In English some of the conjunctions are and, or, but, neither, both, only, etc. In English there are three kinds, 'coordinating' (and, but, or), 'correlative' (either, or) and 'subordinating' (before, after). The first kind are used in phrases like "He <u>and</u> I" or "Bill is big <u>but</u> Tom is bigger". The second kind is used in pairs, "*either* that *or* this". They do not affect word order.

Low German has the 'coordinating' kind (un, ower, oder) and the 'subordinating' kind (before, after), as in Standard German. The following list shows some of the more common conjunction words.

Standard German	English	Low German
und	and	un
aber	but	ower
entweder	either	entweder *
keiner vun	neither	keener vun
beide	both	beide
nur	only	süss
oder	or	oder
auch	also	ok

PRINCIPAL PARTS

The present infinitive, the 1st person singular of the past and the past participle of a verb are called the three 'principal parts'. The full conjugation of a verb, in all six tenses, can be constructed from these principal parts. The conjugation of verbs is done in one of two ways, depending on the type of verb.. In Standard German the verb types are referred to as 'weak' and 'strong', while in English they are referred to as 'regular' and 'irregular'.

The names of the three principal vary. We have used the English terms to describe the Low German terms as well, just for convenience.

Standard German	English	Low German
präsent	present	present
imperfect	past	past
perfect participle	past participle	past participle

Examples for the Standard German principal parts are given below, using the verbs spiel (play) for *weak* and tragen (carry) for *strong*. In the second column is the appropriate verb ending used to conjugate that kind of verb in Standard German. The rules for conjugation will be discussed in more detail in a subsequent section.

Weak:

the *präsent* of spiel (play) is 'spiel'
the *imperfect* of spiel (play) is "spielte'   add -t or -te or -ete
the *perfect participle* of spiel (play) is 'gespielen'   add ge- plus -en

Strong:

the *präsent* of trage (carry) is 'trage'
the *imperfect* of trage (carry) is 'trug'   change vowel
the *perfect participle* of trage (carry) is 'getragen'   ge- & add -en or-n

There are three unusal Standard German verbs that have an 'e' in the present stem - go (gehen), stand (stehen) and do (tun). Their principal parts respectively area: gehen,ging, gegangen (conjugated in the compound tenses with sein); stehen, stand, gestanden (conjugated in the compound tenses with haben); and tun, tat, getan (also conjugated in the compound tenses with haben).

How one constructs the three parts of speech can be seen more clearly from the following example, using the word 'swim'.

The present case: I .... swim   expressed as I do something.
The past case: I ... .swam   expressed as I did something
The past participle: I have ... swum   expressed as I have done something.

An example for the English three principal parts is given now, using the words play (regular - weak) and throw (irregular - strong). In the second column is the appropriate verb ending used to conjugate those verbs in English. In English the two kinds of verb conjugations are referred to as 'regular' (weak in German) and 'irregular' (strong in German). The rules for appropriate endings is discussed in more detail in a subsequent section.

Regular:

> the *present* of play is 'play'
> the *past* of play is 'played'   add -ed
> the *past participle* of play is 'played'.   add -ed

Irregular:

> the *present* of throw is 'throw'
> the *past* of throw is 'threw'   change vowel
> the *past participle* of throw is 'thrown'   nothing or change
>   vowel or add -en or -n

Examples for the Low German three principal parts are given here, using the words speel (play) and **drink** (drink). In the second column is the appropriate verb ending used to conjugate a verb in Low German. In this case, we use the Standard German terms *weak* and *strong*, rather than the English terms regular or irregular.

Weak:

> the *present* tense of play is 'speel'
> the *past tense* of play is "speel '   add -t or -d
> the *past participle* of play is "speelt"   add -t or -d

Strong:

> the *present* of **drink** is '**drink**'
> the *past* of **drink** is '**drunk**'   change vowel
> the *past participle* of **drink** is '**drunken**' change vowel and '-en'

Sometimes the verb types and the endings are very similar in the three languages. Words that are conjugated as *weak* verbs in English, will likely have their cognates also be conjugated as weak verbs in Standard German or Low German. Notice that, for all three languages, the letters 't' or 'd' are used in the suffix. This is not surprising, since within these languages the *sounds* of these two letters are quite often interchangeable. In a manner of speaking, the conjugation of weak verbs is accomplished almost the same way in each language. However, notice that the 'ge-' prefix for creation of the Standard German past participle is not used in Low German.

GENDER

In Standard German a gender is assigned to all objects, whether living or lifeless. All German nouns have a gender.

GENDER	PRONOUN	GENDER ENDING	"THE"
masculine	er	-er ending	der
feminine	sie	-e ending	die
neuter	es	-es ending	das

This rule is largely based on logic (natural male versus female connotations), except for words such as Weib (woman) and Mädchen (girl), which for some reason are treated as *neuter* gender. This curiosity prompted Mark Twain to write "In German, a young lady has no sex, while a turnip has".

In English the nouns are not classified by gender. However, there obviously are conventions regarding gender, such as in the use of personal pronouns for male gender and female gender. Word endings based on gender are not common in English. There are a few, such as actors versus actresses or landlords versus landladies. However, these days female actors invariably refer to themselves as just actors. In English the word "the" applies to all genders.

In Low German, all nouns can be classified by one of three genders, similar to the way they are in Standard German. There are a number of exceptions, where a word is one gender in Standard German and a different one in Low German.. In Low German the gender designations are more in line with English. However, going through and listing all the differences will serve little purpose to the average reader. The gender is just not as important in Low German as in Standard German. There is the following gender difference to be noted regarding articles, as shown in the following table.

	English	*Low German*	*Standard German*
masculine	he	he	er
feminine	she	se	sie
neuter	it	dat	es

The gender is also noted in the declension of the definite article, as shown in a later section discussing definite articles.

DIMINUTIVES

Another distinction between the three languages, and even between the many dialects, is the usage of word endings to describe the diminutive of a noun. This term refers to a special word or word ending that ascribes a smaller or dearer connotation to a noun (little mother or little darling). Specific single words to show this connotation are not common in English.

In Standard German it is normally created by the suffix *-chen,* and sometimes *-lein.* It always has a neuter gender, regardless of the gender of the noun in front of it.

In Low German the diminutives vary by dialect, and are used rarely in certain dialects.. In Low German a word is usually preceded by the word lütt, if one wishes to minimalize a word. In North Saxon the diminutive ending most often used is *-je,* as in the word lüttje (little one). In several other dialects it may be *-ken* (lütken) and in a few it may be *-ing* (lütting). More dialect diminutives are discussed elsewhere, as each dialect is viewed in closer detail. Diminutives are a seldom used but important part of a dialect, in that they help impart a special endearing way of describing beloved person or things.

PLURALIZATION

Sometimes this aspect of a noun is referred to as 'number'. It represents a numerical quantity; either singular or plural.

In English pluralization is very simple. The regular way is to just add an 's', which is also often the method used in Low German. One English exception is a word like child, whose plural is children. In Low German, the corresponding words are kind and kinner. Words that end in *ch, x, s, or sh* take the *es* ending (church - churches, box - boxes, bus - buses, bush - bushes). In Low German, the suffix is more often '-en' rather than '-es'. In some cases the last letter changes (city - cities. leaf - leaves) plus the (-s) ending. The same is true in Low German (breef - breev). And some words are both singular and plural, such as the word fish.

It is a bit more complex in Standard German. In Standard German pluralization usually requires changing the vowel to an umlaut form. Gender is relevant, but knowing which gender doesn't always tell you exactly the appropriate pluralization technique. A masculine noun may have any of a variety of plural forms. In Standard German there are five classes of pluralization.

> Class I - no ending, sumetimes uses an umlaut (bruder - brüder)
> Class II - 'e' ending, often with umlaut (Stadt - Städte)
> Class III - 'er' ending, usually an umlaut (Haus - Häuser)
> Class IV - 'n', 'en' or 'nen' ending, no umlaut (Student - Studenten)
> Class V - 's' ending, no umlaut (Klub - Klubs)

This is fairly complex, but pluralization in Low German can also be complex. And comparisons between the two languages is made difficult by the many stem vowel differences that have arisen over the centuries. However, there are some consistencies, such as if there is an umlaut in the Standard German plural, there is almost always an umlaut in the Low German Plural. This is perhaps because such umlauts were introduced into both languages at about the same time.

In Low German one can describe 8 types of pluralizations (A thru G).

176

Type A - unchanged (similar to Class I above)
Type B - change last letter, with or without adding '-e' (in technical
　　　　terms, the *fortis* consonant becomes a *lenis* consonant, and
　　　　the preceding vowel sound becomes lengthened - *überlange*)
Type C - revise or lengthen the root vowel (no umlaut)
Type D - umlaut the root vowel (similar to Class II above)
Type E - add '-n' or '-en' or '-er' (no umlaut, similar to Class IV
　　　　above)
Type F - add '-n' or '-en' or '-er' or '-e' and change vowel (similar to
　　　　Class III above)
Type G - add '-s' (no umlauts, similar to Class V above)
Type H - use a different word altogether.

These methods of pluralization are listed in the following 8 groupings. The method in question is noted at the end of the first line in each grouping, identifed by the bold text. A single letter shown in bold type (**d, t, n**) somewhere in the list reflects that in this word, at least in the North Saxon dialect, that letter is pronounced with a 'th' sound. Letters that have a short horizontal line through them (đ) can be taken to be silent.

The first column gives the definition of the word in English.

The second column gives the Standard German equivalent word, and shows both the singular and plural words. It is broken up into the five Standard German classes, for comparison purposes.

The third column shows the equivalent Low German word, with both the single and plural versions (except, of course, in the first grouping). There is a good deal of resemblance when it comes to the '-en' endings, but otherwise they tend to follow different paths.

English	*Standard German*	*Low German*
	Class I	**Type A**
drop-drops	Tropfen	droppen
	Class II	
fish	Fisch-Fische	fisch
sheep	Schaf-Schafe	schaap
nut-nuts	Nuss-Nüsse	näärt
leg-legs	Bein-Beine	been
	Class IV	
flower-flowers	Blume-Blumen	bloom
carrot-carrots	Wurzel-Wurzeln	wördel
root-roots	Wurzel-Wurzeln	wördel
berry-berries	Beere-Beeren	beern

English	Standard German	Low German
	Class II	**Type B**
thief-thieves	Dieb-Diebe	deef - deeve
half-halves	Halb-Hälfte	half - halve
sieve-sieves	Sieb-Siebe	seef - seeve
bride-brides	Braut-Bräute	brut - brüüde
horse-horses	Pferd-Pferde	peerd - peerd
town-towns	Stadt-Städte	stadt - städde
yard-yards	Hof-Höfe	hof - hööv
	Class III	
wife-wives	Weib-Weiber	wief - wieve
calf-calves	Kalb-Kälber	kalf - kalve
grave-graves	Grab-Gräber	grab - gräbe
board-boards	Brett-Bretter	brett - breede

English	Standard German	Low German
	Class II	**Type C**
day-days	Tag-Tage	dag - daag
way-ways	Weg-Wege	weg - weeg
	Class II	**Type D**
foot-feet	Fuß-Füsse	foot - fööt
cow-cows	Kuh-Kühe	koh - keih
jacket-jackets	Rock-Röcke	rock - röck
sack-sacks	Sack-Säcke	sack - säck
tree-trees	Baum-Bäume	boom - bööm
	Class III	
wheel-wheels	Rad-Räder	rad - röör
house-houses	Haus-Häuser	huus - hüüs
	Class IV	
bug-bugs	Wanze-Wanzen	bock - böck
potato-potatoes	Kartoffel-Kartoffeln	katuffel - katüffel
turnip-turnips	Rübe - Rüben	roov - rööv

English	Standard German	Low German
	Class I	**Type E**
knife-knives	Messer	mest-mesder *
window-windows	Fenster	finster - finstern *
finger -fingers	Finger	finger - fingern
apple-apples	Apfel-Äpfel	appel - appeln
cork-corks	Pfropfen	propp - proppen
hook-hooks	Haken	hook - hooken
rabbit-rabbits	Kaninchen	haas - haasen

178

Class II

animal-animals	Tier-Tiere	deert - deerder **
ship-ships	Schiff-Schiffe	ship - shippen
hall-halls	Saal-Säle	saal - saaln
knee-knees	Knie-Kniee	knee - kneen
radish-radishes	Rettich-Rettiche	radish - radishen
stone-stones	Stein- Steine	steen - steender **
hill-hills	Berg-Berge	barg - bargen
year-years	Jahr-Jahre	johr - johren
piece-pieces	Stück-Stücke	stück - stücken
part-parts	Teil-Teile	deel - deelen
table-tables	Tisch-Tische	disch - dischen
belly-bellies	Bauch-Bäuche	buuk - buuken
fist-fists	Faust-Fäuste	fuus - fuusen
kiss-kisses	Kuß-küsse	küss - küssen
cabinet-cabinets	Schrank-Schränke	schapp - schappen

Class III

child-children	Kind-Kinder	kind - kinner **
picture-pictures	Bild-Bilder	bild - biller
egg-eggs	EI - Eier	ei - eier
price-prices	Preis-Preise	pries - priesen
roof-roofs	Dach-Dächer	dach - dachen
mouth-mouths	Mund-Münder	mund - munden

Class IV

building-buildings	Bau-Bauten	gebört - gebörder *
doll-dolls	Puppe-Puppen	popp - poppen
car-cars	Karre-Karren	koor - koorn
farmer-farmers	Bauer-Bauern	buur - buurn
nose-noses	Nase-Nasen	nääs - näsen
saw-saws	Säge - Sägen	saag - saagen
cat-cats	Katze-Katzen	katt - katten
bed-beds	Bett-Betten	bett - betten
sun-suns	Sonne-Sonnen	sünn - sünnen
hour-hours	Stunde-Stunden	stunn - stunnen
street-streets	Straße-Straßen	straat - straaten
fly-flies	Fliege-Fliegen	fleeg - fleegen
time-times	Zeit-Zeiten	tied - tieden
dog-dogs	Hund-Hunden	hund - hunden
bridge-bridges	Brücke-Brücken	bröch - bröchen
week-weeks	Woche-Wochen	week - weeken
ox-oxen	Ochse-Ochsen	oss - ossen
lamp-lamps	Lampe-Lampen	lamp - lampen
ape-apes	Affe-Affen	aap - aapen

* When the main word ends with the letter 't' (with a 't' sound),

such as in the words mest and deert, then one should end the plural
with '-**d**' ('-**der**') rather than '-**ter**'. When the suffix of the first syllable
begins with '**t**-' (with a 'th' sound), such as in the word finster, then one
should begin the plural ending with '**t**' ('-**tern**') rather than '**d**', because
the singular of the word already provides the 'th' sound, and thus the
plural ending can keep the '**t**'.

** as mentioned in the beginning, the bold '**d**' or '**t**' is pronunced as
if it were 'th', rather than 'd' or 't'.

English	Standard German	Low German
	Class II	Type F
hand-hands	Hand-Hände	hand - hännen
wall-walls	Wand-Wände	wand - winnen
	Class III	
string-strings	Band - Bänder	band - binnen
chicken-chickens	Huhn-Hühner	hohn - höhne
word-words	Wort-Wörter	woort - wör**d**er
horn-horns	Horn-Hörner	huurn - hüürn
book-books	Buch-Bücher	book - böke
ground-grounds	Grund-Gründer	grund - grünnen

English	Standard German	Low German
	Class I	Type G
life-lives	Leben	leven-lebens
dollar-dollars	Dollar	daler-dalers
key-keys	Schlüssel	slotel - slotels
pillow-pillows	Kissen	küssen - küssens
girl-girls	Mädchen	deern - deerns
plate-plates	Teller	teller - tellers
wagon-wagons	Wagen	wogen - wogens
	Class II	
ball-balls	Ball-Bälle	ball - balls
arm-arms	Arm-Arme	arm - arms
wire-wires	Draht-Drähte	wiern - wierns
	Class III	
stall-stalls	Stall-Ställer	stall - stalls
	Class IV	
boy-boys	Junge-Jungen	junge * - jungs
kitchen-kitchens	Küche-Küchen	köken - kökens
bottle-bottles	Flasche-Flaschen	buddel - buddels
fork-forks	Gabel-Gabeln	gobel - gobels
	Class V	
oven-ovens	Ofen-Öfen	oben - obens

English	Standard German	Low German
	Class III	*Type H*
leaf-leaves	Blatt-Blätter	blatt - blöör *
	Class IV	
person-persons	Person-Personen	minsch - lüüd

* not an '-er' ending, but pronounced as if it had.

The closest thing to a vowel change in English, as it changes from the singular to the plural is shown in the words 'man' and 'woman' (Type H). The 'a' in "woman" changes to 'e' in "women", but it is not in the stressed syllable. Therefore it can't be regard as a vowel change.

	English	Standard German	Low German
Singular:	woman	Frau	früngsminsch
Plural:	women	Frauen	früngslüüd
Singular:	man	Mann	man
Plural:	men	Männer	manslüüd

Some words are used *only* in their plural form. There is no singular for certain Low German words, and the plural form is also used for the singular, e.g. ashen (ashes), tangen (tongs), veeh (cattle), schaap (sheep), swien (swine), hoor (hair), knoken (bones), lungen (lungs) and hooven (oats).

There are also unique circumstances. The masculine noun *arm* (arm) pluralizes to arm*s*, while the other feminine noun *arm* (poor) pluralizes to arm*e*. The plural of doot (dead) is do*den* (dead ones). English does not seem to have just 'one' word that accomplishes this same meaning.

All three languages share the 8 parts of speech, namely noun, article (definite and indefinite), pronoun, adjective, verb, adverb, preposition and conjunction. In the following these will be dealt with in order, analyzing their characteristics within each language.

NOUN

In all three language, a *proper* noun is the name given to a specific person, place or thing. Examples are George and California. Nouns can also be *common*, in that they don't refer to a specific item. Examples are river and book, because they're not referring to a specific river or book.

181

Nouns can possess the four attributes known as gender, person, number and case. The first two (gender and number) have already been discussed.

The third of the four (*person*), refers to the distinction as to to 'direction' of speech which a person is experiencing.

1ˢᵗ person   is the person *speaking*
2ⁿᵈ person   is the person spoken *to*
3ʳᵈ person   is the spoken *about*

The fourth one (*case*), refers to that property of a noun or pronoun which denotes its relation to other words. This relationship can be used to determine the inflections used in the *declension* of a noun or pronoun.. In Old Saxon there were four cases, similar in usage to that described for Standard German, and one fifth case used for articles. Nouns play the same role in each langauge. The cases are covered in the next section, along with the declension of nouns, pronouns and even adjectives.

DECLENSION AND CASE

The term declension describes how a noun or pronoun or adjective is inflected to indicate how it is meant to relate to the word's case, number or gender.

A general rule in Standard German is that feminine nouns add '-en' or '-n' to the singular. All other nouns add '-e' to the singular. In Standard German, declension takes place in four cases. There were also four cases in Old High German.

Nominative: when the *noun* is the *subject* of the verb (who?)
Genitive: when a *noun* expresses possession (whose?)
Accusative: when it's the *direct object* of a verb (whom?, what?)
Dative: when it's the *indirect object* (to whom?)

The nominative case is the same as the subjective case in English. The genitive case corresponds to the possessive case in English. The accusative is the same as objective.

The genitive case is the same as the possesive case in English. Where the Standard German uses the word *des* and a suffix on the object word to denote possession, English uses an 'apostrophe s'. For example, where Standard German might speak of the *Haus des Herrens*, English would say *the fellow's house.*

Low German would instead use a phrase like *de kirls jümehr huus* to say the same thing. There is no genitive or possessive case in Low German.

In English, declension takes place in three cases.

Subjective: when a *noun* is used as the subject of a verb (who?).
Possessive: when a *noun* expresses possession (whose?).
Objective: when a *noun* is used as an object (whom?, what?).

These three cases can be used to describe every syntactic relationship that a noun can have to other words in an English sentence.

In Low German there are, in the main, just two cases. The dative (used with prepositions like 'to' and 'for') is considered to be absorbed into the accusative, and the combination is sometimes referred to as the oblique case. This corresponds to the objective case in English.

Nominative: when a *noun* is used as the subject.
Oblique: when a *noun* is used as the object

One of the few remnants of the possessive case that may exist in Low German occcurs when using family names. It is common to add an -s after a family name, when connecting it to a location or condition. In Low German there's usually a phrase used to indicate possession. In English it is accomplished by using an apostrophe *'s*.

In English, one would say "the Smith's house".
In Standard German one might informally say "das Schmidt Haus".
In Low German it could be the "dat Schmidt*s* huus" (the added 's')
                    but more often one would say "Schmidt sien huus"

The last sentence doesn't involve a genitive case, as such, but it does reflect possession. The primary way of indicating possession in Low German is to use a phrase or a possessive pronoun word (sien). It often uses the word 'sien' (his) or 'ehr (hers). Low German can use a phrase which includes the possessive pronoun *jümehr* (them or their) to indicate possession.

Another example would be, in Low German, when referring to the hired hand (knecht) in the employ of a given family farm, the 's' would be added to the farmer's name. For example, the Panning farm's hired hand would be referred to as "Pannings knecht". In the local community this would be the name by which he would be referred, as opposed to his christian or family name. This special "name" indicates him, of course, but it also indicates his "station in life" or his "role in the community". This was a more important distinction of him as a person than was his own christian or family name.

ARTICLES

The term article, covered in the next two sections, refers to a pronoun that draws attention to another noun. There are two types; definite and indefinite.

The *definite* article is the word that draws specific attention to a particular noun, e.g. *the* or *this* or *that*.

The *indefinite* article draws attention to a <u>non</u>specific group of nouns, e.g. *a* or *an*. The indefinite article, almost by definition, has no plural.

<u>Definite Articles</u>

The earliest version of Old varied the definite article *the* according to gender. This is similar to Standard German, which reflects again how similar the Old Saxon and the Old High German languages were at one time. Note also how similar the neuter form in Old Saxon is to to present day English.

masculine thê   feminine thiu   neuter that

In Old Saxon, the definite article respects gender in both the singular and plural.

	Singular			Plural		
	Masculine	Feminine	Neuter	Masculine	Feminine	Neuter
Nominative	the	thiu	that	thea	thea	thiu
Genitive	thes	thera	thes	thero	then	thero
Accusative	thena	thea	that	thea	thea	thiu
Dative	themu	theru	themu	then	them	them

In English the definite article is always represented by the word *the,* whether referring to a male, female or animal. Standard German varies usage according to the three genders. Low German differentiates between people and objects or animals.

	English	*Low German*	*Standard German*
masculine (man)	the	de	der
feminine (woman)	the	de	die
neuter (dog)	the	dat	das

The *determining* article 'this', which specifies a particular item, often ignores gender. This varies by the Low German dialect. In Standard German it again varies with each gender. In English there is no differentiation.

Gender	*English*	*Low German*	*Standard German*
masculine	this	düsse	dieser
feminine	this	düsse	diese
neuter	this	dütt	dieses

The same is true for the other definite articles, such as *these, those, which* and *every.* These are sometimes referred to as *demonstrative* adjectives, as are *that, many* and *such.*

184

In Standard German the article will also vary to number and case. The definite article is often optional, but when used it takes the form shown here. The nominative singular gender endings are '-er' (masculine), '-e' (feminine) and '-es' (neuter).

	Singular			Plural	
	M.	F.	N.	M. F. N.	English
Nominative	der	die	das	die	the
Genitive	des	der	des	der	of the
Accusative	den	die	das	die	the
Dative	dem	der	dem	den	to the

The word 'der' can be used as a demonstrative pronoun as well, such as 'der Lehrer' (that teacher). In Low German this would be 'de schoolmeester', because Low German doesn't distinguish between 'the' and 'that' ('de' works for both)..

For other Standard German definite articles shown below, the declension differs from the previously mentioned rule - the neuter nominative and accusative ends in '-es' rather than '-as'. These are shown below for the nominative case only, to save space. The accusative forms differ only in the masculine ('-en' ending rather than '-er') gender.

	Singular			Plural		
(English)	Masculine	Feminine	Neuter	Masculine	Feminine	Neuter
(this) nom.	dieser	diese	dieses	-		
(these) nom.	-	-	-	diese		
(that) nom.	jener	jene	jenes	-		
(those) nom.	-	-	-	jene		
(which) nom.	welcher	welche	welches	welche		
(every) nom.	jeder	jede	jedes	alle		
(such) nom.	solcher	solche	solches	solche		
(many) nom.	mancher	manche	manches	manche		

In Low German, gender is not all that significant, but this does vary somewhat by dialect. When gender is utilized, it is usually similar to the gender usage in Standard German.

In Low German, the declension of the definite article *de* (the) is almost as simple as in English.

	Singular			Plural		
	Masculine	Feminine	Neuter	Masculine	Feminine	Neuter
Nominative	de	de	dat	de		
Accus/Dat	den	de	dat	de		

The declension of the definite article düsse (this), which is also a *demonstrative* pronoun, is also simple.

	Singular			Plural
	Masculine	Feminine	Neuter	Masculine Feminine Neuter
Nominative	düsse	düsse	düt or dütt	düsse
Accus/Dat	düssen	düsse	düt or dütt	düsse

The article changes only when referring to a neuter object. With regard to the other Low German definite articles, they do not change at all. This is the same for the group shown below (shown only for the nominative case).

	Singular			Plural
(English)	Masculine	Feminine	Neuter	Masculine Feminine Neuter
(that) nom.	dat	dat	dat	-
(those) nom.	-	-	-	de
(which) nom.	watvun	watvun	watvun	watvun [1]
(every) nom.	jeder	jeder	jeder	jeder
(such) nom.	so	so	so	so [2]
(many) nom.	mannig'n	mannig'n	mannig'n	mannig [3]

(1) The Low German word for which (watvun) represents one of those words that is difficult to correlate exactly into English. In some dialects they use the word 'welke', which is just a variation on the Standard German word 'welche'. In Low German, if you wanted to say "which one", you would use the words 'watvun een', or 'watvun'n'.

(2) In a phrase like "such as that", one would say "so as dat".

(3   The word mannig'n is a contraction of 'mannig een', which would, of course, reduce to just 'mannig' in the plural.

Indefinite Articles

An indefinite article does not indicate number, and is taken as singular.

In English, the articles *a* or *an* are used in all gender and case situations. There is, as mentioned, no plural form for an indefinite article.

	Singular			Plural
	Masculine	Feminine	Neuter	M.F.N.
Subjective	a, an	a, an	a,an	
Possessive	a, an	a, an	a, an	
Objective	a, an	a, an	a, an	

In Standard German, indefinite articles (such as 'a' or 'an') are much less common than definite articles. They are derived from the number 'one' and were meant to refer to an individual member of a group.

| | Singular | | | Plural | |
	Masculine	Feminine	Neuter	M.F.N.	English
Nominative	ein	eine	ein		a
Genitive	eines	einer	eines		of a
Accusative	einen	eine	einen		a
Dative	einem	einer	einem		to a

In Low German, the indefinite article may optionally change with regard to case, but with regard to gender, it changes only with feminine. This is one of the few instances where gender is commonly recognized in Low German.

| | Singular | | | Plural |
	Masculine	Feminine	Neuter	
Nominative	een	eene	een	
Accus/Dat	een	eene	een	

This would also apply to the negative counterpart of eene, which is *keene* (Standard German *keiner* and English *not a one,* or *none*).

| | Singular | | | Plural |
	Masculine	Feminine	Neuter	
Nominative	keen	keene	keen	
Accus/Dat	keen	keene	keen	

PRONOUN

The Latin word pro means "for". Therefore, a pronoun is used "for" a noun. Such a pronoun may refer to yourself, to other people or to animals, in place of the noun.

In Standard German there is a special pronoun used when addressing a person in a formal sense. This is the word *Sie* (capitalized sie, plural Ihrer), which was covered in the previous section on formality.

There are several kinds of pronouns; Possessive, Personal, Indefinite, Interrogative and Relative

These will be covered in turn, in the next five sections.

Possessive

These are the possessive pronouns in Standard German.

187

mein (my)	dein (your)	sein (his)	ihr (her)
unser (our)	euer (your)	ihr (their)	

In Standard German the possessive pronoun must agree with the noun it qualifies, with regard to number, gender and case. The word for 'our' is used as an example.

	Singular			Plural			English
	M.	F.	N.	M.	F.	N.	
nominative.	unser	unsere	unser	unsere			our
genitive	unseres	unserer	unseres	unserer			of our
accustive	unseren	unsere	unser	unsere			our
dative.	unserem	unserer	unserem	unseren			to our

In English, the possessive pronouns change with regard to gender.

	Singular		Plural		
M.	F.	N.	M.	F.	N.
his	our	its	yours, theirs and whose.		

These are the possessive pronouns in Low German.

mien (my)	dien (your)	sien (his)	ehr (her)
uus (our)	juun (your)	jümehr (their)	

In Low German, the possessive pronoun 'mien', for example, changes for gender and number.

	Singular			Plural		
	M.	F.	N.	M.	F..	N.
Nominative	mien	ehr	mien	juun		
Accus/Dat	mienen	ehren	mienen	junn (junen)		

Personal

In Gothic the basic personal pronouns were ik (I) and þu (you). The þ letter is pronounced as 'th'.

In Old Saxon the personal pronouns were ik (I), thû (you), hê (he), siu (she), and it (it). This is very similar to both English and Low German. In Old Saxon, they would be declined as follows, as differentiated by number, case and gender.

188

per = person   m. = masculine   f. =feminine   n. neuter

	Singular					Plural				
	1st Per	2nd Per	3rd Per			1st Per	2nd Per	3rd Per		
	I	YOU	HE	SHE	IT	WE	YOU	THEY		
			m.	f.	n.		m.	f.	n.	
Nom	Ik	thu	hê	sia	it	wi	gî	siû		
Gen	mîn	thîn	is	iro	is	user	iuwar	iro		
Acc	mik	thik	ina	sea	it	us	giû	siû		
Dat	mî	thî	im	irû	im	us	giû	im		

In Standard German, the personal pronoun (such as "I", "you", etc.) takes different forms, when broken down as to gender, number, person and case. The English counterparts (in caps) are placed in each column, to help orient the reader to the relationships between the languages.

	Singular					Plural				
	1st Per	2nd Per	3rd Per			1st Per	2nd Per	3rd Per		
	I	YOU	HE	SHE	IT	WE	YOU	THEY		
			m.	f.	n.		m.	f.	n.	
Nom	ich	du	er	sie	es	wir	ihr	sie		
Gen	meiner	deiner	seiner	ihrer	seiner	unser	euer	ihrer		
Acc	mich	dich	ihn	sie	es	uns	euch	sie		
Dat	mir	dir	ihm	ihr	ihm	uns	euch	ihnen		

In English, these pronouns can also be declined in a similar fashion, using the overall affect of case, person, number and gender.

	Singular					Plural				
	1st Per	2nd Per	3rd Per			1st Per	2nd Per	3rd Per		
			m.	f.	n.		m.	f.	n.	
Nom.	I	you	he	she	it	we	you	they		
Poss	my	your	his	hers	its	your	your	their		
Obj	me	you	him	her	it	you	you	you		

In Low German, the personal pronoun changes with regard to case and person.

	Singular					Plural				
	1st Per	2nd Per	3rd Per			1st Per	2nd Per	3rd Per		
	I	YOU	HE	SHE	IT	WE	YOU	THEY		
			m.	f.	n.		m.	f.	n.	
Nom.	Ik	du	he [1]	se	dat [2]	wi	ji	se		
Dat/Acc	mi [3]	di	ihm [4]	ehr	dat	us	ju	jüm [5]		

(1) hei in some dialects. Notice however that they are pronounced the

189

same. The 'he' is often spoken with a bit of "ee" on the end.
(2) et in some dialects.
(3) mik and dik in Ostphalian.
(4) can be 'em'.
(5) can be 'jem'.

Indefinite

These pronouns draw attention to persons, places, or things, but not specifically just one.

English	Standard German			Low German
M. F. N.	M.	F.	N.	M. F. N.
one, somebody	einer	eine	ein	een
many	mancher	manche	manches	mannig
many a one	manniger	mannige	manniges	mannig een
much	viel	viel	viel	veel
few	weniger	wenige	weniges	wenig
each, every	jeder	jede (1)	jedes	jede (2)
either, anyone	einiger	einige	einiges	eenige
neither, noone, nobody	keiner	keine	kein	keene
all	aller	alle	alles	all

(1) The 'j' has the 'y' sound.
(2) This 'j' has the sound it does in the English word 'joke'.

Interrogative

In Standard German, the interrogative pronouns are wer (who), was (what), wessen (whose) and welche (which). The interrogative pronoun *welcher* is declined like the relative pronoun welcher, except in the genitive singular and plural. Here the forms of the relative pronoun *der* are used instead.

	Singular			Plural	
	masc.	fem.	neut.	masc. fem. neut.	English
Nom	welcher	welche	welches	welche	which
Gen	dessen	deren	dessen	deren	of which
Accus	welchen	welche	welches	welche	which
Dative	welchem	welcher	welchem	welchen	to which

In English, the various interrogative pronouns are who, what, whose and which, and they are used in the process of asking questions (*who* is that? or *which* are those?).

In Low German, the various interrogative pronouns are kehr (who), wokehr (who) , wat (what), welke (which) and welkeen (which one). In the case of wat (what), the

190

following shows the simple forms used. For the accusative/dative case, it is more of a phrase than a word.

	Singular			Plural			
	masc.	fem.	neut.	masc.	fem.	neut.	English
Nominative		watvun			watvun		which
Acc/Dat		watvun vun			watvun vun		to which

Relative

In Standard German, the relative pronoun cannot be omitted. In place of 'who' Standard German uses the pronouns 'der', 'die' and 'das', 'wer', 'welche' and 'was', because it has to recognize gender.. The relative pronoun 'which' changes with gender and case as follows.

	Singular			Plural			
	masc.	fem.	neut.	masc.	fem.	neut.	English
Nominative	welcher	welche	welches		welche		which
Genitive	dessen	deren	dessen		deren		of which
Accusative	welchen	welche	welches		welche		which
Dative	welchem	welcher	welchem		welchen		to which

In English, the relative pronouns are who, whom, which and that. In normal conversation, the use of *whom* is gradually disappearing. If used, the rules 'who' and 'whoever' in the nominative case and 'whom' or 'whomever' in the objective case are as follows.

	Singular			Plural		
	masc.	fem.	neut.	masc.	fem.	neut.
Nominative		who, whoever			who, whoever	
Objective		whom, whomever			whom, whomever	

It is similar in Low German, but even simpler.

	Singular			Plural		
	masc.	fem.	neut.	masc.	fem.	neut
Nominative		wokehr			wokehr	
Accus/Dat		wokehr			wokehr	

ADJECTIVES / COMPARATIVES

An adjective is a word used to "qualify" a noun or pronoun. They can also be used in place of a noun, such as in the phrase "the *good* are respected". Most adjectives can also be used to express degrees of "quality", with the quality changing from 'normal', compared to 'comparative', and further compared to 'superlative'.

191

The <u>normal</u> quality is sometimes referred to as "positive", denoting an adjective's *simple* quality

The <u>comparative</u> quality is used to denote a higher (or lower) degree of quality.

The <u>superlative</u> quality is used to denote the very highest (or lowest) degree of quality available.

In Indo-European the *comparison* between adjective qualities was shown by adding to the stem word; like '-ist' or '-ost'.

In Old High German the *comparative* of adjectives was reflected by adding endings such as '-ir' or '-or'.

In Middle High German there was an unusual "irregular" comparison for the word 'bad' - übel, wirser and wirste. Since then the term übel has come to mean 'evil' or 'unholy', rather than just 'bad'..

In Standard German this becomes lang, länger and längst. Note also the changing of the stem vowel to an umlaut. The stem word here is lang (long).

In English the "er" ending is also used for comparative and "est" is used for superlative. For example; long, longer and longest.

In Low German this becomes groot, gröter and grötste, for large, larger and largest. In some dialects they might prefer spelling groot as grood and gröter as gröder. Note that, in addition to an ending change, the vowel also turns into an umlaut vowel. In Low German, similar to Standard German, the "er" ending is also used for the comparative and the "ste" ending also used for the superlative. The sentence in Standard German, *Sie singt am schönsten*, means in English *She sings the best*. Both require an article preceding the superlative. In the case of Low German, this comes out as *Se singt de schönste*.

As in English, some Low German and Standard German adjectives have an "irregular" comparison structure. The comparative word becomes a different word, instead of just a variation of the stem word. A common example would be the words 'good, better and best'. You wouldn't say 'gooder' or 'goodest'. In Low German this turns out to be good, beter and beste. Though the stem word changes, it still follows the rule for appropriate suffix.

Standard German	*English*	*Low German*
gut - besser - beste	good - better- best	good - beter - beste
viel - mehr - meisten	much - more - most	veel - meehr- meehrste

In the following table are some regular comparisons, using the endings described above. Some 'd' and 't' letters are **bold**. You'll find this in the endings to the root words. This distinction means they should be pronounced with a 'th' sound. For instance, the comparison version of the first word, slechte, should be pronounced as slech-the. The superlative of this word would be pronounced slechs-the. The 't' letter in these endings harks back to when, at the beginning of a syllable, they would have been spelled and pronounced as the ð (th) letter, a ancient form of the 'd' sound. This pronunciation is still evident in the North Saxon dialect.

English			Low German		
Positive	Comparative	Superlative	Positive	Comparative	Superlative
slecht	slech**t**er	slech**t**ste	bad	worse	worst
licht	lich**t**er	lich**t**ste	easy	easier	easiest
hart	har**t**er	har**t**ste	hard	harder	hardest
swor	swor**d**e	swor**d**este	heavy	heavier	heaviest
dicht	dich**t**er	dich**t**ste	near	nearer	nearest
leev	lewer	lewste	dear	dearer	dearest
small	smaller	smallste	small	smaller	smallest
week	weeker	weekste	weak	weaker	weakest
billig	billiger	billigste	cheap	cheaper	cheapest
döstig	döstiger	döstigste	thirsty	thirstier	thirstiest
flink	flinker	flinkste	fast	faster	fastest
sööt	söter	sötste	sweet	sweeter	sweetest

Low German			English		.
breed	bre**d**er	bre**d**ste	wide	wider	widest
dreckig	**d**reckiger	**d**reckigste	dirty	dirtier	dirtiest

As in Standard German, monosyllabic words containing one of the vowels **a**, **o**, or **u** add the umlaut in the comparative. The vowel is also shortened.

Low German			English		.
koolt	köler	kölste	cold	colder	coldest
hooch	höher	höhste	high	higher	highest
lang	länger	längste	long	longer	longest
groot	gröter	grötste	big	bigger	biggest
stiev	stäviger	stävigste	stiff	stiffer	stiffest
glatt	glatter	glattste	pretty	prettier	prettiest
jung	jünger	jüngste	young	younger	youngest
kort	körter	körtste	short	shorter	shortest
oolt	öller	öllste	old	older	oldest

Standard German alt (old) changes to älter (older) in the comparative. The same goes for jung (young) and kürz (short). However, the Standard German for the superlative kürzeste, (shortest) in Low German is körtste, the difference being in the extra letter "e" in the Standard German version. In Standard German there are many monosyllabic words with a, o, u that do not take the umlaut in the comparison.

Low German			English		
froh	froher	frohste	happy	happier	happiest
krank	kranker	krankste	sick	sicker	sickest
dunkel	dunkeler	dunkelste	dark	darker	darkest

German never uses the word *more* (mehr) to form a comparative, as is done in English.

Low German			English		
möör	mörder	mördeste	tired	more tired	most tired
langsom	langsomer	langsomste	slow	slower	slowest
heet	heeter	heetste	hot	hotter	hottest
dicker	dicker	dickste	fat	fatter	fattest
fröh	fröher	fröhste	earler	earlier	earliest
bös	böser	böste	mad	madder	maddest
free	freer	freeste	free	more free	most free
düür	dürder	dürdeste	expensive	more exp.	most exp.

Note that when the stem vowel is umlauted, it remains umlauted throughout the comparative, which is also true in Standard German.

VERB CONJUGATION

In the previous section on "principal parts", two kinds of verb were mentioned, called *weak* and *strong*. It was stated that the concept of weak and strong verbs exists in all three languages, except that in English the strong verb is referred to as *irregular*, while the weak verb is called *regular*. The tenses have different names, as shown below.

The word conjugate means to "unite". In this case what are being united are the *parts* which have been previously described as tense, person and number. The primary ingredients of each conjugation are the three principal parts.

Standard German	English	Low German
präsent	present	present
imperfect	past	past
perfect participle	past participle	past participle

In Old Saxon the *weak* verb formed the past tense with '-te' or '-ta' or '-de' or '-da'. Old Saxon had three classes of weak verbs, differentiated according to how they formed the three principal parts of speech.

In *Standard German*, the conjugation is done as follows.

Weak verbs form the imperfect (the past tense) by adding '-t' or '-te' to the präsent. However, those whose stem already ends in 't' or 'd' form their imperfect by inserting 'e' between the ending and the stem. The perfect participle is formed by adding the 'ge-' prefix plus '-t'. The exception just noted calls for the perfect participle to be formed by adding the 'ge-' prefix plus '-et'. The exception case is shown in this example, using the weak verb arbeit (work)..

präsent:	arbeite	
imperfect (past):	arbeitete	add '-t' or '-te' or '-ete'
perfect participle (past participle)	gearbeitet	add 'ge-' and '-t'

Strong verbs form their imperfect by changing the vowel in the stem syllable, while the perfect participle is formed with a -'ge- prefix and an '-en' ending. The example uses the strong verb schreib (write).

präsent	schreib	
imperfect (past):	schrieb	change vowel
perfect participle (past participle):	geschrieben	add 'ge-' and '-en'

In *English* the verb conjugatons are formed as shown below. Words that are conjugated as *weak* verbs in English, will likely have their cognates also be conjugated as weak verbs in Standard German or Low German. In English the conjugation of verbs that are not compounded is done as follows.

Regular (weak) verbs form their past tense by adding '-d' or '-ed' and form the past participle by adding '-d' or '-ed'.

present:	play	
past:	played	add '-ed' or '-d'
past participle:	played	add '-ed' or '-d'

Irregular (strong) verbs form their past tense by changing the vowel and form the past participle by adding '-en'..

present:	write	
past:	wrote	change vowel
past participle:	written	add '-en'

In *Low German*, the conjugation is done as follows. In Low German, the procedure for conjugation is more similar to English than to Standard German. The term used by Standard German for differentiating between the two verb types will be used for Low German as well.

Weak verbs form the past tense by adding '-t' or '-d', which is similar to English adding '-ed'. They form the past participle also by adding '-t' or '-d', which again is similar to English adding 'ed'. In Low German the past tense hardly every carries a suffix '-d' or '-t', and therefore the main determinant of a weak verb is manner in which the past participle is formed.

present:	speel	
past:	speelt	add '-t' or '-d'
past participle:	speelt	add '-t' or '-d'

Strong verbs fom the past tense by changing the stem vowel, which is similar to both English and Standard German. They form the past participle by doing nothing, by changing the vowel, by also changing a consonant, or by also adding '-en'. In other words, the past participle can under almost any configuration, other than that which is reserved for weak verbs.

present:	shriev	
past:	shreev	change vowel
past participle:	shreben	do nothing or

change vowel and/or change consonant next to vowel or add '-en' or '-t'

Before additional examples are given, the manner of using auxiliary verbs in conjugations will be shown. The auxiliary verbs are more often referred to as *helping* verbs. They are used along with regular verbs, to complete the meaning. The result of the two together is referred to as a *compound* verb

In English, there is just one auxiliary of past time, which is 'have', while in Standard German there are two, which are 'habe' and 'sein'. The Standard German word Sein is used in the conjugation of compound tense forms for all verbs which denote motion to or from a place. Sein is also used with verbs that express a change in condition (die, grow, fall, etc.).

In Standard German, the principal auxiliary verb other than the two just mentioned is 'to become' (werden). Werden is used with the infinitive, to form the future and conditional tenses. Their principal parts are as follows. Note that the perfect participle is formed with the prefix -'ge' and adding '-t' to the present stem (hab).

	'habe'	'sein'	'werden'
präsent:	hatte	war	wurde
imperfect			
perfect participle	gehabt	gewesen	geworden

196

The term 'indicative mood', used in the following lists, refers to a statement with real conditions in the present tense, as opposed to statements that include the word 'if'.

In the next few pages, a number of verbs will be conjugated, to show how the endings are formed for various verbs. They are shown first in Standard German, including the English in the right hand columns. Then there will be examples for the Low German verbs, with the English shown again. The first section will deal with auxiliary verbs, while the remainder will deal with regular verbs. At times certain words will be abbreviated, due to space limitations.

Auxiliary Verb Habe (To Have)

This word is used as an auxiliary with the perfect participle to form the compound perfect tense. Haben shows the same irregularity as in English, because the stem consonant is lost in the 3rd person singular (has vs. have or habe vs. hat). Otherwise, the conjugation is normal.

The conjugation here is a full conjugation, in all the six tenses.

Habe (have)
Indicative Mood

Standard German		**English**	
Present Tense			
Singular	Plural	Singular	Plural
ich habe	wir haben	I have	we have
du* hast	ihr* habet	you have	you have
er,sie,es hat	sie haben	he,she,it has	they have
Past Tense			
ich hatte	wir hatten	I had	we had
du hattest	ihr hattet	you had	you had
er,sie,es hatte	sie hatten	he,she,it had	they had
Future Tense			
ich werde haben	wir werden haben	I shall have	we shall have
du wirst haben	ihr werdet haben	you will have	you will have
er,sie,es wird haben	sie werden haben	he/she/it will have	they will have
Present Perfect Tense			
ik habe gehabt	wir haben gehabt	I have had	we have had
du hast gehabt	ihr habt gehabt	you have had	you have had
er,sie,es hat gehabt	sie haben gehabt	he,she,it has had	they have had

197

Past Perfect Tense

ich hatte gehabt	wir hatten gehabt	I had had	we had had
du hattest gehabt	ihr hattet gehabt	you had had	you had had
er,sie,es hatte gehabt	sie hatten gehabt	he,she,it had had	they had had

g.hab. = gehabt haben **Future Perfect Tense** *h. had = have had*

ich werde g.hab.	wir werden g.hab.	I shall h. had	we shall h. had
du wirst g.hab.	ihr werdet g.hab.	you will h. had	you will h. had
er, sie, es wird g.hab.	sie werden g hab.	h,s,it will h. had	they will h. had

* The familiar forms of address are used here, rather than the formal *Sie*.

The Low German cognate for the Standard German 'haben' (to have) is 'heff'. It is conjugated below for each of the six tenses, along with its English cognate (right hand two columns). Note that here again the 3rd person singular varies from the 1st person singular stem (heff vs. hett).

Heff (have)
Indicative Mood

Low German		**English**	

Present Tense

Singular	Plural	Singular	Plural
ik heff	wi hebbt	I have	we have
du hess	ji hebbt	you have	you have
he, se, dat hett	se hebbt	he,she,it has	they have

Past Tense

ik harr [1]	wi harrn	I had	we had
du harrs	ji harrn	you had	you had
he, se, dat harr	se harrn	he,she,it had	they had

Future Tense

ik schöll [2] hebben	wi schöllt hebben	I shall have	we shall have
du schölls hebben	ji schöllt hebben	you will have	you will have
he,se,dat schöllt hebben	se schöllt hebben	he/she/it will have	they will have

Present Perfect Tense

ik heff hatt	wi hebbt hatt	I have had	we have had
du hess hatt	ji hebbt hatt	you have had	you have had
he, se, dat hett hatt	se hett hatt	he,she,it has had	they have had

Past Perfect Tense

ik harr hatt	ik harr hatt	I had had	we had had
du harrs hatt	ji harrn hatt	you had had	you had had
he,se,dat harrs hatt	se harrn hatt	he,she,it had had	they had had

h.heb. = *hatt hebben*	**Future Perfect Tense**		*h. had* = *have had*
ik will h. heb	wi wütt h. heb.	I shall h. had	we shall h. had
du wulls h. heb	ji wütt h. heb	you will h. had	you will h. had
he,se,dat wullt h. heb	se wütt h. heb	h,s,it will h. had	they will h. had

(1) This could also be written 'du harrst'. The 't' at the end is often forgotten in actual speech and perhaps can be forgotten as well when writing. Note how often in Low German the double 'rr' is used where the Standard German has 'tt' (harr vs. hatt). This is encountered sometimes in the usage of the word wedder (again), where some people might choose to use werrer instead of wedder.

(2) This could be written as either 'shöllt' (shall) or will (will), to represent the future tense, just as the words 'shall' or 'will' are interchangeable in the English future tense. You could say either "du schölls hebben" or "du wills hebben".

There is a syntax (word order) factor at work here, in the spoken langauge, which varies between English and a German language. An English phrase like "I have had that already" would be stated "Ich habe das schon gehabt" and in Low German it would be stated "Ik heff dat al hatt". In English the word 'that' is at the end of the sentence and in the other languages its cognate 'das' or 'dat' is placed in front of the stem verb.

Auxiliary Verb Sein (To Be)

This word *Sein* is used in Standard German to form the compound tense form of all verbs which denote motion to or from a place. It is conjugated here in each of the six tenses. And yet again the 3rd person varies from the 1st person stem (bin vs. ist).

In some areas, such as Munsterland and some East Low German areas, the Low German utilizes a similar verb, which they spell siin. However, usually this verb is not used directly in Low German.

Sein (to be)
Indicative Mood

Standard German		**English**	
	Present		
Singular	Plural	Singular	Plural
ich bin	wir sind	I am	we are
du bist	ihr seid	you are	you are
er/sie/es ist*	sie sind	he/she/it is	they are
	Past		
ich war	wir waren	I was	we were
du warst	ihr waret	you were	you were
er/sie/es war	sie waren	he/she/it was	they were

199

Future

ich werde sein	wir werden sein	I shall be	we shall be
du wirst sein	ihr wirdet sein	you shall be	you shall be
er/sie/es wird sein	sie werden sein	he/she/it shall be	they shall be

Present Perfect

ich bin gewesen	wir sind gewesen	I have been	we have been
du bist gewesen	ihr seid gewesen	you have been	you have been
er/sie/es ist gewesen	sie sind gewesen	he/she/it has been	they have been

Past Perfect

ich war gewesen	wir waren gewesen	I had been	we had been
du warst gewesen	ihr waret gewesen	you had been	you had been
er/sie/es ward gewesen	sie waren gewesen	h/s/it had been	they had been

gew. s. = gewesen sein **Future Perfect** *h.b. = have been*

ich werde gew. s.	wir werden gew. s.	I shall h. b.	we shall h.b.
du wirst gew. s.	ihr wirdet gew. s.	you shall h.b.	you shall h.b.
er/sie/es wird gew. s.	sie werden gew. s.	h/s/it shall h.b.	they shall h.b.

The cognate word in Low German is 'bün', which is conjugated here.

BÜN (am)
Indicative Mood

Low German		**English**	

Present Tense

Singular	Plural	Singular	Plural
ik bün	wi sünd	I am	we are
du büss	ji sünd	you are	you are
he, se, dat iss *	se sünd	he,she,it is	they are

Past Tense

ik weer	wi weern	I was	we were
du weers	ji weern	you were	you were
he, se, dat weert	se weern	he,she,it was	they were

Future Tense

ik will wesen	wi wöllt wesen	I shall be	we shall be
du wolls wesen	ji wöllt wesen	you will be	you will be
he,se,dat woll wesen	se wöllt wesen	he/she/it will be	they will be

Present Perfect Tense

ik bün wesen	wi sünd wesen	I have been	we have been
du büss wesen	ji sünd wesen	you have been	you have been
he, se, dat iss wesen	se sünd wesen	he,she,it has been	they have been

Past Perfect Tense

ik weer wesen	wi weern wesen	I had been	we had been
du weers wesent	ji weern wesen	you had been	you had been
he,se,dat weert wesen	se weern wesen	he,she,it had been	they had been

w. weern = wesen weern	**Future Perfect Tense**		h. been = have been
ik will wesen weern.	wi wollt wesen weern	I shall h. been	we shall h. been
du wolls wesen weern.	ji wollt wesen weern.	you will h. been	you will h. been
he,se,dat wollt w. weern.	se wollt w. weern.	he,she,it will h. been	they will h. been

In Low German the cognate word for the Standard German 'bin' is 'bün', meaning "to be" (also related to 'sein' in Standard German).

* The word 'iss' should perhaps be written 'ist', but it's generally spoken as 'iss'.

Auxiliary Verb Werden (To Become)

This word *Werden* is fully conjugated below in Standard German and English.

Werden (to become)
Indicative Mood

Standard German		**English**	

Present

Singular	Plural	Singular	Plural
ich werde	wir werden	I become	we become
du wirst	ihr werdet	you become	you become
er/sie/es wird	sie werden	he/she/it becomes	they become

Past

ich wurde	wir wurden	I became	we became
du wurdest	ihr wurdet	you became	you became
er/sie/es wurde	sie wurden	he/she/it became	they became

Future

ich werde sein	wir werden sein	I shall become	we shall become
du wirst sein	ihr wirdet sein	you shall become	you shall become
er/sie/es wird sein	sie werden sein	he/she/it shall become	they shall become

gew. = geworden	**Present Perfect**		
ich bin gew.	wir sind gew.	I have become	we have become
du bist gew.	ihr seid gew.	you have become	you have become
er/sie/es ist gew.	sie sind gew.	he/she/it has become	they have become

gew. = geworden	**Past Perfect**		
ich war gew.	wir waren gew.	I had become	we had become
du warst gew.	ihr waret gew.	you had become	you had become
er/sie/es war gew.	sie waren gew.	he/she/it had become	they had become

gew. s. = geworden sein	**Future Perfect**	*h.b. = have become*	
ich werde gew. s.	wir werden gew. s.	I shall h. b.	we shall h.b.
du wirst gew. s.	ihr wirdet gew. s.	you shall h.b.	you shall h.b.
er/sie/es wird gew.s.	sie werden gew. s.	he/she/it shall h.b.	they shall h.b.

In Low German the cognate word for the Standard German word 'werden' in the indicative mood is 'weern'. Possibly it could also be written 'werden', with 'd' as *silent* (or as 'weren'), however it is conventionally written as 'weern'. For the same reason, the word 'worrn' could also be written 'woren'.

Weern (to become)
Indicative Mood

Low German		English	

Present

Singular	Plural	Singular	Plural
ik weer	wi weern	I become	we become
du weers	ji weern	you become	you become
he/se/dat weer	se weern	he/she/it become	they become

Past

Singular	Plural	Singular	Plural
Ik wöör	wi wöörn	I became	we became
du wöörs	ji wöörn	you became	you became
he/se/dat wöör	se wöörn	he/she/it became	they became

Future

ik wüll weern	wi wüllt weern	I will become	we will become
du wülls weern	ji wüllt weern	you will become	you will become
he/se/dat wüll weern	se wüllt weern	he/she/it will become	they will become

Present Perfect

ik bün worrn	wi sünd worrn	I have become	we have become
du büss worrn	ji sünd worrn	you have become	you have become
he/se/dat ist worrn	se sünd worrn	he,she,it have become	they have become

Past Perfect Tense

ik wöör worrn	wi wöört worrn	I had become	we had become
du wöörs worrn	ji wöört worrn	you had become	you had become
he/se/dat wöört worrn	se wöört worrn	he,she,it had become	they had become

w. wes. = weern wesen **Future Perfect Tense** *h. b. = have become*

ik wüll w. wes.	wi wüllt w. wes.	I shall h. b.	we shall h. b.
du wülls h. wes.	ji wüllt w. wes.	you will h. b.	you will h. b.
he/se/dat wüllt w. wes.	se wüllt w. wes.	he,she,it will h. b.	they will h. b.

This completes the look at the helping verbs.

The following text contains a variety of examples for both *weak* and *strong* verbs, in their respective sections. Some of them are fully conjugated in all six tense, but most are conjugated in the more prevalent first three tenses. Some Old Saxon discussion is included, for historical reference regarding Old Low German

Weak (Regular) Verbs

Old Saxon had three *classes* of weak verbs, differentiated according to how they formed the infinitive. An infinitive is created by adding the word 'to' in front of the verb.

Class	English	Low German Infinitive	Old Saxon Infinitive
I	kiss	küssen	kussen
II	pray	beden	bedon
III	live	leben	libbian

In Old Saxon the *weak* verb formed the past tense with '-te' or '-ta' or '-de' or '-da'. All verbs that are *weak* in Old Saxon are also *weak* in Low German (except for the word bring) and most are *weak* in English.

Notice that, when conjugating verbs in all three languages, the letters 't' or 'd' are used in the suffix. This is not surprising, since within these languages the *sounds* of these two letters are quite often interchangeable. In a manner of speaking, the conjugation of weak verbs is accomplished almost the same way in each language. However, notice that the 'ge-' prefix for the Standard German past participle is not used in Low German.

In Low German there are three *classes* of weak (irregular) verbs. The first class has the vowel shortened, from the infinitive to the past participle. The second class has a change in the consonant following the vowel. The third class is similar to the first one, except that the '-en' part is retained.

Class	English	Infinitive	Past Participle
I	bump, push	stöten	stött
II	buy, purchase	köpen	kofft
III	rain	regen	regent

The first example in this weak verb section will a full conjugation for the Standard German verb 'kauf' (buy). This is a weak verb, because of the '*-te*' ending in the imperfect. However, in English, it is a strong verb, as the stem vowel changes from *'u'* in the present tense to *'ou'* in the past tense. The Low German conjugation follows.

The principal parts are kauf, kaufte, and gekauft. A '*-te*' ending makes the imperfect (past) tense and a '*-t*' ending is added (plus a *ge-* prefix) to make the perfect participle.

Kauf (Buy)

Standard German		**English**	
		Present Tense	
Singular	Plural	Singular	Plural
ich kauf	wir kaufen	I buy	we buy
du kaufs	ihr kauft	you buy	you buy
er/sie/es kauft	sie kaufen	he/she/it buys	they buy
		Imperfect (Past) Tense	
ich kaufte	wir kauften	I bought	we bought
du kauftest	ihr kauftet	you bought	you bought
er/sie/es kauftet	sie kauften	he/she/it bought	they bought

203

Future Tense

ich werde kaufen	wir werdem kaufen	I will buy	we will buy
du wirst kaufen	ihr werdet kauften	you will buy	you will buy
er/sie/es werde kaufen	sie werden kaufen	he/she/it will buy	they will buy

Perfect (Present Perfect) Tense

ich habe gekauft	wir haben gekauft	I will buy	we will buy
du hast gekauft	ihr haben gekauft	you will buy	you will buy
er/sie/es hatt gekauft	sie haben gekauft	he/she/it will buy	they will buy

Pluperfect (Past Perfect) Tense   b. = *bought*

ich hatte gekauft	wir hatten gekauft	I had b.	we had b.
du hattest gekauft	ihr hattet gekauft	you had b.	you had b.
er/sie/es hattet gekauft	sie hatten gekauften	he/she/it had b.	they had b.

gek. h. = gekauft haben **Future Perfect Tense**   b. = *bought*

ich werde gek. h.	wir werden gek. h.	I will have b.	we will have b.
du wirst gek. h.	ihr werdet gek. h.	you will have b.	you will have b.
er/sie/es werde gek.h.	sie werden gek.h.	he/she/it will have b.	they will have b.

The Low German cognate word kööp (buy) is conjugated below, in all of its six tenses. This verb changes the stem vowel from 'öö' to 'o' in the past tense and also changes the consonant ('ff') in the past tense. Thus this verb is weak in Standard German but strong in English (changing vowel) and strong in Low German

Kööp (Buy)

Low German		English	

Present Tense

Singular	Plural	Singular	Plural
ik kööp	wi kööpt	I buy	we buy
du koffs	ji kööpt	you buy	you buy
he/se/dat kofft	se kööpt	he/she/it buy	they buy

Past Tense

Ik kofft	wi kofft	I bought	we bought
du kofft	ji kofft	you bought	you bought
he/se/dat kofft	se hebbt kofft	he/she/it bought	they bought

Future Tense

ik will köpen	wi wütt köpen	I will buy	we will buy
du wolls köpen	ji wütt köpen	you will buy	you will buy
he/se/dat will köpen	se wütt köpen	he/she/it will buy	they will buy

Present Perfect Tense

ik heff kofft	wi hebbt kofft	I have bought	we have bought
du hess kofft	ji hebbt kofft	you have bought	you have bought
he/se/dat hett kofft	se hebbt kofft	h/s/it have bought	they have bought

Past Perfect Tense   b. = *bought*

Ik harr kofft	wi harrn kofft	I had b.	we had b.
du harrs kofft	ji harrn kofft	you had b.	you had b.
he/se/dat harrt kofft	se harrn kofft	he/she/it had b.	they had b.

ik sholl köpen h.	wi shöllt köpen h.	I shall have b.	we shall have b.
du sholls köpen h.	ji shöllt köpen h.	you shall have b.	you shall have b.
he/se/dat sholls köpen h.	se shöllt köpen h.	he,she, it shall have b.	they shall have b.

Additional Low German *weak* verb conjugations are shown below. They are conjugated only in the first 3 tenses, because these are the ones most commonly used in speech. An exception is the word for talk (snack), which is so common, and thus conjugated fully.

The first verb dröv (may) is a weak verb because the past participle 'drövt' has the suffix '-*t*' added. The same is true for 'speelt' and 'snackt'. The English verb is a strong verb.

Dröv (May, Permitted)

Low German		**English**	
	Present Tense		
Singular	Plural	Singular	Plural
ik dröv	wi drövt	I may	we may
du drövs	ji drövt	you may	you may
he/se/dat drövt	se drövt	he/she/it may	they may
	Past Tense		
ik drövt	wi drövt	I might	we might
du drövt	ji drövt	you might	you might
he/se/dat drövt	se drövt	he/she/it might	they might
	Future Tense		
ik will dröven	wi wütt dröven	I might	we might
du wolls dröven	ji wütt dröven	you might	you might
he/se/dat will dröven	se wütt dröven	he/she/it might	they might

A verb following a plural pronoun (we, you, they) receives the suffix *t.* If the word already ends in a *t,* it is a problem to add this usual *t* suffix. One solution is to use an apostrophe, to represent the second *t.* Perhaps a more rational solution is to just ignore the second *t,* allowing the context and syntax of the sentence involved to reflect the plural verb situation. An apostrophe could be used to draw attention to the situation, but it isn't recommended.

The verb speel (play) is weak in all three languages.

Speel (Play)

Low German		**English**	
	Present Tense		
Singular	Plural	Singular	Plural
ik speel	wi speelt	I play	we play
du speels	ji speelt	you play	you play
he/se/dat speelt	se speelt	he/she/it plays	they play

ik speelt	wi speelt	I played	we played
du speelt	ji speelt	you played	you played
he/se/dat speelt	se speelt	he/she/it played	they played

Future Tense

ik will speelen	wi wütt speelen	I will play	we will play
du wolls speelen	ji wütt speelen	you will play	you will play
he/se/dat will speelen	se wütt speelen	he/she/it will play	they will play

The next verb is shown in all six tenses only because it is so often used in speech. It is strong in English, because the stem vowel changes from present to past tense. The word can be spelled as 'snak' or as 'snack'.

SPEAK (snak or snack)

Low German		English	
Singular	Plural	Singular	Plural
ik snak	wi snakt	I speak	we speak
du snaks	ji snakt	you speak	you speak
he,se,dat snakt	se snakt	he,she,it speaks	they speak

Past Tense

ik snakt	wi snakt	I spoke	we spoke
du snakt	ji snakt	you spoke	you spoke
he,se,dat snakt	se snakt	he,she,it spoke	they spoke

Future Tense

ik will snaken	wi wütt snaken	will speak	we will speak
du wolls snaken	ji wütt snaken	you will speak	you will speak
he/se/dat will snaken	se wütt snaken	he/she/it will speak	they will speak

Present Perfect Tense

ik heff snakt	wi hebbt snakt	I have spoken	we have spoken
du hess snakt	ji hebbt snakt	you have spoken	you have spoken
he,se,dat hett snakt	se hebbt snakt	he,she,it has spoken	they have spoken

Past Perfect Tense

ik harr snakt	wi harrn snakt	I had spoken	we had spoken
du harrs snakt	ji harrn snakt	you had spoken	you had spoken
he,se,dat harr snakt	se harrn snakt	he,she,it had spoken	they had spoken

Future Perfect Tense *h. spok = have spoken*

ik hatt harr snakt	wi harrn harr snakt	I shall h. spok.	we shall h. spok.
du hatt harr snakt	ji harrn harr snakt	you shall h. spok.	you shall h. spok.
he,se,dat hatt harr snakt	se haarrn harr snakt	h,s,it shall h.spok.	they shall h.spok.

The following are just partial conjugations of additional Low German weak verbs. To conserve space, the preceding pronoun is left out in the last three lines of a grouping. Each one begins with a listing of the principal parts, plus the participle. In German, the participle always ends in '-en'. The *example* format given shows the format that would be normally used, if the preceding pronoun were shown. The example is filled out to show how the word striet (argue) would be conjugated.

Also notice the line through the last 't' in the word striet. This denotes it is a silent 't' in 1st and 2nd person singular. The word is normally pronounced 'stree-ah', with accent on the first syllable. In the plural of the word, the 't' becomes a suffix and is pronounced. The silent 't' is thus activated, to become a pronounced 't'. It is normally pronounced 'stree-et'. The same silent 't' situation exists in the verb arbeit.

<u>Example Format</u>

<u>Singular</u>		<u>Plural</u>	
Ik (I) ...	Ik striet	wi (we) ...	wi striet
du (you) ...	du striets	ji (you) ...	ji striet
he/se/dat (he/she/it) ...	he/se/dat striet	se (they) ...	se striet

The following are *weak* verbs in Low German, but not necessarily so in the other two languages. They are listed in sections. In the first section, the verb is weak in all three languages.

Endure
pres: duur
past: duurt
p.pt: Ik heff duurt
inf: duuren

duur	duurt
duurs	duurt
duurt	duurt

Ask
pres: fraag
past: fraagt
p.pt: Ik heff fraagt
inf: fraagen

fraag	fraagt
fraags	fraagt
fraagt	fraagt

Taste
pres: smeck
past: smeckt
p.pt: Ik heff smeckt
inf: smecken

smeck	smeckt
smecks	smeckt
smeckt	smeckt

Dance
pres: danz
past: danzt
p.pt: Ik heff danzt
inf: danzen

danz	danzt
danzs	danzt
danzt	danzt

Reside
pres: wohn
past: wohnt
p.pt: Ik heff wohnt
inf: wohnen

wohn	wohnt
wohns	wohnt
wohnt	wohnt

Believe [1]
pres: glööv
past: glöövt
p.pt: Ik heff glövt
inf: glöben

glööv	glövt
glövs	glövt
glövt	glövt

Saw
pres: saag
past: saagt
p.pt: Ik heff saagt
inf: saagen

saag	saagt
saags	saagt
saagt	saagt

Study
pres: studier
past: studiert
p.pt: Ik heff studiert
inf: studiern

studier	studiert
studiers	studiert
studiert	studiert

Order, Reserve
pres: bestell
past: bestellt
p.pt: Ik heff bestellt
inf: bestellen

bestell	bestellt
bestells	bestellt
bestellt	bestellt

Say [2]
pres:segg
past: seggt
p.pt: Ik heff seggt
inf: seggen

segg	seggt
seggs	seggt
seggt	seggt

Dream
pres: drööm
past: döömt
p.pt: Ik heff drömt
inf: drömen

drööm	dröömt
drööms	dröömt
dröömt	dröömt

Wish
pres: wünsch
past: wünscht
p.pt: Ik heff wünscht
inf: wünschen

wünsch	wünscht
wünschs	wünscht
wünscht	wünscht

Sweat
pres: sweet
past: sweet [3]
p.pt: Ik heff sweett
inf: sweeten

sweet	sweett
sweets	sweett
sweett	sweett

Work
pres: arbeit
past: arbeit
p.pt: Ik heff arbeit
inf: arbeiden

arbeit	arbeit
arbeids	arbeit
arbeit	arbeit

Inherit
pres: arv
pres: arvt
p.pt: Ik heff arvt
inf: arben

arv	arvt
arvs	arvt
arvt	arvt

Use
pres: bruuk
past: bruukt
p.pt: Ik heff bruukt
inf: bruuken

bruuk	bruukt
bruuks	bruukt
bruukt	bruukt

Thank
pres: dank
past: dankt
p.pt: Ik heff dankt
inf: danken

dank	dankt
danks	dankt
dankt	dankt

make Happy
pres: freih
past: freiht
p.pt: Ik heff freiht
inf: freihn

freih	freiht
freihs	freiht
freiht	freiht

Wait
pres: tööv
past: töövt
p. pt: Ik heff tövt
inf: töben

tööv	tövt
tövs	tövt
tövt	tövt

Argue
pres: striet
past: striet
p.pt: Ik heff striet
inf: strieten

striet	striet
stries	striet
striet	striet

Make
pres: mok
past: mokt
p.pt: Ik heff mokt
inf: moken

mok	mokt
moks	mokt
mokt	mokt

Kiss
pres: küss
past: küsst
p.pt: Ik heff küsst
inf: küssen

küss	küsst
küss	küsst
küsst	küsst

Notify, Inform
pres: kunden
past: kunnt
p.pt: Ik heff kunnt
inf: kunnen

kunn	kunnt
kunns	kunnt
kunnt	kunnt

Search
pres: söök
past: söökt
p.pt: Ik heff socht
inf: söken

söök	sökt
söks	sökt
sökt	sökt

Own	**Show**	**Laugh**
pres: eeg	pres: wies	pres: lach
past: eegt	past: wiest	past: lacht
p.pt: Ik heff eegt	p.pt: Ik heff wiest	p.pt: Ik heff lacht
inf: eegen	inf: wiesen	inf: lachen
eeg eegt	wies wiest	lach lacht
eegs eegt	wies wiest	lachs lacht
eegt eegt	wiest wiest	lacht lacht

Feel	**Cook**	**Smear**
pres: föhl	pres: kook	pres: smeer
past: föhlt	past: kookt	past: smeert
p.pt: Ik heff föhlt	p.pt: Ik heff kokt	p.pt: Ik heff smeert
inf: föhlen	inf: koken	inf: smeeren
föhl föhlt	kook kokt	smeer smeert
föhls föhlt	koks kokt	smeers smeert
föhlt föhlt	kokt kokt	smeert smeert

Pay	**Count**	**Turn**
pres: betohl	pres: tell	pres: dreih
past: betohlt	past: tellt	past: dreiht
p.pt: Ik heff betohlt	p.pt: Ik heff tellt	p.pt: Ik heff dreiht
inf: betohln	inf: telln	inf: dreihn
betohl betohlt	tell tellt	dreih dreiht
betohls betohlt	tells tellt	dreihs dreiht
betohlt betohlt	tellt tellt	dreiht dreiht

In the following second section, the Low German and the English verbs are weak, while the corresponding Standard German verb is strong.

Bake	**Live**	**Load**
pres: bak	pres: leev	pres: lode
past: bakt	past: leevt	past: lodet
p.pt: Ik heff bakt	p.pt: Ik heff leben	p.pt: Ik heff lodet
inf: baken	inf: leben	inf: loden
bak bakt	leev leevt	lode lodet
baks bakt	leevs leevt	lodes lodet
bakt bakt	leevt leevt	lodet lodet

Hear	**Burn**	**Hit**
pres: höör	pres: brinn	pres: hau
past: höört	past: brinnt	past: haut
p.pt: Ik heff höört	p.pt: Ik heff brinnt	p.pt: Ik heff haut
inf: hören	inf: brinnen	inf: hauen
höör hört	brinn brinnt	hau haut

hörs	hört	brinns	brinnt	haus	haut
hört	hört	brinnt	brinnt	haut	haut

In the following third section, *only* the Low German verb is weak.

Dig
pres: graav
past: graavt
p.pt: Ik heff graaven
inf: graben

graav	graavt
graavs	graavt
graavt	graavt

Drive
pres: föhr
past: föhrt
p.pt: Ik heff föhrt
inf: föhren

föhr	föhrt
föhrs	föhrt
föhrt	föhrt

Bleed
pres: blööd
past: blööd
p.pt: Du hess blöd
inf: blöen

blööd	blöödt
blööds	blöödt
blöödt	blöödt

Name, be Called
pres: heet
past: heet
p.pt: Ik heff heett
inf: heeten

heet	heett
hees	heett
heett	heett

Ride
pres: ried
past: ried
p.pt: Ik heff riedt
inf: reiden

ried	riedt
rieds	riedt
riedt	riedt

Cry
pres: shree
past: shreet
p.pt: Ik heff shreet
inf: shreen

shree	shreet
shrees	shreetheet
shreet	shreet

(1) Notice that, in the case of believe and wait, the infinitive vowel changes from 'v' to 'b'. In the infinitive, the word takes on an action quality - to 'do' something. In olden times such an action quality was represented by a special word ending. As an example, let's assume the English noun 'bomb' was to be given an action quality, to denote the action of bombing. By old standards this might have resulted in a spelling like 'bombe'. There is an old reflection of just such a such word change involved when you go from the Low German 'glöv' to the infinitive 'glöben', which causes the change from 'v' to 'b' as the word takes on an 'action' quality. Another good example concerns the very similar Low German words 'boov' (on top) and 'boben' (up above) in Low German. The second one has two syllables, and therefore the 'v' ending in the first version takes the 'b' in the beginning of the second syllable (bo-ben).

(2) This is a case of the doubling of the g, following a short <u>accented</u> vowel.

(3) This is a case of the überlange situation, where the vowel is lengthened and some people want to add an apostrophe at the end (heet'), some would want to double the consonant (heett instead of heet); and some would leave it heet.

<u>Strong (Irregular) Verb</u>

In Old Saxon the *strong* verb formed the past tense by changing the stem vowel. There were 7 classes of strong verbs, differentiated by how they formed the principal parts of speech. In Low German there are 6 classes. The strong verbs in Old Saxon are also strong verbs in Low German, except for the word föhren (which was faran in Old Saxon).

Class	English	Low German Infinitive	Old Saxon Infinitive
I	write	shrieben	skrîban
II	flow	flussen	fliotan
III	throw	smieten	werpan
IV	steal	stehlen	stelan
V	weave	weeven	weban
VI	strike	slagen	slahan
VII	call	ropen	hrôpan

The first example in this *strong* verb section will be for a full conjugation for the Standard German verb 'sehe' (see). This is a weak verb in Standard German, because of the vowel change to 'a' in the imperfect. This change is identical to English, also a strong verb. The Low German conjugation follows in the following section.

The principal parts are sehe, sah, and gesehen. The vowel becomes 'a' to make the imperfect (past) tense and a 'ge-' prefix plus '-en' makes the perfect participle.

Sehen (See)
Indicative Mood

Standard German		**English**	
Present Tense			
<u>Singular</u>	<u>Plural</u>	<u>Singular</u>	<u>Plural</u>
ich sehe	wir sehen	I see	we see
du* siehst	ihr* seht	you see	you see
er,sie,es sieht	sie sehen	he,she,it see	they see
Past Tense			
ich sah	wir sahen	I saw	we saw
du sahst	ihr saht	you saw	you saw
er,sie,es sah	sie sahen	he,she,it saw	they saw
Future Tense			
ich werde sehen	wir werden sehen	I shall see	we shall see
du wirst sehen	ihr werdet sehen	you will see	you will see
er,sie,es wird sehen	sie werden sehen	he/she/it will see	they will see
Present Perfect Tense			
ik habe gesehen	wir haben gesehen	I have seen	we have seen
du hast gesehen	ihr habt gesehen	you have seen	you have seen
er,sie,es hat gesehen	sie haben sehen	he,she,it has seen	they have seen

Past Perfect Tense

ich hatte gesehen	wir hatten gesehen	I had seen	we had seen
du hattest gesehen	ihr hattet gesehen	you had. seen	you had seen
er,sie,es hatte gesehen	sie hatten gesehen	he,she,it had seen	they had seen

g.hab. = *gesehen haben* **Future Perfect Tense**

ich werde g.hab.	wir werden g.hab.	I shall have seen	we shall have seen
du wirst g.hab.	ihr werdet g.hab.	you will have seen	you will have seen
er,sie,es wird g.hab.	sie werden g hab.	he,she,it will have seen	they will hae seen

* The familiar forms of address are used here, rather than the formal *Sie*.

The Low German cognate verb seh (see) is also now fully conjugated. The past participle is 'sehen', which does not end in '-t'. Therefore, this is a *strong* verb.

Seh (See)
Indicative Mood

Low German		English	
Singular	Plural	Singular	Plural

Present Tense

ik seh	wi seht	I see	we see
du sühs	ji seht	you see	you see
he, se, dat süht	se seht	he,she,it sees	they see

Past Tense

ik seh	wi sehn	I saw	we saw
du sühs	ji sehn	you saw	you saw
he, se, dat süht	se sehn	he,she,it saw	they saw

Future Tense

ik schöll* sehn	wi schöllt sehn	I shall see	we shall see
du schölls sehn	ji schöllt sehn	you will see	you will see
he,se,dat schöllt sehn	se schöllt sehn	he/she/it will see	they will see

Present Perfect Tense

ik heff sehn	wi hebbt sehn	I have seen	we have seen
du hess sehn	ji hebbt sehn	you have seen	you have seen
he, se, dat hett sehn	se hett sehn	he,she,it has seen	they have seen

Past Perfect Tense

ik harr sehn	ik harr sehn	I had seen	we had seen
du harrs sehn	ji harrn sehn	you had seen	you had seen
he,se,dat harrt sehn	se harrn sehn	he,she,it had seen	they had seen

s.heb. = *sehn hebben* **Future Perfect Tense**   *h. s. = have seen*

ik will s. heb	wi wütt s. heb.	I shall h. s.	we shall h. s.
du wulls s. heb	ji wütt s. heb	you will h. s.	you will h. s.
he,se,dat wullt s. heb	se wütt s. heb	he,she,it will h. s.	they will h. s.

* This could be written as either 'shöllt' (shall) or will (will), to
represent the future tense, just as the words 'shall' or 'will' are

212

interchangeable in the English future tense

The Low German word brek (break) is conjugated here, in just the first three tenses. This is another verb where the present tense 2nd and 3rd person singular form is made by changing the vowel and adding '-s' or '-t'. The reason that it is a *strong* verb is that the 1st person singular past tense also changes the stem vowel to yet a different vowel (br*e*k .... br*i*ks).

Brek (Break)

Low German		English	
Present Tense			
Singular	Plural	Singular	Plural
ik brek	wi brekt	I break	we break
du briks	ji brekt	you break	you break
he/se/dat brikt	se brekt	he/she/it breaks	they break
Past Tense			
Ik brök	wi bröken	I broke	we broke
du bröks	ji bröken	you broke	you broke
he/se/dat brökt	se bröken	he/she/it broke	they broke

For the future case, there is an '-en' added, along with a helper verb like will or wolls or wütt.

Future Tense			
ik will breken	wi wütt breken	I will break	we will break
du wolls breken	ji wütt breken	you will break	you will break
he/se/dat will breken	se wütt breken	he/she/it will break	they will break

The verb kann (can) is a *strong* verb, because the vowel changes in the past tense.

Kann (Can)

Low German		English	
Present Tense			
Singular	Plural	Singular	Plural
ik kann	wi könnt	I can	we can
du kanns	ji könnt	you can	you can
he/se/dat kann	se könnt	he/she/it can	they can
Past Tense			
Ik könn	wi könnt	I could	we could
du könns	ji könnt	you could	you could
he/se/dat könnt	se könnt	he/she/it could	they could
Future Tense			
ik will können	wi wütt können	I could	we could
du wolls können	ji wütt könnn	you could	you could
he/se/dat will können	se wütt können	he/she/it could	they could

The verb et (eat) changes it's 'e' stem vowel in the present tense to an unusual diphthong 'ee' in the past tense.

ET (Eat)

Low German		English	
Present Tense			
Singular	Plural	Singular	Plural
ik et	wi et	I eat	we eat
du iss	ji et	you eat	you eat
he/se/dat itt	se et	he/she/it eats	they eat
Past Tense			
Ik eet	wi eeten	I ate	we ate
du ees	ji eeten	you ate	you ate
he/se/dat eett	se eeten	he/she/it ate	they ate
Future			
ik will eten	wi wütt eten	I will eat	we will eat
du wolls eten	ji wütt eten	you will eat	you will eat
he/se/dat will eten	se wütt eten	he/she/it will eat	they will eat

The following are the partial conjugations of additional Low German *strong* verbs

Example Format

Singular		Plural	
Ik (I) ...	Ik krieg	wi (we) ...	wi kriegt
du (you) ...	du kriggs	ji (you) ...	ji kriegt
he/se/dat (he/she/it) ...	he/se/dat kriggt	se (they) ...	se kriegt

The following are *strong* verbs in Low German, but not necessarily so in the other two languages. They are listed in sections. In the first section, the verb is strong in all three languages (a few exceptions in English).

Notice that in the case of the verbs may, can and will, when the past participle has an umlauted vowel, the vowel is also umlauted in the plural.

May		**Drink**		**Write** [1]	
pres: mag		pres: **d**rink		pres: shriev	
past: mög		past: **d**rünk		past: shreev	
p.pt: Ik heff mögt		p.pt: Ik heff drunken		p.pt: Ik heff shreben	
inf: mögen		inf: **d**rinken		inf: shreben	
mag	mögt	drink	drinkt	shriev	shrievt
mags	mögt	drinks	drinkt	shriffs	shrievt
magt	mögt	drinkt	drinkt	shrievt	shrievt

214

Sing
pres: sing
past: süng
p.pt: Ik heff sungen
inf: singen

sing	singt
sings	singt
singt	singt

Strike
pres: slaag
past: slögg
p.pt: Ik heff slagen
inf: slagen

slaag	slagt
slags	slagt
slagt	slagt

Ring
pres: ring
past: rüng
p.pt: Ik heff rungen
inf: ringen

ring	ringt
rings	ringt
ringt	ringt

Can
pres: kann
past: könn
p.pt: Ik heff könnt
inf: kannen

kann	könnt
kanns	könnt
kannt	könnt

Bid, Pray
pres: bede
past: boden
p.pt: Ik heff boden
inf: boden

bede	bedet
bedes	bedet
bedet	bedet

Grow
pres: wass
past: wüss
p.pt: Ik heff wussen
inf: wassen

wass	wasst
wass	wasst
wasst	wasst

Throw
pres: smiet
past: smeet
p.pt: Ik heff smeten
inf: smieten

smiet	smiett
smiss	smiett
smitt	smiett

Give [2]
pres: geev
past: geev
p.pt: Ik heff geben
inf: geben

geev	geevt
giffs	geevt
gifft	geevt

Begin
pres: fang
past: füng
p.pt: Ik heff anfungen
inf: fangen

fang	fangt
fangs	fangt
fangt	fangt

Get
pres: krieg [3]
past: kreeg
p.pt: Ik heff kregen
inf: kriegen

krieg	kriegt
kriggs	kriegt
kriggt	kriegt

Fall
pres: fall
past: föll
p.pt: Ik heff fallen
inf: fallen

fall	fallt
falls	fallt
fallt	fallt

Know
pres: weet
past: wüss
p.pt: Ik heff weten
inf: weeten

weet	weett
wees	weett
weet	weett

Think
pres: dink
past: dech
p.pt: Ik heff dacht
inf: dinken

dink	dinkt
dinks	dinkt
dinkt	dinkt

Creep, Crawl
pres: kreep
past: kröpp
p.pt: Ik heff kroppen
inf: kreepen

kreep	kreept
kreeps	kreept
kreept	kreept

Bring
pres: bring
past: bröch
p.pt: Ik heff brocht
inf: bringen

bring	bringt
brings	bringt
bringt	bringt

Fly
pres: fleeg
past: flög
p.pt: Ik heff flogen
inf: flegen
fleeg	fleegt
flüggs	fleegt
flüggt	fleegt

Take
pres: nehm
past: nöhm
p.pt: Ik heff nohmen
inf: nehmen
nehm	nehmt
nihms	nehmt
nihmt	nehmt

Shine, Seem
pres: shien
past: sheen
p.pt: Dat hett sheent
inf: shienen
shien	shient
shiens	shient
shient	shient

Cut
pres: snied
past: sneed
p.pt: Ik heff sneden
inf: sneden
snied	snied
snieds	snied
snied	snied

Steal
pres: stehl
past: stohlen
p.pt: Ik heff stohlen
inf: stehlen
stehl	stehlt
stehls	stehlt
stehlt	stehlt

Weave
pres: weev
past: wööv
p.pt: Ik heff woven
inf: weeven
weev	weevt
weevs	weevt
weevt	weevt

Stick, Prick
pres: stek
past: stök
p.pt: Ik heff stoken
inf: steken
stek	stekt
steks	stekt
stekt	stekt

Stand
pres: stoh
past: stöhn
p.pt: Ik heff stohn
inf: stohn
stoh	stoht
stohs	stoht
stoht	stoht

Go
pres: goh
past: göhn
p.pt: Ik heff gohn
inf: gohn
goh	goht
geihs	goht
geiht	goht

Let, Allow
pres: lat
past: löt
p.pt: Ik heff löten
inf: laten
laat	latt
lass	latt
latt	latt

Run
pres: loop
past: lopen
p.pt: Ik heff lopen
inf: lopen
loop	loppt
lopps	loppt
loppt	loppt

Sit
pres: sitt
past: seten
p.pt: Ik heff seten
inf: sitten
sitt	sitt
siss	sitt
sitt	sitt

Lay
pres: lieg
past: legg
p.pt: Ik heff legen
inf: legen
lieg	liggt
liggs	liggt
liggt	liggt

Find
pres: finn
past: funnen
p.pt: Ik heff funnen
inf: finnen
finn	finnt
finns	finnt
finnt	finnt

Bite
pres: biet
Past: beten
p.pt: Ik heff beten
inf: bieten
biet	biett
biss	biett
bitt	biett

Shoot		**Understand**		**Come**	
pres: sheet		pres: verstoh		pres: koom	
past: shoten		past: verstohn		past: kööm	
p.pt: Ik heff shoten		p.pt: Ik heff verstohn		p.pt: Ik bün kommen	
inf: sheeten		inf: verstohn		inf: kommen	
sheet	sheett	verstoh	verstoht	koom	kommt
shüss	sheett	versteihs	verstoht	kumms	kommt
shütt	sheet	versteiht	verstoht	kummt	kommt

In the following second section, the Low German and the English verbs are strong, while the corresponding Standard German verb is weak.

Will		**Bend**	
Pres: will		pres: böög	
Past: wöll		past: bügg	
p.pt: Ik heff wöllen		p.pt: Ik heff büggt	
inf: willen		inf: bögen	
will	wütt	böög	böggt
wolls	wütt	böggs	böggt
willt	wütt	böggt	böggt

In the following third section, the Low German verb is strong, but the English and Standard German counterparts are in the weak category.

Must		**Wash**		**Tie**	
pres: mutt		pres: wasch		pres: binn	
past: möss		past: wüsch		past: bünn	
p.pt: Ik heff mösst		p.pt: Ik heff wuschen		p.pt: Ik heff bunnen	
inf: mötten		inf: waschen		inf: bunnen	
mutt	mött	wash	wascht	binn	binnt
muss	mött	wasch	wascht	binns	binnt
mutt	mött	wascht	wascht	binnt	binnt

Help		**Pull**		**Carry**	
pres: help		pres: tehg		pres: dreeg	
past: hölp		past: töhg		past: drögg	
p.pt: Ik heff holpen		p.pt: Ik heff tohgen		p.pt: Ik heff drogen	
inf: helpen		inf: tehgen		inf: drogen	
help	helpt	tehg	tehgt	dreeg	dreegt
hölps	helpt	tühgs	tehgt	driggs	dreegt
hölpt	helpt	tühgt	tehgt	driggt	dreegt

217

Look
pres: kiek
past: keek
p.pt: Ik heff keken
inf: kieken

kiek	kiekt
keiks	keikt
kiekt	kiekt

(1) For the word *write*, the 'b' in the infinitive probably comes from the fact that in Old Saxon it was written skrîbun. In Old Saxon the past tense was skêf, which relates to the 'v' ending in Low German, which actually has the 'f' sound.

(2) For the word *give*, the change from 'v' in the present and past to the 'b' in the past participle is reflection of the Old Saxon spelling for this word, geba. This old version of 'b' was pronounced as a 'v'. It was, in Old High German *gebe*, taken as a 'b' but in Low German it was taken as a 'v' except for several inflections of the verb.

(3) In Westphalian, for instance, this would be somewhat different.

present: kriig	kriig	kriigt
past: kreeg	kriigs	kriigt
p.pt: Ik heff kriëgen.	kriigt	kriigt

ADVERB

An adverb is a word used to "qualify" a verb, adjective or other adverbs.

They can be divided into 3 classes.

1. Adverb of place (here, there, near, before, etc.)
2. Adverb of time (today, yesterday, now, often, etc.)
3. Adverb of manner or degree (how, thus, even, almost, etc.)

Examples of adverbs are 'fast', 'quick', 'very' and 'almost', which can be used as they are in the phrases - walking "fast" or moving "quick".

Standard German	English	Low German
schnell	fast	gau
flink	quick	flink
sehr	very	ganz
beinahe	almost	binoh
langsam	slowly	langsom

mehr	more	meehr
glücklich	happily	fröhlig
weitlich	widely	wietlig
zu	too	to
oft	often	oft
täglich	daily	daaglig

PREPOSITION

A preposition is a word that shows the relationship that nouns or pronouns have to other words in a sentence. Literally, it means "place before".

In a sentence it is normally found before the noun or pronoun to which it relates. Examples of such words are 'with', 'for' and 'to', which can be used in the phrases "with" us, "for" him and "to" them. Note that a word like 'to' can also be part of a verbal phrase, such as "to run", at which time it is no longer a preposition.

There are also prepositional phrases, which are a group of words beginning with a preposition and ending with a noun or pronoun (of the house or on the bus).

In Standard German they are referred to as "vorwörter", since they usually precede a phrase. Below are listed some common prepositions, in all three languages.

Standard German	*English*	*Low German*
mit	with	mit
für	for	för
zu	to	to
um	about	vun
über	across	röwer
nach	after	no
an	at	an
zwischen	between	twüschen
bi	by	bi
siet	since	naher
unter	under	ünner
bis	until	bet
ohne	without	ahn or mitut
hinter	behind	achter
neben	beside	blangs

There has been a history of relationship between words and numbers, which is no longer important today. In Indo-European and in Gothic the numbers actually also stood for words. Also, the first several numbers were inflected, so as to reflect gender.

In ancient Greek and Hebrew they used letters of the alpabet to stand for numbers: alpha stood for 'one', beta stood for 'two', etc.

In Standard German you'll sometimes come across the use of 'zwo' for the number 'zwei' (two). It harks back to when 'zwo' was the feminine form of the number. However, today it is used to more clearly differentiate the spoken 'zwei' from 'drei'.

CARDINAL

Included here are the cardinal numbers for several languages. In addition to English, the list shows both the Old High German and the current Standard German. It also shows the older Middle Low German and the current version of Low German, which we have called Platt Düütsch. Comparison of the older and newer forms is quite interesting. For instance, the Primitive German word for eleven was 'elleban' (the b was pronounced much like a 'v'), which is very close to the English word 'eleven'.. In the text following this table is a list of the Old Saxon version of some of these numbers.

	English	*Old H.German*	*Std German*	*Middle L. German*	*Platt Düütsch*
0	zero		null		nuul
1	one	ein	eins	ên	een
2	two	zwei	zwei	twê	twee
3	three	drî	drei	drê	dree
4	four	fior	vier	vêr	veer
5	five	fimf	fünf	vîf	fiev
6	six	sëhs	sechs	ses	söss
7	seven	sibun	sieben	seven	söben
8	eight	ahto	acht	acht	acht
9	nine	niun	neun	negen	negen
10	ten	zëhen	zehn	tein	teihn
11	eleven	einlif	elf	elven	ölben
12	twelve	zwelif	zwölf	twelf	twölf
13	thirteen	drîzëhan	dreizehn	drüttein	dörteihn
14	fourteen	fiorzëhan	vierzehn	vertein	veerteihn
15	fifteen	fimfzëhan	fünfzehn	vêftein	föfteihn
16	sixteen	sëhszëhan	sechzehn	sestein	sössteihn
17	seventeen	sibunzëhan	siebzehn	seventein	söbteihn
18	eighteen	ahtozëhan	achtzehn	achtein	achteihn
19	nineteen	niunzëhan	neunzehn	negentein	negenteihn
20	twenty	zweinzug	zwanzig	twintich	twintig

21	twentyone	einunzweinzug	einundzwanzig		eenuntwintig
30	thirty	drîzzug	dreissig	drüttich	dörtig
32	thirtytwo		zweiunddreissig		tweeundörtig
40	forty	fiorzug	vierzig	vertich	veertig
50	fifty	fimfzug	fünfzig	viftich	föftig
60	sixty	sëhszug	sechzig	sestich	sösstig
70	seventy	sibunzug	siebzig	seventich	söbtig
80	eighty	ahtozug	achtzig	achtsich	achtsig
90	ninety	niunzug	neunzig	negensich	negtig
100	one hundred hunt		hundert	hundert	hunnert
1,000	one thousand zëhanhunt		tausend	dusent	dusend
1,000,000	one million		Million		miljoon
1,000,000,000	one billion		Milliarden		biljoon

In Europe they refer to a billion as a thousand million, thus in German they say
milliarden (a version of million) instead of using the word billion.

The 'lif' ending in Old High German, similar in meaning to the English word 'leave',
expresses the meaning "left over". For instance, the word einlif (eleven) denotes "one
left over beyond ten". The 'zug' ending in Old High German denots 'decade' or 'tens'.
Prior to the early 9th century, this ending was 'zo'.

In Old Saxon the records are unclear as to just how the numbers were written. The
number one was simply ên. In Low German, the gender distinction here is made only
for the feminine (eene Fro), otherwise it is always een. In Old Saxon, the numbers two
and three each had masculine, feminine and neuter forms. As an example, for the
number 'two', these gender forms were twêne, twâ or twô, and twê and for the number
'three' they were thria, thria, and thriu. For the numbers 4 thru 21, they are
(consecutively) fiuwar, fîf, sehs, siƀun, ahto, nigun, tehan, elleƀan, twelif, thriutein,
fiuwartein, fîftein, sehstein, siƀuntein, ahtotein, niguntein, twêntig and ên endi twêntig
(21). You can compare this to the above table. The letter 'ƀ' in these words is the old
version that was pronounced very much like a 'v'.

ORDINAL

English		Standard German	Platt Düütsch
1st	first	Erste	eerste
2nd	second	Zweite	tweede
3rd	third	Dritte	drütte
4th	fourth	Vierte	veerte
5th	fifth	Fünfte	föfte
6th	sixth	Sechste	sösste
7th	seventh	Sebente	söbente
8th	eighth	Ahte	achte
9th	ninth	Neunte	negente

10th	tenth	Zehnte	teihnte
11th	eleventh	Elfte	ölvte
12th	twelfth	Zwölfte	twölvte
13th	thirteenth	Dreizehnte	dörteihnste
14th	fourteenth	Vierzehnte	Veerteihnste
15th	fifteenth	Fünfzehnte	föfteihnte
20th	twentieth	Zwanzigste	twintigste
50th	fiftieth	Fünfzigste	föftigste
100th	hundredth	Hundertste	hunnertste
102nd	hundred and second	Hundertundzweite	hunnertuntweede

In Old High German the ordinals are created by a '-to' ending. Eristo means 'first' and dritto means 'third'. The word for 'second' is very interesting. It is *ander*, which normally means "other" - something *other* than 'first' always thus becomes the 'other'.

DISTINCTIVE

English		Standard German	Low German
1st	firstly	erstens	eerstens
2nd	secondly	zweitens	tweedens
3rd	thirdly	drittens	drüttens
4th	fourthly	viertens	veertens
5th	fifthly	fünftens	föftens
6th	sixthly	sechtens	sösstens
7th	seventhly	siebtens	söbtens
8th	eighthly	achtens	achtens
9th	ninthly	neuntens	negtens
10th	tenthly	zehntens	teihntens
11th	eleventhly	elftens	ölvtens

FRACTIONS

The '*-tel*' ending is a variation of the word *teil*, which means "part".

English		Standard German	Low German
1/2	one half	Hälfte	halvte
1/3	one third	Drittel	drüttel
1/4	one fourth	Viertel	veertel
1/5	one fifth	Fünftel	föftel
1/10	one tenth	Zehntel	teihntel
1/20	one twentieth	Zwanzigstel	twintigtel

TIME

The way time is expressed in the three languages varies considerably. Sometimes Low German is similar to English and sometimes similar to Standard German.

In Standard German one says "Wie viel Uhr ist es jezt?" when one wants to ask for the time. A direct translation into English would yeild "How many watches is it now?". In Low German one would say "Watvun tied is dat nu?", which translates fairly directly into English "What time is it now?". The word 'nu' could be left off, since it is understood that the period for the time is 'now', unless stated otherwise.

In Standard German, the phrase for 5:00 would be "fünf Uhr", which is somewhat similar to the English "five o'clock".. In Low German it would be "klock fiev", which is sort of backwards from the other languages. In Low German the terms 'uhr' and 'klock' both refer to a clock, but one would not say "uhr fiev". The term 'uhr' is a loanword from Standard German, while 'klock' is a basic Low German term.

In Standard German 1:30 would be stated as "halb zwei". Low German would say it similarly; "halvig twee". In English one would just say "one thirty". The German languages refer to the 'next' hour and English refers to the 'previous' hour.

In Standard German 2:15 would be stated as "viertel auf drei" or "viertel nach zwei". In Low German it would be said "veddel no twee". One would not say "twee föfteihn". In English it would be "two fifteen" or "quarter after two".

In Standard German 3:45 would be stated as "viertel vor vier" or "dreiviertel vier". In English it would be "quarter to four". It would never be stated as "three-quarters four". In Low German it would be "veddel vör veer".

ALPHABET

Just for historical purposes, the oldest Germanic alphabet will be described here. It provides an interesting model by which to compare the current alphabet against and earlier version. In the extinct Gothic language, which some consider to be very close to Primitive German, the alphabet letter had *names*, which were also nouns in the Gothic language.

The following table gives the Gothic letter, it's name and then the English translation of the name. There was no letter 'c'. This letter is also almost unknown in Old Saxon and Low German.

There was no letter 'v' (the letter 'u' was used in its stead) or letter 'y'. The Gothic letters also had numerical values, which are shown in the last column.

Gothic		English	Number Meaning
Letter	Name	Word	Number
a	ahsa	axle	1
b	baîrkan	birch	2
d	dags	day	4
e	aîhvs	horse	5
f	faihu	goods	500
g	giba	giving	3
h	hagl	hail	8
hv	hvaîr	cauldron	700
i	eis	ice	10
j	jêr	year	60
k	kusma	boil	20
l	lagus	lake	30
m	manna	man	40
n	nauþs	force	50
o	oþal	inheritance	800
p	paîrþa	dice cup	80
q	qaîrþra	bait	6
r	raida	ride	100
s	sáuîl	sun	200
t	teiws	Tiu, god of war	300
þ	þiuþ	good	9
u	urus	urus, extinct bison	70
w	winja	pasture	400
x	iggws	Ingw, a demigod	600
z	azêti	ease	7

PRONUNCIATION AND SPELLING

A dictionary gives us, besides word definitions, the correct spelling. The larger ones often provide assistance in pronunciation, especially vowel pronunciation. In a dictionary there are *diacritical* marks used to show how a vowel is to be pronounced within a word. The two most common vowel sounds are indicated by the diacritical markings known as the *macron* (long) and the *breve* (short).

The *macron* (-) over a vowel indicates that the vowel is to be pronounced just as that letter is named, which means it is pronounced 'long'.

The *breve* ( ) over a vowel indicates that the vowel is to be pronounced in its 'short' form. It is pronunciation is accomplished in a shorter period of time, with a sound that is unlike its name.

Such diacritical marks are not used much in this book, in order to keep things as simple as possible. Also, these marks are not readily available on a computer and certainly not on a typewriter. However, including some technical terms in the following discussion may help to reveal ways in which the pronunciation of these languages vary.

The differences between *long* and *short vowels* are discussed at various points in this book The long and short vowels in English are pronounced shorter in vocal length than their German counterparts. Notice that the sound of long 'a' in English differs from long 'a' in German. A long Low German vowel is often doubled (oo instead of just o).

Whether the vowel is in an *open* or closed syllable also affects the vowel.

> A *closed* syllable is one that ends with a consonant (krab-bel) In a *closed* syllable, the vowel is usually long, as in tan-te (aunt). But before a doubled (geminated) consonant (not including 'h'), it will be short. Examples of the latter are leggen (lay), katt (cat), kopp (head), shipp (ship), fudder (feed), komm (come) and pott (pot).

> An *open* syllable doesn't end with a consonant (vo-gel). In an *open* syllable, the vowel will usually be short, as in le-sen (to read).

If the concept of short and long vowels is vague, just listen in your head to the different sounds you make when saying the English words 'bead' and 'beat'. Notice how you hold the vowel sounds longer in 'bead' than you do in 'beat'. In Low German, compare the words sied (side) and the longer word wied (wide). In the second word, the 'ie' sound is held much longer than in the first of the two words.

The situation in Standard and Low German is very similar when it comes to vowels, which one might expect of sister languages. In Standard German a vowel is always long when doubled (Meer, Boot). A vowel is *short* when followed by a doubled consonant (Wasser, dumm, Voss). It is generally short when followed by two differing consonants (senden, helfen). A vowel followed by an 'h' is long, as in Hahn (rooster) or Sohn (son). The 'h' takes the place of a second vowel, which is the usual way a long vowel situation arises in Low German (boot).

In Low German, a double vowel doesn't necessarily mean a *long* vowel sound because it may be a diphthong. If it is a monophthong, then it would be *long*. A vowel followed by a single consonant is generally long (hut, grab). A *short* monosyllabic word may have a doubled vowel with a long vowel sound, such as in the words oog (eye), oost (east), ööv (practice), een (one) and uut (out).

There are monosyllabic words that end in 'g', and in these the vowel is *long*. Examples are mag (like), weg (way) and dag (day).

Monosyllabic words are those that are made up of one sound, or one syllable (bag, mud, etc.) Vowels in those monosyllable words that end in 'v', 's', 'd', or 'g' undergo a lengthening of sound (überlange). In older languages these words would have ended with an 'e', which produced a second syllable. Since such unstressed 'e' letters have disappeared (apocope), it is no longer used in spelling but still influences pronunciation. For instance, the word for "our", which is uus in Low German, used to be spelled uuse. In pronunciation, the letter 's' here takes on more of a 'z' sound, as compensation for the missing 'e'. Another example is when a word like 'breef' is pluralized into 'breev'. It is pronounced as if it were spelled 'bree-ve'.

Vowels in ending syllable are unstressed and very short in sound. They are almost silent. Examples are eten (eat), appel (apple), slepen (drag), teken (sign) and lachen (laugh).

In Table Four on the next page are shown the letters, letter sounds, vowel lengths and voice vs. voiceless sounds of consonants. The letter names and sounds differ somewhat between the three languages. Low German and Standard German vowel sounds are quite similar but do vary.

In any technical study the sounds of letters are usually represented by specific symbols. For example, there is the phonetic symbol ç which represents the 'ch' sound. With such symbols, everyone understands the sound in the same way, regardless of their own language. It is certainly more exact to used such symbols. However, they are confusing (at best) to the average reader. Such symbols are not used here, to keep the discussion as simple as possible. However, it may also mean that some comments made here will not conform to technical authorities.

Certain sounds are associated with certain letters. But as the pronunciation (specifically, the sounds) of words change over the centuries, this is often reflected in the spelling of those words. If a sound within a given word - a sound normally associated with, for instance, the letter 'b' - is changed to a sound normally associated with the letter 'p', then that word may become to be spelled with a 'p'. The word's meaning has not changed, just its sound and spelling have changed. Sometimes a sound associated with a letter can be transferred to another letter. In this case, the word's meaning and sound remain the same, just its spelling has changed.

In the table a few technical terms are used, which should be explained. In the second chapter we ran into letter sounds considered to be *'voiced'* because they were sounded with vibration in the vocal chords. Of course, all sounds that come from the throat involve a vibration, but here we're talking about a pronounced vibration affect. For instance, the letters 'd', 'b', 'g', 'z' and 'v' are considered voiced, while the letters 't', 'p', 'k', 's' and 'f' are considered *'unvoiced'* or voiceless. We have taken liberties with this definition and applied it to places where it isn't normally used. This has been done to consolidate varying information into one complete table. The objective is not to be technically correct, but rather to convey to the average reader certain similarities and differences between the languages.

The liquid and nasal consonants (l, r, m, n) are also known as *syllabis* consonants, because just the one letter can often be a syllable all by itself. The liquids (l, r) are often treated as a separate syllable.

The term "*modified*" vowel refers basically to those vowels that have an 'umlaut' sound. These are usually 'ä', 'ö' and 'ü'. They can also be spelled without the double dot above, by placing the letter 'e' behind it (ae, oe or ue). In some dialects the long 'ö' vowels are spelled with 'oe', and the long 'ü' vowels spelled with 'ue'. Modified vowels were added to the German languages about 1200 A.D.

TABLE FOUR — VOWELS AND CONSONANTS

Ltr.	English	Low German	Standard German .

Basic Vowels;

		Long	Short		Long	Short		Long	Short
a *ay*		father	art	*ah*	warm	bak	*ah*	Vater	Wasser
e *ee*		pete	pet	*ay*	lehn	bet	*ay*	sehe	Rest
i *eye*		hi	him	*ee*	ihm	witt	*ee*	Lid	Sinn
o *oh*		toe	got	*oh*	froh	bock	*oh*	loben	Gott
u *yoo*		rule	up	*oo*	schu	bunt	*oo*	Hut	dumm

Additional Semi-Vowels;

å *aw*	paw	*aw*	goh		
ë *ae* [1]	pat	*ae*	beter		
é *eh*	item	*eh*	beter	*eh*	besser

Modified Vowels;

		Long	Short		Long	Short
ä [2]		*ae*	-	hännen	*ae*	zähe	Hände
ö		*oe*	köken	mött	*oe*	schön	könn
ü		*ue*	küken	süss	*ue*	früh	Küsse

Stop (plosive) Consonants;

	Voiced	Voiceless		Voiced	Voiceless		Voiced	Voiceless
d *dee*	dog	-	*day*	dood	wied	*day*	dich	hund
t *tee*	-	tea	*tay*	-	teihn	*tay*	-	hart
b *bee*	ball	-	*bay*	bloot	-	*bay*	ball	-
p *pee*	-	pay	*pay*	-	pann	*pay*	-	dorp
g *gee*	germ	kay	*gay*	goh	weg	*gay*	grün	-
k *kay*			*kah*	-	koh	*kah*	-	klar

TABLE FOUR CONTINUED

Liquid Consonants;

	Voiced	Voiceless		Voiced	Voiceless		Voiced	Voiceless
l *ell*	loud	well	*ell*	laat	hell	*ell*	laut	hell
r *ar*	real	tear	*ar*	rad	dor	*er*	rund	teer

Nasals Consonants;

	Voiced	Voiceless		Voiced	Voiceless		Voiced	Voiceless
m *em*	mute	him	*emm*	mit	ihm	*emm*	mich	ihm
n *en*	new	torn	*enn*	nich	in	*enn*	neu	vorn

Other Consonants;

	Voiced	Voiceless		Voiced	Voiceless		Voiced	Voiceless
c *see*		cafe, certain	*tsay*			*tsay*		Cent
f *ef*		fun	*eff*		fett	*eff*		Fett
h *aich*		hug	*hah*		huus	*hah*		Haus
j *jay*		jug	*jah*		johr	*yot*		Jahr
q *kew*		quiz	*koo*		quatsch	*koo*		Quell
s *ess*	was	mist	*ess*	seep	muus	*ess*	sehe	Saltz
v *vee*	have		*fow*	vun		*fow*	vor	
w *wuh*	wig	new	*vay*		witt	*vay*		wo
x *eks*	box		*iks*	nix		*iks*	xte	
y *wei*	you	boy	*ee*			*ee*		Ypsilon
z *zee*	bozo		*tset*	zigar		*tset*	wiesen	

(1) A remnant of the ancient 'æ' combination letter, similar to a short 'ä'. The word dreg could be written dreeg; but not if used as a *short* vowel.

(2) An example of a Standard German word using the two 'ä' vowels are, respectively, the words Mädchen and lächeln.

The following is a list of comments regarding the sounds that letters as used in Low German words. There are also a few references to Standard German usage of letters. Any references to a 'normal' sound means what would be normal to an English speaking person's ear. Some of the comments are repititious, because the item discussed arises in a number of different conditions.

ɑ This letter 'a' takes the long 'a' sound when followed by 'r' (warm, arm, etc.) or by 'l' (hals).

ƀ This letter originally existed only at the front of words, and perhaps for that reason always takes the voiced 'b' sound at the beginning of a syllable or word.

It takes the unvoiced 'p' sound at the end of a syllable and before a suffix.

Sometimes this letter is found at the end of a Standard German word, and at the end of the corresponding Low German words, it becomes the letter 'v', such as Korb-korv (basket), glaub-glöv (believe), or probe-prööv (prove). The 'v' here has the 'f' sound.

ͨ   This letter, when part of the 'ch' combination at the front of a word, takes the 'k' sound in all Low German words. This letter is rarely found at the beginning of a Low German word.

ð   This letter takes the voiced 'd' sound at the beginning of a syllable, but always takes the voiceless 't' sound when located at the end of a syllable or word.

Due to the second sound shift, it replaces the initial and interior letter 't' or 'tt' found in most corresponding Standard German words, such as Vater-voder (father), weiter-wieder (farther), Kette-kedden (chain), Tisch-disch (table), Teil-deel (part) - except in words that are "loaned" from Standard German, such as Blatt-blatt (leaf), Satz-satz (sentence), Kind-kind (child), or when the letter 't' is part of the letter combination 'st', or when it's the final letter in *some* words, such as Haut-huut (skin) and Wort-woort (word).

A 't' letter in Standard German usually becomes a 'd' letter in the Low German cognate word. But this does not apply to loan words. The word 'arbeit' (work) is loaned from Standard German. Therefore the 't' ending remains a 't' ending in Low German. This changes when an 'active' ending is applied. The phrase 'worker' in Low German is arbeider, where the 't' becomes 'd', and not only that, 'd' is pronounced with the th' sound. Most words that end in '**der**' will follow this example. A similar example, with a true Low German word, is the word 'lüüd (people). The 'd' is silent. On the other hand, the phrase 'a people', which is lüüder in Low German, activates the silent 'd' plus it uses the 'th' sound.

It seems unusual that a Standard German word with <u>one</u> 'd' or 't' (such as Va<u>t</u>er) will sometimes get spelled in Low German cognate (in some Low German dialects), with <u>two</u> 'd' letters (va<u>dd</u>er). There does not appear to be any historical precedent for this spelling, since the older German versions of this word contained only one 'd' or 't' letter; e.g. in Gothic the word was fa<u>d</u>ar. In the opposite direction, the <u>two</u> 't' letters in the Standard German word mutter (mother) show up as just one 'd' in the spelling of its Low German cognate 'moder', because that's how it was in Old Saxon.. When you find two 'd' letters in the Low German, it probably results from the strong influence of Standard German in some Low German areas, especially East Low German.

It takes the 'th' sound when part of the '-de' or '-der' endings of words and when the initial letter of a Low German word just in front of the 'r' letter, such as dröv (may). dreck (dirt), drink (drink), dree (three). The Old Saxon way of spelling dreck would have been ðreck, because þ appeared as 'ð' in Old Saxon. This did not happen in Old English, so it appears that the 'ð' came to be used in Old Saxon after the Anglo-Saxon invasion of Britain.

The English word *father* is spelled voder in Low German which has the two syllables vo-der. The first letter has the voiceless 'f' sound. The letter at the beginning of the second syllable has a voiced sound, which is 'th'. The word was originally spelled, in Old Saxon, as voðer.

The 'd' letter sometimes can have a 'th' sound, when found between vowels. This sound stems from the fact that the letter 'd' was often, in Primitive Germanic and early Old Saxon times, spelled either with a Runic letter called *thorn*, which looked like - þ, or one called *eth*, which like like - ð. Both stood for the 'th' sound. The letter þ was usually used at the front of a word and the letter ð was used within a word. A word like moder (mother) would have, in ancient days, been spelled *moðer* and would be pronounced like mo-the. Now it is easy to see how the original Old Saxon "moðer" becomes "mother" in English. In the Old Saxon version, the 'o' in moðer was a long 'o', so it probably sounded like *moh-the*. The same goes for the English word "other", which in Old Saxon was oðar, which we can now easily convert to its present day 'other'. The English words that correspond to the Old Saxon words erða and weurold aren't hard to figure out either.

Even though the letter 'd' is found within a word like the Low German word tieden (times), it doesn't get the 'th' sound. The reason is that this letter is part of the first closed syllable, rather than beginning the required second syllable.

As just discussed, this 'th' sound was more common in the previous century and was probably more prevalent in the center of North Germany. Current Low German speakers may have lost this sound entirely. And, of course, there are areas in which the 'th' sound was never commonly used or has been long forgotten. And anyone who is primarily familiar with Standard German will find it unusual to associate a 'th' sound with the letter 'd'.

The 'd' letter is *silent* when it is preceded by a vowel and followed by the vowel 'e" (lieden, broder).

e This letter takes the normal 'e' sound when it is the last letter of a stressed syllable or when positioned in a monosyllabic word before a single consonant. It also takes this sound when it is followed by two consonants and in many unstressed prefixes;as well as in the prefixes (be- and ge-) and suffixes.

It takes a weak 'e' sound (like 'uh') when found at the end of a word, in an unstressed position. This sound is called schwa. For example, take the Low German words beste or nexte, where the 'e' ending resembles more of a weak 'uh' sound.

However, the 'e' takes something akin to the German umlauted '*ä*' sound in a Low German word like beter (better), which stems from the Middle High German use of this letter. This '*ä*' can be found in the Standard German word gäste (guests), which to English ears sounds like it should be spelled 'ges-te'.

The vowel 'e' is silent when following the vowel 'i' (ie). In fact, a long 'i' is always written 'ie'.

f This letter takes the normal 'f' sound in a Low German word.

g This letter takes the normal 'g' sound at the beginning of a syllable, except in words of foreign origin.

It takes the "k" sound when at the end of a syllable, except in the case of the Low German '-ig' ending, in which case it has the "ch" sound. You may have noticed that the letters 'b', 'd' and 'g' consistently take their harder 'voiced' sound at the beginning of a syllable and their unvoiced softer sound ('p', 't', 'k') at the end of a syllable.

h This letter takes the normal 'h' sound. It is usually a silent letter when other than the first letter in a word. More specifically, it is silent when following a vowel in a monosyllabic word (mahl, kehr, hohn)

i This letter takes the normal short 'i' sound when it precedes two consonants and in most monosyllabic words. When the long 'i' sound is necessary, it is spelled 'ie'.

j This letter takes the normal English 'j' sound (as in joke), and in the case of words of foreign origin. Originally the letter 'j' was, up until the 15th century, written as 'i'. In Standard German it usually takes a 'y' sound.

m, n   These letters become geminated (doubled) when following a short vowel, e.g. dumm (dumb) or hänn (hands)

o   This letter takes the long 'o' sound when followed by 'h'.

It takes the sound of the 'o' in the English words log or dog, in the cases where the old letter 'å' was used. The Low German word bakåben (bake oven) is shown spelled the old way. The current spelling would be bakoben, where the 'o' has the sound of the letter 'o' in the English word dog, and sounds to the ear like 'aw'.

In most of the current (centrally located) Low German dialects, the long 'o' originally found in these Old Saxon words has become relaxed from an 'oh' sound to an 'aw' sound, so the later dialects might pronounce 'moder' more like something between *maw-the* and *moe-the*. And since the 'o' and 'u' letters are almost interchangeable, it might sometimes sound more like *muo-the*. In fact, in some dialects, it is spelled something like 'mudder' and pronounced more like *muod-the*. Some of this could be due to a strong Standard German influence in the area, because the Standard German word for mother is 'mutter'. In this fashion, it bears little resemblance to Old Saxon.

p   This letter, in Low German words, takes the place of the letter 'f' found at the end of Standard German words, such as Dorf-dorp (village), lauf-loop (run), scharf-scharp (sharp), Seife-seepn (soap), auf-up (up), and hoffe-hopp (hope).

The letter can also be found doubled. In a word like pepper, the vowel is a short 'e', and thus the 'p' letter is doubled. However, the two 'p' letters are split in two different syllables It sometimes has the 'b' sound. The Low German word *pepper*, for instance, can be broken into two syllables; pep-per. The first 'p' is voiceless. The 'p' at the beginning of the second syllable is voiced (has the 'b' sound). The pronunciation would sound like pap-ba, because the second 'p' is at the beginning of a syllable. The use of a voiceless sound at the beginning of a word, and a voiced sound at the beginning of a second syllable is found in many Low German and English words. This is a case which bears some resemblance to the 'th' sound that is applied to the letters 'd' or 't', if they begin the second syllable in a word. This is less evident when spoken in English, but the second 'p' in the English word pepper does have something of a 'b' sound.

If you spelled the previously mentioned English word 'pepper' as peper, the same result would obtain. The second 'p' letter does, after all, begin the second syllable. A medial 'p' is likewise pronounced with a 'b' sound. Therefore, the pronunciation would sound like pa-ba, which is basically indistinguishable from pap-ba.

q   This letter becomes part of the 'qu' letter combination and is always pronounced as 'kw' in all Low German words. It probably stems originally from the Primitive German letter 'qu', which came from the ancient Indo-European letter q^w.

r   This letter takes the normal 'r' sound.

s   This letter takes the normal 's' sound at the end of a word if it is preceded by a short vowel (example hüs).

It also takes the normal 's' sound in front of the letters l, m, n, w, p, t.

It takes the 'z' sound at the beginning of a word (examples söben or sehn or sönnen), or at the beginning of a syllable, or at the end of a *plural* word if it is preceded by a long monophthong vowel (example hüüs) or if medial between two vowels (example lesen).

t   This letter takes the 'th' sound when part of the '-te' or 'ter' endings. Note that the 't' in the Low German word laat (late) has the 't' sound, while the comparative later has the 'th' sound. This results from the fact that the one syllable word laat is turned into the 'comparative' two syllable word later (la-ter) and the probable Old Saxon way of spelling the word was laðer or loðer.

It also takes the 'th' sound when the 't' is the initial letter just in front of the letter 'r', such as in the word trüg (return).

It takes the place of the letter 'z' as found most corresponding Standard German words, such as Zwei-twee (two), Zeit-tied (time) or Zehn-teihn (ten).

And it takes the place of the letter 's' or 'ss' as found in corresponding Standard German words, such as anfassen-anfaten (take hold), Wasser-woter (water), Strasse-straat (street), Distel-diessel (thistle), or muss-mutt (must).

u   Thus letter takes the normal 'u' sound.

v   This letter takes the normal 'v' sound in words of foreign origin.

It takes the normal 'f' sound in most Low German words.

It is replaced with the 'w' letter if the 'v' sound is found at the front of

a syllable in a multiple syllable word, such as leewe (dear) and pulwer
(powder) and halwe (half), but it still uses the 'v' sound.
It uses the 'f' sound at the end of a *verb* (bliev, shuuv, graav, etc.) but
uses 'f' sound at the end of a *noun* (deef, lief, half, kalf, breef, etc.) -
(in English the noun mischief has an 'f' letter ending but its action denoting
counterpart, the word mischievious, instead uses the v' letter).

It takes the place of the letter 'f' as found in some Standard German
words, such as Stiefel-stevel (boot) or Teufel-düvel (devil), although
one may also find the 'b' letter in place of the 'v' or may find the 'b'
sound used with the 'v' letter (a remnant of the ancient ƀ letter).

It normally remains a 'v' spelling if the corresponding Standard
German word begins with a 'v'.

The English word *weaver* has two syllables; wea-ver. In Low German it is
wever. The first letter 'w' has the 'v' sound. The letter beginning the second
syllable has an *almost* 'v' sound, more like a rough 'f' sound.. This sound is a
remnant of the old letter ƀ Normally the 'v' sound requires the lower lip and
teeth to meet. The old letter ƀ was pronounced without touching the teeth, and
the lips were placed close, but not touching, as the air is forced out. The old
way of spelling this word was feb--er. And that's why the letter at the
beginning of the second syllable has the *almost* 'v' sound.

** w** This letter, with a 'v' sound, is used in words that have a 'b' in the
Standard German word, such as the Standard German word ober and
the Low German öwer (over); also aber-ower (but), beliebt-belevt
(dear), rüber-röwer, (across), etc.

Similarly, this letter is used at the beginning of a second syllable, when
the present case stem of the Low German word ends in 'v' or 'f', such as in
the words leev-leewe (dear) or half-halwig (half), and takes the 'v' sound in all
Low German words.

This letter was spelled uu (two 'u' letters) after a consonant, in Old
Saxon, but between vowels it was spelled as 'w'.

x This letter takes the 'eks' sound, such as can be found in nix (nothing) or fix
(nice).

y This letter takes the 'y' sound when it is the last letter of a syllable, in
unstressed syllables, and in words of foreign origin.

It also takes this sound when preceding two or more consonants.

ſ   This letter developed from the 's' letter as used in ancient times, and
            the Primitive German 'z' changed in some words to 'r'.

The following comments regard the sounds of letters not found in English, especially
the umlaut letters.

ö   The letter 'ö' can be pronounced as one pronounces the 'ur' in the
           English word "slur" or close to the 'ir' in the English word "dirt".

ü   The letter 'ü' can be pronounced with a sound that lies about halfway
           between 'o' and 'e'.

There are other special letters and letter combinations that have differing pronunciation
characteristics in English, Low German and Standard German.

The following are comments about letter combinations not common in English, but are
found quite commonly in Low German.

ch   The letter combination 'ch' takes the sound of a 'k' letter after 'a'
           (sack, dack) and is spelled 'ck'.

           It takes the gutteral sound in the German word 'mi<u>ch</u>' after o, e, i, u,
           au, ai, ei, eu, äu (noch, doch). There is no English equivalent sound for
           this gutteral 'ch' at the end of words.

ig   This letter combination, found at the end of Low German words which
           correspond to Standard German have an (-ich) endinge, have a rough
           sound something like a raspy 'clear the throat' sound like that
           mentioned in the preceding paragraph. The (-ich) ending on some
           Standard German words, corresponding to Low German words that
           end in '-ig', is pronounced generally the same.

sch,sh,s These letter combinations involve a particular difference between Low
           German spelling and Standard German spelling. The combination
           'sch' is quite common in Standard German. The 's' is used when it
           precedes 'p' (sprechen) or 't' (strich), in the northern section of Germany.
           The change to'sch' spelling in Standard German began in the 13th century and
           moved northward, but ran out of steam as the change reached the north.

           Which letter combination is used for spelling the Low German word lies with
           the vowel that follows the letter combination. The following are guidelines.

           In corresponding Low German words, the spelling **'sch'** is used when
           these letters are followed by 'a', 'ä', 'o', or 'ö'. It is pronounced with
           the normal 'sh' sound. Example words are schaap (sheep), school
           (school) and schoh (shoe). The 'sch' is retained when also found at the

end of the cognate Standard German word, e.g. wasch.

In corresponding Low German words, the spelling '**sh**' is used when these letters are followed by 'i', 'e', 'u', 'ü', or 'r'. It is pronounced with the normal 'sh' sound. Example words are sheev (crooked), shimp (scold), shuuv (shove) and shriev (write). Does not apply when the 'e' is found in a suffix ('-en' or '-er'). This little rule can be remember with the phrase "shier you", which mean 'sh' is used with 'i','e','r' and 'u'.

In corresponding Low German words, the spelling 's' is used when this letter is followed by any letter not mentioned in the previous two paragraphs (usually 'p', 't', 'l', 'm', 'n'). Examples are speel (play), strick (rope), slaag (strike), smeck (taste) and snuut (snout).

The additional unusual letter combinations 'dt', 'pf', 'ff', 'ph', 'ss (ß)', and 'sz' are used in the Standard German language, but *not* in the Low German language.

Then there is the case of double vowel situations usually result in either diphthongs or monophthongs.

The following section discusses diphthongs and monophthongs. Some are found in Standard German, but many more are found in Low German. In Standard German they sound as follows.

Diphthongs		Monophthongs	.
au	sounds like 'ou' in mouse	aa	sounds like 'a' in father
ai, ei	sounds like 'i' in mine	oo	sounds like 'o' in wrote
eu, äu	sounds like 'oi' in oil	ee	sounds like 'a' in game

Low German diphthongs can be sounded in different ways, even when they involve the same two vowels. In the sounds of diphthongs, the first noted sound *glides* into the second noted sound, with both sounds together in one syllable. Some diphthongs can have a variety of sounds, depending on the derivative history of the word. In Low German they sound as follows.

Diphthongs			Monophthongs	.
			ei	sounds like 'i' in high
aa	'ah' into 'oh'		aa	sounds like 'a' in father
ee	'ae' into 'uh' 'aa' into 'uh'		ee	sounds like 'a' in pay
	'ee' into 'uh' 'ae' into 'ee'			
ie	'ee' into 'uh'		ie	sounds like 'ee' in beet
oo	'aw' into 'uh' 'oo' into 'uh'		oo	sounds like 'o' in wrote
	'ah' into 'oo'			
uu	'oo' into 'uh'		uu	sounds like 'oo' in moose
öö	'oe' into 'uh'		öö	sounds like 'er' in jerk
üü	'ue' into 'uh'		üü	*

236

* There is no English equivalent sound for the monophthong 'üü'. The sound given for the monophthong 'öö is only approximate.

Diphthongs and monophthongs are covered in more detail near the end of this chapter.

Next is discussed the matter of *silent letters.* They exist in nearly every language. The *silent letters* are, of course, not pronounced. Although written, they are not sounded at all in the word.

It is common in English to find the letters 'g' or 'h' written but unpronounced in a word. This is also true sometimes, in Low German, for the letters 'g', 'h', 'd' or 't'.

In Low German, there are differences regarding silent letters that are not found in the other languages. In the ancient versions of the German language there were no silent letters. When there was a doubled letter, such as gg, both letters were given equal weight in pronunciation.

In Standard German the 'd' in the word *zufrieden* (satisfied) is written and pronounced. In its Low German cognate, tofree, the 'd' is gone. However, the word could also be legitimately spelled *tofrede,* with the 'd' as silent. This is an example of a word where it is not necessary to write the silent letter in order for the word to be recognizable. There are other words where recognition is aided and confusion avoided by keeping the silent letter in the spelling of the word. An example of this is the word broder (brother), which would not be easily recognized if spelled broer. These silent letters are identified throughout this book by a short horizontal line drawn through them, which will look like đ for the letter 'd' (not applicable to '-b-', where the longer horizontal line identifies the ancient Primitive German letter that stood for 'v').

Generally speaking, a 'd' letter between two vowels in Low German will be silent. Another example is the Standard German word kneten (knead), which is kneden in Low German, with a silent 'd'.

The 'h' silent letter should be kept in spelling of words, even though it is not pronounced. Another letter falls into the same category. The word arfen (peas) has a letter 'r' that is silent, although some might suggest that it is slightly pronounced. In any event, it should always be spelled.

Whether a 'silent' letter needs to be used in spelling is an important question. Sometimes they should be used anyway, just to make the word clear and unambiguous. One guiding rule might be that, if the letter 'd' is to be pronounced with the 'th' sound, then it should be used in the spelling. In areas where the 'th' pronunciation of 'd' has been lost, then this wouldn't apply. However, there are some words where the 'silent' letter should be kept in the spelling, to avoid confusion between similar words.

The following is a list of words that contain silent letters, but their intelligibility * would benefit from keeping the silent letter in the spelling. The word is shown in both ways, keeping the letter and not keeping it. It appears that the spelling in the last column makes pronunciation difficult to comprehend. It is recommended that the spelling of these words keep the silent letter. You can't, in normal writing, make the use of this silent letter recognizable, as we've done in this book with a short line. It is up to the speaker to *know* that the silent letter shouldn't be pronounced.

* what's the big deal about Mississippi having 4 'i' letters?

Ltr	*Standard German*		*Low German*	
ð	schlitten	(slide)	sle~~d~~en	sleen
	breiten	(widen)	bre~~d~~en	breen
	leiden	(lead)	lie~~d~~en	lieen
	roten	(red one)	ru~~d~~en	ruen
	reiter	(rider)	rie~~d~~en	rien
	bruder	(brother)	bro~~d~~er	broer
	brette	(boards)	bre~~d~~en	breen
	kette	(chain)	ke~~dd~~en	keen
	zeiten	(times)	tie~~d~~ens	tiens
	bedeuten	(mean)	bedü~~d~~en	bedüen
	sneiden	(cut)	snie~~d~~en	snien
t	Posten	(post)	pos~~t~~en	posen
	Gerste	(barley)	gars~~t~~en	garsen
ħ	geh	(go)	goh	go
	jahr	(year)	johr	jor
	geht	(goes)	geiht	geit
	zehn	(ten)	teihn	tein

There are other such words where leaving the letter out still leaves the word as easily recognizable and pronounce-able. It is recommended that the silent letter be left out.

Ltr	*Standard German*		*Low German*	
ð	Wetter	(weather)	we~~dd~~er	weer or wedder
	werden	(become)	wer~~d~~en	weern
	worden	(became)	wor~~d~~en	worrn or woren
t	Kiste	(crate)	kas~~t~~en	kassen
	husten	(cough)	hus~~t~~en	hussen

In the next section some additional letter combinations are discussed, which involved spelling and pronunciation considerations relevant to Low German.

chs - ss   The 'chs' ending of Standard German words is simplified to 'ss in corresponding Low German words: wuchs becomes wuss (grow).

dd   The 'dd' letters appear in Low German in those words that have 'tt' in Standard German. For example, Butter-bodder (butter), wetter-wedder (weather), and kletter-kladder (climb).

The doubling of the letter 'd' is unusual in that both 'd's aren't necessarily pronounced the same. The first 'd' has the normal 'd' sound and the second one has more of the 'th' sound previously described. For instance, the word fudder (feed) would sound like fud-the. The 'd' letter that begins the second syllable is the one that gets the 'th' sound (this does not apply to compound words, like meddag). This also applies in words that don't contain a double 'd'. For instance, the word voder (father); the 'd' begins the second syllable and thus is pronounced with the 'th' sound. The same applies to words like rieder (rider) and kleeder (dresses). This phenomenon also applies to the letter 't'. For instance, there are words like finster (window), swester (sister), Ooster (Easter), and woter (water). The 't' letter gets the 'th' sound. For instance, the word 'woter' is usually pronounced. 'vaw-the'.

dd - ll   There is also a group of words involving the 'dd' combination, where there is an 'e' in front and an 'e' in back of it, where 'dd' can assimilate to 'll' in some dialects. The Standard German word Federn (feathers), for instance, becomes the Low German word feddern, and in some other dialects it becomes fellern. The same happens to the Standard German words Leder (leather) and wieder (again). Its cognate words in Low German are ledder (second 'd' has the 'th' sound) or optionally leller and the second cognate word is weller (again) or optionally wedder.

dr   The 'd' letter that you find at the front of a word and that precedes the letter 'r' is another case of the 'th' sound. One would, for instance, pronounce the Low German word for the English word "three" as 'three', even though spelled as 'dree'. Here again, it is easy to see from where came the English word "three".

ee - eck   The 'e' letter that precedes a 'k' is pronounced differently than one that precedes 'ck'. For instance, in words like dreck (dirt) and eck (corner) and deckel (lid), the 'e' is pronounced as it is in the English word "heck". In words like rek (calculate) and brek

239

(break) and bek (stream), the 'e' is pronounced as the 'a' in the English word "lack". In some dialects, this latter 'e' sound is represented by the letter 'ä'.

en - n   The '-en' endings on certain words are spelled, but not necessarily pronounced. For instance, take as examples such words as eten (eat), buten (outside), meten (measure), töben (wait), glöben (believe, köken (kitchen), tuten (paper sack), klimmen (pinch), dregen (carry), slepen (drag), and teken (badge). The 'e' in the word's ending is not pronounced. Some people show this in the spelling by using an apostrophe in its place (et'n or klimm'n, for example).   However, sometimes when one might expect an '-en' ending, there is instead just an '-n' ending. This applies when the roots of words end with an 'l' or 'r'. Examples of this are muurn (walls), luern (wait), huurn (horns), maaln (draw), worrn (become), uuln (owls), and muuln (mouths).

ff - gg   Double consonants like 'ff' and 'gg' are a special case in Low German, especially after a short vowel. As shown in the separate section on verb conjugation, the use of consonants varies with person and number.

Using 1ˢᵗ person present tense words like bliev (stay), krieg (get), geev (give), fleeg (fly), and leg (lay), the different uses of double consonants will be shown. In the 2ⁿᵈ and 3ʳᵈ person, the ending consonant is *doubled*, but the ending will vary. The 2ⁿᵈ person *singular* (du) in Low German for these words comes out as follows (with an 's' ending).

> du ....bliffs (stays), kriggs(gets), giffs (gives), flüggs (flies), leggs (lays), seggs (say)

The 3ʳᵈ person *singular* (he, se, dat) in Low German for these words comes out as follows (with a 't' ending).

> he, se, dat ..... blifft (stays), kriggt (gets), gifft (gives), flüggt (flies), leggt (lays), seggt (says)

The 1ˢᵗ, 2ⁿᵈ and 3ʳᵈ person *plural* (wi, ji, se) in Low German for these words comes out as follows (without a doubled consonant, but with a 't' ending).

> wi, ji, se......... blieft (stay), kriegt (get), geevt (give), fleegt (fly), leegt (lay), seegt (say)

240

ld -.ll, lt - ll Another small group of words with 'ld' or 'lt' in the Standard German word will assimilate to 'll' in the Low German cognate. Examples for 'ld' are Bilder-biller (pictures) and Schuldig-shullig (guilt). As an aside, the English word children can be heard, in the deep south, pronounced as chillen. In the Louisiana Bayous it can be heard pronounced as chirren. This shows how easy certain sound changes can occur. Examples for 'lt' are Schulter-shullen (shoulder) and halten-hallen (usually written halen).

ou - au These letter combinations have undergone many changes over the centuries. Even in English, they can produce a variety of sounds. Here are several examples, using the 'ou' combination.

OU with "ow" sound	OU with "oh" sound	OU with "aw" sound
noun, south	soul, shoulder	sought, cough

OU with "ur" sound	OU with "uu" sound	OU with "u" sound
nourish	soup, loupe	should

There are similar, but fewer, examples for the 'au' combination.

AU with "aa" sound	AU with "aw" sound	AU with "or" sound
laugh	taught, caught	laurel

Note how often these letter combinations are directly followed by certain letters, e.g. 'r', 'l', 'p' and 'gh'. The latter 'gh' is related to the letter 'h'.

or - ol - oh In Low German, when the letters 'r', 'l' and 'h' follow vowels, a wide variety of sounds is generated. There are several words that seem to have a concensus among the dialects with regard to spelling and pronunciation. This discussion investigates whether they influence the choice of 'a' or 'o'. The cognate Standard words are also given, to see if their spelling might have an impact.

The word johr (year) is always spelled with the 'o' letter, where in Standard German the letter is 'a' (jahr). The Low German pronunciation can be approximated with the sound 'jaw-a'. The same applies to the word wohr (true), which is pronounced 'vaw-a'. Both of these remind one of the å letter, discussed at length elsewhere.

The words hohn (rooster) is almost always spelled with the 'o' letter and it's Standard German cognate is spelled with an 'a' (hahn). Again the pronunciation is widely accepted as approximating

241

"hawn". Similar words are st<u>o</u>h (stand) and g<u>o</u>h (go),
pronunciated as "st<u>aw</u>n" and "g<u>aw</u>n".

Additional words are shown below, broken out by types of
letter combinations.

Low German	Std Ger.		Low German	Std. Ger.

ahl... <u>with the "ah" sound</u>

   prahl (brag)   prahl
   mahl (meal)   mahl
   dahl (down)   nieder
   betahl (pay)   bezahl
   pahl (pole)   pfahl

ohl.. <u>with the "oe" sound</u>

   möhl (mill)   mühle
   föhl (feel)   fühle
   föhr (drive)   fahr

ahn... <u>with the "ah" sound</u>

   ahn (without)   ohne

ohn... <u>with the "aw" sound</u>

   dohn (done)   getan
   lohm (clay)   lehm
   stohn (stand)   stehen
   bohn (lane)   bahn
   gohn (walk)   gehen
   hohn (rooster)   hahn
   ohnung (idea)   ahnung

ahr... *

ohr... <u>with the "aw" sound</u>

   wohr (true)   wahr
   johr (year)   jahr

* no Low German words use this pattern.

o - a   There appears to be no general rule, so the choice of 'o' versus 'a' made
here has been made by virture of the pronunciation of the first syllable. In
some dialects words like dahl and prahl might be written daal and praal.

In some Low German words, the letter 'a' or 'o' appears within
an open syllable. For instance, the Low German word 'm<u>o</u>ken'
(make) is related to the Standard German word 'm<u>a</u>chen'. The
first syllable in mo-ken is an open and stressed syllable. The word
'broken' (broken) is similar. Here the 'o' is pronounced 'aw' and
it is part of an open and stressed syllable. Whether it is part of an
open syllable may have some impact on the choice.

The Old Saxon cognate word for Low German 'moken' is
'm<u>a</u>kon', which has the 'a' letter. One might expect Low German
and its ancestor Old Saxon to use the same letter. So why do most

242

people use the 'o' letter in the Low German moken? While Old Saxon evolved into Middle Low German and later Platt Düütsch, these letters underwent further change. Therefore, Old Saxon will not always agree with Low German with respect to vowels. On the other hand, the similarity between Old Saxon and Norse language suggest that 'makon' may have been spelled with 'å' rather than 'a' and this distinction became lost in the halls of time.

The Low German word woter (water) is also often spelled water, perhaps either because the Standard German cognate is spelled wasser or because it is spelled *water* in English. However, since it is part of an open syllable and it is pronounced 'vaw-the', the spelling should arguably be woter.

This would influence the spelling of the following words as well.

Low German		Standard German
obend	(evening)	abend
ower	(but)	aber
oten	(breath)	atem
dor	(there)	da
gobel	(fork)	gabel
nogel	(nail)	nagel
Voder	(father)	Vater
wogen	(wagon)	wagen

These words have the 'o' followed by 'r', 'l', 'm', or 'n' and the 'o' should have the 'aw' sound.

Low German		Standard German
korden	(card)	Karte
mol	(once)	mal
solt	(salt)	Salz
olt	(old)	alt
homer	(hammer)	Hamer
komer	(chamber)	Kammer

Often the initial 'a' in a Standard German word is also used as the initial letter in the Low German loan words.

Low German		Standard German
appel	(apple)	apfel
as	(as)	as
arbeid	(work)	arbeit
arm	(arm)	arm

And there are some words in which the initial 'o' in Standard German is also the initial letter in the Low German cognate.

Low German	Standard German
oben (oven)	offen
oder (or else)	oder
open (open)	offen
ossen (oxen)	ochsen

Generally speaking, if the sound to be in pronunciation is 'ah', then the 'a' letter should be used. If it has the 'aw' pronunciation, the either 'o' or 'å' should be used in spelling the words.

There are some words that are the same in Low and Standard German and therefore they are spelled the same. The reason for this similarity is the fact that the 'an-' part of the word is just a prefix.

<u>an</u>fang, <u>an</u>kommen, anklogen, and <u>an</u>ker

o - u This relationship has been addressed previously, but the pattern is so strong that further analysis could be helpful. The word 'schuh' in Standard German becomes 'schoh' in Low German. This applies to virtually every dialect as well. Below are further examples, going in both directions.

Low German		Standard German
moder	(mother)	Mutter
bodder	(butter)	Butter
möhl	(mill)	Mühle
föhl	(feel)	Fühle
künig	(king)	König

pp The gemination of the letter 'p' occur at the ends of words that contain a short vowel. To reinforce this, take note of the words saag (saw), daag (days) and loop (run), where the vowels are <u>long</u> and the consonant is not geminated.

Low German		Standard German
stipp	(gravy)	Tunke
lipp	(lip)	Lippe
ropp	(onto)	auf
hopp	(hope)	Hoffe
stopp	(stuff)	stopfen
shipp	(ship)	Schiffe

st - ß The letter combination 'st' in Standard German words becomes 'ss in the Low German cognate.

Low German		Standard German
possen	(post)	Posten
hussen	(cough)	Husten

tt The doubling of the letter 't' functions similarly to the doubling of the 'd' letter. The second 't', because it starts the second syllable, will have the 'th' sound.

The geminated 't' situation comes up usually following a <u>short</u> vowel in a monosyllabic word. Examples are satt (satiated), katt (cat), fett (fat), snitt (cut), glatt (pretty), and bett (bed). By the way, these are also all load words from Standard German. To reinforce this rule about gemination and short vowels, notice that words like kruut (weed) and bööt (alight) have *long* vowels and their 't' isn't geminated.

nd - nn A Standard German word with 'nd' becomes assimilated to 'nn' in the Low German cognate The second 'n' has, for historical reasons associatied with the letter 'd' (especially in North Saxon), the 'th' sound.. For instance, one might pronounce anner as an-the; pretty close to how it would have been pronounced in 5th century Gothic. That aspect of 'n' is why you'll find some '**n**' letters here set out in bold print, as a reminder of this old 'th' sound.

Low German		Standard German
wun**n**er	(wonder)	Wunder
hun**n**ert	(hundred)	Hundert
kin**n**er	(children)	Kinder
wan**n**er	(wander)	wander
bin**n**en	(bind)	binden
an**n**er *	(other)	ander

* in Old Norse it is annar and in Gothic it was anÞar (the Þ is the Runic letter, pronounced 'th').

The 'th' sound of the second 'n' does not apply to some words. For instance, the English word windy is 'winnig' in Low German. The base word 'wind' does end with (-nd). However, the second 'n' does not have a 'th' sound. It is assumed that the reason for this is that the 'th' sound is not sound-compatible with the '-ig' sound that would just follow the 'th' sound. It is just too awkward.

245

Such pronunciation problems have caused variations in languages over the centuries. The same is true for the English word tied, which is bunnen in Low German, but the second 'n' in bunnen is not pronounced 'th'. It is also true for lebinnig (alive), which is lebendig in Standard German.

nt - nn　　A Standard German word with 'nt' becomes 'nn' in the Low German cognate. Here again, the 't' that becomes the 'n' carries with it the old 'th' sound.

Low German		Standard German
ünner	(underneath)	unten
innerest	(interest)	interesse
hinner	(behind)	hinter

au, u - uu
ü　　Standard German words that have 'au' in them often correspond to Low German cognate words with 'u', 'ü' or 'uu' in them. And those with 'äu' often correspond to Low German cognates with 'ü' or 'üü' in them. There seems to be a pattern with regard to whether they become a single versus double vowel and also when they become an umlaut vowel.

First note that when the Standard German word has the vowels in a closed syllable, it will also be a closed syllable in the Low German cognate word. If the word has the vowel within a closed syllable (with no ending or with a simple 'e' type ending, i.e. 'e', er', 'en'), then the Low German will have *two* vowels. If there is an open syllable, then the Low German will have just *one* vowel If there is an umlaut in the Standard German word, it will likely have an umlaut in the Low German cognate word.

The following gives a few examples of these situations.

English	In Closed Syllables Standard GErman	Low German
fence	Zaun	tuun
exchange	tausch	tuusch
belly	Bauch	buuk
hardly	kaum	kuum
mouth	Maul	muul
mouse	Maus	muus
outside	raus	ruut
loud	laut	luut
sour	Sau-er	suur

246

skin	Haut	huut
rejoice	jauchz-en	juuchen
duck	tauch-en	duuken

	In Open Syllables	
English	Standard German	Low German
sad	trau-rig	trurig
thousand	Tau-send	dusend
stumble	tau-meln	tumeln
mildly warm	Lauwarm	lüwarm
thumb	dau-men	dumen

au, oo - öö
üü Standard German words that have 'au' in them can also often Low German words with 'oo', 'öö' or 'üü' in them. There is a pattern as to when the change to one vowel or two vowels. As in the previous section, the existence of an closed or open syllable appears to be influential.

	In Closed Syllables	
English	Standard German	Low German
lice	Läus-e	lüüs
baptize	Tauf	dööp
tree	Baum	Boom
trees	Bäum-e	Bööm
run	lauf	loop
buy	kauf	kööp
seam	Saum	soom
hat	hut	hoot
foot	fuß	foot
sweet	süss	sööt
grape	Traub-e	duuf
speed	saus-en	suusen

	In Closed Syllables	
English	Standard German	Low German
sound	lau-ten	ton
robber	räu-ber	röber
wife	Frau	fro
believe	glau-ben	glöv

There are some loan words that have 'au' in both Standard German and Low German, such as kauen (chew), sau (sow), blau (blue) and dau (dew). The Standard German for the last word mentioned is 'Tau', but all that changes is the normal Low German 'd' substitution for the Standard German 't'.

247

DOUBLE VOWELS

In the section immediately preceding, the discussion of double vowels mentioned that they replaced long vowels in older versions of Low German. There are other double vowel situations that may warrant particular spelling and pronunciation guidelines.

Diphthong

The term diphthong refers to two identical vowels in succession, occurring within one given syllable, and one of the two vowels becomes pronounced differently from its neighboring vowel. For example, the Low German word for beer has a different sound for each of the '*e*' vowels. It has both '*e*' vowels in the first syllable; bee-r. The first '*e*' vowel glides or melts into the second '*e*' vowel, but each has a very distinguishably different sound. You can find diphthongs in English too, such as the 'ou' in "house" and 'oo' in the word "poor".

A particularly interesting case is that of the Low German word 'speeldeel', which refers to a stage play. There are two 'ee' situations in the same word, but they are not pronounced the same. The pronunciation is discussed within the following list.

There is also a kind of diphthong that has just one letter, such as the letter *i*. This is true even in English, although it is seldom noticed. The 'i' in the word hide is an example. There is also the word *live*, as in the infinitive phrase *to live*, and the same word *live*, as it is used as a pronoun in the phrase *it is a live show*. In the first word *live*, the letter *i* has just the one conventional fairly short sound. In the second word *live*, the long *i* sound quickly melts into a short *i* sound, as the sound rolls into the following *v* sound. This kind of sound is caused somewhat by the kind of letter that follows, and the way the mouth has to function to make the sounds.

Diphthongs can be divided into two types, *rising* and *falling*, with regard to the pronunciation of the second vowel.

> If the second of the two vowels is stresses more than the first, than it is a *rising* diphthong. An example might be the diphthong in the Low German word 'fein' or in the word 'book'.

> A *falling* diphthong has the most stress on the first vowel. An example of this might be found in the word 'beer' or in the word 'füür'. Most of them are of the *falling* variety, represented by a sound like 'uh'.

On the next few pages a number of examples of diphthongs and monophthongs area give, along with some indications of preferred pronunciation of the vowels. They are compared to cognate Standard German words.

Diphthong: OO (AR in the Standard German word)

Sounded as ... aw-uh. The first *o* sounds like the *o* in the English word log. The second *o* sounds like the *o* in the English word come (falling).

Platt Düütsch	English	Standard German
boort	beard	Bart
goorn	garden	Garten
hoor	hair	Haar
kloor	clear	Klar
koor	cart	Karre
oort	kind	art
poor	pair	paar
goor	done cooking	gar

In the Low German word the *oo* diphthong is followed by *r* : it has 'or' while the Standard German has 'ar'.

Diphthong: OO (OR or UR in the Standard German word)

Sounded as oo-uh. The first *o* sounds like the *o* in the English word move. The second *o* sounds like the *o* in the English word come (falling).

Platt Düütsch	English	Standard German
doorn	thorn	Dorn
koorn	corn	Korn
pastoor	pastor	Pastor
spoor	spure	spur
toorn	tower	Turm
moor	moor	Moor

In the Low German word the *oo* diphthong is followed by *r* : it has 'or' while the Standard German has 'or' or 'ur'.

Diphthong: OO (U with *oo* sound or A in Standard German word)

Sounded as ah-oo. The first *o* sounds like the *o* in the English word box. The second *o* sounds like 'o' in the English word move (rising).

Platt Düütsch	English	Standard German
book	book	Buch
klook	smart	klug
dook	cloth	Tuch
genoog	enough	genug

ploog	plow	Pflug
hoot	hat	Hut
blood	blood	Blut
good	good	gut
proov	test	prüfen
school	school	Schule
bloom	flower	Blume
knoos	bread heel	(Brotende)
moot	courage	Mut
hook	hook	Haken
goos	goose	Gans
woort	word	Wort

Diphthong: ÖÖ (Ä, Ü or U in the Standard German word)

Sounded as oe-uh. The first *ö* is sounded something like the *i* in the English word g*i*rl. The second *ö* sounds more like the *o* in the English word c*o*me.

Platt Düütsch	*English*	*Standard German*
wöör	was	wäre
döör	door	Tur
böör	lift	(heben)
möör	mushy	(Matsch)
blöör	leaves	Blätter
höör	herd	hüten
röör	tires	Räder

In the Low German word, the *öö* is consistently followed by *r*.

What causes one Low German word to use *oo* and another use *öö*? For historical reasons it seems that an *ä* or *ü* in the Standard German word will see a corresponding *öö* in the Low German word.

Diphthong: UU (EU, AU or U in Standard German)

Sounded as oo-uh. The first u sounds like the *u* in the English word d*u*ke. The second *u* sounds like *u* in the English word b*u*t (falling).

Platt Düütsch	*English*	*Standard German*
geduur	patience	Geduld
duur	last	dauer
suur	sour	sauer
muul	mouth	Maul
luurn	await	lauern

luud	loud	laut
buur	farmer	Bauer
uul	owl	Eule

In the Low German word the *uu* will be followed by *r* or *l* (the d is silent). This serves to differentiate these diphthong words from Standard German words with *u* or *au*, which are instead monophthong words in the Low German.

Diphthong: ÜÜ (EU in the Standard German word)

Sounded as ue-uh. The first *ü* is sounded like the *i* in the English word b*i*rd. The second *ü* sounds like the *u* in the English word b*u*t (falling).

Platt Düütsch	English	Standard German
lüüd	people	Leute
stüür	steer	steuern
füür	fire	Feuer
klüür	color	(Farbe)
düür	expensive	teuer
hüür	hire	(Miete)

In the Low German word the *üü* is followed by *r* (the d is silent). It appears that the *eu* in Standard German corresponds to *üü* in Low German.

Diphthong: EE (E or EE or IE in the Standard German word)

Sounded as aa-uh. The first *e* sound is like the *a* in the English word b*a*d. The second *e* sounds like *o* in the English word c*o*me (falling).

Platt Düütsch	English	Standard German
veel	much	viel
speel	play	spiel
smeer	smear	Schmier
weer	weather	Wetter
geel	yellow	Gelb
peerd	horse	Pferd
steed	location	Stell
beern	berry	Beere

The Low German words have the *ee* diphthong followed by *r* or *l*. The d in steed is silent. A Low German word like speeldeel (stage play) is unique, in that the first 'ee' sounds like aa-uh and the second 'ee' sounds ae-uh.

Diphthong: <u>EE</u> (IE or E in the Standard German)

<u>Sounded as ae-ee</u>. The first *e* sound is like the *e* in the English word g*e*t. The second *e* sounds like *e* in the English word b*e* (falling).

Platt Düütsch	English	Standard German
steev	stiff	Stief
weeg	weigh	wiegen
geev	give	gebe
leev	live	lebe
beev	tremble	beben

Diphthong: <u>EE</u> (IE in the Standard German word)

<u>Sounded as ae-uh</u>. The first *e* sound is like the <u>e</u> in the English word h*e*y. The second *e* sounds like the *o* in the English word c*o*me (falling).

Platt Düütsch	English	Standard German
probeer	try	probier
maneer	manners	Manieren
beer	beer	Bier
veer	four	Vier
beest	beast	Bestie
deep	deep	tief
sheet	shoot	schiess
fleeg	fly	flieg
preester	priest	Priester
deen	earn	dienen
deev	thief	Dieb
sheev	crooked	schief

Diphthong: EE (E or IE in the Standard German word)

<u>Sounded as ee-uh</u>. The first *e* sound is like the *e* in the English word b*e*. The second *e* sound is like the *o* in the English word c*o*me (falling).

Platt Düütsch	English	Standard German
passeer	come to pass	passier
spazeeren	stroll	spazieren
amuseern	amuse	amusieren
weern	become	werden
leehr	learn	lehr
geern	dearly	gern
weert	worth	wert

252

steern	stars	Stern
meehr	more	mehr
kneen	knees	knienn
deern	girl	(Mädchen)
eerd	earth	Erde
steert	tail	(Schwanz)

The *ee* diphthong in the Low German word is followed by an *r* .

Diphthong: EE (EI in the Standard German word)

Sounded as ae-uh. The first *e* is sounded like the *a* in the English word b*a*d. The second *e* is sounds like *u* in the English word b*u*t (falling).

Platt Düütsch	English	Standard German
week	week	(Woche)
nees	nose	(Nase)
heel	whole	heil
deel	part	teil
twee	two	zwei
schree	cry	schrei
free	free	frei
blee	lead	blei
dree	three	drei
fleesch	meat	Fleisch
geest	spirit	Geist
meester	master	Meister

Diphthong: IE (E or EI or I in the Standard German word)

Sounded as ee-uh. The *i* sound is like the *ee* in the English word b*ee*. The *e* sound is like the *o* in the English word c*o*me (falling).

Platt Düütsch	English	Standard German
twiern	twine	Zwirn
shier	sheer	rein
iel	hurry	eil
kiel	wedge	Keil
striet	argue	streit
lieder	leader	Leiter
snieder	tailor	Sneider
rieder	rider	Reiter
shier	shears	Schere
fier	celebrate	feier

biert	appear	(ähneln)
fiel	file	Feile
stiert	tail	Schwanz

It is common for Standard German words with *ei* to have *ie* in the corresponding Low German word. The 'd' letter in bold type in the Low German words call attention to the 'th' sound of this letter.

Diphthong: <u>AA</u> (A in the Standard German word)

<u>Sounded as ah-oh</u>. The first *a* is like the *a* in the English word father. The second *a* is like the *o* in the English word go (rising). Together they can sound very much like the '*ow*' in English words like town or down. Because the first syllable has the 'ah' sound the word will be spelled with 'aa' instead of 'oo'.

Platt Düütsch	*English*	*Standard German*
straat	street	Strasse
fraag	question	frage
slaap	sleep	schlafe
waak	awake	wache
schaad	too bad	Schade
haas	rabbit	Hase
plaaster	plaster	Pflaster
schaal	bowl	Schale
schaap	sheep	Schafe
saak	fact	Sache
daag	days	Tage
salaat	salad	Salat
laat	late	spät
aap	ape	Affe
saag	saw	Säge

<u>MONOPHTHONG</u>

The term monophthong refers to two vowels that have just one vowel sound within a given syllable. For example, the Low German word meen (mean) has one sound for each of the 'e' vowels. It is pronounced as if it were spelled main. The first vowel flows right into the second vowel, but both are used in the sound.

There is no 'aa' monophthong in the Low German language itself, except in *loan* words that it might share with Standard German, such as 'staat' (state).

Only in a few Low Franconian influenced dialects is 'ii' used as a monophthong, and sometimes it shows up as 'iy'.

Monophthong: OO (O with long 'o' in Standard German word)

Sounded as a lengthened 'oh'. The *oo* vowels are sounded together, like the 'o' in the English word j*o*ke, except for the fact that it is drawn out as a long vowel.

Platt Düütsch	English	Standard German
poot	paw	Pfote
dood	dead	tod
schoot	lapq	Schoss
boot	boat	Boot
matroon	matron	Matrone
matroos	sailor	Matrose
doos	dose	Dosis
oost	east	Ost
kanoon	cannon	Kanone
roos	rose	Rose
kroon	crown	Krone
knoop	button	Knopf

Monophthong: OO (A or U or AU in Standard German word)

Sounded as a lengthened 'oh', as in the previous group.

Platt Düütsch	English	Standard German
oog	eye	Auge
kroog	tavern	Kruge
tohoop	together	Zusammen
roop	call	Ruf
soom	seam	Saum
hoof	hoof	Huf
loop	run	lauf
boom	tree	Baum
oolt	old	Alt
droom	dream	Traum

Monophthong: ÖÖ (U, Ü or AU in Standard German)

Sounded as a lengthened 'er'   The öö sounds somewhat similar to the *er* in the English word j*er*k or the 'ur' in sl*ur*.

Platt Düütsch	English	Standard German
söök	search	suche
besöök	visit	besuch
gemöös	vegetables	Gemüse
grööt	greet	Gruss

255

kööm	schnaps	(Branntwein)
rööv	turnip	Rübe
verlööv	permission	Erlaubnis
glööv	believe	glaube
stööv	dust	Staub
drööm	dream	traum
kööp	purchase	kauf
bööt	ignite	entzünden

Monophthong: UU (AU or U in Standard German)

Sounds as oo. Both vowels together sounded much like the *u* in the English word d*u*ke, but lengthened as if it were a long vowel.

Platt Düütsch	*English*	*Standard German*
duuk	duck	ducken
huus	house	Haus
puus	puff	(paffen)
bruuk	utilize	brauch
buuk	stomach	Bauch
huuk	crouch	(Hocke)
kruut	weed	Unkraut
sluut	lock	schluss
huut	skin	Haut
absluut	absolute	absolut
stuuv	room	Stube
shuum	suds	Schaum
kuum	hardly	kaum
duum	drunk	betrunken
suus	rush	sausen
pruusch	sneeze	(Niesen)
tuusch	choose	tausch
kruus	rumpled	krause
ruum	space	Raum
schruuv	screw	Schraube
snuut	snout	Schnauze
muus	mouse	Maus
luun	mood	Laune
shuuv	shove	schub

Note that, in the Low German word, the uu is not followed by *r* or *l*. This differentiates it from similar *uu* diphthongs, where the *uu* is pronounced as if it were just one *u*.

256

Monophthong: EE   (EI or IE in the Standard German word)

Sounded as 'ay'. The vowels are sounded as the *a* in the English word s*a*y, except it is drawn out as a long vowel.

Platt Düütsch	English	Standard German
heemlig	secret	Heimlich
keem	germ	Keim
gemeen	community	Gemein
weeten	wheat	Weizen
meen	mean	meine
been	leg	Bein
feend	enemy	Feind
keen	none	keine
een	one	eine
steen	stone	stein
ween	cry	weinen
alleen	alone	allein
vereen	club	verein
breed	wide	breit
kleed	dress	Kleid
scheedel	partition	scheitel
bescheed	knowledge	bescheid
ünnerscheed	difference	unterscheid
sweet	sweat	schweiss
weet	know	weiß
heet	hot	heiß
geet	pour	giess
deeg	dough	Teig
reeg	row	reihe
eeken	oak	Eichen
leeg	sickly	(Krank)
leed	song	Lied
leev	dear	lieb

Monophthong: ÜÜ   (EU or U or AU or ÄU in Standard German)

Sounded as *ue*. This sound is approximated by the letters e-u-r if they are pronounced in very quick succession. Similar to the 'u' in French.

Platt Düütsch	English	Standard German
tüüg	cloth	tuch
düütsch	german	Deutsch
lüüs	lice	Laus

krüüz	cross	Kreuz
düütlig	clearly	deutlig
müüs	mice	Mäuse

It appears that au and eu in a Standard German word most often equate to üü in the corresponding Low German word. Note that none of these Low German words have either *r* or *l* following the *üü* diphthong.

Monoththong: __EI__ (E or EU or Ü in Standard German)

Sounded as ei. The *ei is s*ounded like the '*i*' in the English word h*i*gh.

Platt Düütsch	English	Standard German
dreih	turn	drehen
bleih	bloom	blühen
strei	scatter	streu
teihn	ten	Zehn
weihen	wave	wehen

Monophthong: __IE__ (EI in Standard German)

Sounded as *ee*. The *ie* is sounded as the *ee* in the English word bee.

Platt Düütsch	English	Standard German
riek	rich	reich
riep	ripe	reif
gries	grey	(grau)
schriev	write	schreib
riet	tear	reiss
kiek	look	(guck)
driev	drive	Treib
lies	soft	leise
knie	knee	Knie
smiet	throw	schmeiss
knieps	shrimp	knirps
striep	stripe	Streife
wiet	far	weit
liek	even	(eben)
flietig	diligent	fleissig
iesen	iron	Eisen
ies	ice	Eis
sied	side	seite
ries	rice	Reis
bewies	proof	Beweiss
wieder	further	weiter

piep	pipe	Pfeif
sliek	sneak	schleichen
shien	appear	schein
bedriev	cheat	(betrugen)
lien	flax	Lein
griep	grip	greif
tied	time	Zeit
dien	yours	deine
wies	show	beweisen
pien	pain	pein
pries	price	preis
swieg	quiet	zweig
stiev	stiff	steif
bliev	stay	bleib
wieldat	because	weil
wiev	wife	Weib
wien	wine	Wein
twiefel	doubt	Zweifel
spieker	granary	Speicher
swien	swine	Schwein
rieb	rub	reib
gliek	similar	gleich
biel	hatchet	Beil
liem	glue	Leim
fien	thin	Fein
krieg	get	greif

It seems to be the common thing to find that Standard German words with *ei* in them will have an *ie* in the corresponding Low German word.

The following summary table shows examples of consonant letters and sounds that existed in older languages. It also shows what has survived in present Low German and Standard German.

Ltr.	Old English	Old Saxon	Low German	Old Norse	Gothic	Std.German
			Extinct Consonant Letters			
þ	þri	oþar	anner, dree	annar, þrir	anþar, dauþs	Tod
ð, d	oðer	faðar	voder	faðir	fadar	Vater
b	giefan	geban	geev, ower	gefa	giban	geben

A unique example is the Primitive German word þeoða, which meant 'people'. It contains both 'th' sounding Runic letters. The 'þ' letter can be found at the beginning or at the end of words. Of similar interest is the past tense singular Gothic word *warþ* and

its past tense plural *wurðum*. Both have a different ´th´ sounding
letter. The first word has the 'þ' at, in this case, the end of the word
and the second one has the 'ð' at the beginning of an unstressed
syllable.

The 'e' ending on words has disappeared (a phenomen known technically as
apocope) on many words, compared to their cognate in Standard German;
Frage-fraag, Tage-daag. The 'e' ending exists in quite a few plurals of words,
such as brill-brille (glasses) and book-böke (books). It also exists in some
comparative word forms, such as böwerste (supervisor) or jüngste (youngest),
or in some infinitives, such as frömde (foreign ones) or dicke (fat one), or in
Standard German loan words, like beide (both) or pause (pause).

STANDARD GERMAN VS. LOW GERMAN

During the period when the various dialects of Old High German began to develop, the
sound of some of its letter changed. Meanwhile, Old Saxon also continued to evolve,
but in a different direction. There were also some vowel changes in Old Saxon, as it
developed into Low German, but these were far fewer and less dramatic than in Old
High German.

Both languages underwent a transitory "middle" phase in their development, at about
the same time. The "middle" phases of the two languages have been discussed in
Chapter Two. The list on the next page takes a look at the current versions of the two
langugages. Some of the changes represented in the list beginning on the next page
took place during the "middle" phase, as opposed to happening early or late.

When, how and why these changes took place can only be estimated. Which letters
changed depended often on the context. Especially relevant was the location of a vowel,
and whether it preceded a particular consonant. The consonants r, l, m, and n have
always been particularly important, going all the way back to the Indo- European
language. The previous discussion about monophthongs and diphthongs often
mentioned the letters 'r' and 'l' which just followed the double vowels. The most
common change happened in the vowels, and sometimes they'd change one way in one
century and then back again in a subsequent century.

As in all languages, these changes do not apply without exception. There are times
when something you expected would happend, does not, or sometimes it happens to a
letter. However, these are in the minority and, for the most part, the changes do follow a
pattern. Unfortunately, the pattern is far too complex to explain in a few paragraphs.
However, some of it can be seen in the following list, especially the word examples in
the third column. The letter in the first column, in Standard German, will have
changed to the letter in the second column. The cognate words are shown, to point out
these changes. Following the list are some comments to explain idiosyncracies, and also
to discuss how the results may vary amongst dialects.

The following list attempts to summarize some of the relationships that exist between the changes in Low German and Standard German. This may be helpful to those that understand the basic of Standard German and wish to use this knowledge to help them write Low German.

STANDARD GERMAN	LOW GERMAN	EXAMPLES
a	e,ee	sagen-seggen, habe-heff, tragen-dregen, sah-sehn, war-weer.
a *(not end -e)*	o	Abend-obend, mache-mok, bezahl-betohl, klagen-klogen, Vater-voder, schaden-shoden, aufladen-uploden.
a (followed by r or l)	o	Fahr-föhr, da-dor, sogar-sogor, Karte-korden, Jahr-johr, Wahr-wohr, Saltz-solt halten-holen.
a *(not end -e & before r,l,m,n)*	oo	Garten-goorn, klar-kloor, Karre-koor, alt-oolt, Bart-boort, Hafen-hooven, Hafen-hoob, Gans-goos, art-oort, zusammen-tohopen, kalt-koolt, gar-goor.
a *(ending -e)*	aa	Strasse-straat, frage-fraag, sache-saak, Affe-aap, Säge-saag, Schafe-schaap, wache-waak, schlafe-slaap, Hase-haas,
ä	öö [1]	Blätter-blöör
aa (followed by r)	oo	Haar-hoor, Paar-poor
au	u, uu. [2]	auf-up, Raum-ruum, laut-luud, Faust-fuus, bedauer-beduur, sauer-suur, Mauer-muur, Haut-hoot, kaum-kuum, aus-uut, sausen-suus, Maul-muul, Maus-muus, dauer-duur, Schraube-shruuv, brauch-bruuk. Bauch-buuk, Bauer-buur, Maus-muus, Haus-huus, Unkraut-kruut
au	o,oo [2]	Baum-boom, lauf-loop, auch-ok, Saum-soom, Urlaub-urloob, auf-op.
au, äu	ö,öö [2]	Sau-sög, Glaub -glöv, glaube-glööv, kauf-kööp, Erlaubnis-verlööf, Staub-stööv,
äu	ö	träumen-drömen, Räuber-röber.
b	f	ab-af, abgehen-afgohen, Weib-wief
b	v	treiben-driev, geben-geev, glauben-glöven, Sieb-seev, schub-shuuv, Stube-stuuv, Korb-korv, leben-leven, Kalb-kalv, Rabe-raav.
ch	ck	Dach-dack, Loch-lock.
ch	k [3]	Milch-melk, Kirche-kerk, machen-moken, kochen-koken, reich-riek, Sich-sik, Ich-ik, woche-week, brechen-breken.

e	a	Berg-barg, Herz-hart, erb-arv Herbst-harvst, Mark-mark, Farbe-farv
e	ee	Stern-steern, gebe-geev, werden-weern, Wetter-weer, Gelb-geel, Stell-steed, gern-geern, Wert-weert, mehr-meehr, Erde-eerd, lehr-leehr.
e	i	Gestern-gistern
e	ei	drehe-dreih, wehen-weihen.
e	o,oo,ö	gehe-goh, sechs-söss, schwer-swoor.
ei	ee	Teil-deel, heil-heel, Gemein-gemeen, bleich-bleek, drei-dree, ein-een, frei-free, allein-alleen, Fleisch-fleesch, Zwei-twee, nein-nee, bescheit-besheed, Eisen-iesen, Heiss-hitt, kein-keen, Geist-geest, Meister-meester, schweig-swieg.
ei	i, ie	meine-mien, treiben-drieven, schreiben-shriev, bleib-bliev, dreist-driest, gleich-gliek, greif-griep, Eis-ies, Preis-pries, Leise-lies, bei-bi, Weiss-witt, Zeit-tied.
eu	uu	Eule-uul, Beule-buul, heulen-huulen, Treu-truu, Scheu-shuu.
eu	ü,üü	bedeuten-bedüden, deutlich-düdlig, Leute-lüüd, Heute-hüüt, Kreuz-krüüz, teuer-düür,Feur-füür, Steuer-stüür, Deutsch-düütsch.
f	v	Briefe-breev, Schorfe-schorv, schief-sheev.
f,ff	p	Dorf-dörp, Reif-riep, treffen-drepen, offen-open, Pfeffer-peper.
i	e [4]	Kirche-kerk, Himmel-heven, Hilf-help, sicher-seker, Ihm-em.
i	ü	Zwischen-twüschen, Ihm-üm, bin-bün, immer-jümmer.
ie	e, ee	Bier-beer, Lied-leed, tief-deep, giebe-geev, viel-veel, Tier-deert, Schiessen-sheeten, passier-passeer, probier-probeer, flieg-fleeg, schief-sheev, Vieh-veh, Ziege-zegen, Diebe-deev, Liebe-leev.
ld	ll	Bilder-biller, geduldig-gedullig, schuldig-shullig.
nd,nt	nn	Wunder-wunner, ander-anner, finden-finnen, Stunde-stunn, unter-ünner, Kinder-kinner, Handel-hannel, lebendig-lebennig, hinter-hinner, windig-winnig.
o	a,aa	ohne-ahn, Vogel-vagel, Mond-maand
o	oo [5]	wort-woort, Tod-dood, gross-groot, Ost-oost, Knopf-knoop, Koch-kook, rose-roos,

		Kanon-kanoon, Korn-koorn, Dorn-doorn, Krone-kroon, Pfote-poot, Pastor-pastoor.
o	u [6]	voll-vull, von-vun, komme-kumm, beklommen-beklumm.
o	ü	Sonne-sünnen, sonst-süss.
o	öö	Orgel-örgel, vor-vör, vorn-vörn.
ö	üü	höre-hüür
pf	p	Kopf-kopp, Pferd-peerd, hüpfen-hüppen, Apfel-appel, Knopf-knoop, Pfad-padd, Pfand-pand, Pfanne, pann, Pfosten-posten.
sch *(l,w,m,n)*	s [7]	Schmied-smitt, Schnecke-snick, schwer-swoor, Schwager-swager, Schlüssel-slotel schlafen-slaapen, schlecht-slecht,Schnabel-snabel, Schwester-swester, Schlittschuh-slittschoh, Schlange-slang, Schlank-slank. Schweigen-swiegen, schluss-sluut, Schwein-swien, Schwert-sword, schwach-swaak, Schwalbe-swoolk, Schwarm-swoorm, Schwarz-swatt, Schwan-swoon, schlabber- slabber, schlacht-slacht,
sch *(e,i,r,u)*	sh [8]	Schiessen-sheeten, Scheiss-shiet, Schrei-shree, schelte-shimp, Schramm-shramm Schein-shien, Scheune-shüün, schieben-shuuben, schier-sheer, schief-sheev, Schiff-shipp, schimmer-shimmer, Schirm-shirm, Schraube-shruuv, Schreck-shreck.
sch (a,o)	sch [9]	Schafe-schaap, Schule-school.
ss,s,z	t	lassen-laten, Fuss-foot, messen-meten gross-groot, nass-natt, Wasser-Woter, ziel-teel, bezahl-betohl, Zehn-teihn, Katz-katt, Zucht-tucht, Zinn-tinn, Zahm-tamm.
t [10]	d	Taube-duuv, Taler-daler, Tag-dag, Tau-dau, Tannen-dannen, Mutter-moder bett-bedd, Vater-voder, Trink-drink tief-deep, Tausend-dusend, tun-doon, Sorte-sorde, Zeit-tied, Tisch-disch.
t	s	husten-hussen, pusten-pussen.
u	o	Kuh-koh, Stuhl-stohl, rufen-ropen zu-to, burg-borg, Zug-tog.
u	oo	Blut-blood, Buch-book, tun-doon, klug-klook, gut-good, Glut-gloot, Schule-school, Turm-toorn, Mut-mood, Hut-hoot ruf-roop, Schnur-snoor, Spur-spoor, Blume-bloom, Tuch-dook, genug-genoog, Pflug-ploog.

u	öö	Tur-döör, suche-söök, besuch-besöök.
u	uu	Krug-kruuk, absolut-absluut, Schluk-sluuk, Stube-stuuv, ducken-duuk.
u	uo	brochen-bruoken, Knochen-knuoken. [6]
u	ü	Kuss-küss.
ü	ö,öö [11]	Kühl-köhl, Bürger-börger, für-för, Mühl-möhl, Schütze-shörten, Grün-grön, entzünden-bööt, Gemüse-gemöös, spüle-spööl, Rübe-rööv, müde-möör.
ü	u	wünsch-wunsh

The following notes apply to Low German in general. Those with an asterisk apply primarily to dialects influenced by Low Franconian, such as Westphalian, Ostphalian or East Low German.

(1). When pluralized, the Standard German 'ä' becomes 'öö' in Low German (blätter-blöör).

(2). In singular, the Standard German 'au' becomes 'uu' or 'oo'. When pluralized, the standard German 'äu' becomes 'üü' in Low German, such as in the words Mäuse-müüs and Läus-lüüs.

(2).* In the Westphalian dialect, the Standard German 'au' may stay 'au'. An example is Lauf-laup. It may also change to 'iu', as shown in brauchen-briuken. And then again, it may change to 'ue', as shown in Bauer-buer, Mauer-muer.

(3). Some words do not change from 'ch' to 'k', such as nich-nich, tauschen-tuschen, dicht-dicht, lachen-lachen, largely because they are used the same in both languages.

(3).* In the Westphalian dialect, this change to 'k' takes place much oftener. For example, review these these additional words -- Kelch-kelk, Fisch-fisk, Mensch-mensk, Wasche-waske, wisch-wisk, tauschen-tiusken and westlich-westlik. This is also true for Ost Frisian, where you can find bischen-bitken.

(4).* In the Westphalian dialect, the Standard German 'i' often changes to 'iä', rather than to 'e'. And often the 'e' also may change to 'iä', such as in bischen-biäten, Kirch-kiärk, while examples of the latter are hegen-hiägen, Herz-hiärt, lesen-liäsen, treffen-driäpen, and fressen-friäten.

(5).* In the Westphalian dialect, the Standard German 'o', instead of changing to 'oo', it may change to "au", such as in Tod-daut.

(6).* In the Westphalian dialect, the Standard German 'o' often changes to the combination 'uo'. This doesn't happen in North Saxon, but may also happen in Mecklenburgisch and Pommersche Platt (East Low German dialects in general).

(7). Standard German words in which the 'sch' is *not* followed by a, o, e, i, r, or u is spelled with 's' in Low German.

(8). Standard German words in which the 'sch' is followed by e, i, r, or u is spelled with 'sh' in Low German.

(9). Standard German words in which the 'sch' is followed by a or u is spelled with 'sch' in Low German.

(10). Some words keep the 't', such as Tasse-tass, Tee-tee, Tüte-tuten and Teller-teller. Again, these are words used by both languages.

(11). Some words do not change the 'u' vowel, such as nun-nu and pusten-pussen.

This glossary lets you look up the Low German word, to find both the Standard German and the English interpretation.

The first column contains the Low German word. The middle column (in italics) is the Standard German word. In a few cases a corresponding word in Standard German was not readily available. The corresponding English word or phrase is given in the last column. In some cases there are several words of meaning, or a second way of spelling (separated by the word 'or'), that is also used. In some cases, this alternative meaning or spelling is one that is favored in another dialect. Letters which are *silent* are indicated by a short horizontal stroke through the middle, e.g. -d- or -t-

There are some letters that are in **bold** type. This concerns letters that are usually pronounced a bit differently than one might normally expect. The term normal here means how it would be pronounced in English. This alternate pronunciation is based on dialects that existed about 150 years ago, in the general center of the Low German speaking areas of north Germany (spread around the City of Hamburg). It is still pronounced that way today. This difference may not be germain to every other area, and perhaps it has been lost in some areas. This distinction is a remnant of the Primitive German Runic letters ð and þ, which were used then in places where today we use the Latin letters 'd' or 't'. The letter '**d**' is such a special case. For example, in some Low German words the '**d**' should be pronounced as a 'th', when beginning the second syllable or preceding an 'r'. In ancient times it was spelled with a ð or þ. This can also apply to the letter '**t**' (except when preceded by an 's') and, in a few cases, to the letter '**n**'. The letter 'n' has, in some cases, taken the place of the letter 'd', and thus inherited the 'th' sound. In some earlier language forms, the 'nn' doubled consonant was actually 'nd'. The thickened letter (i.e. the **bold** effect) used to denote this distincton may even help one remember that the sound of the letter should be 'thickened'.

A '**d**' letter at the *beginning* of a word is pronounced 'th' if it precedes the consonant letter 'r', otherwise it is pronounced with the normal 'd' sound. For example, the word for dirt in Low German is **d**reck. It is phonetically pronounced as threck.

A '**d**' letter that might begin the second syllable *within* a word is also pronounced with the 'th' sound. For example, the Low German word for 'father', which is vo**d**er. This is pronounced faw-the (the letter 'v' is, as usual, pronounced with an 'f' sound).

When the letter 'd' is found at the *end* of the word, then the 'd' is pronounced as it if were a 't'.

A double 'd' in a word is a special case. The first 'd' is pronounced as a normal 'd' and the second '**d**' is pronounced with the 'th' sound, because it starts the second syllable. For example, the word for 'feed' in Low German is fudder.

Similarly, when a word that ends in 't' is lengthened by a suffix, the 't' is changed to a '**d**' and is given the '**th**' pronunciation. For instance, when the Low German word deert, meaning animal, is pluralized to animals, it becomes deerde. It is pronounced dee'r-the. Some may prefer to keep the 't' letter, but still pronounce it with the 'th' sound, as in deerte.

The letter å is used in Danish and Swedish, and its *sound* is used also in old Low German.

> Danish: åben (open), år (year), årsag (cause), gå (go)
> Swedish: mål (meal), åldes (age), stå (stand), gå (go)

It was used in Danish starting about 1250 and didn't take hold in the north Low German territory until about 1400. This is the area in which the North Saxon Low German is spoken.

The 'å' letter has the sound, in English, that is found in the 'o' letter of words like *log* or *dog*. It is a sound about halfway between a long 'o' and a long 'a'; though closer to 'o'. In Low German it is used in such words as goh (go) and stoh (stand) and oben (oven). These words could just as easily and correctly be spelled gåh or ståh or åben. But the 'å' letter is uncommon for most Germans because it isn't in their alphabet, though its sound is used in Tochter and Kopf. It is also unfamiliar for Americans. If instead the 'å' sound was spelled with 'a', most Germans and Americans would ascribe to it an 'ah' sound that is normally associated with 'a', not the more appropriate sound of 'o' in log or dog. These words are often spelled with an 'a' in some Low German dialects, but people using those dialects are likely already aware of the correct sound to be attached to this letter.

In the following glossary, the letter 'o' is used to represent this å sound, because it has basically the same sound as the 'o' in log or dog. And also because, in Standard German, the 'o' letter in words like Tochter and Kopf also have the same sound.

There are many words which produce this problem of deciding whether to spell with an 'a' or an 'o' letter. Two of the most common are the Low German words goh (gah) or stoh (stah). In dialects where gah or stah has been the spelling norm for centuries, it should perhaps be continued. After all, there's little chance of a reader being confused, since stah and stoh are so similiar anyway. However, if a dialect's normal way of *pronouncing* the word stoh (stah) sounds more like "staw" or "stauh" than "stah", then spelling it goh instead of gah would be in line with the *original* sounds assigned to the letter 'o' and 'a'.

aal	*Aal*	eel
aant	*Ente*	duck
aanten	*Enten*	ducks
aantenkruut	*Entenunkraut*	duckweed
abscharlig	*abscheulich*	abominable, terrible
acht	*acht*	eight
achteih	*achtzehn*	eighteen
achtel	*achtel*	eighth
achter	*hinter*	behind or after
achterbeen	*hinterbein*	hind leg
achterdöör	*hintertür*	back door
achterklapp	*Folge*	consequence
achterkommen	*ausfinden*	figure out
achterkopp		back of my mind
achternolopen	*nachjagen*	chase after
achterrüm	*hinterrum*	around back
achterrut	*hinten aus*	out the back
achtzig	*achtzig*	eighty
acker	*Acker*	acre or field
ackerknecht	*Feldknecht*	field hand
ackerland	*Ackerland*	farmland, plowed land
adder	*Gift Schlange*	giftslang
adebor	*Storch*	stork
adrett	*fein*	adroit
af	*weg*	away
af un an	*aus und ein*	off and on
af un to	*ab und zu*	now and then
af	*ab*	off
afbeden	*abbitte*	apologize
afbestelln	*abbestellen*	cancel
afbetohln	*abbezahlen*	pay off
afbieten	*abbeissen*	bite off
afbild	*abbild*	copy
afbleben	*abgebeiben*	stayed away
afblosen	*abblasen*	blow off
afbörsten	*abbürsten*	brush off
afbreken	*abbrechen*	break off
afbrinnen	*abbrennen*	burn off
afdanken	*abdanken*	resign
afdeel	*Abteilung*	compartment
afdoon	*abgetan*	dismissed
afdreihn	*abwenden*	turn off or shut off

afdrieben	*abwehren*	drive off
affleegen	*abfliegen*	fly off
affragen	*anfragen*	inquire or question
affragen	*anfordern*	request of
afgas	*abgas*	exhaust
afgeev	*Abgabe*	tax
afglans	*Reflexion*	reflection
afgunst	*Neid*	envy
afgünstdig	*missgünstig*	envious or jealous
afhacken	*abhacken*	hack off
afhalen	*einsammeln*	collect or pickup
afhalt	*abgeholt*	picked up
afhauen	*abspalten*	chop off
afjagen	*wegjagen*	drive off
afkanzeln	*ermahnen*	admonish
afkat	*Anwalt*	attorney or lawyer
afkat	*Fürsprecher*	advocate
afköhlen	*abkühlen*	cool off
afköhlt	*abgekühlt*	cooled off
afkommen	*Abkommen*	agreement
afköpen	*abkaufen*	buy from
afkratzen	*abkratzen*	scratch off
aflaten	*ablassen*	leave off
afleehrn	*ablernen*	unlearn
afleggen	*abiegen*	lay off
aflesen	*ablesen*	read off
aflicken	*ablecken*	lick off
aflieden	*ableiten*	divert or lead away
aflopen	*ablaufen*	run off or drain
afmeten	*abmessen*	measure
afmoken	*zumachen*	shut off
afmokt	*Abkommen*	agreed
afnehmen	*abnehmen*	take off
afplücken	*abpicken*	pick off
afputzed	*abbürstet*	finished or brushed off
afreken	*abrechnen*	deduct
afropen	*absagen*	call off
afrümen	*abräumen*	clear off or clear away
afsaagen	*absägen*	saw off
afsatz	*Absatz*	paragraph or heel
afschoonst	*obgleich*	although
afschoten	*abgeschossen*	discharged, shot off
afschuum	*Abschaum*	scum
afschüürn	*abreiben*	rub off
afschüürt	*abgerieben*	rubbed off

afseggen	*abschlagen*	refuse or turn down
afsehn	*abgesehn*	recognize
afsheed	*Abschied*	farewell or parting
afsheeden	*verabschieden*	leave or depart
afsheeten	*Abschuss*	discharge or shoot off
afshrifft	*handgeschrieben*	hand written copy
afsicht	*Absicht*	intent
afsichten	*Absichten*	intention
afsnacken	*aufschwatzen*	talk out of something
afsneen	*abschneiden*	cut off
afsnitt	*Abschnitt*	part cut off
afspannen	*ausspannen*	unharness
afstammt	*abstammen*	descended from
afstiegen	*absteigen*	dismount
afsunnerlig	*Bemerkenswert*	remarkable, odd
aftecken or afteken	*Abzeichen*	badge
aftehn	*abziehen*	pull off
aftellen	*Zählen*	count off
aftog	*Abzug*	deduction
aftogen	*abgezogen*	pulled off
aftwiegen	*abzweigen*	branch off
afwickel	*abwickeln*	unwind
afwiesen	*hervorstechen*	show off
afwiesen	*abweisen*	turn away
afwinnen	*abwenden*	turn away
afwinnen	*ntziehung*	get rid of a habit
afwischen	*abwaschen*	wash off or wipe off
afworen	*abgenutzt*	worn off
ahn	*ohne*	without
ahnfarv	*farblos*	colorless
ahnglieklig	*unvergleichlig*	incomparable
ahnhen	*ohnehin*	anyhow or besides
ahnklüür	*farblos*	colorless
ähnlig	*ähnlich*	similar
ahnmachtig	*ohnmächtich*	powerless or weak
ahoorn	*Ahorn*	maple
ahren	*Ernte*	harvest
akkediern	*Feilschen*	haggle
akraat or akraot	*genau*	accurate
akschoon	*Aktion*	action
aksen	*Ächzen*	groan
al	*schon*	already
alkohol	*Alkohol*	alcohol
alkoov	*Wandbett*	wall bed
all or alls	*alles*	all or everything

alldaags	*Wochentag*	weekday or everyday
alldaagstüch	*Arbeitskluft*	work clothes
alledings	*allerdings*	above all or to be sure
allee	*Allee*	avenue
alleen	*allein*	alone
aller beste	*besten Wünschen*	best wishes
allerhand	*allerhand*	lots or all kinds of
allerwegens	*überall*	every place, everywhere
alltied	*immer*	all the time
alvern or mall or dwallerig	*albern*	silly
Amerikoner	*Ami*	American
aminn	*vielleicht*	perhaps or maybe
ammel	*Eimer*	pail
ammel	*Eimer*	bucket or pail
ampel or immicken	*Ameise*	ant
ampelhumpel	*Ameisen Haufen*	anthill
amusieren	*amüsieren*	amuse
an	*an*	to or toward
anbakken or ankleben	*ankleben*	glue on
anbeden	*nbieten*	offer or make an offer
anbieten	*zubeissen*	take a bite
anbinnen	*verbinden*	tie up
anböten or ansteken	*anzünden*	light a fire
anbott	*Angebot*	an offer
anbreken	*öffnen*	open it
andacht	*gedacht daran*	thought of
andeel	*Rolle*	part in play
andinken	*Andenken*	souvenir
andregen	*aufmerksam geworden*	become aware
andreihn	*aufdrehen*	turn on
andrepen	*Treffen*	encounter
androgen	*aufmerksam geworden*	became aware
andüden	*andeuten*	indicate
anduuren	*beharren*	persist
anfang	*anfang*	beginning or start
anfangen	*anfangen*	begin
anferdigen	*Anfertigung*	manufacture, produce
anföhr	*Transport*	transport
anfoten	*anfassen*	take ahold
anfung	*angefangen*	begun or started
angeev	*Angabe*	statement
angeiht	*nimmt platz*	goes on
angeln	*angeln*	fishing
angewickst	*wütend*	angry
angohn or angahn	*geschah*	occurred, happened

angreepsch	*verlockend*	enticed or seduced
angriepen or anfoten	*anfassen*	grab on
angst	*Angst*	fear
angsthaas	*bange Katz*	fraidy cat
angstig	*ängstlich*	anxious
angüng	*geht vor sich*	went on
anhäng	*Anhang*	appendix
anhebben	*anhaben*	have on or wear
anholen	*anhalten*	hold on
anhören	*zuhören*	listen to
ankeken	*anschauen*	looked at
anker	*Anker*	anchor
ankieken	*chau*	look at or view
ankieker	*Zuschauer*	spectator
ankleben	*Ankleben*	stick to
anklogen	*anklogen*	accuse
anknöpen	*verknüpfen*	attach or fasten
ankommen	*ankommen*	arrive
anköteln	*einschmeicheln*	ingratiate
ankünnigen	*Ankündigen*	make announcement
anküren	*ansagen*	speak to
anlöden	*löten*	weld
anmellen	*anmelden*	enroll
anmoken	*befestigen*	attach or turn on
änner	*ändern*	alter or change
anner	*andere*	other
anner sorde	*anders sorte*	other kinds
annerde	*anderen*	others or other one
anners	*anders*	different or otherwise
anners moken	*revidieren*	revise
annerwegens	*anderswo*	somewhere else
annerwegens	*anderswo*	elsewhere
annogeln	*annageln*	nail on
anroden	*empfehlen*	recommend
anropen	*anrufen*	call on or call up
anseggen	*konsultieren*	ask or consult
ansehn	*Ansehen*	reputation
ansheten	*betrügen*	deceived
anshieten	*anscheissen*	play trick on
anshrieben laten	*anschreiben lassen*	on credit
ansluut	*Anschluss*	connector or connect
ansmusen	*anschmiegen*	snuggle up
ansnacken	*anreden*	speak to or address
anspruk	*Sprache*	speech
ansprungen	*ansprungen*	jumped at

ansteken	*anstecken*	infect
anstellde	*Angestellte*	employee
anstellen	*darstellen*	act or behave
anstellt	*aufgetragt*	ordered in advance
anstiken	*Feur stiften*	light or set fire to
anstött	*gestossen*	bumped against
anstrek	*Anstrich*	coat of paint
anstrieken	*anstreichen*	paint
anstringen	*anspannen*	strain or exert
anstringt	*anstrengt*	exerted
antehn or antrecken	*anziehen*	dress or put on
antern	*anworten*	to answer
antohgen	*nziehen*	put on or dressed
antruut	*verlobt*	engaged
antuuten	*versäufen*	get drunk
anwies	*Anzeichen*	indication
anwiesen	*anzeigen*	notify
anwinn	*gewöhnen*	get used to
anwinnen	*mache zur Regel*	make a habit of
anwoort	*Antwort*	answer
anwörde	*Antworten*	answers
anwunnen	*dran gewöhen*	accustomed, used to
anwuss	*Zuwachs*	an increase to
anwussen	*anwachsen*	grown onto
apatt	*aber*	however or but or indeed
app or aap	*Affe*	ape
appel	*Apfel*	apple
appeldwatsch	*albernheit*	foolishness or silliness
appelgoorn	*Apfel garten*	apple orchard
appelhof	*Apfel Hof*	apple yard
appelmoos	*Apfelmus*	apple sauce
appeln	*Äpfel*	apples
April	*April*	April
apteek	*Drogerie*	drugstore or pharmacy
apteker	*Drogist*	druggist
aptiet	*Appetit*	appetite
arbeider	*Arbeiter*	worker or employee
arbeiders	*Angestellten*	workers
arbeit	*Arbeit*	work or job
arbeitsteed	*Arbeitstelle*	workplace
arfen	*Erbse*	pea
ärgerlig	*Ärgerlich*	disturbing
arm	*Arm*	arm
arm huus	*Armenhaus*	poor house
arm	*arm*	be poor

274

aʀmbost	*Armbuss*	cross bow
aʀme	*Armen*	the poor
aʀmoot	*armut*	poverty
aʀms	*Armen*	arms
arnten	*Ernte*	harvest
aʀv	*erben*	inherit
aʀvdeel	*Erbteil*	inherited share
aʀvschop	*Erbschaft*	inheritance
aʀvt	*geerbt*	inherited
as	*so*	as
asheboom	*Esche*	ash tree
Ashemiddeweeken	*Aschermittwoch*	Ash Wednesday
ashen	*Asche*	ashes
ashenbeker	*Aschbecher*	ash tray
asig	*Schrecklich*	horrible
ass (in korden)	*Ass*	ace (in cards)
assen (in korden)	*Ässen*	aces (in cards)
aswenn	*alswenn*	as if
August	*August*	August
aukschoon	*Auktion*	auction
avion	*Flugzeug*	airplane
baars	*Barsch*	rude
baas or boos	*Chef*	boss or company head
backen	*Backe*	cheek
backentähn	*Backenzahn*	molars
backhuus	*Toilette*	outside toilet (back-house)
bak	*backen*	bake
bakd	*gebacken*	bakt
baken	*backen*	to bake
baker	*bäcker*	baker
bakeree'	*backerei*	bakery
bakhuus	*backhaus*	bake house
bakmehl	*Back Mehl*	baking flour
bakoben	*backofen*	bake oven
bakpulwer	*backpulver*	baking powder
baksteen	*backstein*	brick
bald	*bald*	soon
balje	*badewanne*	bathtub or tub
balkun	*Balkon*	ledge or balcony
ball	*ball*	ball
ball	*ball*	dance
baller	*knall*	bang
ballersweep	*peitschen*	switch
bammel or bummel	*Besorgnis*	anxiety

band	*Band*	string
banduhr	*Armbanduhr*	wrist watch
bang vun	*bange*	afraid of
bang	*bange*	afraid
bangbüx or bangorse	*Feigling*	fraidy cat
bangmoken	*bange machen*	scare or frighten
bank	*Bank*	bench
bankrott	*bankrott*	bankrupt
bannig veel	*sehr viel*	very much
bannig	*sehr*	very or great
banoon	*Banane*	banana
bar	*Bär*	bear
bärdel	*Fass*	barrel
barft or barfoot	*barfuss*	barefoot
barg	*Menge*	a lot of or a heap of
barg	*Berg*	slope
barg	*Hügel*	hill
bargdohl	*Berg herunter*	downhill
bargen	*scheuen*	avoid
bargig	*Bergig*	hilly
bargup	*Berg auf*	incline or uphill
baschaan (shippen)	*Pik Dame*	queen (spades)
bass	*Tiefe*	deep or deeply
bassenpitten	*Wurzelstock*	rhizome
batz or bootz	*unmittelbar*	right away
baut or boot	*baut*	built
bedacht	*betrachtet*	considered
bedd or bett	*Bett*	bed
bedddecken	*Decke*	blankets
beddelt	*kämpft*	battled
bedden	*Betten*	beds
beddlaken	*Bettlaken*	bedsheets
beddlaken	*Leintuch*	bed sheet
beddstell	*Bett gestell*	bedstead
beddtied	*Bettzeit*	bedtime
beddtüüch	*Bettzeug*	bedclothes
bedeende	*Angestellte*	employee
bedel	*Meissel*	chisel
beden	*beten*	pray
bedingen	*bedingungen*	conditions
bedregen	*betragen*	fraud or swindle
bedriev	*Betrieb*	company
bedrog	*Betrug*	fraud
bedrogen	*Betrugen*	cheated
bedrööv	*betriebt*	dejected

bedröövt	*traurig*	sad
bedüden	*erschein*	seem like or symbolize
bedüdet	*scheint als*	seems like
beduur	*Bedauer*	pity
beduurlig	*bedauerlich*	pitiful
beeden	*bieten*	bid or make offer
beedsch	*bissig*	sarcastic
been	*Bein*	leg
beer	*Bier*	beer
beern	*Beere*	berry
beest	*Biest*	beast
beestig groot	*gewaltig*	enormous
beestig	*schrecklich*	horrible or horribly
beev or beven	*Zittern*	shiver
beevt	*bebt*	trembles or shivers
befeel	*Befehl*	order or decree
begegen	*begegnen*	meet
begin	*beginnen*	begin
begnögt or tofree	*genügsam*	content
begöösch	*kümmern*	tend to or take care of
begrebnis	*Begräbnis*	funeral
begrebnissen	*Begräbnisse*	funerals
begriepen	*begreifen*	comprehend or grasp
begroben	*begraben*	buried
behaupt	*behaupten*	contend
behol or behool	*behalten*	keep
beholen	*behalten*	remember
behoopt, behaupt	*behaupten*	both
beinflott	*Einfluss*	an influence
bek	*Bach*	brook or stream
bek	*Bach*	stream
bekannt	*wohlbekannt*	familiar
bekannte	*Bekanntschaft*	acquaintences
beker	*Kanne*	beaker or cup
bekiek	*inspizieren*	inspect or look over
beklumm	*beklommen*	dank oder sultry
bekommt	*wird*	will become
beköpen	*bestechen*	bribe
bekümmern	*nachfragen*	ask or inquire about
beleben	*Erfahren*	to experience
belevnes	*Erlebnis*	experience or adventure
belevt	*geliebt*	beloved
bemarkt	*bemerken*	observed or mentioned
bemööt	*treffung*	encounter
benaut	*deprimiert*	depressed

benehmen	*annehmen*	accept
benieden	*beneiden*	envy
benzin	*Benzin*	gasoline
bereek	*Bereich*	area
bereken	*berechnen*	assess
berichtig	*berechtig*	entitled
bescheed	*Bescheid*	aware of, knowledgeable of
bescheed seggen	*Informieren*	inform
besett	*besetzen*	occupied
beshriev	*Beschreiben*	to describe
besinnen	*nachsinnen*	ponder or re-think
besinnen	*erinnern*	remember
besinnlig	*denkwürdig*	memorable or profound
besitter	*Besitzer*	owner
beslagnohmen	*beschlagnahmen*	confiscated
besloten	*beschlossen*	decided
besluut	*Entschluss*	decision
besocht	*besucht*	visited
besök or besöken	*Besuch*	visit
besöker	*Gast*	visitor
besopen	*ertrunken*	drunk
bessen	*Besen*	broom
bessensteel	*Besenstiel*	broomstick
bestännig	*beständig*	constant
bestellen	*Bestellung*	order
besten	*beste*	best
bestimmt	*übereinstimmt*	agrees
bestmoder, bestemor	*Grossmutter*	grandmother
bestvoder or bestevo'r	*Grossvater*	grandfather
besunners	*besonder*	special or exceptional
bet herto	*bis jetzt*	until now
bet	*bis*	until
betel	*Meissel*	chisel
beten or betken or bäten	*ein wenig*	little bit
beter or biäter or bäter	*besser*	better
betieds	*zeitig*	in time
betohl	*Zahlen*	to pay
bewies	*Beweis*	proof
bewohr	*bewahren*	protect
billebeern	*Heidelbeern*	bilberry
bi misülms	*mirselbst*	by myself
bi rinkieken	*besichtigen*	visit or drop by
bi wesen	*Bei sein*	be at it
bi wesen	*Bei sein*	was at it
bi	*an*	at

bi	*bei*	by
biarbeiden	*arbeiten am*	work at
bibel	*Bibel*	bible
biblieben	*bestehen*	stick with it or persist
bicht	*beichte*	confession
bidaags	*während des Tages*	during the day
bidagstied, bidaagslicht	*Tageslicht*	day time
bidd or bede	*bitte*	request
bidder	*bitter*	tart or bitter
bidregen	*beitragen*	contribute
biel	*Beil*	hatchet or axe
bienoh	*beinahe*	almost
biernsteen	*Bernstein*	amber
biesterföhren	*beschwindeln*	deceive
biet	*beiss*	bite
bifall	*Beifall*	applause
bihuus oder tohuus	*zuhause*	at home
bild	*Bild*	picture
bileggt	*Beilagen*	enclosed
biljoon	*Milliarden*	billion
biller	*Bilder*	pictures
billig	*billig*	cheap
billjet	*Billet*	ticket
bilöpig	*gelegentlich*	incidental
bilüttens	*nach und nach*	little by little
bimmel	*klingel*	toll or knock or bang
binaam or binoom	*Spitzname*	nickname
binder	*Binder*	binder
binder	*Binder*	binder
bindertweern	*Binder Zwirn*	binder twine
binn	*verbinden*	string tie
binnen	*Innenseite*	inside or within
bis	*sind*	(you) are
bisitter, mitsitter	*Mitglieder*	member
bislapp	*Nachtrag*	supplement
bispeel or bispill	*Beispiel*	example
bistohn	*beistehen*	support
blamieren	*blamieren*	disgrace or expose
blangdöör or sieddöör	*Seitentur*	side door
blangs or blang to	*neben*	beside, alongside
blank	*blank*	shiny or clean
blanksteert	*Leuchtkäfer*	glow worm
blarren	*brüllen*	bawl or bleat
blatt	*Blatt*	leaf or page
blatt	*Zeitung*	newspaper

279

blau	*Blau*	blue
blaubeern	*Blaubeere*	blueberry
bleck	*Blech*	metal or tin
blecksmied	*Schmidt*	potsmith
blee	*Blei*	lead
bleek or blass	*bleich*	pale
bleestick or pensil	*Bleistift*	pencil or lead pencil
bleih	*Blüten*	bloom
bleiht	*blühend*	flowering or blooms
blenkern	*glitzen*	glisten or twinkle
bless or vörkopp	*Stirn*	forehead
bliev	*bleib*	remain or stay
blifft	*bleibt*	remains or stays
blind	*blind*	blind
blitz	*Blitz*	lightning
blockdreiher	*Kurbel*	winch
blocken	*Block*	block
blöd	*beschränkt*	stupid
blödsinn	*Unsinn*	nonsense
blokhuus	*Blockhaus*	log cabin
blööd or blööt	*Blutung*	is bleeding
blööd	*Blutung*	bleeds
bloom	*Blume*	flower
bloomenstruss	*Blumenstrauss*	bouquet
blöör	*Blüten*	blooms
blöör	*Blätter*	leaves
bloos	*blasen*	blow
blooskapell	*Blasorchester*	brassband or orchestra
bloot	*Blut*	blood
blootdrück	*Blutdruck*	bloodpressure
blootloorn or heiteck	*Zecke*	tick
bloot	*bloss*	naked
blots or bloss	*bloss*	except or merely
blubbern	*sprudeln*	bubble or gush
bluchtern		bluster
bluus	*Bluse*	blouse
boben or boven	*oben*	above
bobenop or bovenup	*oben drüber*	up above
bobento	*zuzätzlich*	in addition or on top of
böck or boek	*Insektin*	bugs
bock	*Bock*	buck or bench
bock	*Käfer*	bug
bock	*Ramme*	ram
bodder	*Butter*	sandwich
bodderbloomen	*Löwenzahn*	dandelion

bodderbrot	*utterbrot*	bread & butter
bodderflegen	*Schmetterlinge*	butterflies
bodderköken	*Speisekammer*	pantry
bodderköken	*Butter Küchen*	butterkitchen
bodderlicker	*Schmetterling*	butterfly
boddermelk, karnmelk	*Buttermilch*	buttermilk
boddern	*Butter*	butter
bögel	*Steigbügel*	stirrup
böhn	*Dachboden*	ceiling or upstairs
bohn	*Bahn*	highway
bohnen	*Bohne*	bean
böke	*Bücher*	books
bökeree	*Bücherei*	library
bökerschapp	*Bücherschrank*	bookcase
bölk	*Geheul*	yell
bölken	*schreien*	yelling
bolz	*Kater*	tomcat
bood	*Bad*	bath
boodbüx	*Badehose*	swim trunks
bόόg	*beugen*	bend
boog	*Bug*	bow
book	*Buch*	book
bookbrett	*ücherbrett*	bookshelf
bookdeckel	*Buchdeckel*	bookcover
bookdrücker	*Drucker*	printer or publisher
bookschapp	*Bücherschrank*	book case
bookstov	*Buchstabe*	letter or character
bookweten pannkoken	*Pfannkuchen*	Buckwheat pancakes
bomms	*Krach*	crash or splat
boom	*Baum*	tree
boomgoorn	*Obstgarten*	orchard
boon	*bauen*	build
bόόr	*heben*	lift or raise
boots or batz	*sofort*	right away
boov	*oben*	above
börgen or lehn	*borgen*	borrow
borg	*Burg*	castle
börger	*Einwohnern*	citizens
borger	*Bürger*	citizen
börgerkrieg	*Bürgerkrieg*	civil war
Börgermeester, Schulte	*Bürgermeister*	mayor
börgerschop	*Bürgerschaft*	citizenry
börgersinn	*Gemeinsinn*	public spirit
börgt	*bückt*	bends
bork	*Borke*	bark

born	*Quell Brunnen*	spring fountain
börst	*Bürste*	brush
bort	*Bart*	beard
bös	*böse*	mad or angry
bös	*Übel*	evil
bosem	*Busen*	bosom
bösorrig	*bösartig*	vicious or angry mood
bost	*bersten*	burst
bost or boss	*Brust*	chest or breast
bostdook	*Schürzenlatz*	bib
bostmoder	*Milchmutter*	foster mother
bosttashen	*Brust Tasche*	chest pocket
bott	*Gebot*	bid
böwerste	*Vorstand*	department head, highest
braadt	*braten*	broil
Braakmaand	*Brachmonat*	June
brauk	*Bruch*	marsh or wet area
brede	*Planken*	boards or planks
breedbiel	*Breite Axt*	broadaxe
breede	*breit*	wide
breede	*Breite*	width
breef	*Brief*	letter
breefdreger	*Briefträger*	mailman or postman
breefkassen	*Briefkasten*	mailbox
breev	*Briefe*	letters
bregen or brägen	*Gehirn*	brain
brek	*brechen*	break
brenn	*Weinbrand*	brandy
brenneree	*Brennerei*	distillery
brett	*Brett*	board
bries	*Brise*	breeze
brill	*Brille*	glasses or eyeglasses
brille	*Brille*	glasses or spectacles
brillianten	*Diamanten*	diamonds
bring	*bringen*	bring
brink	*am Rande*	edge of village
brinn	*brennen*	burn
brinnnettel	*Brennnessel*	burning nettle
brocht	*brocht*	brought
broder or broer	*Bruder*	brother
broderschop	*Bruderschaft*	brotherhood
broderswester	*Schwägerin*	sister-in-law
brögam	*Bräutigam*	bridegroom or fiance
bröh	*Suppe*	broth
broken	*gebrochen*	broken

brölen	*kochen*	boil
bröör	*brauen*	brew
brööree	*Brauerei*	brewery
brot or broot	*Brot*	bread
brotkist	*Brotkorb*	bread box
brotmest	*Brotmesser*	bread knife
brüch or brügg	*Brücke*	bridge
bruddig	*launisch*	sultry or moody
brüdjen	*plagen*	tease
brüllen	*brüllen*	bellow
brüllsch	*läifig*	in heat
brummel	*brummen*	grumble
brummelbeern	*Brombeere*	blackberry
brummsen	*zermalmen*	bruise
bruuk	*gebrauchen*	use
bruun	*Braun*	brown
brüür or brüden	*plagen*	tease
bruus	*Brause*	storm or rage
bruuswoter	*Sturmwasser*	stormwater
bruut	*Braut*	bride
bruutföhrer	*Brautführer*	best man
bruutjungfro	*Brautjungfer*	maid of honor
bück	*bücken*	bend down
buddel	*Flasche*	bottle
buddels	*Flaschen*	bottles
büdel	*Beutel*	bag or pouch
büdelneiher	*egelmacher*	sailmaker
bül	*Beil*	hatchet
bullenkopp	*Krug*	jug (7 liters)
bullenstöter	*Stichling*	stickleback
bullerjahn	*Polterei*	wedding celebration
bült	*Hügel*	hill
bums	*dröhnen*	thud
bün	*bin*	am
bünnel	*Bündel*	bundle
bunneln	*bündeln*	tie into bundle
bunnen	*gebunden*	tied or bound
bunt	*farbenreich*	colorful
bunte	*Volkstanz*	german square dance
bunte	*Viereckig*	quadrille
bürker	*Holtzhammer*	wooden hammer or mallet
buro	*Kommode*	dresser
busch	*Busch*	bush
buschig	*buschig*	bushy
bush or holt	*Wald*	woods

283

bussdag	*Öffnungstag*	opening day
büssenflint	*Schrotflinte*	shotgun
büst	*sind*	are
buten	*Aussenseite*	outside
butenbord	*über Bord*	overboard
butendöör	*Aussentür*	outside door
butenhannel	*Aussenhandel*	foreign trade
butenkant	*Umkreis*	periphery
butenland	*Auslands*	foreign land
butenrüm	*Radius*	aroundoutside
butt	*frech*	impudent
buttfisch	*Flunder*	flounder
buuk knoop	*Nabel*	belly button
buuk	*Bauch*	belly
buukörgel	*Harmonika*	accordion
buukpien	*auchschmerz*	stomach pain
buuksnaker	*Bauchredner*	ventriloquist
buukweh	*Magenschmerz*	bellyache
buul	*Beule*	dent
buur	*Bauer*	farmer
buuree	*Meierei*	dairy farm, farming
buurfro or buurfru	*Bäuerin*	farmer's wife
buurhuus	*Bauernhaus*	farmhouse
buurschop	*Bauerntum*	peasantry, township
buursteed	*Bauerstelle*	farmstead
büx or büxen	*Hosen*	pants
büxendregers	*Hosenträger*	suspenders
büxenshieter	*Hosenscheisser*	baby
chaff	*Spreu*	hacksel
chef	*Chef*	chief
chor	*Chor*	choir
christlig	*christlich*	christian
dä	*getan*	did
daag	*Tage*	days
daagsblatt	*Tagesblatt*	daily paper
daagslicht	*Tageslicht*	daylight
daakig	*Tauig, Dunstig*	cloudy or foggy
daame	*Dame*	lady
dään	*sie tun*	they did
Daansch	*Dänisch*	Danish
dacht	*gedacht*	thought
dack	*Dach*	roof
dag	*Tag*	day

284

däglig	*Täglich*	daily
daglohner	*Taglohner*	day laborer
dahl or daal	*nieder*	down
dahlblosen	*niederblasen*	blow down
dahlbreken	*zusammenbrechen*	break down
dahlbroken	*zusammenbrochen*	broken down
dahlfallen	*niederfallen*	fall down or fail
dahlhuken	*Hocken*	squat
dahljagen	*ubertrieben*	drive over
dahllaten	*niederlassen*	let down
dahlmarken	*abschlagen*	mark down
dahlrieten	*niederrissen*	tear down
dahlsackt	*versanken*	sank or sunk
dahlsluken	*verschluken*	swallow
dahlsluten	*verschliessen*	shut down
dal	*Tal*	valley
damp	*Dampf*	steam
damper	*Dampfer*	steamship
dank	*Dank*	thank
dankbor	*dankbar*	thankful
dann	*Tannen*	pine
dannboom	*Tannenbaum*	pine tree or fir tree
dannhäger	*Eichelhäher*	jay
dansen	*tanzen*	to dance
danz	*Tanz*	a dance
darm	*Därme*	intestines
daswegen	*deswegen*	that's why
dat or et	*es*	it
dat	*das*	that
dau	*Tau*	dew
de	*der*	the
deck	*Boden*	floor
deck	*Deck*	deck
deckel	*Deckel*	lid
deckelblatt	*Titelseite*	cover page
deef	*Dieb*	thief
deeg	*Teig*	dough
deel	*Diele*	hall floor or barn floor
deel	*Ding*	thing or article
deel	*Fall*	instance
deel	*Handel*	deal
deel	*Teil*	part or portion
deelbor	*Teilbar*	partially
deelen	*austeilen*	deal cards
deelen	*Dinge*	things

285

deelwies	*Teilweis*	partial
deenen	*dienen*	serve or earn
deenenstunnen	*Werkstunden*	working hours
deenstdeern	*Magd*	maid
deent	*verdient*	works or earns
deep	*Tief*	deep
deern or diern	*Mädchen*	girl
deerns	*Mädchen*	girls
deert	*Tier*	animal
deesel		wood shaping hatchet
deev	*Diebe*	thief
defdig	*kernig*	durable or robust
dehnbor	*dehnbar*	vague or elastic
deiht	*tut*	(he,she,it) does
deiht mi leed	*tut mir Leid*	I'm sorry
denk	*denken*	think
denkmol	*Denkmal*	monument
denn	*dann*	then
denntied	*zu Zeit*	that time or at that time
dennweg	*dassweg*	that way
Dezember	*Dezember*	December
di	*du*	you
dibbern	*Nörgeln*	nag
dicht fallen	*zugefallen*	fallen shut
dicht	*dich*	close or near
dichtbi	*dicht bei*	close by or nearby
dichtel	*Gedicht*	poem
dichter	*ichter*	closer or nearer
dick	*dick*	thick
dickdohn	*gross getan*	showed off
dickdoon	*ich grosstun*	show off
dicke frünnen	*Busenfreunde*	close friends
dicke tied	*heiterkeit*	high old time
dickeschütt	*Schmollen*	pout
dickliev	*fleischig*	corpulant or fat
didrik	*Nachschlüssel*	skeleton key
diek	*Deich*	dike
diek	*Teich*	pond
dien	*ihre*	yours
diesig	*hartnäckig*	stubborn
ding	*Ding*	thing
Dingsdag	*Dienstag*	Tuesday
dinn	*dieser or jene*	that one
dint	*tinte*	ink
direkschoon	*Richtung*	direction

direkt	*direkt*	direct
disch	*Tisch*	table or plate
dischdecken	*Tischtuch*	table cloth
discher	*Kunsttischler*	cabinet maker
discheree	*ischlerei*	cabinet shop
dischlaken	*Tischtuch*	table cloth
dischlappen	*Spüllappen*	dish rag
dischler	*Tischler*	carpenter
dischschuuf	*Schublade*	table drawer
disken	*scheiben*	disc
dissel	*Distel*	thistle
disselboom	*Deichsel*	wagon tongue
do	*tu*	do
do	*dann*	then
doch	*doch*	anyhow or nevertheless
dochter	*Tochter*	daughter
doden	*Toden*	dead ones
doh	*tue*	do it
dohn	*fertig*	done
dohn	*getan*	did it
dokter	*Arzt*	doctor
dokters	*Ärzte*	doctors
doler	*Taler*	dollar
dömelig	*gedankenlos*	thoughtless
domols	*damals*	then or at the time
döntje	*Kurzgeschichte*	tall tales
dood or doot	*Tod*	dead
doof or dief	*taub*	deaf
dook	*lappen*	cloth
doon	*gefertigt*	done
doon	*hat getan*	have done
dööp	*Tauf*	baptize
dööpkleed	*Taufkleid*	baptism dress
dööpnaam	*Taufname*	christian name
dööpshien	*Taufschein*	baptismal certificate
döör	*Tür*	door
döörlock	*Torweg*	doorway
döörpingel	*Türklingel*	doorbell
doorn	*Dorn*	thorn
doos	*Dose*	box
doot gohn or doot bleben	*sterben*	die or died
doot mööd	*tot müde*	dead tired
doot	*tut*	we, they) do
dor or doar	*dort*	there
dör or dörch	*durch*	through

dorbi	*dabei*	thereby
dorblieben	*dableiben*	stay there
dörbreken	*durchbrechen*	break through
dörbrinnen	*durchbrennen*	burn through
döreenanner	*chaotisch*	chaotic or confused
döreenannern	*Verwirrt*	muddled
dörfallen	*fehlgeschlagen*	failed, fell through
dörfohren	*durchfahren*	drive through
dorgegens	*dagegen*	against that
dörgeneiden	*streitsüchtige*	cantankerous people
dörhaalt	*ausgebildet*	accomplished
dörhalen	*erlangen*	achieve
dorhen	*daüber*	over there
dorhin	*dahin*	that way
dorin	*drin*	in there
dörkieken	*durchblicken*	look through
dörmet	*Durchmesser*	diameter
dormit	*damit*	therewith
dorno	*dazu*	according to
doröwer	*daüber*	about that
dorp or dörp	*Dorf*	village
dörpen	*Dörfer*	villages
dörplüüd	*Dorfleute*	village people
dörrecken	*durchreichen*	reach through
dörshienig	*Transparent*	transparent
dörslag	*Durchschlag*	strainer
dörsnee	*durchgeschnitten*	was cut through
dörsnie	*durchschneiden*	cut through or slice
dörsnittlig	*Durchschnitt*	average
dörsteken	*durchstechen*	pierced
dörtehn	*durchziehen*	pull through
dörteihn	*Dreizehn*	thirteen
dörtig	*dreissig*	thirty
dorto	*dazu*	thereto
dorüm	*darum*	that's why
dorup	*darauf*	up there
dorvun	*davon*	from there
dörweihen	*durchblasen*	blow through
döschen	*dreschen*	threshing
döschflegel	*Dreschflegel*	hand thrasher
döschmaschin	*Drescher*	thrash maschine
dosen	*dösen*	day dream
döskopp	*Idiot*	dummy or idiot
döst	*Durst*	thirst
döstig	*durstig*	thirsty

288

dotomal		at that time
dotum	*Datum*	date
draad	*bald*	soon
draak	*Drache*	dragon
draaken	*Drachen*	kite
drak	*Enterich*	drake
drall	*schwach*	plump or bloated
drang	*Drang*	distress or pressure
drapen	*treffen*	meet
drapp	*treff*	hit
dreck	*Dreck*	dirt
drecklock	*Dreckloch*	mudhole
dree eck	*Dreieck*	triangle
dree eckig	*dreieckig*	triangular
dree	*Drei*	three
dreebeen	*Milchhocker*	milkstool
dreefak	*dreifach*	triple
dreeg	*tragen*	carry
dreerad	*Dreirad*	tricycle
dreih	*drehen*	turn or screw
dreihdings	*Drehung*	wrench
dreihörgel	*Drehorgel*	barrel organ
drempel	*Schwelle*	doorstep
driest	*dreist*	safely or boldly
driev	*antrieb*	urge
driev	*trieben*	drive
driewersch	*vertriebt*	reckless or driven
driggt	*trägt*	carries
drink	*Trink*	drink
drinksegg	*Trinkspruch*	toast
drög or dröög	*trocken*	dry
drogen	*tragen*	carried
dröhnbuddel	*langweilen*	bore
dröhnig	*langweilig*	boring
drömen	*Traume*	dreams
drömt	*geträumt*	dreamed
dronken or drauhen	*bedrohen*	threaten
drööm	*Traumen*	to dream
droom	*Traum*	dream
droot	*Faden*	thread
droppen	*Tropfen*	a drop
drossel	*Drossel*	thrush
dröv or dröf	*darf*	may
drück	*Druck*	pressure or print or press

drunken	*getrunken*	drank
drüppel	*Tropfen*	drops or dribble
drüs	*Drüse*	gland
druseln	*leichtes Regen*	drizzle
drütte	*Dritte*	third
drüttel	*Drittel*	one third
druuf	*Traube*	grape
du lewe strohsack	*du liebe zeit*	good heavens!
du	*du*	you
dübel or düvel	*Teufel*	devil
dübelig	*teufelig*	devilish
duddigkeit	*Trägheit*	inertia
dudelkassen	*Drehorgel*	barrel organ
duff	*schwach*	dull or feeble
duldsom	*geduldig*	tolerant
dull	*reizig*	exasperating
dull	*schnell*	fast or quick
dull	*zu viel*	too much or beyond me
dullen	*dulden*	tolerate
dullhuus	*Asyl*	asylum
dumen	*Daumen*	thumb
dumm	*dumm*	dumb
dumm	*Stumm*	mute
dumm snack	*Geschnatter*	ridiculous talk
dumm tüüch	*Unsinn*	nonsense
dummhaftig	*dumm*	stupid
dummheit	*dummheit*	dumbness or stupidity
dünen	*Dünen*	dunes
dung	*Mist*	manure
dünn	*dünn*	thin
dunner	*Donner*	thunder
Dünnersdag	*Donnerstag*	Thursday
dünnerslag	*Blitz*	lightning or thunderbolt
dunst	*Dunst*	haze
dunstig	*Dunstich*	hazy
duppel	*Doppel*	double
dusend	*Tausend*	thousand
dusenmol	*Tausendmal*	thousand times
dusenshelm		real idiot
düsig	*schwindlig*	dizzy
düsse or disse	*diese*	these
düsse	*diesen*	this one
düsstied	*diese zeit*	this time
düt or dütt	*dieses*	this
dütig	*hurtig*	quickly or greatly

dütjohr	*dieses Jahr*	this year
dütlig	*deutlich*	clearly
dütmol	*diesesmal*	this time
dutt	*menge*	heap or mass
dutz	*Dutzend*	dozen or twelve
duuken or duken	*Tauchen*	duck down, stoop
duum or duun	*betrunken*	drunk
duun	*Düne*	dune
düür	*teuer*	expensive
duurt	*dauert*	lasts
düüster	*dunkel*	dark
düüsterbrill	*Sonnenbrille*	dark glasses
düüsterdeern	*Callgirl*	callgirl
düüsterrot	*Sonnenuntergang*	sunset
düütlig	*deutlich*	distinct, simply, clear
düütsch or dütsk	*Deutsch*	german
duuv	*Taube*	dove
dwars	*diagonal*	diagonal or crosswise
dweerfeld	*querfeldein*	cross country
dweerholt	*Schlegel*	cross beam
dweerstraat	*Abendrot*	cross street
eben	*eben*	even
eben	*gleich*	in a moment
ebengliek	*dennoch*	nevertheless
ebensoveel	*in gleicher eben*	as much as
eck	*Ecke*	corner
eckel	*Eichel*	acorn
eckernsäbeln	*Maikäfer*	cockchafer or scarab
ecken	*Ecken*	corners
ecko	*Echo*	echo
edelmann	*Edelmann*	nobleman
eder	*früher*	earlier
ederkaun	*widerkauen*	chew cud
eeg	*schulden*	owe
eegen	*eigen*	own
eegennutt	*eigennutz*	self interest
eegensinning	*eigensinnig*	stubborn
eeken	*Eiche*	oak
eekkat or katekel	*Eichhörnchen*	squirrel
een	*eine*	a
een gohn laten	*Furz*	fart
een reeg vun	*einige*	some or a row of
een vun or eenner vun	*einer von*	one of
een	*ein*	one

eenanner	*einander*	one another
eendütlig	*unmissverständlich*	unequivocal
eenerlei	*einerlei*	monotonous or all the same
eenfaak or eenfach	*einfach*	simple, plain
eenheemig	*einheimisch*	local
eenige	*einige*	some
eenigt	*einigt*	agreed
eenmol or eemol	*ein mal*	one time
eenmolig	*einmalig*	unique
eenner	*einer*	one
eensige or eensigste	*einsige*	only one
eensom	*einsam*	solitary or lonely
eenspanner	*Junggeselle*	bachelor
eenverstoh	*einverstanden*	agree
eenweg	*irgenwe*	gone way, somehow
eerd	*Erde*	earth
eerdappel	*Heidecker*	potato
eerdbeern	*Erdbeere*	strawberry
eerdbeven	*Erdbeben*	earthquake
eerdöl	*Erdöl*	petroleum
eerdpik	*Asphalt*	asphalt
eerdsch	*weltlich*	worldly
eerkröppel	*Eidechse*	lizard
eersen		little bit ago
eerst	*erst*	first
eerste or eersten	*erste*	first one
egelig	*ekelhaftich*	ugly
egenortig	*ungewohnt*	unusual
egol	*gleich*	alike
egol	*gleichmässig*	equal
egolweg	*ebenso*	evenly
ehe	*Ehe*	marriage
ehefro or ehefru	*Ehefrau*	wife
ehekirl	*Ehemann*	husband
ehekrach	*Zank*	quarrel
ehelüüd	*Eheleute*	married people
ehepoor	*Ehepaar*	married couple
eher or eder	*eher*	before
ehesheeden	*Scheidung*	divorce
ehr	*ihr*	her
ehr sülbens or ehr sülms	*ihrselbst*	herself
ehr	*ihr*	their
ehr	*ihrer*	hers
ehrbor	*ehrbar*	honorable
ehre	*Ehre*	honor

292

ehrlig	*ehrlich*	honest
ei	*Ei*	egg
eier	*Eier*	eggs
eiergeel	*Eigelb*	egg yellow
eierklock	*Eieruhr*	egg timer
eierkopp	*Intellektueller*	egghead
eierrund	*Oval*	oval
eierschuum	*Eiweiss*	whipped egg white
eiershel	*Eierschale*	eggshell
eierwitt	*Eiweiss*	egg white
eisch	*artig*	naughty or mischievous
elektrik	*elektrisch*	electric
elennig	*elend*	miserable
elk	*alle*	every
elkeen	*jedermann*	everyone
ellbogen or ellentipp	*Ellbogen*	elbow
eller	*Erle*	alder
ellerboom	*Erlenbaum*	alder tree
em or üm	*ihm*	him
enerwegens	*irgendwo*	somewhere
enkeldochter	*Enkelin*	granddaughter
enn	*Ende*	end
ennlig	*endlich*	finally
enweder	*entweder*	either
erbärmlig	*Erbärmlich*	pitiful
ermel	*Armel*	sleeve
ernst	*ernst*	earnest
ernst	*ernsthaft*	serious
erstenmol or eerstenmol	*erstenmal*	first time
esch	*Esche*	ash
eschboom	*Eschenbaum*	ash tree
escher	*Spaten*	spade
esel	*Esel*	donkey
essig	*Essig*	vinegar
et	*essen*	eat
etdisch	*Essentisch*	dinner table
eten or äten	*essen*	to eat
eten or spies	*Speise*	food or eats or meal
etenkorden or spieskorden	*Speisekarte*	menu
etgeshirr	*Tischgeschirr*	dinner service
etlepel	*Esslöffel*	tablespoon
etoje	*Etage*	story or floor
etwas	*etwas*	some or something
ever	*Eber*	boar
ewig	*ewig*	ever

ewig	*ewigkeit*	forever
extro	*extra*	extra
fack	*Fach*	subject or specialty
fackel	*zaudern*	hesitate
facklüüd or faklüüd	*Fachleute*	experts
fackminsch or fakminsch	*Fachmann*	expert
fall	*Fall*	fall
fall	*Falle*	trap
fallen	*gefallen*	fell
falsch	*falsch*	false
falten	*Runzeln*	wrinkles
familje	*Familie*	family
famos	*famos*	famous
fantasie	*Phantasie*	fantasy
farken	*Ferkel*	piglets
farv	*Farbe*	color or dye
fason	*Fasan*	pheasant
fast	*fest*	firm
Fastelobend	*Fastnacht*	Shrove Tuesday
fastmoken	*befestigen*	fasten
Februor	*Februar*	February
feeg	*Fegen*	sweep
feend	*Feind*	enemy
feendlig	*feindlich*	hostile
fehlt	*fehlend*	missing or is wrong with
fein	*fein*	fine or nice
feld	*Feld*	field
fell	*Fell*	skin
fellenhoot	*Federhut*	featherhat
fellenveeh	*Federvieh*	poultry or chickens
fellerbedd	*Federbett*	featherbed
fellern or fedder	*Feder*	feather
ferdig	*fertig*	finished or done
fesen	*Fasen*	fiber
festdag	*Feiertag*	holiday
fett	*Fett*	fat or lard
fettbuuk	*Bauch*	paunch
fettcakes	*Fettgebackenes*	donuts
fewers	*Fieber*	fever
fiecheln	*streicheln*	stroke or caress
fief or fiev or fiiv	*Fünf*	five
fiefadernblöör	*Wegerich*	plantain
fieg	*Feige*	fig
fiegboom	*Feigenbaum*	fig tree

fiel	*Feile*	file or rasp
fien moken	*dekorieren*	decorate or dress up
fien	*leicht*	fine or thin
fienbeker	*Tortekoch*	pastry cook
fienkost	*Feinkost*	delicacy
fier	*feiern*	celebrate
fierdaag	*Feiertage*	holidays
fierdag	*Feiertag*	holiday
fiftel	*Murmel*	murmur
figur	*Figur*	figure
figuren	*Zahlen*	figures
finanz	*Finanzwesen*	finance
finger	*Finger*	finger
fingerhandshen	*Handschuh*	glove
fingerhoot	*Fingerhut*	thimble
fingern	*Fingern*	fingers
fingerspitz	*Fingerspitz*	fingertip
finnen	*finden*	find
finster	*Fenster*	window
finsterbank	*Fenstersims*	window sill
finsterbrett	*Fensterbrett*	window sill
finsterklappen	*Fensterladen*	shutters
finsterschief	*Fensterscheibe*	window pane
fipsig	*schwach*	feeble
fisch	*Fisch*	fish
fix	*fix*	quick or neatly
flaak or flach	*flach*	shallow or plain
flammen	*Flammen*	flames
flaschappel	*Kürbis*	pumpkin
flass	*Flachs*	flax
flau	*Flau*	faint
flaukopp	*Blond*	blonde
fleder	*Flieder*	lilac
fleeg	*Fliege*	fly
fleehan	*Fliehan*	flee
fleesch	*Fleisch*	flesh or meat
flegenklopper	*Fliegenschlager*	flyswatter
fleiche	*Pfeifen*	whistle
fleichepiepen	*Flöte*	whistle pipe
flick	*flicken*	mend
flicken	*Flicken*	patch
flicken	*reparieren*	repair
fliddermuus	*Fledermaus*	bat
fliddermüüs	*Fledermäuse*	bats
flietig	*fleissig*	hardworking or industrious

flink	*rasch*	quick
flint	*Gewehr*	gun
flintpulwer	*Schiesspulver*	gunpowder
flister	*Geflüster*	whisper
flitterkraam	*Putz*	finery
flitzboogen	*Schleuder*	slingshot
flock	*Flocke*	flake
flogen	*geflogen*	flew
floh or flei	*Floh*	flea
flohtpiepen	*Flöte*	flute
flöög	*flögen*	flew
floot	*Flut*	flood
flortsche	*Libelle*	dragonfly
flott	*Flotte*	navy
flott	*Flussen*	flowed
flött	*Rahm*	cream
fluch	*Fluch*	cuss or curse
fludderig	*veränderlich*	fickle
flüh	*Flöh*	fleas
flunk	*Flügel*	wing
flünken	*Flügel*	wings
flunken	*flunkern*	fib
flunkert	*flunkert*	fibs
flussig	*verstellbar*	variable or liquid
flutt	*Fluss*	the flow
fluug	*Flucht*	flight
fluur	*Fussboden*	floor
foder	*Fuder*	cartload
föffteihn	*Fünfzehn*	fifteen
föfftel	*Fünftel*	fifth
föfftig	*Fünfzig*	fifty
fohl	*Fohlen*	foal
föhl	*Fühl*	feel
föhlbor	*wahrnehmbar*	noticeable
föhlen or geföhlen	*Fühlen*	feelings
fohn or flagg	*Fahne*	flag
föhr or jaag	*Fahren*	drive
föhrbohn	*Fahrbahn*	driving lane
föhrgast	*Fahrgast*	passenger
föhrkorden	*Fahrkarte*	travel ticket
föhrmann	*Fahrer*	driver
föhrshien	*Führerschein*	drivers license
föhrstohl	*Fahrstuhl*	elevator car
foken or faken	*häufig*	frequent or often
foorts	*sofort*	right away or at once

foot	*Fuss*	foot
fööt	*Füsse*	feet
footganger	*Fussgänger*	pedestrian
footpadd	*Fusspfad*	footpath
footspur	*Fussabdruck*	footprint
footstohl	*Fussbank*	footstool
foppen	*necken*	tease
för	*für*	for
förbeden	*verbieten*	forbid
Först	*Fürst*	Prince
förwoort	*Fürwort*	pronoun
fot an or fat an	*Halt*	hold
fot or fat	*gegriffen*	grasped
fotkriegen or fatkriegen	*Griff*	grab
fraag or froog	*Frage*	a question
fraag	*fragen*	ask
fraagsteert		questioning pest
fraagt	*Fragt*	asks
Franzoos	*Französisch*	French
Fredag or Freedag	*Freitag*	Friday
free	*frei*	available
free	*frei*	free
freed	*verheiratet*	married
freeden	*Freiheit*	freedom or peace
freedhof	*Friedhof*	graveyard or cemetery
freegewig	*freigebig*	generous
freeholen	*Reserve*	reserve
freemödig	*aufrichtig*	candid
freen	*Heiraten*	to marry or to court
freer	*frieren*	freeze
freetied	*Freizeit*	liesure
freewillig	*freiwillig*	voluntary
freiht mi	*erfreut mich*	makes me happy
frenschen or frensken	*wiehern*	neigh
freten	*fressen*	eat
fretsack	*Fresser*	glutton
frisch	*frisch*	fresh
fro or fru	*Frau*	wife
froh	*glücklich*	happy
froh	*froh*	glad
fröh	*früh*	early
fröher tieden	*früher Zeiten*	past times
fröher	*früher*	earlier or in the past
fröhjohr	*Frühling*	spring
fröhriep	*`frühreif*	precocious

fröhstück	*Frühstück*	breakfast
fröhtiedig	*frühzeitig*	early or premature
frömd	*fremd*	foreign
frömde	*Fremde*	stranger
frömdwoort	*Fremdwort*	foreign word
fröngslüüd	*Frauen*	women
fröngsminsch	*Frau*	woman
froom	*fromm*	devout
froren	*gefroren*	frozen
frost	*Frost*	frost
frucht	*Frucht*	fruit
fruchtbor	*fruchtbar*	fruitful
fründ	*Freund*	friend
fründjen	*flirten*	to flirt
fründlig	*freundlich*	friendly
fründschop	*Freundschaft*	friendship
frünnen	*freunden*	friends
fuchtig	*gesund*	fit or in shape
fudder	*futter*	to feed
fudder	*Futter*	food
fuddertied	*futterzeit*	feeding time
fuget	*mogeln*	cheat
führpelig	*furchtbar*	tremendously
funkschoon	*Funktion*	function
funnen	*gefunden*	found
futsch	*ist weg!*	suddenly gone
fuul	*faul*	lazy
fuulheit	*Faulheit*	laziness
fuulheit	*Torheit*	silliness
fuulsnuut	*Strolch*	bum
füünsch	*bewegt*	agitated or peeved
füür or füer	*Feuer*	fire
füürbaas	*Feuerchef*	fire chief
füürböter	*Brandstifter*	arsonist
füürböter	*Hirschkäfer*	stag beetle
füürsteed or füürplatz	*Herd*	fire place
fuus	*Faust*	fist
füüs	*Fäuste*	fists
fuushandshen	*Fausthandschuh*	mitten
gadder	*Gitter*	trellis
gadderwark	*Gitterfenster*	grillwork
gagel	*Zahnfleisch*	gums
gallsüchtig	*cholerisch*	choleric
galopp	*Trott*	trot

galsterig	*ranzig*	rancid
gang or gangweg	*Gang*	aisle
ganner	*Gänserich*	gander
gans beten or gans bäten	*zehr viel*	quite a bit
gans un gor	*ins gesampt*	totally
ganse	*ganz*	entire
ganslig	*gänzlich*	entirely
garv	*gerben*	to tan hide
gassen oder grube	*Gerste*	barley
gast	*Gast*	guest
gasten	*Gäste*	guests
gau	*schnell*	fast
geben or gebem	*gegeben*	given
geben	*geben*	deal cards
geböhr	*Gebühr*	fee
gebööt	*Bau*	building
gebörde	*Gebäude*	buildings
gebott	*Gebot*	command
gebruuk	*Gebrauch*	custom or tradition
gebruuk	*gebrauch*	use
geburen	*geboren*	born
geburt	*Geburt*	birth
geburtsdag	*Geburtstag*	birthday
gedanken	*Gedanken*	thoughts
gedeen	*gedeihen*	thrive
gedibber	*Plauder*	chatter
gedicht	*Gedicht*	poem
gedullig	*geduldig*	patient
geduur	*Geduld*	patience
geel	*Gelb*	yellow
geelimmick	*Goldammer*	yellow hammer bird
geern	*gern*	gladly or with pleasure
geest	*geist*	spirit
geet	*giessen*	pour
geetkann	*Giesskanne*	watering can
geev	*geben*	give
geev in	*nachgeben*	give in
geev	*Dosis*	dose
gefähr	*Gefahr*	danger
gefährlig	*gefährlich*	unsafe or dangerous
gefallen	*Gefallen*	favor
gegend	*Gegend*	area or region
gegendeel	*Gegenteil*	contrary or opposite
gegens	*gegen*	against
gegensiedig	*Gegenseitig*	opposite

299

gegenspeeler	*Opponent*	opponent
gegenspruk	*Einspruch*	objection
gegenstohn	*widerstehen*	resist
gegensweern	*gegensetzen*	oppose
geheel	*Gesampt*	totality
gehoorsom	*gehorsam*	obedient
gehörig	*zehr viel*	a lot
gehüür	*Argwohn*	suspicion
geihs	*geht*	is going
geiht an	*gescheht*	occurs
geiht los	*einfallen*	get started
geiht	*geht*	goes
geld	*Geld*	money
geldkassen	*Geldkassette*	cashbox
geldknipp	*Geldbeutel*	purse
gellt	*Gültig*	valid
gelööf	*geloben*	vow
gelött	*Geläuten*	chimes
gelovet	*geliebt*	beloved
gemeen	*Gemein*	congregation
gemeensom	*gemeinsam*	common
gemellig	*langsam*	slow
gemöös	*Gemüse*	vegetables
genau	*genau*	exact
genehm	*angenehm*	pleasant
generatschoon	*Generation*	generation
genral	*General*	general
geneten	*geniessen*	enjoy or relish
gereide	*Schmuck*	jewelry
geren	*gären*	ferment
gerichtsholder	*Richter*	judge
geruch or rüük	*Geruch*	smell or odor
gesangbook	*Gesangbuch*	hymnal
gesegge	*Gerede*	rumor
gesell	*Junggeselle*	bachelor
gesell	*Lehrling*	apprentice
gesellschop	*Gesellschaft*	association
gesett	*Gesetz*	act or statute or law
geshichte	*Geschichte*	history
geshichte	*Geschichte*	story
geshink	*Geschenk*	present or gift
geshirr	*Geschirr*	horse equipment
gesicht	*Gesicht*	face
gesicht	*Grimas*	expression
gesichten	*Gesichten*	faces

gesmack	*Geschmack*	taste
gespöös		empathy
gesprek	*Gespräch*	discussion or dialog
gest	*Gischt*	yeast
gestank	*Gestank*	stench or stink
gestell	*Bausystem*	framework
gesund	*gesund*	healthy
gesundheit	*Gesundheit*	health
geswister	*Geschwister*	siblings
gewees	*Getue*	attitude
geweten	*Gewissen*	conscience
gewicht	*Gewicht*	weight
gewidder	*Sturm*	storm
gewinn	*Gewinn*	win
gewinnt	*gewöhnt*	accustomed or used to
gewiss	*allerdings*	certainly or for sure
gewiss or wiss	*gewiss*	certain or sure
gewöhnlig	*gewöhnlich*	usually
gewonnen	*gewonnen*	won
gewrögel	*Tumult*	tumult
giezhals	*Geizhals*	miser or tightwad
giezig or nährig	*geizig*	miserly or stingy or thrifty
gifft	*giebt*	gives
gift	*Gift*	poison
gild or gill	*Gilde*	guild
gilt	*Sau*	sow
giraap	*Giraff*	giraffe
gistern or güstern	*gestern*	yesterday
gittigitt	*hu!*	ugh!
glas schap	*Glaskasten*	glass cupboard
glas	*Glas*	glass
gläs	*Gläser*	glasses
glatt	*glatt*	smooth or shiny
glatt	*hübsch*	pretty
glatties	*Glatteis*	black ice
glattsnacker	*Schmeichler*	flatterer
glemlig	*glimpflich*	lenient
glemmer	*Glimmer*	glimmer
glieck	*gleich*	even or alike
glieden	*Gleiten*	glide
gliek or mag lieden	*gefallen*	like
gliekentied	*gleicherzeit*	contemporaneous
glieks	*bald*	soon
glind	*Geländer*	railing
glinnig	*glänzig*	glinty

301

glinster	*Glitzern*	twinkle
glipp	*ausgleiten*	slip
glöhnig	*glühnig*	glowing
gloot	*Glut*	ardor
glösen or glötern	*Glühen*	glow
glöv	*glaub*	believe
glück	*Glücksfall*	luck
glücken	*gelingen*	succeed
glücklig	*glücklich*	lucky
gnaad	*Gnade*	mercy or grace
gnaasten	*knirschen*	grind
gnibble	*benagen*	nibble
gnick	*Genick*	neck
gniggle	*kichern*	chuckle or giggle
gnitt	*Mücke*	mayfly or gnat
gnuur	*knurren*	growl
gobel	*Gabel*	fork
gockelhohn	*Hahn*	rooster or act like a rooster
Godd	*Gott*	God
goddesdeenst	*Gottesdienst*	religious service
gode or goode	*ein gute*	good one
goden dag	*Guten Tag*	good day
goden moren	*Guten Morgen*	good morning
goden obend	*Guten Abend*	good evening
godendagstock	*Spazierstock*	cane
gödig	*gütig*	kind
goh man to	*geh zu*	go ahead
goh mitut	*entbehren*	go without
goh or gah or gaoh	*geh*	go or walk
gohn	*gegangen*	went
göl		swale
gold	*Gold*	gold
golden	*golden*	golden
good	*gut*	good
goodhartig	*gütig*	kind or kindly
goodheit	*Gutheit*	goodness
goodstuuv	*Gastzimmer*	parlor
goor or goar	*gar*	fully cooked or done
göör or gör	*kind*	brat or kid
goorn or goarn	*Garten*	garden
goos bloomen	*Gänseblümchen*	daisy
goos	*Gans*	goose
gördel	*Gürtel*	belt or girdle
goren	*Garn*	yarn
gören	*Zicke*	brats or kids

302

görgel	*Gürgel*	throat
görgeln	*gurgeln*	gargle
gorkeen	*kein*	none
gössel	*Gänseküken*	gosling
gött	*strömend*	pouring
gotten	*gegossen*	poured
grab	*Grab*	grave
graben	*Graben*	ditch
grabsteen	*Grabstein*	grave stone
graleeren	*gratulieren*	congratulate
grapsen		grab quickly
gras	*Gras*	grass
grasen	*weiden*	graze
gräsig	*furchtbar*	awful
gräsig	*sehr*	greatly
gresen	*Schaudern*	shudder
grien	*grinsen*	grin
griep	*greif*	grab or grasp
gries	*grau*	gray
grieselig	*grausig*	gruesome
grod	*gerade*	straight
grod	*Grad*	degree
grode knacker		big shot
grode	*gerade*	straight one
gröder	*grösser*	larger
grodmuul	*Lautmaul*	loudmouth
grodordig	*grossartig*	splendid or imposing
grodshrieben	*gross schreiben*	capitalize
grodsporig	*grotspurig*	self important
grodsporig	*hochmütig*	arrogant
Grof	*Graf*	Count
groff	*grob*	coarse or rough
Grofin	*Grafin*	Countess
grömen	*sich grämen*	grieve
grön or gröön	*Grün*	green
grönhöke	*Gemüsenhändler*	vegetable trader
grönkroom	*Gemüse*	vegetable
grönsnobel	*Grünschnabel*	greenhorn
grood	*erschrocken*	afraid of
grööt	*grüssen*	greet
groov or graav	*graben*	dig
gropen or grapen	*Topf*	iron pot on 4 legs
gröt or grött	*Grösse*	size
gröten	*Gruss*	greetings
grötste	*grösste*	biggest or largest

grube	*Rübe*	turnip
grübel	*murren*	grumble or complain
grund	*Basis*	basis or reason
grund	*Grund*	ground
gründen	*begründen*	found or establish
grundsteen	*Gründung*	foundation
grundstock or grundfluur	*Erdgeschoss*	ground floor
grundswien	*Murmeltier*	ground hog
grünsen	*murren*	groan
grusel	*ekel*	disgust
grüsom	*grausam*	cruel
grusskinner	*Enkelkinder*	grandchildren
grussmoder or Oma	*Grossmutter*	grandmother
grussvoder or Opa	*Grossvater*	grandfather
grütt	*Grütze*	gruel
gud	*Gut*	wealth
gummiband	*Gummiband*	rubberband
gummiwogen	*Gummiwaggon*	rubbertired wagon
güng	*geht*	went
günn	*günsten*	favor with
günner	*Gönner*	patron
Gunsdag	*Mittwoch*	Wednesday
günseln	*Geheul*	howl
günstig	*günstig*	favorable
gurk	*Gurke*	pickel or cucumber
gurren	*gurren*	coo
guts noch mol!		what's going on, son-of-gun!

haas	*Kaninchen*	rabbit or hare
haasenfoot	*Feigling*	coward
habbelig	*verkommen*	disheveled
habbock	*Hirsch*	stag
hacken	*Ferse*	heel
hagel	*Hagel*	hail
hak	*hacken*	to hoe
haken	*Hacke*	hoe
halen	*abholen*	fetch or go get
halfweg	*annähernd*	halfway
hals	*Hals*	throat
halsdook	*Halstuch*	kerchief
halsjük	*Halsjoch*	yoke
halskedden	*Halskette*	necklace
halv	*halb*	half
halvestunn	*halbe Stunde*	half an hour
halvig s'morrns	*morgendlich*	mid morning

halvig s'nammidag		mid afternoon
hälvscheed	*halb Portion*	half portion
hälvstetied	*halbe Zeiten*	half the time
hand	*Hand*	hand
handdook	*Handtuch*	handcloth
handlink	*Handgelenck*	wrist
handshen or handsken	*Handschuhe*	gloves
handshrift	*Handschrift*	handwriting
handstock	*Spazierstock*	cane
handvull	*Handvoll*	handfull
hängt an	*abhängig*	depends on
hannel	*handel*	handle
hannel	*Handel*	trade
hännen	*Hände*	hands
hännig	*geschickt*	handy
hansworst	*Hanswurst*	clown
happig	*begeistered*	enthused
harbarg	*Herberge*	inn
Hardemaand	*Januar*	January
hark	*Harke*	hoe or rake
harken	*harken*	to hoe
harp	*Harfe*	harp
harr dat geern	*gern haben*	adored that
harr	*gehabt*	had
harrn	*sie haben*	(we, they) had
hart	*Herz*	heart
harten (korden)	*Herz*	heart (in cards)
hartenlust	*herzenslust*	heart's desire
hartklopp	*Herzschlag*	heart beat
hartlig	*herzlich*	cordially or heartily
hartpuckern, hartslag	*Herzanfall*	heartattack
harvst	*Herbst*	all or autumn
harvstied	*Ernte Zeit*	harvest time
Harvstmaand	*September*	September
hass	*Hass*	hate
hasskater	*Waldameise*	red ant
hatt or hart	*hart*	hard
hatthüren	*schwerhörig*	hard of hearing
hau	*Schlag*	hit or pound or strike
hau fork	*Heu Forke*	hay fork
hau or hai	*Heu*	hay
haufeld	*Weide*	hay field or pasture
Haumaand	*Juli*	July
haupt or hoopt	*Haupt*	main
hauptdings	*Hauptfach*	main thing

hauptsaak	*Hauptsache*	important thing
hauptseklig	*Hauptsächlig*	primarily
hauraaker	*Heuharker*	hay rake
he or hei	*Er*	he
hebben	*habenn*	have
hebbt	*gehabt*	they have
hecken	*Hecke*	hedges
heeg up	*ersparen*	save up
heeg	*sparen*	save
heek or hekt	*Hecht*	pike
heel moken	*heilen*	heal
heel	*hei*	whole or healthy
heelen	*heil*	cure
heem or heimot	*Heim*	home
heemgeburen	*einheimische*	native
heemig	*hiesig*	local
heemsch	*unwillig*	indignant
heer	*her*	ago
heer	*hier*	over here
heet	*heiss*	call
heet	*heiss*	hot
heeten	*heissen*	called
heff	*haben*	have
heff dat geern	*gern haben*	adore that
heff geern	*entzückend finden*	adore
hegen	*hegen*	cherish
hehn	*Huhn*	chicken
hehn	*Henne*	hen
heide	*Heide*	heath
heide	*Moor*	moor
heidelbeern	*Heidelbeere*	bilberry
heiroden	*heiraten*	marry
heister	*Elster*	magpie
hekeln	*häkeln*	crochet
hell	*hell*	bright
hell	*hell*	light
hellrot	*Scharlach*	scarlet
hemmet	*Hanf*	hemp
hengt	*hängt*	hangs
her or heer	*lang her*	ago
herd	*Herd*	hearth
herkommt	*Herkunft*	origin
hermel	*Hermelin*	ermine
Hertog	*Herzog*	Duke
herünner	*unter hier*	under here

herup	*hier oben*	up here
hetje	*Axt*	hatchet
hett	*hätte*	(he,she,it) has
hett klappt	*hatt geklappt*	worked out,successful
hevel	*Hebel*	lever
heven or heben	*Himmel*	heaven
hex	*Axt*	axe
hex	*Hexe*	witch
hexenkruut	*Dill*	dill
hiddelig	*aufgeregt*	excited
hier	*hier*	here
hier un dor	*hier und dort*	here and there
hierher	*dieser weg*	this way
hierrüm	*hier um*	around here
hill or hild	*hektisch*	hectic or busy
hillig or weih	*heilig*	holy
himbeeren	*Himbeere*	raspberry
himd	*Hemd*	shirt
himphamp	*flatterhaft*	muddle head, scatterbrain
hin un her	*hin und her*	here and there
hin un trüg	*hin und zurück*	back and forth
hin un weller	*manchmal*	sometimes
hinfinnen	*weg gefinden*	find the way
hing	*hängen*	hang
hingen	*Scharnier*	hinge
hings	*Hengst*	stallion
hinken	*hinken*	limp
hinlang	*entlang*	along
hinlangen	*erlangen*	reach for
hinner	*hinter*	behind
hinnergrund	*hintergrund*	background
hinnern	*hinten*	backside
hinnern	*Rückseite*	hinder
hinrecken	*ausstrecken*	reach for
hinsetten	*nachlassen*	relax
hinstellen	*stellen*	put in place
hinto	*Annährung*	towards or approaching
hinünner	*daunter*	under there
hinwies	*Hinweis*	reference
hinwiesen	*hinzeigen*	point to
hinwiest	*hingezeigt*	pointed
hirschkoh	*Reh*	doe
hitt	*Hitze*	heat
hittkopp	*Hitzkopp*	hothead
hittöl	*Heitzöl*	heating oil

hitzig	*hitzköpfig*	hot tempered
hobe	*Nabe*	hub
hoben or hoven	*Hafen*	harbor
hochnäs	*eingebildet*	conceited
höchstens	*höchstens*	primarily
hochtied	*Hochzeit*	wedding
hochtiedbitter	*Hochzeitsbitter*	wedding inviter
hochtiednödiger	*Hochzeitsbitter*	wedding inviter
höden or hödjen	*Hüten*	herd
hof or hoff	*Bauernhof*	barnyard
höflig	*höflich*	courteous
höflig	*höflich*	polite
hofsteed	*Hof*	farmyard
hög, höög	*amüsieren*	be amused, be pleased
högel	*Hobel*	plane
högelig	*freudig*	joyful
hogen	*Gehölz*	thicket
höglig	*froh*	cheerful
hoh düütsch or hoch dütsk	*Hoch Deutsch*	high german
hoh inbild	*einbildet*	conceited
hoh	*hoch*	tall or high
höh	*Höhe*	height
höhger	*höher*	higher
hohn	*Hahn*	cock or rooster
höhner	*Geflügel*	poultry or chickens
höhnerglöben	*Aberglaube*	superstition
höhnerstall	*Hühnerstall*	chicken coop
höker	*Händler*	trader
hokus pokus	*Zauber*	magic
hol dien klapper	*halt Maul*	shut up
hol dien muul	*Mund halten*	hold your tongue
hol fast	*fest halten*	hold tight
hol or holen	*Halten*	hold
hol wiss	*hol fast*	hold tight
höld	*gehalten*	held
höll	*Hölle*	hell
hölp	*Hilfe*	help
hölschen, hölsken	*Holz Schuhe*	wooden shoes
holt	*Bauholz*	lumber or woods
hölten been	*Höltzenbein*	wooden leg
hölten	*höltzenen*	wooden
holthomer	*Höltzenhammer*	wooden mallet
holtkohl	*Holzkohle*	charcoal
holtkopp	*Holzkopf*	blockhead
homer or hommer	*Hammer*	hammer

hönken	*Hahn*	spigot
hönken	*Zapfen*	faucet
höög	*Freude*	pleasure
hook or haaken	*Haken*	hook
hool or hol	*abholen*	fetch , carry, retrieve
hoor	*Haar*	hair
höörd	*Hürde*	hurdle
hoormütz	*Perücke*	wig or hairpiece
hoorn	*Horn*	horn
höörn	*Hörner*	horns
hoornadel or Hoornodel	*Haarnadel*	hair pin
hoot	*Hut*	hat
hoov	*Huf*	hoof
hooven or hoowen	*Hafen*	oats
hooviesen	*Hufeisen*	horseshoe
hopp or hoff	*Hoffnung*	hope
hoppen	*hopfen*	to hope
hops	*hopsen*	hops
horken	*Hornisse*	hornet
Horning	*Hornung*	February
horr	*Hure*	whore
hörsaal	*Horsaal*	auditorium
hovegrütt	*Haferflocken*	ground oats
hoven	*Hafen*	oats
hübben vull	*völlig*	full to the top
huchel	*Kichern*	giggle
hüft	*Hüfte*	hip
hülse	*Stechpalme*	holly
hummer	*Hummer*	lobster
humpel	*Haufen*	pile
humpeln	*Humpeln*	hobble
humung or hummuken	*Hummel*	bumble bee
hund or rüe	*Hund*	dog
hundenhuus	*Hundehütte*	doghouse
hüng	*gehangen*	hung
hunger	*Hunger*	hunger
hungertied	*Hungersnot*	famine
hungrig	*hungrig*	hungry
hunnenbloom	*Löwenzahn*	dandelion
hunnert	*Hundert*	hundred
hunnig	*Honig*	honey
hüren	*hören*	hear
hüret	*gehöret*	hears
hüs	*heiser*	hoarse
husen or hussen	*Husten*	cough

hütt	*Hütte*	hut
huuf	*Haube*	hood
huuken	*hocken*	crouch
huul	*Geheul*	howl
hüün	*Riese*	giant
huupen	*gehäuft*	heaping
hüür	*anhören*	listen or hear
hüür	*Miete*	hire
hüüren	*Miete*	rent
hüürmann	*Mieter*	tenant
hüürt or gehüret	*gehören*	belong
huus	*Haus*	house
hüüs	*Häuser*	houses
huusfro or huusfru	*Haushälterin*	housewife
huushold or huusstaub	*Haushalt*	household
huusholen	*Haushalten*	keep house
hüüsling	*Häusler*	tenant
huusschoh	*Hausschuhe*	slippers
hüüt or vundaag	*Heute*	today
huut	*Haut*	skin
hüütigendaags	*Heutzutage*	these days
idea	*Idee*	idea
iedelig	*eitel*	vain
ieland	*Insel*	island
ies	*Eis*	ice
iesbeen	*Eisbein*	pigs knuckles
iesbohn	*Kunsteisbahn*	skating rink
iesen	*Eisen*	iron
iesenbleck	*Eisenblech*	sheet iron
iesenhoot	*Helm*	helmet
ieskold or ieskoold	*Eiskalt*	ice cold
iestappen or jökel	*Eiszapfen*	icicle
ievrig	*eifrig*	eager or enthusiastic
iggen or ingen	*Egge*	harrow
igitt	*schlecht*	nasty
ik or ick	*Ich*	I
iloov or ieloof	*Efeu*	ivy
imm	*Honigbiene*	honey bee
immen	*Bienen*	bees
immenkorf	*Bienenkorb*	beehive
impen	*impfen*	vaccinate
in a iel or ielig	*eilig*	in a hurry or busy
in a'luft	*Luftraum*	in the sky
in shick or shicklig	*sauber*	proper, in fashion

310

in sinn	*absicht*	intention
in	*in*	in
in'a büx stöven	*eilig*	hurry up
inbilden	*sich vorstellen*	imagine
inbreken	*einbrechen*	break in
inbreker	*Einbrecher*	burglar or criminal
indruck or indrück	*Eindruck*	impression
infallen	*behalten*	come to mind or remember
inflott	*Einströmung*	inflow
influtt	*Einfluss*	influence
infohr	*Einfuhr*	import
inföhr	*Eingang*	entrance
infohren	*einfahren*	drive in
ing or iggen	*Egge*	farm implement
ing	*Eng*	narrow or small
ingang	*anfungen*	started
ingel	*Engel*	angel
Inglisch or Engelsch	*Englisch*	English
ingroben	*begraben*	bury
inhoken	*einhaken*	hook in
inholen	*einhalten*	hold in
inholt or inhold	*Inhalt*	content
inkoken or inmoken	*einmachen*	preserve, can
inkommen	*Einkommen*	income
inköpen	*einkaufen*	shop or shopping
immeesch	*Blaumeise*	bluetit
innehm	*Einkommen*	income
innehm	*Einnahme*	intake
innern	*erinnern*	remember
innerste	*innerst*	innermost
inpacken	*einpacken*	pack up
inpackt	*gepackt*	packaged
inrichten	*einrichten*	furnish
insetten	*einsetzen*	install
insetten	*festsetzen*	appoint
insied	*Innenseite*	inside
inslaap	*schlafend*	asleep
inslaapen	*geschlafen*	fall asleep
insloten	*einschlossen*	locked in
insloten, mit insloten	*einschliessen*	included
insmeern or infetten	*abfetten*	grease up
insnacken	*einreden*	persuade or convince
insnitt	*Einschnitt*	incision
inspritt	*einspritz*	injection
inspritten	*einspritzen*	inject

insprütt	gespritzed	injected
instippen	einstippen	immerse or dip in
instött	Einsturz	collapse
intogen	eingezogen	pulled in
invorut	im voraus	ahead of
inwand or vörwand	vorwand	excuse
inweihen	einweihen	dedicate
inwickeln	einwickeln	wrap or wrap up
inwohner	Einwohner	inhabitant or occupant
inwussen	einwärts wachsend	ingrown
is	is	is
jagen	Führen	drive or herd
jaagen	jagen	hunting
jaapen	gaffen	gape
jack	Jacke	coat or jacket
jager	Jäger	hunter
jagt	Jagt	hunt
jagtecken or jagshien	Jagdschein	hunting license
jammer or jank	jammern	whine
jammer or sörge	klagen	complain
Jan Moot	Seefahrer	mariner
janken	murren	groan
jannever	Gin	gin
Januor	Januar	January
jark	Jucken	itch
jaulen	Geheul	hoot
jedentied	jeden Zeit	every time
jedenweg	jedesweg	everyway
jeder	jeder	each
jeder	jeder	every
jedereen	jedermann	each one or everyone
jedesmol	jedesmal	everytime
jemols	jemals	ever
ji	Sie, Ihr	you
jichens	vielleicht	possibly
jidder	Euter	udder
jiep	Gequiek	squeek
jo or jup or jao	ja	yes
johr	Jahr	year
johrhunnert	Jahrhundert	century
johrlig	jährlig	annual
johrn	Jahren	years
ju or jo	euer	you
juchen	erfreuen	rejoice

juffer	*alte Jungfer*	spinster
Jul or Julklapp	*Weihnachten*	Christmas
Juli	*Juli*	July
jüm or se	*sie*	them
jümehr	*ihr*	theirs
jümme or jümmeto or ümmer	*immer*	always
jump or spring	*spring*	jump
jung	*Junge*	boy
jung	*jung*	young
jungen	*Bursche*	youngsters
jungfro or jungfru	*Jungfrau*	virgin
jungkirl	*Junggeselle*	young bachelor
jungs	*Jünge*	boys
jüngste	*jüngste*	youngest
Juni	*Juni*	June
jüst or jüss	*eben als*	just
Juud	Jude	Jew
juun or jo'n	*eure*	your or yours
kaane	*Dohle*	jackdaw crow
kaat or kott	*Katte*	cottage
kabbelig	*rastlos*	restless
kabin	*Kabine*	cabin
kacheloben	*Kachelofen*	heating stove, tile stove
kaff	*Spreu*	chaff
kaffe or koffi	*Kaffee*	coffee
kaffebohnen	*Kaffeebohne*	coffeebean
kaffekoken	*Kaffeekuchen*	coffeecake
kaffemöhl	*Kaffeemühle*	coffee grinder
kaffepott or kaffeputt	*Kaffeekanne*	coffeepot
kaffetied	*Kaffee Zeit*	coffeetime
kahl or kahlkopp	*kahl*	bald
kaih	*Kühe*	cows
kakelbeern	*Johannisbeere*	currant
kalb	*Kolben*	cob
kalf	*Kalb*	calf
kalinner	*Kalender*	calendar
kalinners	*Kalender*	calendars
kalwe	*Kälber*	calfs
kamm	*Kamm*	comb
kämmen	*Kämme*	combs
kamp	*Lager*	field or camp
kanditel	*munter*	merry or joyful
kanditer	*Zuckerbäcker*	candy maker
kaneel	*Zimt*	cinnamon

313

kann	kann	can or able to
kannedat	Kandidat	candidate
kannen or kanns	Büchse	metal cans
kann	Dose	tin can
kanol	Kanal	canal
kanon	Kanone	cannon
kant	Kante	edge
kanten	lehnen	tilt or lean
kantsteen	Kantstein	borderstone
kaputt	kaputt	tired or broken
karbe	Kerbe	notch
karben	Kerben	carve
Karfreedag	Karfreitag	Good Friday
karp	Karpfen	carp
kartuffel	Kartoffel	potato
kartüffel utkriegen tied	Kartoffel Ernte	potato harvest time
Kartuffeldaansch		Low Danish
kassbeer	Kirsche	cherry
kassbeern	Kirschen	cherries
kassbeernboom	Kirschbaum	cherry tree
kassen	Kiste	chest or crate
katechissen	Katechismus	catechism
katoolsch	Katholik	catholic
katt	Katze	cat
katten	Katzen	cats
kattenkees	Malve	mallow
kattuul or uul	Eule	owl
kau	kauen	chew
kaugummi	kaugummi	gum
kaut	kaut	chewed
kautabak	Kautabak	chewing tobacco
kaver	Käfer	beetle
keddel	kitzeln	tickle
keddelig	Kitzlig	ticklish
kedden	Kette	chain
keek	sah	looked
keekster	Elster	magpie
keem or kömm	gekommen	came
keen or geen	kein	none
keeneen or keene	keiner	no one
keenwegens	keines wegs	no way
kees or käs	Käse	cheese
keesblatt	Lokalblatt	local paper or flyer
keeswei	Molke	whey
kegeln	Kegeln	bowling

kehr or wokehr or wo	*wer*	who
kei or keih	*Kühe*	cows
keken	*anschaut*	looked
kelk	*Kelch*	goblet
kell	*Schöpflöffel*	ladle
keller	*Keller*	basement
keller	*Keller*	cellar
kenn or kinn	*anerkennen*	recognize or know
kennbor	*kennbar*	recognizable or knowable
kerk or kark	*Kirche*	church
kerkhof or karkhof	*Kirchhof*	cemetery
kerkspell or karkspell	*Kirchspiel*	parish
kerktoorn, karktoorn	*Kirchturm*	churchtower
kesen	*gerinnen*	curdle
ketel or kettel	*Kessel*	kettle
ketelflicken	*Klempnen*	kettle repair
ketelklopper	*Klempner*	kettle fixer or kettle repairer
kiehr or ankiehren	*märken*	pay attention to
kiek	*schau*	look
kiekkassen	*Fernseher*	tv set
kiekt ähnlig	*ähnlich sein*	resembles
kiekut or pass up	*pass auf*	watch out
kiel	*Keil*	wedge
kiem	*Kiemen*	gill
kiepenkirl	*Kiepenkerl*	wandering peddler
kiewitthohn	*Eule*	owl
kimm	*Horizont*	horizon
kimmen	*kämmen*	to comb
kind	*Kind*	child
kind or blagen or gör	*Baby*	baby
kinn	*Kinn*	chin
kinnelbeer	*taufen*	christening
kinner	*Kinder*	children
kinnerbett or krüff	*Krippe*	crib
kinnergoorn	*Kindergarten*	kindergarden
kinnerkoppig	*kindisch*	childish
kinnerkroom	*Spielzeug*	toy
kinnerskinner	*Grosskinder*	grandchildren
kinnertied	*Kindheit*	childhood
kinnerwohren	*Kinder hüten*	babysit
kinnig	*Bonbon*	candy
kinnmark	*kennzeichen*	characteristic
kipp	*kippen*	tip
kippkoor or kippkoar	*Kippwagen*	dumptruck
kirl or keerl	*Kerl*	fellow or chap

315

kirls	*Kerle*	fellows
kirschen or kassbeern	*Kirsche*	cherry
kirse	*Kerze*	candle
kittel	*Rock*	coat
kitza		scat
kitze	*Rehlamm*	fawn
klaffekatt	*Angeber*	informer or spy
klamüstern	*ausbrüten*	brood
klap	*Klaps*	clap
klappbrüch	*Zugbrücke*	drawbridge
klappdisch	*Klapptisch*	folding table
klappen	*Klappe*	flap or lid
klapperkassen		old car
klapps	*Klaps*	spank or spanking
klapps kregen	*geklappt*	was spanked
klass	*Klasse*	class
klatter	*erklettern*	climb
klau	*stehlen*	swipe
klaus	*Klaus*	hermit
klaveer	*Klavier*	piano
klebe	*Klebstoff*	glue
kledaasch	*Kleider*	clothes
kleed	*Kleid*	dress
kleede	*Kleider*	dresses
kleedschap	*Kleiderschrank*	wardrobe closet
kleen	*kleine*	small
kleev	*Kleister*	glue
klei or kratz	*kratzen*	scratch
klemmvogel or hafke	*Habicht*	hawk
klever or kleehau	*Klee*	clover
kleverblatt or klewerblatt	*Kleeblatt*	clover leaf
kleverveer or klewerveer	*Glücksklee*	four leaf clover
kliester	*Kleister*	paste
klimp or klemp	*Klampe*	clamp
klimpner	*Klempner*	plumber
klimmt	*klemmt*	pinched
klingel	*Klang*	ring
klingelbüdel	*Sammelbeutel*	collection bag
klingelgeld	*Kleingeld*	coin or change
klingt so	*Klangt*	sounds like
klink	*Türgriff*	door handle
klippeken	*Holzpantoffel*	wooden slippers
klöben or klöven	*Bruch*	split
klock	*Uhr*	clock
klocken	*Uhren*	clocks

316

klogen or kloogen	Klagen	claim or sue
klönen	plaudern	chat
klönsnak	Klatschen	story telling or gossip
klook	klug	smart
klooker	kluger	smarter
klookmoken, wiesmoken	benachrichten	inform
klookshet	Klugscheisser	smarty pants
klöönkassen or telefon	Telefon	telephone
kloor or kloar	klar	clear
klooster	Kloster	cloister
klopp	klopfen	knock
klor or kloar	klar	distinct
klottergeld	Kleingeld	small change
klotterig	unordentlich	messy
klotz	Klotz	blockhead
klövtig	klug	clever
kluckhehn	Glucke	brooding hen
klumm	dumpf	damp
klump	Klumpen	clump
klumpen	Hölzken	wooden shoes
klüsen	Stampfen	stomp
kluster	Traube	cluster
klüten	Kloss	dumpling
klüten	Klumpen	dirt clods
klüür	Farbe	color
kluusner	Einsiedler	recluse
kluuten	Klump	a clod or a dumpling
knabbel	Zwieback	hard bread
knack	knacken	crack
knäckebroot		hard bread
knall dor rin	einrammen	ram
knall	knallen	bang
knapp	dünn	scarce or meager
knapp	mager	barely
knass	Knacker	old man
knast or knass	Astloch	knothole
knast	gefängnis	jail
knassenstöter	Zimmermann	carpenter
knecht	Diener	servant
knecht	Knecht	farmhand
kneden	kneten	knead
knedet or knattert	knattern	crackle
knick	Knick	border hedge
knickbeenig	krummbeinig	bowlegged
knicker (speeldings)	Murmel	marble (game)

knie	*Knie*	knee
knien	*knien*	kneel
kniep	*kneifen*	pinch
knieper	*Wäschklammer*	clothes pin
kniepogen	*Wink*	wink
knieps	*Knirps*	shrimp
knieptang	*Kneifzange*	pincers
knieptasch	*Tasche*	purse
kniff	*Kniff*	fold
knipp	*Klipp*	clip or swipe
knippelsteen	*Marmor*	marble
knippt	*gestohlen*	swiped
knob	*Knopf*	knob
knöf	*Muskel*	muscle
knokel	*Enkel*	ankle
knökel	*Knöchel*	knuckle
knoken	*Knochen*	bone
knokenhauer	*Metzger*	meat marketer
knokenkirl	*Gerippe*	skeleton
knoop	*Knopf*	button
knööp	*Knöpfer*	buttons
knoopnodel	*Sicherheitsnadel*	safety pin
knoos	*Knäppche*	bread end slice or heel
knopp	*Knospe*	bud
knöwig	*muskelös*	muscular
knubben	*Kuppe*	knob or bump
knubberig	*knaufig*	knobby
knuffel	*Bausch*	wad
knüpel	*Keule*	club
knütt	*gestricht*	knitted
knutt	*Knoten*	knot
knütten or stricken	*strichen*	to knit
knuublok	*Knoblauch*	garlic
kobbelsteen	*Kieselstein*	cobblestone
kocheloben	*Kachelofen*	tile stove
ködel	*Kot*	turd
kofft or inkoft	*gekauft*	bought or purchased
koh	*Kuh*	cow
kohfell	*Kuhfell*	cowhide
kohkamp	*Kuhweide*	cow pasture
kohl or kabuus	*Kohl*	cabbage
kohl or kool	*Kohle*	coal
köhlig	*Kühle*	cool
kohschiet	*Kuhfladen*	cow pie
köken or kök or bakstuuv	*Küche*	kitchen

koken	*Kochen*	cooking
koken	*Kuchen*	cake
köksch	*Koch*	the cook
kold or koolt	*kalt*	cold
kölnwoter	*Kölnischwasser*	cologne
kombüüs	*Schiffsküche*	galley
komer or kamer	*Kammer*	chamber
komil	*Kamille*	camomile
kömm or keem	*kam*	came
komm or kumm	*komme*	come
kommodig	*bequem*	comfortable
kommt an	*kommt an*	comes on or appears
kommt or kummt	*kommt*	comes
komood	*Kommode*	chest of drawers
komplett	*vollständig*	complete
komplizeert	*kompliziert*	complicated
könn weren, könn wesen	*könn sein*	could be
könn	*könn*	could
könnt	*sie können*	(we, they) can
kontroll	*Kontrolle*	control
kook or kok	*Koch*	cook
kook	*Kochen*	boil
kookt	*gekocht*	cooked or cooking
koolteföten	*kalte Füsse*	cold feet
kooltsüster or kooltswester	*Halbschwester*	half sister
kööm	*Weinbrand*	brandy
kööm or keem	*gekommen*	came
koom	*kumme*	(am) coming
kööp	*kauf*	buy or purchase
kööploden or koophuus	*Kaufhaus*	department store
kööpman, inköper	*Käufer*	buyer, businessman
koor or koar or kaar	*Karre*	cart or car
koorn or korn	*Mais*	corn
koornkalb	*Maiskolben*	corncob
koornkribben	*Maisspeicher*	corncrib
kopie	*Kopie*	copy
kopp	*Kopf*	head
koppdook	*Kopftuch*	headscarf
koppel	*Koppelung*	link or connection
koppel	*koppeln*	couple
koppel	*Herde*	flock
köppen	*Kelch*	cup
kopper	*Kupfer*	copper
koppgeld	*Kopfgeld*	reward
koppjen or kupp	*Tasse*	cup

319

koppöwer	*auf dem Kopf*	incorrect, upside down
koppöwer	*umgekehrt*	overturned
koppral	*Korporal*	corporal
koppsteen	*Kopfstein*	headstone
koppswaak	*schwachköpfig*	feeble minded
koppverkölt	*Kopfkält*	head cold
koppweh	*Kopfschmerzen*	headache
kopteen or käppen	*Kaptein*	captain
korv	*Korb*	basket or hamper
korden	*Karte*	card
korn or koorn	*Korn*	grain or corn
kornbloomen or ruschelpen	*Korn Blume*	cornflower
kornuhren	*Korn Ähre*	ear of corn
kort anbunnen	*verschroben*	cranky or testy
kort or kuort	*kurz*	short
körtens	*kürzlich*	shortly
körv	*Körbe*	baskets or hampers
kost	*kosten*	cost
köst	*kostet*	costs
kostbor	*kostbar*	expensive or precious
köstenbidder	*Hochzeitsbitter*	wedding inviter
kösthuus	*Pension*	boardinghouse
kotner or kattner	*Hütter*	cottager
kotterig	*quengelich*	crabby
kotz	*Kotze*	puke
kraagem	*Kragen*	collar
kraam or kroom	*sachen*	stuff
kracker	*Gaul*	old nag
krall	*Kralle*	claw
krank	*krank*	sick
krankenhuus	*Krankenhaus*	hospital
krankenswester	*Krankenschwester*	nurse
kratz	*Kratz*	scratch
kratzeln	*kritzeln*	scribble
kreatur	*Kreatur*	creature
kreep	*kriechen*	creep
kreepen or krabbeln	*kraulen*	crawl
kreeshen	*kreischen*	scream
kregel	*Munter*	cheerful
kregen	*bekommen*	got
kreih	*Krähen*	crow
kreiht	*kräht*	crows
kreun	*Wasserhahn*	crane
kribble	*zittern*	tremble or shudder
kride	*Farbstift*	crayons

kried or kalk	*Kreide*	chalk
krieg	*krieg*	get
krieg	*Krieg*	war
kriegel oder kregel	*heiter*	lively
kriegen	*kriegen*	to get
kriggt	*gekriggt*	gets
krimp	*Falte*	crease
krimpstebel, krimpstevel		work boots
krimskraam	*Kehricht*	rubbish
kring	*Kreis*	county
kringbaas	*Kreis Vorsitzender*	county chairman
krink	*Kreis*	district
kritt	*zanken*	bicker
kröger	*Kröger*	innkeeper or tavernkeeper
kröken	*Runzel*	pickle
krömer	*Geschäftsinhaber*	shopkeeper
kronik	*Chronik*	chronicle or history
kroog	*Taverne, Kneipe*	tavern
kroon	*Krone*	crown
krööt or üüz	*Kröte*	toad
kropp	*kropf*	crop
kröpt	*gekriecht*	is creeping
krosch	*Knusperig*	crisp
krückeln	*rünzeln*	to wrinkle
krüderee	*Gewürz*	seasoning or spice
krüff	*Krippe*	manger
krück	*Krücke*	crutch
krüll	*Kräuselung*	curl
krüllig	*Kräuselig*	curly
krüllt	*Kräuselt*	curls
krumm	*Krümm*	bent or curved
krümmel	*Krume*	crumb
krümelig	*krumelig*	crumbly
krüpelig or krükelig	*verkrüppelt*	infirm
krüppel	*Krüppel*	cripple
krüsel	*Kreiselachse*	orbit or gyroscope
kruuken	*Steinkrug*	stone jug
kruup	*Diphterie*	diptheria
kruus	*Runzelt*	wrinkled or rumpled
kruuskopp	*Krauskopp*	curly head
kruut	*Unkraut*	weed
krüüz	*Kreuz*	cross
krüüzadder	*Viper*	viper or adder
krüüzweg	*Kreuzweg*	cross road
küern or snacken	*reden*	talk

kuffer	*Koffer*	bag or suitcase
kugel	*Kugel*	bullet
kühl	*Kälte*	chill
kühlken	*Grübchen*	dimple
küken	*Küken*	chicks
kukuk	*Kuckuck*	cuckoo
kukuksbloomen	*Knabenkraut*	wild orchid
kulengräber	*Totengräber*	gravedigger
kultur	*Kultur*	culture
kumfermation	*Konfirmation*	confirmation
kumfermiert	*Konfirmiert*	confirmed
kumm or komm	*komm*	come
kümme or kümmer	*Kummer*	pay attention to
kümmel	*Kümmel*	caraway
kummt an	*kommt an*	comes on or appears
kummt or kommt	*kommt*	comes
kump	*Kelch*	large coffee cup
kump	*Bowle*	bowl
kumpan or kumpel	*Kamerad*	comrade
künig	*König*	king
künigfro	*Königin*	queen
kunne	*Kunde*	customer
kunnen	*Künden*	customers
künnig	*Bericht*	report or notice
kunnigmoken	*verkünden*	proclaim
kunstabler or schandarm	*Polizist*	policeman
kunstdungen	*Düngemittel*	artifical fertilizer
kunterdans	*Kontertanz*	contra dance
kur or leehrgang	*Kurs*	course, course of study
küren	*Kern*	kernel
kürenig	*körnig*	granular
kusde	*Küste*	coast
küssel	*kreiseln*	spin or whirl
küssen	*Kissen*	pillow or cushion
kuster	*Küster*	sexton
kutsch or kutschwogen	*Wagen*	carriage
kuul	*Grab*	ditch
küül	*Keule*	club
kuum	*kaum*	hardly
küüschheit	*Keuschheit*	chastity
kuusen	*Backenzahn*	molars
laad or kuffer	*Lade*	chest
laat	*spät*	late
laater	*später*	later
lach	*Lachen*	laugh

lächel	*Gekicher*	giggle
lachen	*Gelächter*	laughter
lächerlig	*lächerlich*	laughable
lacht	*lacht*	laughs
lamb	*Lamm*	lamb
lampen	*Lampe*	lamp or lamps
land	*Land*	country or land
landdeel	*Gebiet*	district
landschop	*Landschaft*	landscape
landstraat	*Landstrasse*	country road
landstrieker	*Landstreicher*	tramp, vagabond
lang	*lang*	long
langenweg	*längsweg*	lengthwise or long way
langfinger	*Taschendieb*	pickpocket
langs	*Verlangen*	longing
langskommen	*vertragen*	get along
langsom	*langsam*	slow
lappen	*Lappen*	rag
lapperig	*rachitisch*	rickety
lärmt	*Lärm*	noise
lastig	*lästig*	troublesome
lat' falln	*lassfallen*	let fall or drop it
lat	*lassen*	let
later hin or loter hin	*späterhin*	later on
later or laater	*späterhin*	later
latern or lüchen	*Laterne*	lantern
latt	*erlauben*	allow
latten	*Querholz*	slat
lausbub or lümmel	*Rüpel*	lout
lauwarm	*lauwarm*	luke warm
leben or leven	*Leben*	life
lebenlang or levenlang	*lebenslang*	lifelong
lebennig	*lebendig*	alive
lebennig	*hurtig*	spry
lebens tied	*Lebenszeit*	lifetime
lebensgefähr	*Gefahr*	danger or extreme anger
leckersnuut	*Leckermaul*	picky eater
leckertähn	*Feinschmecker*	gourmet
leddig or ledig	*leer*	empty
leder or leller	*Leder*	leather
leeben	*leb*	lives or lifetimes
leed	*Leid*	song
leed	*Leid*	sorrow
leeg	*unwohl*	poorly or bad or sick
leegen	*lügen*	to lie

leeger	*schlechter*	worse
leegheit	*slecht Benehmen*	mischievness
leegholt	*Unfug*	mischief
leegt	*liegen*	is lying
lehn	*borgen*	borrow
leehrjohr or schooljohr	*Schuljahr*	school year
leehrn	*erlernen*	learn or study
lees	*lesen*	read or decipher
leesbor	*Lesbar*	legible
leev	*Lieber*	dear
leevste	*Liebste*	dearest
leevt	*geleben*	living
leevt	*lebt*	lives
legg	*legen*	lay or put
lehn	*Darlehen*	loan
lehnen	*lehnen*	lean
lehnstohl	*Lehnstuhl*	easy chair or armchair
lek	*Leck*	to leak
leken	*lecken*	leak or drip
leksen	*Vortrag*	lecture
leller or ledder	*Leiter*	ladder
lengd	*länge*	length
lenk	*Gelenk*	link
Lenzmaand	*März*	March
lepel or läpel or liäpel	*Löffel*	spoon
lesen or liäsen	*lesen*	read or perused
lett so	*scheint*	seems so or seems to be
lettich	*Lattich*	lettuce
letz johr	*vergangenen Jahr*	last year
letz	*letzt*	last
letzthin	*vergangenen Zeit*	some time ago
lever	*Leber*	liver
leverworst	*Leberwurst*	liverwurst
lewe	*Lieber*	dear
lewer	*lieber*	rather
licht	*Leuchte*	light or lamp
lichtferdig	*leichtsinnig*	frivolous
lick	*belecken*	lick
lie	*Schiefer*	slate
liecht	*leicht*	light
liecht	*leicht*	easy
liedenhaftig	*leidenschaftlich*	passionate
lieder	*Leiter*	leader
liedsom	*sozial*	social
lief	*Leib*	body

324

liefkniepen	Bauchweg	stomach ache
liekdeel	gleichmässig	equal
liekdoorn	Hühneraugen	corn (on foot)
liekers	dennoch	nevertheless
liekers or ahnhin	irgendwie	anyway
lieklopen	parallel	parallel or run parallel
liekmodig	ungetrübt	serene
liekut, grodut, richtut	geradeaus	straight out
liem	Leim	glue
lien	Leine	line
lienöl	Lack	varnish
lies	leise	quiet or soft
liggen gohn, lingen gohn	siedlegen	lay down
liggt	legt	lays
linkpoot	Linkshände	lefthanded
links	links	left
linn	Linde	linden
linnen or lienen	Leinen	linen
lion	Löwe	lööv
lirk	Lerche	lark
lipp	Lippe	lip
lippen	Lippen	lips
lirkenklemmer	Sperber	sparrow hawk
list	Liste	list
lock	Loch	hole
lockerig	löcherig	porous or holy
loden	einladen	to load
löden	Lot	solder
logen	gelogen	lied
logisch	logisch	logical
lohm	lahm	lame
lohn or daglohn	Lohn	pay
lohnt sik	lohnt sich	pays
lohntuten	Lohn Tüte	pay envelope
lö'k (glöv ik)	Ich glaube	I believe
lood	laden	load
loop	lauf	run
lööp	laufen	ran
loos	Laus	louse
lööv	glaube	believe
loov	Laube	garden shed
loppt	läuft	runs
los	lose	loose
los laten	loslassen	let go
los moken or los maken	loslösen	loosen

losbreken	*losbrechen*	break loose
losgeiht	*losgehen*	starts
loswieren or losweern	*loswerden*	get rid of
lotz	*Litze*	lace
löv or löf	*Lob*	praise
lüchen	*Lampe*	lamp or gas lamp
lücht or lucht	*luster*	candle light or brightness
lüd	*Leute*	people
luft	*Luft*	air
luftmatratz	*Luft Matratze*	air mattress
lüggbuddel	*Lüger*	lier or fibber
lüggt	*lügen*	lieing
luk	*Schnittlauch*	chives
lümmel	*Racker*	scamp
lungen	*Lunge*	lungs
luss	*Laus*	louse
lust	*Lust*	desire
lüsten or lustern	*lauschen*	eavesdrop or listen
lustig	*aktiv*	active or lively or merry
lustig	*kraftvoll*	energetic
lustwannern	*Schlendern*	stroll
lütt	*klein*	little
lüttje or lütting	*Kleine*	little one
lüttste	*kleinste*	smallest
lüüd or lüer or lüür	*Leute*	people
lüüde or lüer or lüür	*Volk*	all people
lüüdlütt	*sehr klein*	tiny
lüüdsnak, klönsnak, snakaree	*Klatsch*	gossip
luukuhren	*horchen*	eavesdrop
luun or loon	*laun*	mood
lüün	*Sperling*	sparrow
luur or luer	*lauern*	wait on
luurt or luert	*lauernd*	waits on
lüüs	*Läuse*	lice
luut	*laut*	loud
luuthals	*lauthals*	very loud
lüwarm	*Lauwarm*	lukewarm
maad	*Wurm*	maggot
maag or mäke	*Magd*	maid
maagen	*Magen*	stomach
maal	*zeichnen*	draw
maaler	*Künstler*	artist
maand or moond	*Mond*	moon
maand or moond	*Monat*	month

maandag or mondag	*Montag*	monday
maandshien	*Mondschein*	moonshine
maat	*Maat*	mate
maatschop	*Genossenschaft*	cooperative
mach or müch	*möchte*	might
machangel	*Wacholder*	juniper
macht	*Macht*	might or power
mackelig	*gemächlich*	cosy
macker	*Genosse*	buddy
maddick	*Wurm*	earthworm
mag or möch	*hab gern*	like
mahl	*Mahl*	meal
mahltied	*Mahlzeit*	mealtime
mahne	*Mähne*	mane
Mai	*Mai*	May
maike or mäke	*Mädchen or Magd*	girl or maid
mais	*Mais*	corn
mal	*einfältig*	silly
mal	*wahnsinning*	mad
malen or maleree	*Malen*	painting
maleree	*Kunst*	art
malör	*Unglück*	misfortune
man to	*nur zu!*	go ahead or let's go
maneeren	*Manieren*	manners
maneerlig	*zivilisiert*	civilized
mang or mank	*zwischen*	among
mann	*Mann*	man
mann or mien mann	*Mann*	husband
mannel	*Mandel*	almond
mannig	*manch*	many
mannigeen	*manch ein*	many a one
mannigmol	*manchmal*	often
mannschop	*Mannschaft*	team
mannslüüd	*Männer*	men
mantel	*Mantel*	overcoat or cape
mardel bloom	*Gänseblümchen*	daisy
mark	*Marke*	brand or mark
märken	*Märchen*	fairy tale
markt	*Markt*	marketplace
marmeln	*Marmor*	marble
marmelood or fruchtmoos	*Marmelade*	jam
marsch	*Moor*	lowlands
marschen, rümtrampen	*marschieren*	march
Märtmaand	*März*	March
März	*März*	March

327

märzbloomen	*Huflattich*	coltsfoot herb
mashien	*Maschine*	machine
masse	*viel*	much
masseln	*Masern*	spots
massiv	*massiv*	solid
maten	*Glied*	members
matrass	*Matratze*	mattress
matten	*Hammelfleisch*	mutton
meddag	*Mittag*	noon
meddageten	*Mittagessen*	dinner or lunch
medizin	*Medizin*	medicine
meehr	*mehr*	more
meehrfak	*vielfaltig*	multiple
meehrheit or miehrdeel	*Mehrheit*	majority
meehrmol	*mehrzahl*	oftener
meehrmol	*ständig*	repeatedly
meehrst or miehrsten	*meist*	most
meehrstens	*meistens*	mostly or most of the time
meen	*meinen*	imply or mean
meent	*meint*	means
meenung	*Meinung*	meaning
meeschen	*Meise*	titmouse
meester	*Meister*	master
meestern	*herrschen*	dominate
mehl	*Mehl*	flour
mehlsack	*Mehlsack*	flour sack
meih	*mähen*	cut oder mow
meihdöscher	*Mähdrescher*	combine
meihen	*mähend*	to mow
meihmashien	*Mähmaschine*	mower
meist	*beinahe*	almost
melk	*Milch*	milk
melkammel	*Milcheimer*	milkpail
melkbock	*Milchstuhl*	milking stool
melkhuus	*Milchhaus*	milkhouse
melkkann	*Milchkanne*	milkcan
melkkirl	*Milch Kerl*	milk man
melkmashien	*Melkapparat*	milk machine
melktähn	*Baby Zähne*	baby teeth
mellen or anmellen	*anmelden*	report to
melodie	*Melodie*	melody
mengeleern	*Mischung*	blend
mengeln or misheln	*mischen*	mix
Mennoniten	*Mennonite*	Mennonites
merken	*Regenwurm*	earthworm

mess barg	*Misthaufen*	manure pile
mess fork	*Forke*	manure fork
mess	*Mist*	manure
messe	*Messe*	fair
messelig	*Messing*	brass
mess smieter		manure spreader
mest or mess	*Messer*	knife
meten or mäten	*messen*	measure
metstock	*Lineal*	ruler or standard
mettworst	*Wurst*	summer sausage
mi	*mich*	me
Micheelismaand	*September*	September
midde	*Mieder*	waist
midde	*Mitte*	middle
middelsmann	*Agent*	agent
middeöller	*Mittelalter*	middle ages
middernacht	*Mitternacht*	midnight
Middeweken	*Mittwoch*	Wednesday
middewiel, middetied	*mittlerweile*	meanwhile
miege	*Harn*	urine
miel	*Meile*	mile
mien	*meine*	mine
miendaags	*Meines Tages*	my days or my life
mienhalben, mienwegens	*meinetwegen*	my sake
miessen	*Sprühregen*	sprinkle
miesst, de müngen de pisst	*bespritzen*	misting
miljoon	*Million*	million
minnächtig	*verächtlich*	contemptuous
minnhaftig	*unbedeutend*	slight
minnheit or minnedeel	*Minderheit*	minority
minsch	*Mensch*	human being or man
minsch	*Herr*	gentleman
minschheit	*Menschheit*	mankind
minschlig	*Menschlich*	human
minschrecht	*Menschenrecht*	human rights
minuten	*Minute*	minute
miss	*vermissen*	miss
mistroo or mistruu	*Misstrauen*	mistrust
misülbens or misülms	*mirselbst*	myself
mit dör kommen	*vollbringen*	achieve, get away with
mit kind or swoorfoot	*Schwanger*	pregnant
mit togang	*engagiert*	engaged
mit utholt or mit dörholt	*aushalten*	endured
mitdregen	*mittregen*	drag along
mitmoken, mitsnacken	*mitmachen*	participate

mitsitter	*Mitglied*	member
mitslepen	*mitschlepen*	drag along with
mitspelen	*mitspielen*	play along
mitünner	*zuweilen*	sometimes
mitut	*mitaus*	without
mitwegkommen	*entkommen*	get away with
mode	*Mode*	custom or fashion
moder or mudder	*Mutter*	mother
moderne	*modern*	modern
möer	*müde*	tired or sleepy
mög or müch	*mögen*	like or like to
möglig	*möglich*	possible
mohl or maal	*Mahl*	meal
möhl	*Mühl*	mill
möhlen	*mahlen*	grind
möhler	*Müller*	miller
mohltied	*Mahlzeit*	mealtime
mohnen	*Mahnen*	remind
moi or moj	*Freude*	joy or gladness
moi papeer	*pack papier*	holiday wrapping
moin moin	*Hallo*	hello
moin, morrn	*Guten Morgen*	good morning
mok open mak open	*offenmachen*	open up
mok or mak	*mache*	make or construct
mok to	*mach zu*	close it
mokt or makt	*macht*	makes
mölle		shallow wooden bowl
molt	*Malz*	malt
momang	*Moment*	moment
mood or moot	*Mut*	courage
mööd	*Müde*	tired
möödsom	*ermüdend*	tiresome
möör	*weich*	tender
moor	*Maure*	bog
moorbock	*Bekassine*	snipe
moorhehn	*Waldhuhn*	grouse
moos	*Maische*	to mash potatoes
moos'de kartuffel	*Kartoffelbrei*	mashed potatoes
mööv	*Seemöwe*	seagull
moren or morrn	*Morgen*	tomorrow
morrnrot	*Sonnenaufgang*	sunrise
morslicker	*Schmeichler*	sycophant
mott or ulenkind	*Motte*	moth
mött	*müssen*	(we, they) must
motten	*Motten*	moths

mottenkugel	*Mottenkugel*	mothball
mucken	*klagen*	complain
müerker, muurman	*Maurer*	bricklayer or mason
müggen	Mücke	mosquito
mulen or muulen	*Schmollen*	sulk
mund örgel	*Harmonika*	harmonica
mund or muul or muulwaɍk	*Mund*	mouth
munkelig	*trüb*	gloomy
münnel	*Mündel*	ward
muschel	*Muschel*	shell
musik	*Musik*	music
muskant	*Musiker*	musician
muskanten	*Musikanten*	musicians
muskel	*Muskel*	muscle
muster or vörbild	*Muster*	pattern
mutt	*muss*	must
mütz or kappen	*Mütze*	cap
muul	*Maulesel*	mule
muulbeeren	*Maulbeere*	mulberry
muulkorf	*Maulkorb*	muzzle
muulsch	*halsstarrig*	stubborn
muur	*Mauer*	masonry wall
muus	*Maus*	mouse
müüs	*Mäuse*	mice
müüsenstill or muusstill	*Mäuschen still*	very quiet
muusfall	*Mausefalle*	mousetrap
myrtel kranz	*Myrtel Kranz*	myrtle wreath
naakt or splitternaakt	*nackt*	naked
naam or noom	*Name*	name
naart or nöört	*Nuss*	nut
nachher	*nachher*	after while
nacht	*Nacht*	night
nachtigall	*Nachtigall*	nightingale
nachtuul	*Nachteule*	night owl
nacken	*Nacken*	neck
nägelken	*Nelke*	carnation
nämlich	*nämlich*	namely
naɍms de weg or keenweg	*keinweg*	noway
naɍms	*nirgendwo*	nowhere
naɍmsdeweg	*keineswegs*	noway
narrsch or tövelig	*närrisch*	foolish
naɍv	*Narbe*	scar
näs or nääs or snuut	*Nase*	nose
näschierig, neeschierig	*neugierig*	nosy or curious
naschkroom	*Naschwerk*	sweets

naschkroom	*Süssigkeiten*	candy
nasicht or nosicht	*Nachsicht*	indulgence
natschoon	*Nation*	nation
natt	*nass*	wet
nattorse	*Laubfrosch*	tree frog
nebel or daak or dauk	*nebel*	fog
neddelst	*niedrigste*	lowest
nedder	*nieder*	low
Nedderdüütsch	*Niederdeutsch*	Low German
Neddersassisch	*Niedersachsisch*	Low Saxon
neden or neern	*unter*	below
nee johr or nei joor	*Neu Jahr*	new year
nee	*nein*	no
neeg	*Nähe*	nearn
neeg bi	*nahe*	close or nearby
neegde	*Nähe*	vicinity
neeren or nejen	*neuen*	new one
neest	*Nest*	nest
neet or neje	*neu*	new
negelken	*Gewürznelke*	clove
negen	*neun*	nine
negenteihn	*neunzehn*	nineteen
negentig	*nuenzig*	ninety
nehm	*nehmen*	take
nehmlig	*nehmlich*	specifically
neih	*Nähen*	sew
neihen	*nähen*	to sew
neihkorf	*Nähenkorb*	sewing basket
nerven or närven	*Nerven*	nerves
nervös	*nervös*	nervous
nett	*Netz*	net
Nevelmaand	*November*	November
nexte	*nächts*	next one
nich bekannt	*unbekannt*	unfamiliar
nich nödig	*unnötig*	unnecessary
nich or neet	*nicht*	not
nichde	*Nichte*	niece
nichs för ungood	*nicht für ungut*	no offense taken
nichs weert or sleef	*wertlos*	worthless
nickkopp	*Nicken*	nod
niedisch	*neidisch*	jealous
niemols	*nie*	never
nierig	*übertrieben*	fussy
nimmt	*nimmt*	takes
nipp	*genau*	exact

332

nix or nams or nichts	*Nichts*	nothing
no	*nach*	after
no	*nach*	toward
nobetohl	*nachschuss*	pay extra
noch	*noch*	yet
nodeel	*Nachteil*	disadvantage
nodel	*Nadel*	needle
nödeln	*trödeln*	loiter
nodem, nodat, achter dat	*nachdem*	after that
noden	*Noten*	notes
nodenken	*nachdenken*	contemplate or think about
nödichen	*einladen*	invite
nödig	*Einladung*	invitation
nodisch	*Nachtisch*	dessert
nodrücken	*ausdrücken*	emphasize
noföhlen	*nachfühlen*	trace
noföhrnen	*Nachfahre*	descendants
nogeben or nogeven	*Nachgeben*	give in
nogel	*Nagel*	nail
nöger or neger	*näher*	nearer
nogevig	*nachgiebig*	compliant or flexible
nogohn oder nagahn	*nachgehen*	go after
nögste or negste	*nähste*	nearest
nohber or naober	*Nachbar*	neighbor
nohberschop	*Nachbarschaft*	neighborhood
nohberslüüd	*Nachbarleute*	neighbor people
nöhm	*hat genommen*	took
nohmen	*genommen*	taken or took
nohuus	*zuhause*	to home
nohuus gohn	*zuhause gehen*	go home
nokieken or oppassen	*nachsehen*	look after
nokriegs tied	*Nachkriegs*	postwar
nolopen	*nachlaufen*	run after
nolot or nolat	*Verminderung*	reduction
nomalen (bi hand)	*nachmachen*	copy (by hand)
nomiddags, s'nomiddags	*Nachmittag*	afternoon
nomoken or namaken	*nachmachen*	imitate
nonn	*Nonne*	nun
noog or genoog	*genug*	enough
noord	*Nord*	north
noot or not	*notwendig*	necessity or emergency
nootutgoh	*Notausgang*	emergency exit
nordwest	*Nortwest*	northwest
nörgeln	*klagen*	complain
noricht	*Nachricht*	news

normol	*normal*	normal
noseggen, wellerseggen	*wiederholen*	repeat
nosehn or nokieken	*besichtigen*	inspect
noshuuv	*versorgung*	supplies or replenishment
nosichtig	*nachsichtig*	lenient
nosliepen, wellersliepen	*nachschärfen*	resharpen
nospören	*erforschen*	explore
notreken or nokommen	*nachgehen*	follow
notürlig	*natürlich*	naturally
notüür	*Natur*	nature
notwennig	*Notwendig*	necessary
November	*November*	November
nowies	*Nachweis*	proof or evidence
nowoort or noschrift	*Nachschrift*	postscript
nu	*nun*	now
nüksch	*mürrisch*	moody
nuddelig	*müssig*	lazy
null	*Null*	zero
nummer	*Nummer*	number
nummershild	*Nummernschild*	license plate
nüms	*niemand*	nobody
nützlig	*nützlich*	useful
nüüdlig	*nett*	nice
ob	*ob*	whether
oben or oven	*Ofen*	stove or oven
obend or ovend or aobend	*Abend*	evening
obendbrot	*Abendbrot*	supper or evening meal
obendmohl	*abendmahl*	communion service
obendstied	*abendzeit*	evening
obsluut	*absolut*	absolute
October	*Oktober*	October
oder	*oder*	or
öfter	*öfter*	oftener
öfters or mannigmol	*öfters*	often
ogbrau	*Augenbraue*	eyebrow
ogen	*Augen*	eyes
ogenblick	*Moment*	moment
ogendeckel	*Augenlid*	eyelid
ogenplinkern or ogenslag	*blinken*	blink
ogenshienlig	*augenscheinlich*	evidently
ogenwasch	*Augenbad*	eyewash
ohm or unkle	*Onkel*	uncle
ohnung	*Idee*	idea
ohnung	*Kenntnis*	awareness

334

ok or ook	*auch*	also
ökelnaam	*Spitzname*	nickname
öl lampen	*Öl Lampe*	oil lamp
oldgesell	*Haupt Lehrling*	first apprentice
olendeel or ollekraam	*Gerümpel*	old stuff
olentieden	*Alte zeiten*	early times
öller	*Alter*	age
öller	*Alter*	older
öllern	*Eltern*	parents
öllernhuus	*Eltern Haus*	parent's house
öllste	*Alteste*	oldest
olsche	*"Alte"*	the old lady
oltmodisch	*Altmodische*	oldfashioned
ölven or ölben	*Elf*	eleven
omasbroder, opasbroder		great uncle
omaswester, opaswester		great aunt
oog	*Auge*	eye
oogappel	*Augapfel*	eyeball
ooghoor	*Augenwimper*	eyelash
oogklappen	*Augenfleck*	eyepatch
ööl or öl	*Öl*	oil
oole	*Alte*	old man
oolt	*Alt*	old
oolt johrs obend	*Neu Yahr*	new years eve
oort or maneer	*Art*	manner
oort	*Ansicht*	meaning or opinion
oost	*Osten*	east
ööv or öwen	*Ausübung*	practice
op	*an*	on
op af gohn or op af gahn	*bauen auf*	rely on
op mien halben		on my behalf
op	*um*	about
op'n böhn	*oben*	upstairs
open moken	*offen machen*	open up
open	*offen*	open
openbor	*offenbar*	obvious
openbreken	*offenbrechen*	break open
openholen	*offenhalten*	keep open or hold open
openlaten	*offenlassen*	leave open
openlig	*Offentlich*	public
openrieten	*offen rissen*	tear open
opensmieten	*offen schmeissen*	throw open
operien	*einwirken*	operate
oppassen or worren	*wachen*	watch
oprichten	*aufrichten*	erect

opsammeln	*sammeln*	gather up
opseher	*Vorgesetzte*	supervisor
opsternaatsch	*aufsässig*	hostile or rebellion
ördnen or örnen	*orden*	bring to order or arrange
örgel	*Orgel*	organ
orkan	*Orkan*	hurricane
örnig or orig	*sauber*	proper
örnung	*Ordnung*	order
orrig	*charmant*	charming or tasteful
orse or morse	*Arsche*	butt or arse
orsebacken	*Arschbacken*	buttock cheeks
orsefreter	*aasfresser*	scavenger
oss	*Ochse*	ox
ossen	*Ochsen*	oxen
ossenfleesch	*Ochsenfleisch*	ox steak
Osten	*Ostern*	Easter
osterbloomen	*Anemone*	anemone
osterbloomen	*Narzisse*	narcissus
Osterhaas	*Oster Hase*	Easter rabbit
Ostermaand	*April*	April
oten or ooten	*Atem*	breath
otenpiep	*Luftröhre*	windpipe
övermann or vörsitter	*Vorsitzende*	chairman
övrig	*übrig*	left over or remaining
öwer or röver	*uber*	over
öwer or um or vun	*um*	about
ower, awer, apatt	*aber*	but or however
öwerbett	*Steppdecke*	quilt
öwerbleben	*übrigbleiben*	remained
öwerdacht	*nachgedanken*	thought over
öwerdoon	*ubertrieben*	over done or done over
öwerdregen, röverdregen	*ubertragen*	carry over
öwerdrieven	*übertrieben*	exaggerate
öwerdrieven	*überwältigen*	overcome
öwereenstimmen	*übereinstimmen*	harmonize
öwerfall	*Überfall*	sudden attack or raid
öwergeld	*Ertrag*	profit
öwergloben	*Aberglaube*	superstition
öwergohn or öwergahn	*übergehen*	go over
öwerhand	*Überlegenheit*	advantage or control
öwerjagen, röwerjagen	*übertrieben*	drive over
öwerkieken	*betrachten*	examine or look over
öwerkommen	*überwinden*	get over it
öwerleben	*überleben*	survive
öwerleggen	*nachsinnen*	contemplate or consider

öwerleggen	*uber liegen*	lay over
öwerleidig	*übermässig*	redundant
öwerlevt	*überlebend*	survived
öwernacht	*über Nacht*	overnight
öwernachten	*übernachten*	stay overnight
öwernehmen	*übernehmen*	take over
öwerrock	*Mante*	overcoat
öwersetten	*übersetzen*	translate
öwersheerig	*zuviel*	overdone or too much
öwersluken	*verschlucken*	swallow
öwersnacken	*besprechen*	discuss
öwerste	*Werkmeister*	foreman or section head
öwerstimmt	*überzeugt*	convinced
öwerstöten	*überstossen*	knock over or bump over
öwerstött	*übergestossen*	knocked over
öwertüügen	*überzeugen*	convince
öwrig	*übrig*	leftover or remaining
paad or padd	*Pfad*	path
paat or voderstohn	*Pate*	sponsor
pack	*Pack*	pack
packelausch, gepack	*Gepäck*	baggage or luggage
padden	*Pfoten*	paws
pageluun	*Pfau*	peacock
pahl or pohl	*Pfahl*	pole
pahl	*Stange*	pole
pahlbörger		bourgois
pahlholen	*feststellen*	stand firm
pakeet	*Paket*	package
palm	*Palme*	palm
pamp	*Fruchtmark*	pulp
pampig	*frech*	brazen or insolent
pand	*Pfand*	pledge
pandhuus	*Pfandleihe*	pawnshop
paneel	*Füllung*	panel
pankoken	*Pfannkuchen*	pancake
pankschoon	*Pension*	pension
pann	*Pfanne*	pan
panner	*Gerichtsdiener*	bailiff
panner	*Sheriff*	sheriff
pantuffel	*Pantoffel*	slipper
papp	*Pappe*	cardboard
pappbeker	*Pappbecher*	papercup
pappel	*Pappel*	poplar
parat	*bereit*	ready or prepared

337

pass or to pass kommen	*passend*	suit
pass up or kiekut	*gib acht*	look out
pass	*Pass*	pass
passeer oder passeern	*passieren*	happen
passeert	*passiert*	happens
passt	*passt*	fits
pastoor or pastor or paster	*Paster*	pastor
patroon	*Patrouille*	patrol
patschen	*Feuerlöscher*	fire extinguisher
pause	*Unterbrechung*	intermission
pech	*slechten Glück*	bad luck
pedd	*tretent*	step
peddt	*schreiten*	stepping
peddut	*austreten*	step out
peek	*Spitzestock*	pike
peenlig or schenerlig	*peinlich*	embarrassing
peer or peerd	*Pferde*	horses
peerd	*Pferd*	horse
peerhannel	*Pferdhandel*	horse trading
peerstall	*Pferdestall*	horsestall
pelz or pelt	*Filz*	felt
pepper	*Pfeffer*	pepper
peppernaart	*Pfeffernütze*	peppernuts
petersill	*petersilie*	parsley
pick	*wahl*	pick
piek	*spähen*	peek
piel or pielup	*aufrecht*	upright
piel	*Pfeil*	arrow
pieler	*Pfeiler*	pillar
piep	*Piep*	peep
piepegol	*egal*	all the same
piepen or piep	*Pfeife*	pipe
piependeckel	*Spitzbube*	rascal
piknik	*Picknick*	picnic
pill	*Pille*	pill
pillen	*Pillen*	pills
pimperlig	*überempfindlich*	squeemish
pingel	*klingel*	bell ring
Pingsten	*Pfingsten*	Whitsunday or Pentecost
Pingstvoss	*PfingstFuchs*	Pentecost Fox
pinn	*Pinne*	tiller
pirsch or peeschen	*Pfirsich*	peach
plaag	*piesacken*	pester or disturb
plaag	*Plage*	plague
plaan	*Plan*	plan

338

plack	*Fleck*	spot
placken	*Acken*	farm fields
plackerwark or plackerarbeid	*Feldt arbeit*	field work
plakeet	*Plakette*	plaque
plant	*Pflanze*	plant
pläster or plaaster	*Pflaster*	plaster
platschen or palschen	*platschen*	splash
platt dütsk	*Platt Deutsch*	Low German
platt düütsch	*Platt Deutsch*	Low German
platt	*platt*	flat
platz	*Platz*	place or location
plätz	*Plätze*	places
plege or pleeg	*Pflege*	care
plegen	*erhalten*	care for or maintain
plegöllern	*Pflege Eltern*	foster parents
pletten or strieken	*Plätten*	iron clothes
plettiesen	*Bügeleisen*	iron
plicht	*Verpflichtung*	obligation
plieren	*Schielen*	squint or blink
plietsch	*schlau*	smart or crafty or canny
plinkern	*funkeln*	sparkle
plögen	*pflügen*	to plow
ploog	*Pflug*	plow
plöög	*Pflügen*	plows
ploogiesen or ploogschar	*Pflugschar*	plow share
plörig	*dünn*	thin
ploster	*Pflasterung*	pavement
plosterweg	*Bürgersteig*	sidewalk
plöterig	*armselig*	wretched
plück	*pflücken*	pick or pluck
pluck	*Klotz*	block
plückfidel	*Gitarre*	guitar
plumm	*Pflaume*	plum
plumpsen		plop
plünnen tohopen smieten	*Heiraten*	to marry
plünnen	*Lappen*	rag or rags
poesie	*Poesie*	poetry
pogg	*Frosch*	frog
poggenslick	*Wasserlinse*	duckweek
pökelt	*gepökelt*	pickled
pomodig	*ruhig*	calm
pool	*Pfuhl*	puddle
poor	*paar*	pair
poot	*Pfote*	paw
popeer or popier	*Papier*	paper

popiergeld	*Vermögen*	paper money
poppen	*Puppe*	doll
poppenlustig	*damen lustig*	girl crazy
poppenwogen	*Puppenwagen*	doll carriage
port	*Pforte*	gate
portschoon	*Portion*	portion
porzellan	*Porzellan*	porcelain
posten or possen	*Pfosten*	post
postkirl	*Postträger*	postman or mailcarrier
pott	*Topf*	pot
pött	*Töpfen*	pots
pottdicht	*sehr dicht*	very tight
pottdüüster		very dark
pottegol	*ganz gleich*	even steven
pöttjer or püttjer	*Töpfer*	potter
pottshrapels	*übrigen*	leftovers
praat	*bereit*	ready
praatschen	*Geplapper*	prattle
prahl	*prahlen*	brag
praktische	*praktisch*	practical
predig	*Predigt*	sermon
predigen	*predigen*	preach
preen	*Stanze*	punch
preester	*Priester*	priest
pries	*Preis*	price or prize
pries	*Preis*	prize
priesdreger	*Preisträger*	prizewinner
prieselbeeren	*Preiselbeere*	cranberry
priesen	*Preisen*	prices
problem or pech	*Problem*	problem
pröddels		breakfast meat
profeschoon	*Beruf*	profession
project	*Projekt*	project
prökeln	*stochern*	poke
prööv	*Probe*	test
propp	*Propfen*	cork
prügel	*schlagen*	beat
prünjen		tobacco chaw or plug
prüük	*Perücke*	wig
pruusch	*Niesen*	sneeze
puch or puuch	*plädieren*	plead or pester
puckel	*Rücken*	back
puckel weh	*Rückenschmerzen*	backache
puddelmütz		woolen cap
pudel smieten	*Kegeln*	bowling

puff	*Puff*	puff
pugge	*Ferkel*	piglets
pulterig	*ärmlich*	humble
pulterobend	*Pulterabend*	wedding eve party
pulwer	*Pulver*	powder
pummelig	*rundlich*	chubby
pumpen	*Pumpen*	pump
pund	*Pfund*	pound
punk	*Punkt*	dot or point
punklig	*pünktlich*	dotted
puter	*Truthahn*	turkey
puthehn	*Truthenne*	turkey hen
püttjerkunst	*Töpferkunst*	ceramic
püttscherig	*umständlich*	fussy or huffy
putz börst	*Rasier Pinsel*	shaving brush
putzbüdel	*Friseur*	barber
putzen	*Rasieren*	shave
putzen	*polieren*	polish
putzen oder rein moken	*putzen*	to clean
putzfro or putzfru	*Putzfrau*	cleaning woman
putzig	*lieblich*	cute
puuch	*Bett*	bed
puulkraam or puulkroom	*Lappalie*	trifle
puur	*unverfälscht*	pure
puus	*blasen*	blow
puusbacken	*pausbäckig*	chubby cheeks
puust	*blasend*	blows
puuster	*Luftgewehr*	air rifle
quarkbuddel	*Querulant*	quackgrass
quarken	*quälen*	nag
quarteer	*Quartier*	quarter
quatsch	*Quatsch*	nonsense
quecke	*Quecke*	quackgrass
quesen	*klagen*	complain
quesig	*klagten*	complaining or nagging
raad or ord	*Rat*	advise or advice
raaken	*harken*	to rake
raar or rarr	*selten*	rare
raasch or ärger	*Wut*	rage or anger
raav or rook	*Kolkrabe*	raven
rad or fohrrad	*Fahrrad*	bicycle
rad	*Reifen*	tire or wheel
radel	*Rätsel*	riddle

rafstöten	*abstürzen*	knock off
rake	*Harke*	rake or hoe
ran	*an*	against
rang	*Sprosse*	ladder rung
rangeern	*umherstreifen*	roam around
rankel	*rankel*	rankle
raphohn or feldhohn	*Rebhuhn*	partridge
rappelsnuten	*Plaudertasche*	chatter boxes
rasien	*Rosine*	raisin
rasiern	*rasieren*	shave
rassel	*Rascheln*	rustle
rast or rest	*rasten*	rest
rebeet	*Bereich*	area
recht	*Recht*	right or fair
reck	*Strecke*	reach
redden	*retten*	rescue or save
redder	*Retter*	saver or savior
redig	*Rettich*	radish
reeg	*Reihe*	row
reem	*Riemen*	thong
reep	*Tau*	rope
regeeren	*regieren*	govern or rule
regeerung	*Regierung*	government
regeln	*regulieren*	regulate
regen or riägen	*Regen*	rain
regent	*regnen*	raining
reh	*Reh*	doe
rein	*rein*	clean
reis	*Reise*	trip
reken	*berechnen*	figure or calculate
rekenbook	*Rechnenbuch*	account book
rekent	*betrachtet*	considered
rekner	*Kalkulator*	computer or calculator
remeln	*Reimen*	to rhyme
rennen or rasen	*Renne*	race
rennpeerd	*Rennpferd*	racehorse
rente	*Pensionierung*	retirement
repareeren	*Reparatur*	repair
respekt	*Respekt*	respect
rest	*Rest*	rest
reten	*zerissen*	torn
reve	*Ranke*	vine
revolutschoon	*Revolution*	revolution
rezept	*Rezept*	recipe
ribben	*Rippen*	ribs

richter	*Richter*	judge
richtig	*berechtigen*	correct
rickers	*Stangenbohnen*	runner bean
riebiesen	*Reibeisen*	grater or rasp
rieden	*reiten*	ride
rieder	*Reiter*	rider
riederee	*Kavallerie*	cavalry
riedstebel	*Reitstiefel*	riding boot
riek	*reich*	rich
riekdom	*Reichtum*	kingdom
riemel	*Reim*	rhyme
riep	*reif*	ripe
ries	*Reis*	rice
riet	*zerreissen*	tear
rietsticken	*Streichholz*	match
rietversluut	*Reissverschluss*	zipper
riez	*Reiz*	charm
rin	*in*	into
rinbetohln	*einbezahlen*	pay in
rinblosen or rinpuusen	*einblasen*	blow into
rinbreken	*einbrechen*	break into
rinbringen	*einbringen*	bring in
rinbrocht	*eingebrocht*	brought in
rindanser	*Eintänzer*	gigolo
rinder or rindveeh	*Rinder*	beef cattle
rindfleesch	*Rindfleisch*	beef
rindrieben	*treiben*	lead into or drive into
rinföhren	*einfahren*	drive into
ring	*Ring*	ring
ringeldans	*Ringeltanz*	round dance
ringoh or ringah	*Eingang*	entrance
ringohn or ringahn	*eingehen*	enter into
ringriepen	*eingriffen*	intervene
rinholen	*einhalten*	hold in
rinjagen or rindäbeln	*einkrachen*	crash into
rinkieken	*herein sehen*	look into
rinknallen	*einrammen*	slam into or smash into
rinkomen or kommrin	*reinkommen*	come in
rinkommen	*hereinkommen*	enter
rinlat	*Eintritt*	admission
rinlaten	*einlassen*	let in
rinleggen	*herein legen*	place into or lay into
rinleggen	*einlegen*	insert
rinlopen	*einlaufen*	run into
rinnehm	*einkassieren*	collect

rinrieden	herein reiten	ride into
rinschruben	einschrauben	screw in
rinstippen	einstippen	dip into or dunk
rinstoppen	einpaucken	stuff into
rintehn	einzogen	pull into
rintritt	Einlass	entryway
riskiern	riskieren	risk
robber	Gummi	rubber
robberstebel	Gummistiefel	rubber boots
röben	rauben	rob
röber	Räuber	robber or pirate
rock	Frauenrock	skirt
rock	Rock	coat or jacket
rod or rad	Rute	rod
rodbosten	Rotkehlchen	robin redbreast
rodder	Ruder	rudder
rodkrüüz or rotkrüüz	Rotenkreuz	red cross
roen	erraten	guess
rögen	hasten	to hurry
rögen	Schwungen	movement
roggen	Roggen	rye
rögt	bewegt	moved
roh or rauh	Ruhe	rest
rohig	ruhig	calm
rohm or room	Rahm	cream
röhr	rühren	stir
röhreier	Rührei	scrambled eggs
rohrstohl	Rohrstuhl	cane chair
rohstunn	Nickerchen	nap after noon, rest time
roken	Rachen	jaw
rollstohl or rullstohl	Rollstuhl	wheelchair
rolltreppen or rulltreppen	Rolltreppe	escalator
röög or rög	beeilen	hurry
röög or rög	bewegen	move
rooh	Ruhe	quiet
rook	Rauch	smoke
roop	ruf	call
röör	Reifen	tires
roos	Rose	rose
root or rot or rood or rod	Rot	red
rööv	Rübe	turnip
ropp or rupp	auf	onto
roppt	ruft	calls
rorr or bullern	brüllen	roar
rot	Rat	council

rötern or rökeln	*röcheln*	rattle
rothuus	*Rathaus*	city hall
rott	*Ratte*	rat
röwer	*herüber*	over or across
röwerbringen	*überbringen*	bring over
röwergeben	*übergaben*	hand over
ruden (in korden)	*Karo*	diamond (in cards)
rudekohl	*Rotkohl*	red cabbage
ruden	*roten*	red one
rüe	*Hund*	hound
ruhriep	*Rauhreif*	hoarfrost
rükelbusch	*Blumenstrauss*	bouquet
rüken	*riechen*	smell
rükerkaat	*Rauchhaus*	smokehouse
rükt	*gerüch*	smells
rükwoter or rükwater	*Parfüm*	perfume
rull or roll	*Roll*	roll
rulladen	*Jalousie*	venetian blind
rüm	*um*	around
rumatis	*Rheumatismus*	rheumatism
rümdriewer	*Chauffeur*	chauffeur
rümdüm	*ringsherum*	all around
rümen or rümmen	*raumen*	clear away
rümflegen	*umfliegen*	fly around
rümflitzen	*umgaukeln*	scurry
rümfragen	*umfragen*	ask around
rümgohn or rümgahn	*umgehen*	go around
rümhüppen	*umhüpfen*	hop around
rümig	*geräumig*	spacious
rümkieken	*umschauen*	look around
rümlopen	*umlaufen*	run around
rumpelkroom	*Kehrricht*	junk
rümsnacken	*klatschen*	spread word or gossip
rümsnuben	*umschnüffeln*	snoop around
rümstebeln or rümsteveln	*Taumeln*	stagger
rümwickelt	*umwickelt*	wrapped around
rund	*Runde*	round
rundloop	*Rotation*	rotation
rundmest		wood shaping rounded knife
runksen or rütschen	*schlottern*	slouch
rünnen or dackrünn	*Dachrinne*	gutter
rünner	*unten*	underneath
rupstiegen or ropstiegen	*aufsteigen*	climb on
russel	*rauschen*	rustle
rust	*Rost*	rust

rustig	*rostig*	rusty
rut	*aus*	out of
rutblieben or rutblieven	*ausbleiben*	stay out of
rutbloosen	*ausblasen*	blow out
rutfallen	*ausfallen*	fell out or fallen out
rutflegen	*ausfliegen*	fly out
rutflogen	*ausgeflogen*	flew out
rutholen	*ausholen*	keep out
rutlaten	*auslassen*	leave out
rutlopen	*auslaufen*	run out
rutnehmen	*ausnehmen*	take out
rutnohm	*ausgenohmen*	took out
rutrieten	*ausreisen*	tear out
rutsch	*rutschen*	slide
rutschig	*glitschig*	slippery
rutsluten	*ausschliessen*	lock out
rutsmeten	*ausgezwirnt*	thrown out
rutsmieten	*ausschmeissen*	throw out
rutspringen	*ausspringen*	jump out
rutstiegen	*aussteigen*	climb out
rutstohn	*ausstehen*	stick out or stand out
ruttohgen	*ausziehen*	pulled out
rüük	*Geruch*	smell
ruum	*Raum*	room or space
ruut	*raus*	get out
s'morens or vörmiddag	*Morgen*	morning
sä	*sagen*	(he,she,it) said
saag	*Säge*	saw
saagenbock	*Sägenbuck*	saw buck
saagmehl	*Sägestaub*	sawdust
saagmöhl	*sägenmühl*	sawmill
saak	*Grund*	reason
saak	*Sache*	thing
saakmodig	*bedächtig*	deliberate or cautious
saal	*Saal*	dance hall or large room
saalhund	*Seehund*	seal
sään	*sagten*	they said
saat	*Saat*	seed
saatland	*Saatland*	seeded ground
Saatmaand	*October*	October
sabbelig	*gesprächig*	talkative
sabben	*sich beklagen*	complain
sabel	*säbel*	sabre
sack dahl	*sanken*	sink down

346

sack	*Sack*	sack
sack	*sinken*	sink
saddel	*Sattel*	saddle
saddler	*Sattler*	saddler
saft or sapp	*Saft*	juice or sap
saftwoder or saftwater	*Cola*	softdrink
sahl	*Sohle*	shoe sole
salmbook	*Psalmbuch*	psalmbook
salv	*Salbe*	salve
sand	*Sand*	sand
sandborg	*Sandburg*	sand castle
sanduhr	*Sanduhr*	hourglass
sapp	*Saft*	sap
sappholt	*Saftholz*	green wood or sapwood
sarg	*Sarg*	coffin
satt eten	*Sattessen*	eat your fill
satt	*Satt*	done eating
satt	*Vull*	full
satt	*zufrieden*	satisfied
satz	*Satz*	sentence
schaaf	*Hubel*	carpenter's plane
schaal	*Schale*	shallow dish
schaap	*Schaf*	sheep
schaapschieren	*Schafschur*	sheep shearing
schaapsködel	*Schafskot*	sheep raisins
Schaapskopp	*Schafskopf*	sheepshead (cardgame)
schaapswull	*Schafswolle*	sheeps wool
schaar	*Aktie*	share
schaarwarken	*zusammenarbeit*	cooperation
schabbig	*Schäbig*	unfriendly
schacht or shaft	*Schaft*	shaft
schadden	*Schatten*	shade
schaff	*schaffen*	operate or work or create
schall	*solle*	shall
schallen	*Sprosse*	shoots or sprouts
schallott	*Schallott*	shallot
schäm di	*Schäm dich*	shame on you
schäm	*Scham*	shame
schämlos	*schamlos*	shameless
schandal	*Skandal*	scandal
schandarm	*Polizei*	police
schangs	*Chance*	chance
schännen	*Schande*	disgrace
schännen or unehrn	*unehren*	dishonor
schapp	*Küchenschrank*	cupboard

347

schapp	*Kabinett*	cabinet
scharp	*scharf*	sharp
scharpen	*verschärfen*	sharpen
schass or schalls	*sollte*	(you) should
schatt	*Schatz*	treasure
schaukelpeerd	*Schaukelpferd*	rocking horse
schoben	*geschoben*	shoved
schoden	*Schaden*	harm or damage
schodet	*schaden*	harms
schoh	*schuh*	shoe
schohbörst	*Schuhbürste*	shoebrush
schohlepel	*Schuhanzieher*	shoehorn
schohster	*Schuhflicker*	shoemaker or shoe cobbler
schok or bult	*Stoss*	stack of wheat
schock	*Schock*	shock
schokolad or kakao	*Schokolade*	chocolate
schöler	*Schuler*	student
scholl or schall	*soll*	(I) should
schöllt	*sollen*	(we, they) should
schön	*schön*	lovely or nice
schon	*schon*	already
school	*Schule*	school
schoolbank	*Schulbank*	school desk
schoolen	*Schulen*	schools
schoolgrund or schoolhof	*Schulhof*	playground
schoolkind	*Schüler*	pupil
schoolkinner	*Schulkinder*	pupils or schoolchildren
schoolleehren	*Schulaufgabe*	homework
schoolmeester	*Schullehrer*	teacher
schoolrot	*Schulrat*	school board
schoot	*Schoss*	lap
schor or küst	*Küste*	shore or coast
schorsteen	*Schornstein*	chimney
schorv	*Schorf*	scab
schoten	*Schuss*	shot
schöttel	*Schüssel*	dish or bowl
schötteldook	*Spültuch*	dishrag or washrag
se	*Sie*	she or they
see	*See*	sea or lake
see	*Sieb*	sieve
seehdook	*seihtüch*	straining cloth
seehen	*seihen*	to strain
seel	*Seele*	soul
seemann or mariner	*Matrose*	sailor
seemlig	*ziemlich*	fairly

seepen	*Seife*	soap
seepsteen	*Speckstein*	soapstone
seesel	*Sichel*	scythe
seet	*sass*	sat
seetung	*Seezunge*	sole
segel	*Segel*	sail
segel	*Siegel*	seal or crest
segen	*Segen*	blessing
segg	*sagen*	say
seggen	*sagen*	to say
seggt	*gesagt*	says or said
seggwoort	*sprichwort*	saying
seh	*sehen*	see
sehn	*gesehen*	seen
sehnweert	*sehenswürdig*	worth seeing
sei	*säen*	sow
seien	*aussaat*	to sow
seker	*sicher*	sure or secure
sekerheit	*Sicherheit*	security
sekerlig	*sicherlich*	surely
sekund	*Sekunde*	second
sellschop	*Gesellschaft*	company
sellschop or gesellschop	*Gesellschaft*	society
selten	*selten*	rare or seldom
sement	*zement*	cement
sengeln	*glimmen*	smoulder
seten	*gesessen*	sat
sett	*setzen*	set or place
shedel	*Scheitel*	partition
sheed	*Abschied*	leave
sheedel	*Scheitel*	hair part
sheeden	*scheiden*	divide or separate
sheeden	*Scheidung*	divorce
sheedkunst	*Chemie*	chemistry
sheef or krumm	*schief*	crooked
sheel	*Unterschied*	difference
sheel	*Schielen*	squint
sheel	*seitlich*	lateral
sheel	*Teil*	share or portion
sheet	*Schiessen*	shoot
sheeten	*Schiessen*	shoot
sheevbeenig	*scheifbeinig*	bowlegged
shell	*schälen*	peel
shell	*Schale*	shell
shelm	*Halunke*	rascal

shelmstück	*Schelmerei*	prank
sheneren	*verwirren*	embarrass
sheper	*Schäfer*	shepherd
sheret or sheert	*Konzern*	concerns
sheurn or shüün	*Scheune*	barn
shicht	*Schicht*	layer
shick	*Schick*	shape or fitness
shick	*Feinheit*	elegance
shick	*schicken*	send
shien	*Schein*	shine
shienbor	*scheinbar*	seemingly
shiensmieter	*Scheinwerfer*	searchlight or headlight
shient or lett so as	*es stellt sich heraus*	appears
shient so	*erscheint*	seems as if
shier	*Schere*	scissors or shears
shier or shiev	*schlicht*	smooth or even
shier	*schlicht*	smooth
shierwark or schievwark	*Eggewalze*	use cultipacker
shiet	*Scheiss*	shit
shiethuus	*Plumpklosset*	out house
shietkraam	*Auswurf*	garbage
shiev	*Scheibe*	pane
shild	*Schild*	shield or badge
shiller or schilder	*Maler*	painter
shillern	*schildern*	portray
shimmel or spaak	*Schimmel*	mold
shimmel	*Schimmel*	white horse
shimmer or schummer	*Schimmer*	gleam
shimpas	*Schelte*	scolding
shimpen	*verwarnen*	admonish
shimpen	*schelten*	scold
shimplig	*schimpflich*	disgraceful
shimpt	*schelten*	scold
shinkel	*Schenkel*	thigh
shinken or swiensmors	*Schinken*	ham
shinnen	*abbalgen*	skin or scrape skin
shinner	*Schinder*	shingler
shipp	*Schiff*	ship
shippen (in korten)	*Pik*	spade (in cards)
shirm	*Schirm*	umbrella
shohster	*Schuhmacher*	shoemaker
shörten	*Schürze*	apron
shörtenjager	*Schürzenjäger*	skirt chaser
shraap	*Scharren*	scrape
shramm	*Schramme*	scratch

shreck	*Schreck*	fright
shrecken	*Schrecken*	scare
shrecklig	*schrecklich*	frightening or terrible
shree	*Geschrei*	scream
shree	*Schrei*	cry or screem
shreeg		out of line
shreen	*schreien*	cry
shreen	*Weinen*	crying
shrewegoorn	*Schrewegarten*	small alloted garden
shriev	*schreib*	write
shrievmaschin	*Schreibmaschine*	typewriter
shrievschapp		writing desk
shrievwies, rechtshriev	*Schreibweis*	proper spelling
shriewer	*Sekretär*	secretary
shriewerslüüd	*Autoren*	authors
shriewersmann	*Schriftsteller*	author
shrink	*schrinken*	shrink
shroot		tobacco plug
missing	*Kleie*	bran
shrot	*Kügelchen*	shotgun pellets
shrott	*Abfall*	junk
shrott	*Schrot*	crushed grain
shrunk	*schrumpf*	shrunk
shruuf	*Schraube*	screw
shrüüv	*Schraube*	screws
shruuvslotel	*Schraubeschleuse*	wrench
shu	*scheu*	shy
shüchte	*schüchtern*	bashful
shüddel	*Schüttel*	shake
shüffel	*Schaufel*	shovel
shüffelploog	*Bodenbearbeitungsgerät*	cultivator
shuld	*Schuld*	blame
shuldig or shullig	*schuldig*	guilty
shuldig or shullig	*schuldig*	owed
shulden or shulen	*Schuldend*	debt or obligation
shullern	*Schulter*	shoulder
shulls	*sollte*	should
shümer	*Schaumlöffel*	skimmer
shummertied	*Dämmerung*	dusk
shunt		skiff
shuppen	*schaben*	scrape
shutt	*Geröll*	rubble
shüttkopp	*abschlagen*	deny
shuuf	*Schublade*	drawer
shuum	*Schaum*	foam or froth or suds

351

shuumwien	*Champagner*	champagne or sekt
shüür or shüer	*scheuer*	rub
shuuv	*Schub*	shove
shuuvkoor	*Schubkarren*	wheelbarrow
shüün	*Scheuene*	barn
shüür	*Reiben*	rub
shüürpahl		rubbing post or scratching post
sied	*Seite*	side
sied	*Seite*	page
siedendöör	*Seiteltü*	side door
siedmoken	*beseitigen*	reduce or eliminate
sieg	*Sieg*	victory
sien or wesen or west	*sein*	be
sien	*Sein*	his
siet	*seicht*	ow
sik or sik sülms	*es selbst*	itself
sik sülbens or sik sülms	*er selbst*	himself
sik vertüren	*zanken*	squabble
sik	*sich*	self
simmlig or teemlig	*ziemlich*	rather
simp	*Senf*	mustard
sims	*Sims*	ledge
sing	*Singen*	sing
singhönken	*Zirpe*	cricket
sinksanken	*Zickzack*	zig zag
sinn	*Gesinnung*	mind or sense
sinnbild	*Sinnbild*	symbol
sinnig or insichtig	*verständig*	sensible
sinnig or nodenklig	*nachdenklich*	thoughtful
sinnig	*sorgfältig*	thoughtful or deliberate
sinnlig	*sinnlich*	sensual
sinnlos or kopplos	*kopflos*	mindless
sinnlos	*sinnlos*	senseless
sinnriek	*freimütig*	ingenious
sinnspruk	*Sinnspruch*	motto
sinnverwand	*sinnverwandt*	synonymous
sinnvull	*sinnvoll*	meaningful
sippen	*Nippen*	sip
sippschop	*Sippschaft*	community or clan
sirup	*Sirup*	syrup
sitt	*sitzen*	sit
sittung or samlung	*Sitzung*	meeting
sitz	*Sitz*	seat
skat (kordenspeel)	*Skat*	skat (card game)
sketts	*Skizze*	sketch

slaag or slag	*Schlag*	strike or hit
slaan or slagen	*betroffen*	struck
slaap or sloop or slaop	*Schlaf*	sleep
slaapkist or sloopkist	*Wandbett*	bunkbed
slaaplos or slooplos	*schlaflos*	sleepless or insomnia
slaapmütz or sloopmütz	*Schlafmütze*	nightcap
slaapstuuv,sloopkomer	*Schlafzimmer*	bedroom
slaav	*Sklave*	slave
slacht	*schlachten*	slaughter
slachter	*Schlächter*	butcher
slachtmest	*Schlachtmesser*	butcher knife
slakker	*vergiessen*	spill
slakkerbüx	*Schmutzflecker*	sloppy person
slang	*Schlange*	snake
slanggift	*Gift*	venom
slank	*schlank*	thin or slender
slapp	*schlaff*	slack
slapp		hog feed
slecht or slimm	*schlimm*	bad
slecht	*schlecht*	poor
sleden	*Schlitten*	sled
sleden	*schlittern*	slide
sleier	*Schleier*	veil
sleiht	*erschlagen*	strikes
sleng	*Schlinge*	sling
slepp or shlepp	*schleppen*	drag
Sleswig	*Schleswig*	Schleswig
slicht	*Schlicht*	plain
sliek	*sleichen*	sneak
sliem	*Schleim*	slime
sliepsteen	*Schleifstein*	whetstone
sling	*Schlinge*	loop
slingdook	*Schal*	shawl
slips or kravat	*Krawatte*	tie
slittschoh	*Schlittschuh*	skates
slobber	*Schlabber*	slabber
slön	*Schwarzdorn*	blackthorn
slotel	*Schlüssel*	key
sloten	*geschlossen*	ocked
slott	*Schloss*	lock
slucht	*Bergschlucht*	ravine
sluckup	*Schlucken*	hiccup
slüngel or sleef	*Schlingel*	imp or rascal
slusig	*unvorsichtig*	careless
sluuk	*Schluck*	swallow

smacht	Hunger	hunger
smachtig	hungrig	hungry
smal	schmal	small
smeck	schmeck	taste
smecklos	geschmacklos	tasteless
smeckt	schmeckt	tastes
smeer or smier	schmieren	smear or spread
smeer	schmier	smear
smeer	Schmiere	grease
smeerdig	formbar	malleable
smeergeld	Schmiergeld	bribe
smeerkees	Schmierkäse	cheese spread
smeerpistol	Schmierpistole	grease gun
smeten	gewurft	thrown or tossed
smied or smitt	Schmied	blacksmith
smiede	Schmiede	forge
smiel	lächeln	smile
smiet	schmeiss	toss or throw
smok or damp	Rauch	smoke
smöken	rauchen	to smoke
smokhuus	Räucherhaus	smoke house
smölt or upsmölt	geschmolzen	melted
smolt	schmalz	lard or grease
smölt	schmelzen	melt
smölten	schmelzen	to melt
smuck	attraktiv	attractive or pretty
smuck	Schmuck	cute or dapper
smuck	Schmuck	jewelry
smuddelig or schieterig	schmutzig	dirty
smuggel	schmuggeln	smuggle
smuseree	Schmeichelei	flattery
smüstern or smustergrienen		smirk
smutz	Schmutz	dirt
snaaksch	auffallend	strange
snackt or küert	redet	speaks or talks
snack or sprek or küer or proten	reden	speak or talk
snall	Schnalle	buckel
snappen	Rotze	snot
snappenlicker		snot nosed kid
snatern or kackeln	gakkern	cackle
snee	Schnee	snow
sneeantog or sneebüx	Schneeanzug	snowsuit
sneeball or sneeklüten	Schneeball	snowball
sneefall	Schneefall	snowfall
sneeflaken	Schneeflocke	snowflake

sneeflock	*Schneeflocke*	snowflake
sneekirl or sneekadel	*Schneeman*	snowman
Sneemaand	*Januar*	January
sneen or sneden	*geschneiden*	cut or sliced
sneewittshe	*Schneewittchen*	snow white
snick	*Schnecke*	snail
snickelfritz	*Spassvogel*	rascal
snie or snien or snieden	*schneiden*	cut
sniedbrett	*Schneidebrett*	cutting board
sniedemester	*Schnittmeister*	editor
snieder	*Schneider*	cutter
snieder	*Schneider*	tailor
sniedspaden	*Torfgraber*	peat spade
snippel	*Brocken*	scrap
snippel	*Schnitzel*	shred
snitt	*Schnitt*	a cut
snitzeln	*schnitzeln*	whittle or carve
snobben	*Mistkäfer*	dung beetle
snobel	*Schnabel*	beak
snoben	*geschnupft*	sniffed
snodderig	*unverschämt*	brash
snodderig	*Schnodderig*	brash or snotty
snoken	*Ringelnatter*	grass snake
snoor	*Schnur*	braid or string
snoosbort	*Schnauzbart*	mustache
snork	*Schnarch*	snore
snorken	*schnarken*	to snore
snöterwark	*Klatsch*	gossip
snuckel	*Näseln*	sniffle
snudderegen	*nieseln*	drizzle
snüffel	*Näseln*	sniffle
snüffelhund	*Schweisshund*	tracking dog
snuller	*Schnuller*	baby fooler or pacifier
snurren	*betteln*	beg
snurrer	*Bettler*	beggar
snut upsetten or snut moken		make a face
snuten	*Schweine*	pickled pig nose
snuup	*schnüffeln*	snoop
snuut	*Schnauze*	nose or snout
snuuv	*schnauben*	snort
snuuv	*schnupfen*	sniff
snuuvtabak	*Schnupftabak*	snuff
so draad as	*so bald wie*	as soon as
so to seggen	*so zu sagen*	so to say
so un soveel	*so und so viel*	so much

so wat as dat	*so was wie das*	stuff likethat
so	*so*	so or thus
söben	*Sieben*	seven
söbente	*siebente*	seventh
söbentein	*siebzehn*	seventeen
söbentig	*siebzig*	seventy
socht	*socht*	looked or searched
sock	*Socke*	sock or stocking
söcken	*Socken*	socks or stockings
sodennig	*so wie*	that's how
sög	*Sau*	sow
sogor as	*sogar als*	as soon as
sogor or sogoor	*sogar*	even
sogor or woll or egentlig	*tatsächlich*	actually
sogrode as or sobald as		soon as
söhn or jung	*Sohn*	son
söken	*suchen*	searching
solang as	*solange wie*	so long as
solat	*Salat*	salad
solo or zolo (kordenspeel)	*Solo*	solo (card game)
solt	*Salz*	salt
so'n	*solche*	such a
söök	*Suche*	search
soom	*Saum*	seam
soot or pütte	*Brunnen*	well
sööt	*süss*	sweet
sootswang	*Schwengel*	pump handle
sootswiengel	*Schwengel*	well sweep
sopper	*Abendessen*	supper
sorde	*Art*	type
sorde	*Sorte*	kind
sörge or sögge	*klagen*	complain
sorge	*Sorge*	care or worry
sorgen oder pech	*plaggen*	worries
söss	*Sechs*	six
sössbeente	*Laus*	louse
sösstein	*Sechszehn*	sixteen
sösstig	*sechzig*	sixty
söten or küss	*Kuss*	kiss
sötwater or frischwoter	*Süsswasser*	fresh water
sowatts or sowat as dat		such as that
sowiet as	*insofern*	as far as
spaas	*Spass*	fun
spadel	*Spatel*	spatula
spaden or küffel	*Spaten*	spade

356

spandelje (in korden)	*Kreuz Dame*	queen clubs
spann peer	*Gespann*	team
spann	*anspannen*	hitch up
spann	*Paar*	pair
spann	*Spanne*	span
spannt	*gespannt*	tense
spatz	*Spatz*	sparrow
spazeern	*Spaziergang*	stroll
speck	*Speck*	bacon
speckaal or rökeraal	*Räucheraal*	smoked eel
spee or spae	*Spucke*	spit
speegel	*Spiegel*	mirror
speel	*Spiel*	play or play a card
speelbaas	*Spiel Direktor*	play director
speeldeel	*Bühnenspiel*	playlet
speeldings	*Spielzeug*	toy
speelkorden	*Spielkarte*	playing card
speelruum, speelstuuv	*Spielstube*	playroom
speelsoken or speeldingen	*Spielwaren*	toys
speer	*Speer*	spear
spegeln	*reflektieren*	reflect
spektokel	*Spektakel*	spectacle
spennen	*geben*	donate
sperrstunn	*Abendglocke*	curfew hour
spieker	*Speicher*	granary
spies	*Speis*	food
spietsch	*sarkastisch*	derisive or sarcastic
spijöök	*Posse*	farce
spinnbock	*Spinne*	spider
spinnweev	*Spinngewebe*	cobweb
spinrad	*Spinnrad*	spinning wheel
spinwark	*Spinngewebe*	spiderweb
spitz (in korten)	*Sieben*	seven clubs (in cards)
spitz kommen	*gewahr worden*	become aware
spitz	*spitz*	pointed or sharp
spitz	*Gipfel*	summit
splidder	*Splitter*	sliver or splinter
splienigkeit	*Heiterkeit*	craziness
spliet or spleten	*spalten*	split
splitternaakt or splitternokt		stark naked
spöhl	*spülen*	rinse
spökenkieker	*Wahrsager*	clairvoyant
spökig or pukkelig	*schäbig*	shabby
spöllappen	*Spüllappen*	dish rag
Sponsch	*Spanisch*	Spanish

spöök	*Spuken*	spook
spool	*Spule*	spool
sporbook	*Bankbuch*	bankbook
sporkass or bank	*Sparkasse*	savings bank
sporren	*sparen*	save
sporsom	*selten*	rare
sposig or spasig	*spasshaft*	funny
spott	*Beleidigung*	insult
spöttsch	*spotten*	mocking
spreen	*Star*	starling
spreegen	*Starren*	stare
sprickwoort	*Motto*	motto
spring or jump	*springen*	spring or jump
springer, grasspringer	*Heuschrecke*	grasshopper
spritt	*spritz*	spray
sproch or sprok	*Spruch*	language
sprööd or krümmelig	*spröde*	brittle
sprungen	*Sprungen*	sprung
sprütt	*Spritze*	squirt
sprütt	*sprühen*	to spray
sprüttling	*Spross*	offspring
spundlock	*Spundloch*	bung hole
spuur or spoor	*Spur*	trail or track
staak	*aufstellen*	to stack
staat	*Staat*	state
staats	*anstatt*	instead
staatsch	*prachtvoll*	magnificent
stackelsminsch	*armer Teufel*	bum or wretch
stadt	*Stadt*	city or town
stadtlüüd	*Stadtleute*	city people
stadtlüüd or stadtlüer	*Stadtleute*	townspeople
stadtrot	*Stadtrat*	city council
stahl	*Stahl*	steel
stalk or spier	*Stiel*	stalk
stall	*Bude*	stall
stamm	*ableiten*	derive
stammboom	*Stammbaum*	family tree
stammt vun	*stammt aus*	stems from
stang	*Stange*	pole
stännig	*ständig*	constant
stark	*stark*	strong
statschoon	*Standort*	station
stebel or stevel	*Stiefel*	boot
stebelknecht	*Stiefelknecht*	bootjack
steen	*Stein*	stone

steenkruug	*Krug*	jug
steenöl	*Steinöl*	petroleum
steentied	*Stein zeit*	stone age
steern	*Sterne*	stars
steernkieker	*Fernrohr*	telescope
steert	*Schwanz*	tail
steertpogg or pielepoggen	*Kualquappe*	tadpole
steertrock	*Frack*	frock coat
steevig	*stämmig*	stable or sturdy
stehl	*stehlen*	steal or rob
steiht	*steht*	stands
steihtup	*aufstehen*	stands up or gets up
stek	*Stich*	stab or stick
steken (in korten)	*stichen*	take trick (in cards)
stekfleeg	*Stechmücke*	mosquito
steknodel or steknadel	*Sicherheitsnade*	safety pin
stekrööv	*Stekrübe*	turnip
stell or steed	*Stelle*	place
stempel	*Stampfen*	stamp
stich	*Stich*	a score (in cards)
stich	*Stich*	stitch
stickelree	*Stickerei*	embroidery
stickendüster	*Stockdunkel*	pitch dark
stickrööv or kohlrööv	*Kohlrübe*	rutabaga
stiefmarieken	*Stiefmütterchen*	pansy
stiegen	*steigen*	climb
stier	*Stier*	bull
stiev or stief	*steif*	stiff or rigid
stievbroder	*Stiefbruder*	stepbrother
stievfroren	*Steifgefroren*	frozen stiff
stievkind	*Stiefkind*	stepchild
stievmoder	*Stiefmutter*	stepmother
stievnacken or stievkopp	*hartnäckig*	stubborn
stiggt	*stiegt*	climbs
stikbeern,stickelbeern	*Stachelbeere*	gooseberry
still	*still*	silent
still	*regungslos*	motionless
Stillfreedag	*Karfreitag*	Good Friday
stillken	*Geheimniss*	secret
stimm or stimmen	*Stimme*	voice
stimmel	*stemmen*	stem or shaft
stimmt mit	*übereinstimmen*	agrees with
stimmt	*einstimmen*	agrees or checks out
stingel	*Stachel*	stinger
stingel	*Stengel*	stem

stinnen or utstohn	*aushalten*	to stand or endure
stipp	*Tunke*	gravy
stippen		dip into
stobble	*Stoppel*	stubble
stoff	*Staub*	dust
stoff	*Stoff*	stuff
stoh	*Stehen*	stand
stöhl	*Stühl*	chairs
stohl	*Stuhl*	chair
stohlen	*gestohlen*	stolen
stohn	*gestanden*	stood
stohwoter		standing water
stok	*Stock*	stick
stökern	*stochern*	poke or stir
stolt or krönsch	*Stolz*	proud
stolterboltern	*Sturz*	tumble or somersault
stöör	*stören*	bother or disturb
stoot or stood	*Stute*	mare
stopp	*Stoff*	stuff
stopp	*Halt*	stop
stoppen	*stopfen*	darn sock
stoppshild	*Halteschild*	stopsign
storb or storv	*sterben*	die
stött	*stossen*	bump
stöttaf or vun stöten	*abschlagen*	knock off
stotter	*Stottern*	stutter
stötterbüx	*Stammeler*	stutterer
stövig	*staubig*	dusty or stuffy
straaf or stroof	*Strafe*	punishment or sentence
stramm	*straff*	taut
strand	*Strand*	beach
streben	*streben*	strive
strei	*ausstreuen*	scatter
strek or streck	*Strecke*	stretch
strick	*Strick*	rope
strickjack	*Strichjacke*	cardigan
stricknodel	*Stricknadel*	knitting needle
stricktüüg, stricktüch	*Stricktuch*	knitwear
striek	*Strich*	streak
strien, quelen, vertüren	*Streit*	quarrel or argue
striep or striek	*Streifen*	stripe
striepelt	*streifig*	striped
strietbor	*streifbar*	contentious
stroh	*Stroh*	straw
strohdack	*Strohdach*	thatched roof

strohl	*Strahl*	ray of light or sunray
strokel	*streicheln*	stroke
strom	*Fluss*	stream or river
stroot or straat	*Strasse*	street
stropp	*Riemen*	strap
strümp	*Strumpf*	stocking
strütchen or miegen	*pissen*	piss
strukeln	*schreiten*	stride or stroll
struus	*Strauss*	ostrich
strüven	*sträuben*	russle or bristle
stück	*Stück*	piece
stücken	*Stücke*	pieces
studiern	*studieren*	study
stüer or stüür	*Steuren*	steer
stüern	*Steuern*	taxes
stühn	*gestanden*	stood
stumm	*stumm*	mute
stummel	*Stumpf*	stub
stump	*stumpf*	blunt
stump	*Stumpf*	stump
stumpsinnig or langwielig	*langweilig*	tedious
stün	*gestanden*	(he,she,it) stood
stünn	*gestanden*	(we, they) stood
stunn	*Stunde*	hour
stuur or loden	*Laden*	store
stuurm or gewidder	*Sturm*	storm
stüürmann, stüermann	*Steuermann*	helmsman
stüürrad or stüerrad	*Steuerrad*	steering wheel
stüüts	*Steiss*	rump
stuuv	*Stube*	room
sucker or sukker	*Zucker*	sugar
suckerrööv	*Zuckerrübe*	sugar beet
suckersnuut	*Zuckerpuppen*	sweet girl
südoost	*Südosten*	southeast
südwest	*Südwesten*	southwest
sugen or suchten	*Saugen*	suck
süh	*sieh*	see or so
süht ut as, kiekt so, lett so		seems to be
sui sui		here piggy
suldot or suldat	*Soldat*	soldier
suldoten	*Soldaten*	soldiers
süll	*Schwelle*	sill
sülve	*Silber*	silver
sülvig or övereen	*selbe*	same
sülvige	*selbigste*	same one

summer	*Sommer*	summer
summertied	*Sommerzeit*	summertime
sumpheid	*Sumpf*	swamp
sünd	*sünd*	(we, they) are
sungen	*gesungen*	sang
sünn	*Sonne*	sun
sünnbrill	*Sonnenbrille*	sunglasses
sünndag	*Sonntag*	sunday
sünnen	*Sünden*	sins
sünnenkind	*Marienkäfer*	ladybug
sünnerbor	*sonderbar*	odd or strange
sunnerlig	*besonderlich*	particularly
sünnfall	*Sonnenuntergang*	sundown
sünnküken	*Marienkäffer*	ladybug
sünnobend or saterdag	*Sonnabend*	saturday
sünnobend obend	*Samstagabend*	saturday evening
sünnshien	*Sonnenschein*	sunshine
sünnsprütten	*Sommersprossen*	freckles
suppen lepel	*Suppenlöffel*	soup spoon
suppen	*Suppe*	soup
süss so or genau so	*ganz richtig*	just so or exactly so
süster or swester	*Schwester*	sister
süüd	*Süd*	south
suup	*saufen*	drink
suupmichel	*Besoffene*	drunkard
suupt		gets drunk or drinks
suur	*Saure*	sour
suurkohl	*Sauerkraut*	sauerkraut
suurmuul	*Sauertopfl*	sourpuss
suus	*sausen*	dash or rush around
süüs	*sonst*	otherwise
suust	*sausen*	speeds
swaak	*schwach*	weak
swaaken	*Schwalbe*	swallow
swaan	*Schwan*	swan
Swabig	*Schwabe*	Swabian
swager	*Schwager*	brother-in-law
swalken	*Schunkeln*	sway
swanz or steert	*Schwanz*	tail
swarm	*Schwarm*	swarm
swart	*Schwarz*	black
swartbrot	*Pumperncke*	pumpernickel
swarthannel	*Schwarzhandel*	black market
swartkopp	*Schwartzkopf*	sap or dope
Sweed	*Schwede*	Swede

sweep or wipp	*Peitsche*	whip
sweet	*Schweiss*	sweat
sweeten	*schwitzen*	to sweat
swell	*schwellen*	swell
swengel	*Schwengel*	handle
swerd	*Schwert*	sword
swetschen	*Backpflaume*	prune
swewel	*Schwefel*	sulphur
swewelsuur	*Schwefelsäure*	sulphuric acid
swieg or still	*Stille*	quiet
swiegen	*schwiegen*	keep silent
swiegerdochter	*Schwiegertochter*	daughter-in-law
swiegermoder	*Schwiegermutter*	mother-in-law
swiegervoder	*Schwiegervater*	father-in-law
swielen	*wunden*	sores
swien	*Schwein*	pig
swien	*Schweine*	pigs
swienbroden	*Rost Braten*	roast pork
swienegel or orsewöttel	*Spitzbube*	rascal
swienegel	*igel*	hedgehog
swienfleesch	*Schweinfleisch*	pork
swienribben	*Schweinerippchen*	pork chops
swiensglück	*Sonntagsglück*	great luck
swienshoor	*Hartgras*	hardgrass
Swies	*Schweiz*	Swiss
swimm	*Schwimm*	swim
swimmbüx	*Schwimmhosen*	bathing suit
swindel	*Schwindel*	swindle
swing	*schwingen*	swing
swinnelig or düsig	*schwindelig*	dizzy
swÖÖp	*Peitsche*	whip
swoor	*schwer*	difficult
swoor	*Schwer*	heavy
swoorheit	*Schwierigkeit*	difficulty
swör	*Schwur*	swear or oath
swören	*schwören*	swear
sworfoot	*Schwanger*	pregnant
swümm	*Pilze*	mushroom
taach	*Fackel*	torch
taag	*Zähe*	tough
taak	*Tempo*	tempo
tabel	*Tablette*	tablet
tack	*Takt*	beat
tacknogel	*Reissnagel*	tack

363

tähn	*Zähne*	teeth
tähnfleesch	*Zahnfleisch*	gums
tähnknieper or tähndoktor	*Zahnarzt*	dentist
tallig	*Talg*	tallow
tamm	*zahm*	tame
tang	*Drahtzange*	pliers or tong
tang	*Tang*	seaweed
tank	*Tank*	tank
Tante Meier	*Bade Zimmer*	bathroom or toilet
tante or möhm or medder	*Tante*	aunt
tapeed	*Tapete*	wallpaper
tapig	*ungelernt*	unskilled
tapp	*Zapfen*	plug or bung
tapper or modig	*tapfer*	brave
tappet	*Teppich*	carpet
tapsig	*plump*	clumsy
taschen or tasken or tashen	*Tasche*	pocket
tashendöke	*Taschentüche*	handkerchiefs
tashendook	*Taschentuch*	handkerchief
tashenuhr or tashenklock	*Taschenuhr*	pocket watch
tass	*Tasse*	cup
tau	*Zäh*	chewy or tough
täw	*Hündin*	bitch
teckel	*Dackel*	dachshund
tecken	*Zeichen*	sign or mark or signal
tee	*Tee*	tea
teel	*Ziel*	aim
teelepel	*Teelöffel*	teaspoon
teelt	*zielt*	is aiming or aims
teer	*Teer*	tar
teetass	*Teetasse*	teacup
tegel	*Ziegel*	tile or brick
tehg	*ziehe*	pull
tehn	*Ziehen*	pull
teihn	*Zehn*	ten
teihntel	*Zehntel*	tenth
telgen or telling or twieg	*Zweig*	branch or twig
tellen	*zählen*	count
teller	*Teller*	plate or dish
tellt oderr gellt	*zählig*	counts
telt	*Zelt*	tent
tev	*Weibsbild*	bitch
theoter	*Theater*	theater
throon	*Thron*	throne
tidel	*Titel*	title

tied or tiet or tiit	*Zeit*	time
tiedlang	*zeitlang*	awhile
tiedlangs hin	*nach geräumer Zeit*	after a while
tiedlig	*zeitlig*	timely
tiedloop	*Zeitlauf*	course of events
tiedlos	*zeitlos*	timeless
tiedpunkt	*Zeitpunkt*	moment
tiedshrift	*Zeitschrift*	magazine
tiedsnitt	*Zeitraum*	time interval
tiedverdriev	*Zeitvertrieb*	pass the time or amusement
tiedwoort	*Zeitwort*	verb
timmeree	*Zimmerei*	carpenter shop
timmerman	*Zimmerman*	carpenter
timmern	*Zimmerhandwerk*	carpentry
tinn	*Zinn*	tin
titt	*Zitse*	nipple
tja	*ja*	yeah
to or no or tau	*zu*	to
to or tomokt	*zugemacht*	shut or closed
to dull	*sehr*	too much or too fast
to enn or to'n enn	*Schluss*	over or ended
to	*allzu*	too
tobak	*Tabak*	tobacco
tobehör	*Zubehör*	accessory
töben	*Warten*	waiting
tobieten	*zubeissen*	take a bite
tobinnen	*zubinden*	tie shut
toblieben	*zubleiben*	stay shut
tobott	*Subvention*	subsidy
todecken	*zudecken*	cover or cover up
todeelt or togeben	*addierend*	added to
todenn	*zudem*	to
todoh	*Bestandteil*	ingredient
todreihn	*zudrehen*	turn shut or twist shut
toeenannern	*zueinander*	to one another
toeerst	*zuerst*	initially or at first
tofällig or tofellig	*zufällig*	accidental or coincidental
toföhren	*versorgen*	supply
tofoot	*zufuss*	by foot
tofoten or anpacken	*angreifen*	grip or grip onto
tofree	*zufrieden*	satisfied or content
tog	*Zug*	train
togeev or bidregg	*Beitrag*	contribution
togeev or extro	*zusatz*	additional
tögel	*Zügel*	reins

togliek	*gleichzeitig*	simultaneous or immediate
tohl	*zahl*	pay
töhn	*Zehen*	toes
tohopen dreihn	*zusammen drehen*	twist together
tohopen or tosamen	*zusammen*	together
tohopenbakken	*kleben*	glue together
tohopenbinnen	*Verbinden*	tie together
tohopenbunnen	*gebunden*	tied together
tohopengohn	*zusammengehen*	go together
tohopenholen, tosomenholen	*zusammen halten*	hold together
tohopenklappen	*zusammenklappen*	fold up
tohopenkommen	*zusammenkommen*	come together
tohopenkunft	*zusammenkunft*	meeting or conference
tohopenspeeln	*zusammenspielen*	play together
tohören	*gehorchen*	obey or listen to
töht	*zieht*	pulls
tohüren	*zugehören*	belong to
tohuus or bihuus	*Zuhause*	at home
tokieker	*Zuschauer*	viewer or onlooker
toknöpen	*zuknöpfen*	button up
tokommt or tokunft	*Zukunft*	future
tokünftig	*Zukunftig*	in the future
tolette	*Toilette*	toilet
toletzt	*letzte*	last
toll	*Zoll*	inch
töller	*Teller*	plates
toloop	*zulauf*	run to or run after
tominnen or minnern	*vermindern*	diminish
tomööt kommen or begegen	*treffen*	meet
ton or toon or klang	*Ton, Lauten*	sound
tonaam or tonohm	*familien Name*	family name
tonichts moken	*demolieren*	demolish
töög	*gezogen*	pulled
toom or togel	*Zügel*	bridle
toorn	*Turm*	tower
toost	*Toast*	toast
tööv	*warten*	wait
topass	*passend*	convenient
topp	*Topp*	top
torv or torf	*Torf*	peat
torvsteken	*Torf Ernte*	peat harvesting
toschannen	*verderben*	ruin or damage
toschännt	*verunstalten*	disfigured
toschüffeln	*vollbringen*	fill up or shovel full
toseggen	*Zusage*	promise

toseggt	*Versprochen*	promised
tosehn	*wachten*	see to or wait and see
toshick moken		do chores
toslag	*zuschlag*	surcharge
tosloten	*zugeschlossen*	locked up
tosluten	*zuschliessen*	lock up
tosmeck or tosmecken	*schmecken*	sample or taste
tosnacken	*einhauchen*	inspire or support
tostand	*Zustand*	condition
tostännig	*zuständig*	competent or authorized
tostimm	*billigen*	approve
tostohn or bistohn	*beistehen*	support or defend
tostüür	*anweisen*	direct or indicate
total or heel	*total*	total or completely
toveel	*zuviel*	too much
töven or töben	*warten*	waiting
tövlig	*zaudernd*	hesitant
tövt	*erwartet*	waits
towass	*Wachstum*	growth
traditschoon	*Tradition*	tradition
tramp	*treten*	tread
trauun	*Ziviltraung*	marriage
trechtmoken or trechtstellen		make proper
treck	*Schlep*	haul
trecken	*Schleppen*	pull or move
treckpadd	*Schlepppfad*	tow path
treckter or trekter	*Trecker*	tractor
tred	*Pedal*	treadle
trek	*gehen*	walk
trekfidel or trekörgel	*Ziehharmonika*	accordion
treppen	*Treppen*	stairs
trietsen	*berieseln*	irrigate
tritt	*Treppen stufen*	front steps
tritt	*Schritt*	steps
troddel	*Troddel*	tassel
trog	*Trog*	trough
tru	*treu*	loyal
trubel or pech	*Plage*	trouble
truen or vertruun	*Vertrauen*	trust
trüg or trüch	*Rück*	back
trügbetohln	*Rückzahlen*	pay back
trügfallen, falltrüg	*rückfall*	fall back
trügfohren	*Rückfahren*	drive back
trügfohrkorden	*Rückfahrkarte*	roundtrip ticket
trüggeben or trüggeven	*Wiedergeben*	return

trügholen	*Rückhalten*	hold back
trügkieken	*Rückblicken*	look back
trügkommen	*wiederkehren*	come back
trügköpen	*Rückkaufen*	buy back
trügleggen	*rücklegen*	lay back
trügloten or trügsett	*zurückhaltend*	reserved or left behind
trügnehmen	*wiedernehmen*	take back
trügpedden	*rückschritt*	step back
trügstohn	*rückstanden*	stand back
trügwards or trüchwards	*rückwärts*	backwards
truhardig	*ernsthaftlig*	earnestly
trulig or truulig	*getreu*	faithful or trustworthy
trummel	*Trommel*	drum
trump	*Trumpf*	trump
trumpen (korden)	*übertrumpfen*	trump (cards)
trumpett	*Trompete*	trumpet
trünnel	*walzen*	roll
trünnen	*Trännen*	tears
trurig	*traurig*	sad
trüsel	*schunkel*	sway
truu	*treu*	true
truupand	*Pfand*	pledge of allegiance
truurn	*trauren*	mourn
truut	*vertraut*	familiar
tschüss	*Aufwiedersehn*	goodbye or so long
tuchhuus	*Zuchthaus*	penitentiary
tucht	*Zucht*	discipline
tucht	*Zucht*	breed
tuchtpeerd	*Zuchtpferd*	breedhorse
tucken	*zurückweichen*	flinch
tüdelband	*Rad*	wheel or band
tudu		toy car
tügen	*bezeugen*	testify
tühnkraam	*Wahnsinn*	madness
tüksch	*tückisch*	spiteful
tulp	*Tulpe*	tulip
tulpen	*Tulpen*	tulips
tumelig	*taumelig*	giddy
tumeln	*taumeln*	stagger
tumpig	*verwirrt*	confused
tungen	*Zunge*	tongue
tungenknieper	*Zungen brecher*	tongue twister
tunn	*Tonne*	ton
tunn	*Tonne*	barrel
turnier	*Turnier*	tournament

turnüster	*Tornister*	knapsack
tüschen or tüsken	*zwischen*	between
tuten	*Tüte*	bag or paper sack
tüüch or tüüg	*Tuch*	clothes or cloth material
tüüchloden	*Tuchladen*	clothing store
tüügen	*Zeugen*	witness
tuun	*Zaun*	wooden fence or wire fence
tuunkroom	*Unsinn*	nonsense
tuunkrüper	*Zaunkönig*	wren
tuunpahl or tuunpohl	*Zaunpfahl*	fence post
tuunsinger	*Zaunsinger*	warbler
tuur or reis	*Reise*	tour or trip
tuur		a period of time
tuusch	*tauschen*	trade
tuuschen	*tauschen*	to trade
tuuschen or vertuuschen	*eintauschen*	exchange
tüüschen	*täuschen*	disappoint
twalen oder spazeern	*Schlendern*	stroll
twee	*Zwei*	two
tweeback	*Zwieback*	biscuit
tweede	*Zweite*	second
tweedeelig	*zweiteilig*	two piece
tweedrüttel	*Zweidrittel*	two thirds
tweemol	*Zweimal*	twice
tweerlie	*doppeltlig*	doubly
tweern or twiern	*Zwirn*	twine or string
tweeweg or tweeler	*Weggabel*	fork in the road
twei moken	*brechen*	break
twei	*gebrochen*	broke or broken
twiefel	*Zweifel*	doubt
twieg	*Zweig*	twig
twilling	*Zwilling*	twin
twintig or twentig	*Zwanzig*	twenty
twölf	*Zwölf*	twelve
twüschen or tüsken	*Zwischen*	between
twüschenkommen	*Zwischengekommen*	come between
twüschentied	*Zwischenzeit*	in the meantime
uhr	*Ohr*	ear
uhr	*Uhr*	watch
uhrlappen	*Ohrlappen*	earlobe
uhren	*Ohren*	ears
üm	*ihm*	him
üm'a eck gohn		take a dumper
ümarbeidet or ümdohn	*revidiert*	revised

ümbringen or afmorken	*umbringen*	kill
ümbrocht or doot mokt	*umgebracht*	killed
ümdoon	*revidieren*	to revise
ümdreihn	*umkehren*	turn back or turn around
ümfoten or ümfaten	*umarmen*	hug
ümfraag	*Umfrage*	questionnaire
ümkant	*Rand*	periphery
ümkieken	*zurückzehen*	look back
ümkippen	*tippen*	tip over or capsize
ümkommen	*umkommen*	died
ümmerlos	*fortlaufend*	continuously
ümstand or item	*Umstand*	fact or circumstance
ümstiegen	*umsteigen*	get off or get on
umsüss	*umsonst*	free of charge or for nothing
ümtog or ümweg or ümdriev	*umweg*	detour
ümtog or wannelbohn	*Umzog*	procession
ümwinnen or ümdreihn	*umwenden*	turn or turn around
un	*und*	and
unachtsom	*unachtsam*	unnoticed
unbesichtlig	*unabsichtlich*	unintentional
unarsch	*unbändig*	unruly
unbedüdend	*unbedeutend*	insignificant
unbewiss	*unverdächtig*	unsuspecting
uneben	*uneben*	uneven
unehrlig	*illegal*	illegal
ungliek	*ungleich*	unequal
unglück	*Unfall*	bad luck or accident
ungood	*lieblos*	unkind
unheelbor	*unheilbar*	incurable
unkommodig	*unbequem*	uncomfortable
unmöglig	*unmöglich*	impossible
ünner or ünder	*unter*	under or below
ünnerbüx	*Unterhosen*	underpants
ünnerdack	*Obdach*	shelter
ünnerdrieben, ünnerdrieven	*vernichten*	defeat
ünnereerdsch or dwargen	*Zwerg*	dwarf
ünnergohn	*nachlassen*	fail or go under
ünnerhimd	*T-shirt*	T-shirt
ünnerkleed	*Unterrock*	slip
ünnernehm	*Unternehmen*	undertaking
ünnerricht	*Unterricht*	instruction
ünnerrock	*Unterrock*	petticoat or slip
ünnersatz or grund	*Grundlage*	basis
ünnersheed moken	*unterscheiden*	differentiate
ünnersheed or sheel	*Unterschied*	difference

ünnershrieben	*Unterschrift*	sign or signature
ünnersied	*Unterseite*	underside
ünnersöken	*untersuchen*	investigate or do research on
ünnerstriecken	*unterstreichen*	underline
ünnertidel	*Untertitel*	subtitle
ünnertüch	*Damenwäsche*	lingerie
ünnerweeg	*unterweg*	under way
ünnerwegens	*unterwegs*	on the way
unoort	*Unart*	vice
unrecht	*Unrecht*	injustice
unschuldig or ahnschuld	*unschuldid*	innocent
unseggen	*entsagen*	renounce
unsowieder u.s.w.	*und so weiter*	etcetera or and so on
unvergliekbor	*unvergleichbar*	incomparable
unverschämt	*ohne scham*	unashamed
unwedder or unweer	*Unwetter*	bad weather
up	*auf*	up
up'n kopp fallen	*verrückt*	crazy
upblosen	*aufblasen*	blow up
upboot	*aufbaut*	builtup
upbörn	*aufheben*	raise up
upbört	*aufgehoben*	raised up
upbreken or opbreken	*aufbrechen*	break up
upbringen	*aufwurfen*	bring up
upbrocht	*aufgebracht*	brought up
upbruken	*verbrauchen*	consume or use up
upbunnen	*aufgebunden*	tied up or bundled
updeelen	*aufteilen*	divide up
upeenmol, miteens, batz	*plötzlich*	suddenly or all at once
upeten	*aufessen*	eat up or eaten up
upfreten	*zerfressen*	eaten up (by animals)
upgeben or upgeven	*aufgeben*	give up
upgriepen, begriepen	*schnell ergreifen*	snatch
upheegen	*ersparen*	save up
upheeten or upwarmen	*aufwarmen*	warm up
uphelpen	*aufhilfen*	help up
uphoken or ophoken	*anhaken*	hook up
upholen	*aufhalten*	hold up or support
upholen	*halten*	stop
upholt	*auf halten*	held up
uphung	*aufhungen*	hung up
upinnern	*sich erinnern*	remember or remembering
upkieken	*aufblicken*	look up
upkloren or verkloren	*erklären*	explain
upkloren	*aufklären*	clarify or clear up

uplaten	*auflassen*	leave up
uplodet	*aufladen*	loaded
upluurn or upluern	*aufwarten*	wait on
upmokt	*aufgemacht*	made up
upmucken	*rebellieren*	rebel
upnehmen	*aufnehmen*	take up
uppietschen	*anreizen*	stimulate
uppustern or upbloosen	*aufblasen*	inflate
uprieten	*aufreissen*	tear up
upringen	*aufrufen*	call (telephone) or ring up
uprollen or oprullen	*aufrollen*	roll up
upsässig or wrevelig	*widerspenstig*	rebellious
upschuben, upschuven	*aufschieben*	delay,defer
upsett	*aufgesetzt*	put on
upshrieben	*anpreisen*	write up
upshrift or opschrift	*aufschrift*	inscription
upsnien	*zerschneiden*	cut up
upsocht	*auf gehoben*	picked up
upsöken	*aufpicken*	pick up
upspeen	*aufspucken*	spit up or barf
upsteed	*Heutzutage*	these days or now a days
upstellen	*anstellen*	begin or do
upstellt	*vorbereitet*	prepared
upstiegen or opstiegen	*aufsteigen*	climb on
upstohn	*aufstehen*	arise or get up
upstohn	*aufstiegen*	stood up or got up
upstöten	*aufstossen*	belch
upstunns	*anwesend*	presently
uptellen or tohopentellen	*summieren*	add up
upwashen	*aufwaschen*	wash up
upwiesen	*beweisen*	show up
upwook or upwaak	*erwachen*	awake
urgrussmoder	*Urgrossmutter*	great-grandmother
urgrussvoder	*Urgrossvater*	great-grandfather
urhohn	*Waldhuhn*	grouse
urloob	*Urlaub*	leave or vacation
uroolt	*uralt*	ancient
ursaak	*Ursache*	cause
ur-ur-grussmoder	*Ururgrossmutter*	great-great-grandmother
ur-ur-grussvoder	*Ururgrossvater*	reat-great-grandfather
us	*uns*	us
ut or uut	*aus*	out
ut or uut	*aus*	out
ut'e büx gohn		defecate
ut'n kopp	*auswendig*	from memory

utbilden	*ausbilden*	educate
utblieben	*ausbleiben*	stay out
utblosen or utpusten	*ausblasen*	blow out
utboon	*ausbreiten*	expand
utbreden	*ausbreiten*	widen out
utbreken	*ausbrechen*	break out
utdacht	*durchdacht*	reasoned or considered
utdeelen	*austeilen*	deal out or hand out
utdeelen	*erteilen*	assign
utdrögen	*austrocknen*	dry out
uteenanner	*auseinander*	apart
uteenannerbreken	*auseinanderbrechen*	break apart
uteenannerdrieven	*auseinandertrieben*	drive apart
uteenannern	*getrennt*	to separate
uteenannertehn	*auseinanderziehen*	tear apart
utenweg	*auf umwegen*	out of the way
utfegen	*ausfegen*	sweep out
utfinnen	*ausfinden*	find out or discover
utföhrbor	*ausführbar*	feasible
utföhren	*sozialisieren*	socialize or go visiting
utföhren	*ausführen*	export
utföhrlig	*ausführlich*	detailed
utfreten	*schlecht benehmen*	misbehaved
utgang oder utgoh or uttritt	*ausgang*	exit
utgeev	*Ausgabe*	expenditure
utglieken	*ausgleichen*	equalize
uthebben	*Wort streit*	face off or have it out
uthelpen	*aushilfen*	help out
utholen	*aushalten*	hold out or tolerate
utkiek or utsüht	*Ausblick*	outlook
utklooken or utkeesen	*ausklügen*	figure it out
utkloppen	*ausklappen*	knock out
utknippen	*nachgeben*	bug out
utkoken	*auskochen*	boil over
utkomm	*Ergebnis*	outcome
utkommen or afsluut	*Beschluss*	conclusion
utlachen	*auslachen*	laugh at
utlanner	*Ausländer*	foreigner
utledigen	*leer*	empty
utleggen	*anlegen*	invest or pay out
utlicken	*auslecken*	lick out
utlopen	*auslaufen*	run out
utluud or luuthals	*laut stark*	outloud
utmalen	*abmalen*	describe or depict
utmeten	*abmessen*	measure out

utnehm	*Ausnahme*	exception
utnehmlig	*ungewöhnlich*	exceptional
utnohm	*ausgenohmen*	took out
utoosen	*schimpfen*	discipline or chew out
utpuuser or utsuuser	*auspuff topf*	muffler
utpuust or otenlos	*Atemlos*	breathless
utrohn	*Ruhen*	rest
utropen	*ausrufen*	call out
utrotten or utverrott	*verrotten*	rotted out
utschreen	*ausschreien*	cry out
utschutt	*Ausschuss*	committee
utschüddeln	*ausschütteln*	shake out
utshellen	*ausschimpfen*	scold or discipline
utsicht or utblick	*blick*	view
utsied or butensied	*Aussenseite*	outside
utsied rüm	*am Randen*	around the outside
utsnitt	*ausschnitt*	clip
utsnuben	*schnäuzen*	blow your nose
utsocht or utplückt	*ausgesucht*	picked off
utsöken	*auswählen*	select or choose
utspeen	*ausspucken*	spit out
utspruk	*Aussprache*	pronunciation
utstellen	*ausstellen*	exhibit
utstiegen	*aussteigen*	step out
utstohn or verdregen	*ausstehen*	abide
utstrecken	*ausstrecken*	stretch out
utstüürn	*Brautausstattung*	trousseau
utsüht or süht as	*erscheint*	appears as
utteckend	*ausgezeichnet*	excellent
uttohgen	*ausziehen*	undressed
uttosetten	*kritisieren*	criticize
uttrekbor	*vergrösserbar*	extendable
utwanner	*Auswanderer*	emigrant
utwannern	*auswandern*	emigrate
utwickel	*auswickeln*	unwrap
utwickelt	*ausgewickelt*	develops
utwies	*Ausweis*	identification
uul	*Eule*	owl
uulenspegel	*witzbold*	ractical joker
uus or uusen	*unser*	our
üüz or ütz	*Kröte*	toad
üüz	*Tor*	teaser of fool
üzen	*uzen*	tease
vaagt	*Vogt*	governor

374

vagel	*Vogel*	bird
vagel bülo	*Pirol*	oriole
vagelhuus	*Vogelhaus*	bird house
vagelnest	*Vogelnest*	bird nest
vagels	*Vögel*	birds
veddel or vertel	*Viertel*	quarter
vedder or kusine	*Vetter*	cousin
veeh or veh	*Vieh*	cattle
veel	*viel*	many or much
veel mals'n dank	*vielen dank*	thanks a lot
veer	*Vier*	four
veerdig	*viertzig*	forty
veereckig	*viereck*	square
veerteihn	*vierzehn*	fourteen
vehdokter	*Tierarzt*	veterinarian
veleren	*verlieren*	lose
verantwoordig	*verantwortlich*	responsible
verärger or verdrütt	*ärger*	annoy or annoys
verbaast	*verwirrt*	confused
verbeden	*verbieten*	prohibit
verbetern	*verbessern*	improve
verbrinnt	*verbrennt*	burned
verdaag	*Heute*	today
verdamte	*verdammt*	damned
verdarben	*Verdorbenheit*	corruption
verdattert or verbiestert	*verwirrt*	confused or puzzled
verdeen	*verdienen*	earn
verdorri	*verdamt*	dammit
verdrag	*Vertrag*	contract or commission
verdregen or utholen	*ertragen*	endure
verdreiht	*verdreht*	screwed up or twisted
verdreihte or verdullte	*verwünscht*	darn or doggone
verdrütt	*Verdruss*	bothers or annoys
verdübelt	*verteufelt*	bedeviled
verduldnochmol		hey, have a little patience
vereen	*Verein*	club
vereenigen	*vereinigen*	unite
vereenschop	*Vereinigung*	union
verflixt	*verflixt*	confounded
verföhren	*abwenden*	divert
verfroren	*gefroren*	frozen
vergeben	*vergeben*	forgive
vergeiht	*besorgt*	concerns
vergeiht	*vergeht*	passes by
vergellung	*Rache*	revenge

375

verget	*vergiess*	forget
vergeten	*vergessen*	forgotten
vergeterig	*vergesslich*	forgetful
vergeterig	*zerstreut*	absent minded
verglieken	*vergleichen*	compare
vergnögen or pläsier	*vergnügen*	enjoyment or pleasure
vergnögt	*vergnügt*	pleased
vergohn	*vorbeigehen*	pass it by
vergreglig	*widerwillig*	reluctantly
vergrellt or füünsch	*aufreizen*	irritated
vergrödensglas	*vergrössungsglas*	magnifying glass
verhungern	*verhungern*	starve
verinnern	*erinnern*	remember or recall
verjog or verjoog	*erschrecken*	surprise
verjogen or verjoogen	*erschrecken*	to surprise
verjogt or verjoogt	*erschreckt*	surprised
verkeehrt	*falsch*	wrong
verklogen	*verklagen*	sue
verkloppen or verspenn	*spenden*	spend
verknusen	*verdauen*	digest
verkölt	*erkältet*	a cold
verköp	*verkaufen*	sell
verleden	*vergangen*	former
verleevt	*geliebt*	loved
verlehn or vermieten	*Pachte*	rent
verlengen	*verlangen*	long for
verlööf or verlööv	*erlaubnis*	permission or authorization
verloop or ümgohn	*umgehen*	bypass
verloren or verschwunn	*verloren*	lost
verloten or verlaten	*verlassen*	depend on
verlütt	*verliert*	loses
vermeehren or vermiehren	*vermehren*	increase
vermeten	*urteilen*	judge or make judgement
vermisst	*vermisst*	missed or overlooked
vermorrn	*heut Morgen*	this morning
vernommiddag	*heut Nachmittag*	this afternoon
vernünftig	*vernünftig*	sensible or careful
verrott	*verfaulit*	rotten
verrückt or dwatsch or maal	*verrückt*	crazy
vers	*Vers*	verse
verschämt	*verschämt*	ashamed
verschiedene	*verschieden artig*	various
verschüttgohn	*verscherzt*	forfeited
verschuuben	*aufschieben*	postpone
versekern	*versichern*	assure

376

versetten	*ersetzen*	replace
vershimmelt	*schimmelig*	moldy
versocht	*erprobt*	tried
versök or probeer	*Versuch*	try or attempt
versopen	*ertrunken*	drowned
verspeeln	*verspielen*	lose (at cards)
verspennen	*spenden*	spend
verstand	*Verstand*	sense or common sense
verstek	*verstecken*	hide
versteken or verstekt	*versteckt*	hidden
verstoh or begriep	*begreifen*	understand
verstohn or bigrepen	*begriffen*	understood
vertell	*erzählen*	tell or relate
vertellsel	*Geschichte*	story
vertelstunn	*viertelstunde*	quarter of an hour
vertohl or vörhebben	*absichten*	intend
vertörn or striet	*ausweichen*	quibble or argue
vertroot	*vertraut*	trusts
vertrüg geben	*rückgeben*	give back
vertrüg kommen or retuur	*Rückkehr*	return or come back
verwand	*verwandt*	related
verwandschop	*verwandtschaft*	relatives or relationship
verwunnen	*verwunden*	wounded
vigelett	*Violett*	violet
vigeliensch	*Komplex*	complex
vigelin	*Geiger*	violin
villicht	*vielleicht*	maybe or perhaps
voder or vader or voer	*Vater*	father
voderstohn	*Gevatter*	stand as godfather
vör or vörher	*vor*	before
voran	*voraus*	ahead or in front of
vörbi gohn, vörbigahn	*Vorbeigehen*	passed by or bypassed
vörbi	*Vorbei*	ended or done
vörbringen	*vorbringen*	bring up or bring to
vörbrocht	*vorgebracht*	brought up or presented
vördeel	*Vorteil*	advantage
vorföhrnen	*Vorfahren*	ancestors
vörgistern	*Vorgestern*	day before yesterday
vörhang	*Vorhang*	curtain
vörherseggen	*voraussagen*	predict
vöriger	*vormals*	former
vörkommen	*vorkommen*	come up or come before
vörkopp	*Stirn*	forehead
vörlogen	*vorlügen*	lied to
vörmiddag or vörmiddags	*Vormittags*	before noon or forenoon

377

vörmiddags, s'morrns	*Morgen*	in the morning
vörn an	*vorn*	in front
vörn	*vorder*	front
vörnaam	*Vorname*	first name
vörnehm	*vornehm*	noble
vörnohmen	*angenohmen*	accepted
vörreed or vörred	*Vorrede*	introduction
vörschutt	*Vorschlag*	proposal
vörseggen	*aufsagen*	recite
vörshriev	*vorschreiben*	prescribe
vörsitter	*Vorsitzer*	chairperson
vörslagen or vörslaan	*empfehlen*	suggested or recommended
vörsmieten	*vorwerfen*	accuse or blame
vörstellen	*sich vorstellen*	imagine
vörstellen	*vorstellen*	introduce or present
vörstenruum	*Gastzimmer*	parlor
vorut	*voraus*	ahead
vörwarts	*vorwärts*	forward
voss	*Fuchs*	fox
vosskatekel	*Eichhörnchen*	fox squirrel
vulkaan	*Vulkan*	volcano
vüll	*Fülle*	fill
vull	*voll*	full
vüllig	*vollig*	completely or fully
vüllig	*gefült*	filled
vullmoken or uptankern	*voll machen*	fill it up
vullstännig or heel	*vollständig*	complete
vullwussen	*erwachsen*	adult
vun nu af, vun nu avant	*von nun an*	henceforth
vun	*von*	from
vunachtern	*vonhinten*	from behind
vunafgohn or vunafgahn	*von ausgehen*	go away from
vundaag or vondage	*Heute*	today
vundag or hüüt or hüüttodags	*Heute*	today
vundenntied or nodem or siet	*seit*	since
vunobend, vanovend	*Heutabend*	this evening
waad	*Wade*	calf of leg
waag	*Waage*	scales
waagen	*gewogen*	weighed
waaghals	*Wagehals*	daredevil
waagschaal	*Waageschale*	weight scale bowl
waak or wook	*wachen*	awake
waak up or wook up	*erwachen*	wake up
waak	*wach*	awake

378

wachhund	*Wachthund*	watchdog
wachsom	*wachsam*	watchful
wackel or jackel	*schlottern*	wobble
wackelig	*wackelig*	wobbly or shaky
wackelpeter	*Gelee*	jelly
waden	*Baumwolle*	cotton
wadertulpen	*Schwertlilie*	iris
walfisch	*Walfisch*	whale
walnaart	*Wallnüsse*	walnuts
wand	*Wand*	wall
wandklock or hangklock	*Wandklock*	wallclock
wanneer or watvuntied	*wie viel uhr*	what time
wanner	*wander*	migrate or wander
wannern	*wandern*	hiking or traveling
ward	*werden*	becomes
wark	*Werk*	work
warksteed	*Werkstatt*	workplace or shop
warm holen	*warm halten*	keep warm
warm	*warm*	warm
warms	*Wärme*	warmth
wasch	*waschen*	wash
wasch or wäsch	*Wäsche*	laundry or the wash
waschlappen	*Waschlappen*	wash cloth
waschschaal	*Waschbecken*	washbowl
waschbalje	*Waschkübel*	washtub
waschknieper, klimper	*wäschklammer*	clothes pin
waschköken	*Waschraum*	laundry room
waschmashien	*Waschmachine*	washing machine
wasel	*Wiesel*	wiesel
wass	*wachsen*	grow
wass	*Wachs*	wax
wat	*Was*	what
wat nees or wat nejes	*was neues*	something new
wat vun tied	*wieviel uhr*	what time
wecke or wegge	*einige*	some
wecketiedens or biweglanglig	*irgenwann*	sometimes, occasionally
wedder or weller	*wieder*	again
wedderdöper		Anabaptist
weeg	*weg*	is gone
weeg or wääg	*wege*	ways
weeg	*abwiegen*	weigh
weege	*Wiege*	cradle
week or swaak or swiemelig	*weich*	weak
week or möör or saftig	*sanft*	soft
week	*Woche*	week

weekenenn	*Wochenende*	weekend
ween or wesen or west	*war*	has been or was
weenen or schreen	*weinen*	weep
weer or widder or wäär	*Wetter*	weather
weer	*war*	was
weerglas	*Barometer*	baromenter
weern	*wahren*	(we,they) were
weern	*gewerden*	became
weerst	*werden*	become
weert	*Wert*	worth
weertschop	*Restaurant*	restaurant
weertshuus or harbarge	*Wirtshaus*	inn or tavern
weertsmann	*Gastwirt*	landlord
weertvull or uprichtig	*würdig*	worthy
wees	*Weise*	meadow
weet	*weiss*	know
weeten	*Weizen*	wheat
weev	*weben*	weave
weevstohl or weegenstohl	*Schaukelstuhl*	rocking chair
weg	*fort*	away or gone
weg	*weg*	way or means
wegblieben	*wegbleiben*	stay away
wegbloosen	*wegblasen*	blow away
wegbreken	*wegbrechen*	break away
wegen or wegens	*wegen*	because
wegen	*Wiegen*	rock back and forth
wegenweg	*welchen weg*	which way
wegfallen	*wegfallen*	fall away
weggeben or weggeven	*weggeben*	give away
weggohn or weggahn	*weggohn*	leave or go away
weghalen	*wegholen*	haul away
wegjagen	*wegtrieben*	drive away
wegkommen	*verloren*	lost (at cards)
wegleggen or wegsetten	*wegliggen*	put aside
weglopen	*weglaufen*	run away
wegnehmen	*wegnehmen*	take away
wegropen	*wegrufen*	call away
wegsheen or wegshäen		shoo away
wegslieken	*wegschleichen*	sneak away
wegsluten	*wegschliessen*	lock away
wegsmeten'de geld	*Weggeworfenes Geld*	thrown away money
wegsmieten	*wegschmeisse*	throw away
wegspöhln	*wegspülen*	rinse away
wegvun	*af*	away from
wegwieser	*Wegweiser*	directional sign

wehdaag or pien	*Pein*	pain
wehdoon	*weh tun*	hurt
weih	*wehen*	blow
wekke or welke	*einige*	some
wekker	*Wecker*	alarm clock
welkomm	*Willkomm*	welcome
weller or wedder	*wieder*	again or come again
weller beholen	*behalten*	remember
wellerwussen	*regenerieren*	regrew
welpen	*Welpe*	pups
welt or werld	*Welt*	world
wemmern	*Gewimmer*	whimper
wenig	*wenige*	a few
weniger	*weniger*	fewer or a lesser amount
wenigsten	*wenigste*	least
wenigstens or tominnst	*mindeste*	at least
wenn	*wann*	when
wenn or wanneer	*wann*	when
wenn or ob	*wenn*	if
weren or weeren or wäen	*waren*	were or became
weret or weret nich ut	*dauernd*	lasts or doesn't wear out
wersen	*gewesen*	was or were
wesen or west or wään	*gewesen*	was or has been
wesseln	*wechseln*	change
wessen oder wespen	*Wespe*	wasp
west	*West*	west
west	*Weste*	vest
wetenlig	*bewusst*	deliberate
wetenschop	*Wissenschaft*	knowledge or science
wett	*Wette*	bet
wettlopen	*Wettrennen*	race
wever	*Weber*	weaver
wi	*wir*	we
wichel	*Weide*	willow
wicht	*Mädchen*	girl
wichtig or notwennig	*wichtig*	important
wickel	*wickeln*	roll up or wind
widfro or widfru	*Witwe*	widow
wied	*Weide*	pasture
wieder	*weiter*	farther or further
wief	*Weib*	wife
wiehnachten	*Weihnachten*	christmas
wiehrook	*Weihrauch*	incense
wiel	*Weile*	while
wieldat	*wiel das*	because of that

381

wieldes	*unterdessen*	in the meantime
wien	*Wein*	wine
wienbuur	*Weinbauer*	wine grower or vineyardist
wienerhund	*Dachshund*	dachshund
wientapper	*Winzler*	wine merchant
wiern or iesendrood	*Draht*	wire
wies	*anzeigen*	show or indicate
wieser	*Bienenkönigin*	queen bee
wies moken	*zeigen*	show how
wies worrn or spitz worrn	*gewahr worden*	became aware
wiesemoder or moder griepsch	*Hebamme*	midwife
wiesen	*zeigen*	show
wieser	*Uhrzeiger*	clock hand
wiesfinger	*Zeigefinger*	index finger
wiespahl	*Wegweiser*	signpost
wiet af	*entfern*	remote or faraway
wiet or afstand	*fern*	distance
wiet un siet	*fern und weit*	far and wide
wiet	*weit*	far
wietkieker	*Teleskop*	telescope or binoculars
wietvun	*weit von*	far from
wild	*wild*	wild
wilddeev	*Wilddieb*	poacher
wilden bookweeten	*Winde*	bindweek
wildnis	*Wildnis*	waste land or wilderness
wildswien or bass	*Eber*	wild boar or wildpig
will	*will*	will
will	*will*	want
wille swien	Kelleraffel	wood louse
willn	*willen*	way
wimmworm	*Maulwurf*	mole
wind	*wind*	wind
windhund	*Windhund*	greyhound
wink	*Winken*	wave
winkel	*Winkeleisen*	square
winnel or kinnerdook	*Windel*	diaper
winneln	*Windeln*	swaddling or diapers
winnen	*wenden*	turn
winnig	*windig*	windy
winter	*Winter*	winter
wippsteert	*Bachstelze*	wagtail bird
wisch or weise or moor	*Wiese*	meadow
wisch	*Wischen*	wipe
wiss or hol wiss	*fest*	tight
wissheit	*Weisheit*	wisdom

wissholen or fastholen	*festhalten*	hold fast
witfro or witfru	*Witwe*	widow
witmann	*Witwer*	widower
witt	*Weiss*	white
witz or döntje	*Witze*	joke
wo or woneem	*woher*	where
wo bass		cow - hold still
wo or wegenweg or wodennig	*wie*	how or in what way
woanners, wonehm anners	*woanders*	where else
woans	*wie sonst*	how or how else
wöddel or wörtel	*Karotte*	carrots or roots
wodennig	*wie dann*	how come or how then
wogen or wagen	*Wagen*	wagon
wohin or woneemhin	*wohin*	to where or where to
wöhl	*sich eingraben*	burrow or wallow
wohn	*wohn*	live or reside
wohnplatz	*Wohnsitz*	residence
wohnstuuv	*Wohnzimmer*	living room
wohnt	*gewohnen*	lived
wohnt	*wohnt*	lives
wohr	*wahr*	true
wohren or worren	*schützen*	protect
wohrhaftig	*Wahrhaftig*	truthful
wohrheit	*Wahrheit*	truth
wohrnehmen or afsehn	*wahrnehmen*	perceive
wohrtecken	*Kennzeichen*	emblem or symbol
wokeen or watvun	*welche*	which or which one
wokeen	*wem*	whom
wokehr sien	*wessen*	whose
woll or müch	*Woll*	would like
woll	*Wohl*	well
woller	*wieder*	coming again
wollerwesen or wedderwest	*zurückkommen*	returned
wollerwöör	*überdies*	furthermore
wollklang	*Einklang*	harmony
womit or wokehrmit	*mit wem*	with who
woneem an	*woran*	on what or what on
woneem bi	*wobei*	by which or by what
woneem för	*wofür*	for what
woneem her	*woher*	where from
woneem mit	*womit*	with what
woneem vun	*wovon*	from what
wöör	*wäre*	would be
wöörn	*würden*	(we, they) were
woort	*Wort*	word

woren or worden or worrn	*geworden*	became
woren	*verbraucht*	worn
wörgen	*erwürgen*	choke or strangle
worm	*Wurm*	worm
wörme	*Würme*	worms
wörmk	*Wermut*	wormwood
worr	*achtgeben*	beware
worr	*vermeiden*	avoid
wörrn or weern	*würden*	were
worrn	*warnen*	warn
wörte or wöör	*Wörte*	words
wörtebook	*Wörterbuch*	dictionary or glossary
wörtel or wöddel	*Wurzel*	root
worüm or wieso	*warum*	why
woso	*wieso*	why or how come
wost	*Wurst*	sausage
woter or woder or water	*Wasser*	water
woterbett or waterbett	*Wasserbett*	waterbed
woterdicht	*Wassdichte*	waterproof
wotermöhl, watermöhl	*Wassermühle*	watermill
woveel	*wieviel*	how many or how much
wowiet	*wie weit*	how far
wrack	*Wrack*	wreck
wulf	*Wolf*	wolf
wulken	*Wolken*	clouds
wull	*Wolle*	wool
wund	*Wunde*	wound
wunner	*Wunder*	wonder
wunner	*Wunder*	miracle
wunnerbor	*Wunderbar*	wonderful
wunnerlig	*wanderlich*	restless
wünsch	*Wunsch*	wish
würklig	*Wirklich*	really
wuschen	*gewoschen*	washed
wüss	*wusste*	knew
wussen	*wuchsen*	grew or grown
zeddel	*Zettel*	note or scrap of paper
zegen	*Ziege*	goat
zeidung or blatt	*Zeitung*	newspaper
zibbel or zippoln	*Zwiebel*	onion
zigar	*Zigarre*	cigar
zigarette	*Zigarette*	cigarette
zipollen or zibbel	*Zwiebel*	onion
zitron	*Zitrone*	lemon

zolo or hombre	*Solo*	solo (card game)
züchten	*Saufzen*	sigh or moan

This chapter contains a review of the various Low German and High German dialects, and a discussion of their *evolution*. These dialects are the precursors of the current Low German (Platt Düütsch) and High German (Standard German) languages. Textual examples of some of the old languages are given, along with examples of some of the more current dialects. The 800 page book entitled *Handbuch zur niederdeutsch Sprach- und Literatur Wissenschaft,* edited by Gerhard Cordes and Dieter Möhn, is an excellent source of information about dialects.

The *evolutionary* process resulted in significant language and dialect changes over time. However, during these many centuries, there are some words that have remained pretty much the same in English, Low German and Standard German. For example, there are the words 'still', 'tank', 'sand', 'ring', 'mark' and 'spring', which don't vary at all amongst these languages.. There are words that are the same in Low German and Standard German, but different in English; for example (in the respective language order) 'strick', 'strick', 'rope' or 'prügel', 'prügel', 'beat' or 'luft', 'luft', 'air'. There are other words that are the same in English and Low German, but different in Standard German; for example 'swing', 'swing', 'schwung'. Having the same words in several languages doesn't make one language a dialect of another. One would expect some words to be the same in both Germans, because they came from the same original word and coining a new word just didn't seem necessary.

Nonetheless, it's beens said that Platt Düütsch is just a dialect of High German. If that were true, then all the words in Platt Düütsch would be just variations of High German. In fact, however, there are words in Platt Düütsch that don't even exist in Standard German. A few examples are (respectively) 'smiet' vs. 'werfen' or 'so een' vs. 'solche' or 'losmoken' vs. 'lockern' or büx vs. Hosen or lütt vs. klein.

There are words that are spelled the same, such as the word for noise, which is Lärm in Standard German and lärm in Low German. However, the 'ä' has a different sound. And, if one were to look at gender, then Lärm is masculine in Standard German and lärm is neuter in Low German. In the same way, Lappen is masculine and lappen is neuter. There'd be no opportunity to modify gender if one was a dialect of the other.

It is common for Standard German words and Low German words to have a consistent pattern of differentiation. For instance, the Standard German words 'Teil', 'Gebe', 'Tief', 'treff', 'vor', 'Zehn' and 'Zeit' have, as their respective cognate words in Low German, the words 'deel', 'geev', 'deep', 'drepp', 'vör', 'teihn' and 'tied'. The differences possess a pattern as regards consonant and vowel variation. Many examples of this appeared at the end of Chapter Four (grammar).

The age old debate about what is a language versus what is a dialect will be sidestepped here. Except to say that the most cogent response to this question may be the old saying "a language is a dialect that has an army behind it". In other words, what can or can't be called a language has less to do with linguistic quality or history than it does with the 'political' power of its practicioners. Sometimes it happens just as an accident of history; one dominates because it was around at the right time. Had Hannover prevailed, rather than Prussia, then things might be somewhat different today. Had Denmark not continually battled against the Hansa, things would definitely be different today.

In Chapter Two we learned that English derived from Old Saxon, which derived from Primitive German, which itself derived from Indo-European. Once could say possibly that English is thus a dialect of German, but not in earnest. English is a language partly because Britain had not only a strong army, but a pretty good navy as well. In that chapter we also learned about the various ancient German tribes, the Goths, Vandals, Saxons, Alemanni, Bavarii, Lombards, Franks, etc. After they had finished migrating and absorbing other tribes, there emerged about 6 main German tribes throughout Germany. They are often geographically grouped into the North, Middle and South (Upper) Germans. The North and the South each contained dialects which later formed into individual languages.

This map shows a Germany that was once split linguistically into three areas. Today it is just split into a north area and south area. Such a language split has happened in other countries as well. France has a north-south linguistic division, running east and just north of Bordeaux. Spain has the Castilians in the north and the Andalusians in the south. England has a Northumbrian

MAP I   MAJOR LANGUAGE AREAS

north and a Saxon south. Scotland has the Highlanderss in the north and the Lowlanders in the south. America has northerners and southerners, who have to listen close to understand each other.

North Germans

The *North Germans* included mainly the Saxon and Frisian tribes, who remained in northern Germany. One could also include in this geographical category the Low Franconians, which are basically the West Franks. The majority of the Low

Franconians settled in Belgium and the Netherlands. They strongly influenced both the West and East Low German dialects.

We should include among the North Germans the easterly Low German people. Their dialects, such as Mecklenburg, Pommersch and Brandenburg, are not directly derived from these old tribes. Rather, they are a mixture of broad tribal influences that ebbed and flowed through their area. The North Germans dialects that survived until today are all part of the Low German language, known today as Platt Düütsch.

Middle Germans

The *Middle Germans* include the <u>Franks</u> and <u>Thuringians</u> . The East Franks can be further divided into Rhenisch Franks, Ripaurian Franks and Moselle Franks. The East Franks settled in the valleys of the Lower Rhine and Meuse. The Thuringians were squeezed into a small area between the Saxons and Franks. Their Middle High German dialects provided the nucleus for the standard adopted by Martin Luther (1483-1546).

The line dividing Middle from Upper German is called the Germersheim Line. Above this line the 'p' to 'pf' change did not materialize. Here you'll find appel instead of apfel and pund instead of pfund.

Upper Germans

The *Upper (southern) Germans* include the Alemanni <u>Swabians</u> and <u>Bavarians</u>. This also includes the Alsatians. The Swabians were spread along the waters of the Upper Danube and the Upper Rhine. The southern Swabians settled in Switzerland. The Bavarians were spread along the middle Danube, and some of the Bavarians settled in what is now Austria. Their dialects provided a framework for a subsequent Standard High German (which participated in the Second Sound Shift).

In Chapter Two it was stated that the Second Sound Shift did not affect any of the North Germans. The Saxons, Friis and the Low Franks were among those not affected in any significant way. This Shift, which started with the Swabians and Bavarians, obviously affected the Upper German language the most.

Each of the major High German and Low German dialects will be discussed in the remainder of this chapter, along with their related ancient and their current languages.

Each of these languages coexist with a number of their own family dialects. History has bound these languages and dialects so tightly together, that their differences become accepted as necessary as colors in a quilt. Unfortunately the two languages, Low German and Standard German are not seen that way; it's often a tense coexistence.

HIGH GERMAN

These are mainly the dialects and languages of southern Germany.

GOTHIC

The Gothic language is considered the oldest written example of ancient German. It is certainly reminiscent of Primitive German, although in fact it is a language that branched away from Primitive German. The following text, taken from R.E.Keller's *The German Language* (1978), is the Lord's Prayer in Gothic, along with an English transliteration.

> *Atta unsar þu in himinam,*
>> Our Father, who art in heaven,
> *weih nái namo þein.*
>> hallowed be Thy name.
> *Qimái þiud in assus þeinsg, wair þái wilja déins*
>> Thy kingdom come, Thy will be done
> *swe in himina jah ana aírþái.*
>> On earth, as it is in heaven.
> *Hláif unsarana þana sint einan gif uns himmi daga.*
>> Give us this day our daily bread.
> *Jah aflet uns þater skulans sijáima,*
>> and forgive us our trespasses,
> *swaswe jah weis afletam þáim skulam unsaráim*
>> as we forgive those
> *Jah ni briggáis uns in fráistubnjái,*
>> who trespass against us,
> *ak lausei uns af þumma ubilin*
>> and deliver us from evil
> *unte þeina is þiudangardi jah mahts*
>> for Thine is the kingdom, the power
> *jah wullþus in aiwins.*
>> and the glory forever.

Note the prolific use of the Runic letter 'þ' (Thorn), which has a 'th' sound. The beginning sentence starts with 'Atta', which is reminiscent of the Old High German version of this same prayer, which starts with 'Abba Vater'.

Another example of Gothic can be seen in this excerpt from Matthew 6:25.

> *Duþþ giþa izwîs hi maùrnàiþ sàiwalài,*
>> Therefore, I tell you, be not anxious for your life,
> *izwarài hwa matjàiþ*
>> what you will eat

> *jah hwa digkàiþ*
>> or what you drink.

Of particular interest here is the word 'hwa' - meaning "what". The letters are transposed, which happened to several other words. For instance, the word for horse was originally spelled 'hros'. The Gothic language is old, and is the least *familiar* looking of all those German languages with which we are familar today.

There is some disagreement about how much influence Gothic had on the later Old High German. Gothic died out about the 4th century, and the Goths were then assimilated and disappeared. The Gothic tribes had, by this time, migrated to southern Germany, which makes one think they might have begun or influenced the southern High German dialects. But the apparent dissimilarities are great enough to make the experts wonder about its actual relationship to Old High German. Old High German text is traced back only to the 8th century, by which time Gothic had all but disappeared. On the other hand, southern German tribes were the target of evangelizing missionaries from the 5th century on, and the Gothic Arian religion was its primary message. The Goths certainly did influence the Lombards, but they became part of Italy. The modified Greek alphabet of the Goths paved the way for Greek loan words being accepted in High German, such as the Greek kyrikon (becoming Kirche) and daupjan (becoming taufen).

OLD HIGH GERMAN

The East Franconian language is taken as the best example of Old High German. This was one of the four main dialects of High German; the others being Bavarian, Alemannic and Langobardic. The latter became extinct about 1000 A.D. In Old High German there was less stress applied to any particular syllable, which made it a softer and more melodic language than present day German. The earliest known surviving texts date back to 750 A.D.

An example of Old High German would be this excerpt from the pre-christian epic poem "Hildebrandslied", written about 920 AD. Unfortunately, it also has some Old Saxon mixed in.

> *Ik gehorta þat seggen þat sih urhettun aenon muotin*
>> I heard it told, that they challenged one another
> *Hiltibraht enti Haþubrant untar heriun tuem.*
>> Hildebrand and Haubrand, between the two armies

Note the use of the þ letter (sounded as 'th') in the word 'þat', which means it would have been pronounced nearly the same as we would today pronounce its modern version... 'that'. In those days it have been unusual for even the average nobleman to be able to read or write. This was revealed by Hartmann von Aue, in his "Der arme Heinrich", when he wrote the following poem.

Ein ritter so geleret was
daz er an den buochen las.

This knight was so learned
that he even read books.

Note the use of the word 'was', so similar to the English word 'was'.. The 's' would later turn to 'r', to become the Standard German word 'war'.

MIDDLE HIGH GERMAN

In the 13th century, The Middle High German language looked something like the following prose. It is taken from the folk epic Nibelungenlied. Included is an approximate translation into English.

Nu lat iuch unbilden, sprach do Hagene,
> Now let me warn you, said Hagen,

niht mine rede darumbe, swie halt iu geschiht,
> not because of my speaking, as to what may happen to you,

ich rat iu an den triuvan, welt ir uch wol bewarn,
> I advise you very sincerely, if you take good care,

so sult ir zuo den Hiunen vil gewaerliche varn.
> you will be mighty against the Huns

Note here that the use of the Runic letter þ, reminiscent of Gothic and Old High German, appears to be gone. However, it did survive in Old Norse and Old Saxon (and its daughter language Old English). Old Norse and Old Saxon quite probably predate Old High German. It is fairly well established that that Gothic and Old Norse and Old Saxon were contemporaneous. There are other oddities in this example. Note the use of 'iu' where we might expect 'eu'. Also the letter 'h' is used where we would expect 'ch'. In the word "vil" the long letter 'i' stands for what later in time would be spelled 'ie'.

Some southern German dialects of the High German language became part of the standard, due in great degree to the German which was adopted by Martin Luther for his translation of the Bible. Here is an example from the beginning of the 23rd Psalm, as found in the written 16th century records of Martin Luther.

Der herr ist meyn hirte, myr wirt nichts mangeln
> The Lord is my Shepherd, I shall not want

er lesst mich weyden da nicht gras steht
> He maketh me to lie down in green pastures

und furel mich zum wass das mich erkulet
> He leadeth me beside still waters.

Er erquickt meyne seele
> He anointeth my soul

Und er furet mich auff rechter strasse umb seyns names willen
> He leaded me on the path of rightiousness

Notice the use of the letter 'y' where we would expect the letter 'i'. The word 'erquickt' is also interesting because of how close it is to the English word "quick". The word for water is curiously "wass", rather than "wasser". Over time, Martin Luther made adjustments to the language he chose, so this doesn't represent the final version. In fact, he worked at this language all his life. Below are examples of some 16ᵗʰ century High German dialect variations. They use roughly the same text, for ease of comparison.

UPPER GERMAN

The following is an example (from Matthew 14: 23) of an old Upper Central German dialect. This dialect was used in the first German Bible ever printed, in 1466.

> *Vnd do er hett gelasses die geselschaffte,*
>> After he had dismissed them,
> *er staig auf allein bettent an dem berg.*
>> He went up on a mountainside to pray.
> *Wann do der abent wart gemacht er was allein do.*
>> When evening came, He was there alone.

Notice the use of the letter 'v' in place of the letter 'u', as it was used in Greek.

The following is an example of an old East Central German dialect, as taken from Luther's *Septembertestament* (Matthew 14: 23), from his first edition of the New Testament as printed at Wittenberg in 1522.

> *Vnd da er das volck von sich gelassen hatte,*
>> After He had dismissed them,
> *Steyg er auff synen berg alleyne, das er bette.*
>> He went up on a mountainside by himself, where He prayed.
> *Vnd am abent was er alleyn daselbe.*
>> When evening came, He was there alone.

Notice that the nouns are not capitalized, as they would be if written in today's Standard German. Capitalizing the first letter of a *major* word was first picked up by royal persons in the 13ᵗʰ century. This usage increased throughout the population until th 17ᵗʰ century, when *all* nouns were capitalized. This is about the same time when overall spelling rules first became recognized.

The following is an example from *Das gantz Nüw Testament*, printed by Christopher Froschauer in Zürich (1524) using an Old Swiss German dialect, which is the High Alemmanic version of the Alemmanic Upper German dialect. It is a translation of Luther's text into the Old Swiss dialect.

> *Vnd do er das volck von jm gelassen hat,*
>> After He had dismissed them,

steig er uff einen berg allein, das er bettette.
>He went up on a mountainside by himself, there to pray.

vnd am abend was er allein da selbe.
>When evening came, He was there alone.

The Swiss have now developed their own version (koine) of High German, which differs somewhat from Standard High German. It is spoken by 70% of the population. The Swiss became strong enough to develop their own version of German when they wrested their own independent country from the clutches of the Holy Roman Empire in the late 13th century. The Swiss today write Standard German but speak their own version of German, which is very difficult for German nationals to comprehend.

For comparison purposes, the following is a translation of this example text from Matthew, into Standard High German and in English.

Und da er das Volk von sich gelassen hatte,
>And after He had dismissed them,

stieg er auf einen Berg allein, daß er betete.
>He climbed on a hill alone, to pray.

Und am Abend war er allein daselbst.
>And by evening he was by himself, alone.

Again, just for further comparison purpose, here is a Middle Low German version of this same text.

Vn do he hadde vorlaten de schare,
>After He had dismissed them,

he ghink vp allenen bedende an enen berghe.
>He went up on a hill, to pray alone.

Vn do dat avent ward he was allenen dar.
>And when evening came, He was alone there.

Note here the use of the letter 'v' for the letter 'u', the use of the letter 'd' in place of the letter 't', the use of the letter' v' in place of the letter 'b' in "avent" (abend), the use of the letter 't' in place of the letter 's' in "vorlaten" (verlassen), and the overall simpler phraseology. These are all still characteristic of the normal differences between High German and Low German.

The following is a textual example of the <u>Voralberg</u> dialect, located in Austria along the border with Switzerland.

Dà goht ar î si und seit: Wie viel Taglüehner mi's Vaters
>He reflected and said: How many employees my father had

heand z'iësset gnug, und ih hië gaär nünt.
>that had enough to eat, and not to go hungry.

Especially interesting here is the word 'goht' (went), which is very similar to Low German. Here the dialect phrase containing 'goht' means "went into himself", which evidently means "reflecting within himself".

The following is an example of the <u>Old Allemannic</u> dialect of High German, from southwest Germany, in a partial text of the Lord's Prayer.

> *Fater unseer, thu pist in himile, wihi namun dinan*
>> Our Father, Who art in Heaven, hallowed be Thy name,
> *qhueme rihhi diin, were willo diin, so in himile so sa in erdu.*
>> Thy kingdom come, Thy will be done, as in Heaven so on earth
> *Prooth unseer emezzihic kip uns hiutu,*
>> Give us this day our daily bread
> *oblaz uns sculdi unseere, so wir oblazem uns sculdikem,*
>> Forgive us our trespasses, as we forgive those
> *enti ni unsih firleiti in khorunka*
>> who trespass against us
> *uzzer losi unsih funa ubile*
>> and deliver us from evil

Note the use of the letter 'p' (pist) where one would expect the letter 'b' (bist); as well as the use of the letter 'c' where one might expect 'k' and finally 'z' where one might expect 's'. Also interesting is the word 'kip', for the word "give". In this area, they use the curious word 'schwätzen', meaning 'to speak'. The Allemans dialect is the ancestor of Swiss German. and has also influenced Austrian. Some additional words in this dialect are...

I (I)	zritt (step)	d (the)	dine (yours)
au (also)	obe (over)	chunt (comes)	s (it)
barg (hill)	häd (had)	e (one)	unde (under)
mögl (possible)	han (have)	do (then)	bissel (little bit)

Some words in Swabish, another south Germany dialect, are strossa (street), net (not), ka (can), ghe (go), en (one), i (I) and boh (track). They also tend to leave out the unaccented 'e' in word endings; such as mockn (make) and bliebn (stay).

Here is an example of the <u>Old Bavarian</u> dialect of High German from southeastern Germany, also with a *partial* text of the Lord's Prayer (somewhat similar to the above Alemannic dialect).

> *Fater unser, du pist in himilum, kawihit si namo din,*
>> Our Father, Who art in Heaven, hallowed be Thy name,
> *piqhueme richi din, wesa din willo, sama so in himile est, sama in erdu.*
>> Thy kingdom come, Thy will be done, as in Heaven, so on earth

Pilipi unsraz emizzagaz kip uns eogawanna enti flaz,
　Give us this day our daily bread,
compare uns unsre sculdi sama so wir flazzames unsrem scolom
　Forgive us our trespasses, as we forgive those who trespass against us

Austrian German has links to the Bavarian dialect. It's Catholic heritage caused the area to resist Martin Luther's new High German, so they've hung on to certain old words. When Luther wrote "Ich war", the Bavarians much prefered their "Ich was".

In some cases, the souther German dialects bear a strong resemblance to Low German, probably because in those olden days, there wasn't that much difference between Middle High German and Middle Low German. Austrian also has much in common with south German and Swiss. Here are examples of words in the <u>Austrian</u> version of the German language.

bua (boy)	diandl (girl)	kloan (small)
våtta (father)	gnack (neck)	kopfweh (headache)
gaudi (fun	johr (year)	was (was)
büchl (book)		

Note especially the word for 'girl', or in this case a 'little girl'. The diminutive in Austrian uses the '-l' ending, such as in the word for 'little book', which is Büchl (Büchlein in Standard German).

Here are examples of words reported to be in a <u>Bavarian</u> dialect, most of which have similarities with Low German..

wern (to become)	zwo (two)	olls (all)
I (I)	glabet (believe	holt (halt)
bauen (to plow)	ross (horse)	henn (chicken)
paradaiser (tomato)	stadel (barn)	stoppel (cork)
wonns (when)	häär (hear)	nomittag (afternoon)

Generally speaking, it remains a fact that south Germany never did accept all of Martin Luther's recommendations, or even today doesn't fully adopt the subsequent Standard High German. They prefer, when they have the choice, their own dialect version of southern High German. Here are some examples of current Austrian or south Bavarian local dialect words.

ins (us)	bua (boy)	diandl (girl)
våtta (father)	gnack (neck)	kopfweh (headache)
reden (speak)	nomittag (afternoon)	bauen (to plow)
ross (horse)	stadel (barn)	henn (chicken)
stoppel (cork)	paradaiser (tomato).	kloan (small)
samstag (saturday)	spengler (plumber)	

The words of the Lord's Prayer can be found in about every language and dialect, making it a good reference point for word and spelling comparisons. Some of them are shown in the following list of words, adapted from R.E. Keller, *The German Language*.

Gothic	Old Norse	Old English	Old Frisian	Old Saxon	Old Rhen. Franc. High German
atta	faþer	faeder	feder	fadar	fater
unsar	varr	ure	user	usa	unser
þu	þu	þe	þu	þu	thu
in	i	on	in	an	in
himinam	hifne	heofonum	himile	himilq rikea	himilom
weihnai	helgesk	gehalgod	ewied si	geuuihid si	giuuihit si
namo	nafn	nama	nama	namo	namo
qimai	tilcome	tobecume	kume	cuma	quæme
warþai	verþe	geweorþe	werthe	uuuerða	uuerdhe
wilja	vile	willa	willa	uuilleo	uuilleo
gif	gef	syle	jef	gef	gib
uns	oss	us	us	us	uns
daga	idag	to-dæg	hui-dega	dago	hiutu
hlaif	brauþ	hlaf	hlef	rad	broot
Jah	Ok	And	And	And	endi
aflet	fyrerlat	forgyf	forjef	alat	farlaz
skulans	skulder	gyltas	skelda	mensculdio	sculdhi
weis	ver	we	wi	uue	uuir
briggais	eiþ	galæd þu	led	lat	gileidi
fraistubnjai	freistne	costnunge	forsekinge	farledean	costunga

The use of the letter 'w' in the above examples is incorrect, but it used here merely for clarity purposes. The double letter 'uu' was actually used then to represent what we today think of as the letter 'w'.

In 1300, a dialect researcher named Hugo von Trimberg summarized some of the variety among dialects in Germany in a poem called *Der Renner*.

Swâben ir wörter spaltent	Swabians split their words up
Die Franken ein teil si valtent	The Franks run them together
Die Baire si zerzerrent	The Bavarians tear them to pieces
Die Düringe si ûf sperrent	The Thuringians open them out
Die Sachsen si bezückent	The Saxons cut them short
Die Rînliute si verdrückent	The Rhinelanders suppress them
Die Wetereiher si würgent	The Wetterau speakers throttle them
Die Misner si wol schürgent	The Meissen emphasize them strongly

Egerlant si swenkent	Egers say them with a sing-song voice
Oesterriche si schrenkent	Austrians weave them together
Stirlant si baz lenkent	Styrians speak them with a rising tone
Kernte ein teil si senkent	Carinthians speak with a falling tone

Attitudes toward such a great variety in speech vary greatly. For most people, dialect has always been associated with the peasant, and for them it became a class issue. This was reinforced in the 18th century when the elite attempted to produce a supra-standard German language. However, many authors have reveled in the richness of the various dialects; not the least of which was Goethe. Low German, although a language as well as a panoply of dialects, has also been put into the lower classes of speech by many Germans.

LOW GERMAN

There was a long period of time when Old Low German and later Middle Low German were used widely and daily in north Germany. It was used in speech, business and literature. When it ceased to be a prominent literary language, after the decline of the Hansa, the recognition of Low German as a separate language dissolved somewhat into a sea of of Low German dialects. These dialects have continued to develop and change over the centuries.

OLD SAXON

Written records of Old Saxon, the oldest form of Low German, date back to the late 8th century A.D. This does not mean that the language began at that point. It means only that these particular 8th century written records have survived to this day, and earlier records evidently have not survived. There surely were earlier records written, but probably not many of them. There was not much writing done in those days, so finding even these examples of Old Saxon writing is something of a miracle in itself. How much earlier would one have to go, prior to the 8th century A.D. to find the language's origination? The actual point of origin in time of most languages will never be known.

Our knowledge of the oldest Low German is based on the Old Saxon language. The following is a 10th century magical charm that was recited to cure a horse's lameness.

> *Visc flot aftar themo uuatare,*
>> A fish was swimming through the water,
> *verbrustun sina vetherun*
>> it fins broken;
> *tho gihelida ina use druhtin.*
>> then our Lord healed it.
> *The selve druhtin, thie thena viscgehelida,*
>> The Lord himself, who healed the fish,
> *thie gihele that hers thern spurihelti.*
>> may he cure the horse of its lameness.

Notice the interesting spelling of fish (visc) and horse (hers), plus the use of 'uu' for 'w'. The word 'gihelida' obviously means "the holy one".

There are documents available in Old Saxon, dating from the 9th century to the 12 century, and the most well known of these documents is a poetic narration of the Life of Christ, referred to as Der Heliand (the Saviour), written about 830. Below are lines 2906 to 2908.

> *Thô lêtun sie suî ðean strôm, hôh hurnidskip*
>   Then they caused the high prowed ship to part the
> *hluttron ûðem, skêðan skir uuater. Skrêd lioht dages,*
>   strong current, the pure water with clear waves. The light of day passed

Der Heliand also contained a poetic version of the Lord's Prayer, of which the first line looked as follows.

> *Fadar usa, þu bast an þem hohonhimila rikea*
>   Our Father, who art in heaven

It was presumably written by a Saxon Monk, sometime between 822 and 843. However, experts point out that the entire text contains what seems to be a mixture of Old Frisian, Old Saxon and High German dialects. With this limitation, it is difficult to determine from Der Heliand the exact vocabulary of Old Saxon itself.
One should not forget that an early version of Old Saxon is the language that migrated to Britain in the 5th century, becoming first Anglo-Saxon, then Old English, Middle English and finally became English

Old Saxon differed somewhat from Primitive Germanic, its antecedent language. It is this lineage which explains its similarity to Old High German (compare Old Saxon 'kalf' to Old High German 'kalb'). The change in pronunciation and use of letters we find here is a constant factor in any language.

MIDDLE LOW GERMAN

This verson of Low German became the *lingua franca* of the internationally based Hanseatic League. Just what was this Hansa? Where did the Hansa come from. It seems that Hansa is an Old French word for an association. Creation of the Hansa was preceded, about 1150, by the development of a trading group among the towns around the lower Rhine. This perhaps became the seed for later developing a much broader "Hansa".

Lübeck, shown in the center of the following map, the first city to secured an imperial trading charter from Frederick II, became the administrative center of the Hansa. This city was founded by Henry the Lion in 1143, on what was then Slavic soil.

MAP J   THE HANSEATIC CITIES

The city of Hamburg was next. In 1241 these cities formed an alliance to protect their
Baltic trade routes. The term Hanseatic League was first used in 1344. It was always a
very loose confederation, with members being quite independent. This was one of its
weak points. They could only agree when the same enemy was threatening their
pocketbook. In time, the Hansa grew to include cities in England, Sweden, Norway,
Denmark and Russia. At its height, it included 160 towns and cities, some of the larger
ones shown on the map. Consequently, the Lübeck area Low German language
strongly influenced these neighboring countries and their language, especially the
Swedish and Danish languages. Low German was such a prominent language then that
it was used for international treaties and city histories.

The Hansa cities in all these countries made interlocal agreements regarding exclusive
trade rights, hoping to discourage outside (primarily Dutch) trade influence. They
traded in metals, wood, pitch, tar, terpentine, horses, wool, linen, leather, salted cod and
herring, beer, amber, drugs, grain, olive oil, salt and silk. Their chief business centers
were at Wisby (Gothland), Bergen, London and Bruges. Some of the member cities
were powerful city-states, and thus could raise their own armies. The Hansa even had
their own navy, by virtue of hiring the military ships of neighboring countries.. During
the 12th to 14th century, the Teutonic Order of Knights gave military assistance to the
Hansa. Waldemar IV of Denmark fought the Hansa. In 1362 he deafeated the Hansa
fleet, but they fought back. The Peace of Stralsund, in 1370, between the temporarily
defeated Denmark and the Hansa, was negotiated and written in Low German. Internal
Hansa organizational problems caused them to be divided into thirds; the Wendish-
Saxon, the Prussian-Westphalian and Gothland-Livland. However, the struggle with
Denmark continued. The Hundred Years War also weakened the Hansa. Denmark
began letting Dutch trade in, and during the subsequent battles the Hansa began to lose
influence in the 15th and 16th century: officially gone in 1669.

Hamburg and Lübeck established branch offices as far away as London and Novgorod. In all of these offices, the business language was Low German. It was used and understood in major cities all along the North Sea and Baltic Sea coasts.

The following is an example of Middle Low German, from a 1294 ordinance excerpted from the City Statutes of the City of Lübeck. This could be taken as an example of the Low German language as used by all the Hanseatic League participants.

> *We ratmen van Lubeke prowet in maneghen saken, de vor vs komet, dat bewilen et eleke vormunden nicht des an sic hebbet, dat se nutte vormunde wesen kunnen; bewilen sint se nicht so vlitich vnde so weruesam ofte so truwe also dar to boret, vnde bewilen scheppet se dar vnder eres silues nut vnde nicht uan rechte der nut, des vormunde se sin gheworden.*

The words 'maneghen saken' probably means "many things". The letter 'v' is used where one would expect a 'u' today. The word 'vlitich' evidently means "busy" or "industrious" (fleissig). Some words are borrowed from High German, such as 'vormunde' and 'gheworden', perhaps because these were common loan words in the Lübeck dialect.

Although somewhat different from any of today's dialects, a Low German reader could study this and come up with the gist of the matter. Here is an approximate English transliteration of the ordinance, wherein they seem to be speaking of their limitations as *guardians* of the citizens..

> We, the City Councilmen of Lübeck, have many things come before us, that sometimes the guardians don't have the ability, to be useful guardians; sometimes they aren't as industrious or reliable as they should be, and sometimes they do things for their own benefit and not for the benefit of those for whom they have become guardians.

Several large city chronicles (histories) were written in Low German. In 1380, the Magdeburg Schöppenchronik recorded not only the city history in Low German but traced the history of all of Upper Saxony and the Saxons, up to the 14th century. The following is an example of Middle Low German as found in a this *Weltchronik*, written by Hermann Korner.

> *Dô it quam vor middernacht, dô sach dê jungelinc, dat sik des vogedes graf up dede unde dê dôde lîcham richtede sick up unde nam dat laken, dar hê inne gewunden was, unde want dat to hôpe unde leide dat in ênen horne des graves.*

There are strong hints of Middle High German here, which was somewhat similar to Middle Low German. This is shown in a word like 'sach' for "saw" (past tense of 'see'), which is like the Standard German past tense word 'sah' but not at all like the corresponding Low German phrase 'hett sehn'. On the other hand, a very typical Low

German word in this text is 'to hôpe' for "together", which would not be found in High German. In ancient times, ' to hôpe' referred to a making a "heap", meaning to pile something up together in one "heap". Today 'tohopen' means just "together".

Also note the word 'horne', which here means "corner". It makes one wonder if whoever penned the nursery rhyme "little Jack Horner, sat in a corner", was aware of therelationship between these words? Note here also the indication of a possessive case (des graves), which is no longer used in Low German. Add to this the fact that Weltchronik was written by a man named Korner.

In the Middle Ages, people using Middle Low German and Middle High German could understand each other fairly easily. For instance, the word 'laken' would have been spelled as a very similar 'lachen' in Middle High German. The following is an English translation of the *Weltchronik*.

> As midnight approached, the lad saw the bailiff's grave open and the
> dead body got up and took the shroud it was wrapped in and folded it
> up and laid it in a corner of the grave.

A Priest named Everhart wrote a rhymed chronicle, about 1216-1218 at Gandersheim, in a Middle Low German which might have come out of Ostphalia.

> *Do de grote könnich Otto sinen ende genam,*
> When the great King Otto anticipated his end,
> *sin sone her Otto na eme an dat rike quam*
> his son Otto came upon acquiring the kingdom
> *ein eddel vrouwe was sin moder, Edith, de was*
> a noble woman was his mother, Edith, who was
> *als ek an dem boke wol hebbe bekannt,*
> as I learned of her from books
> *von vadere to vadere von negen köninigen geboren.*
> from father to father from 9 kings born.

This text is closer to today's dialect. It is quite readable, to anyone familiar with both Low German and Standard German. The following are some of the more reasonably recognizable Middle Low German words.

kêse (cheese)	klêt (dress)	vlês (flesh)
klên (small)	dêp (deep)	blôt (blood)
bôm (tree)	grôt (large)	dôk (cloth)
laken (sheet)	was (was)	dôd (dead)

Notice the common use of long stressed vowels, which have been largely replaced by monophthongs in the later Low German.

The following is another example of the Low German used in the Hansa era. It is an excerpt from one of those beautifully illlustrated bibles one sees pictures of, printed by Steffen Arndes at Lübeck in 1495. The text describes how, after Jeses sent the disciples across the lake in a boat, he prayed a while and then proceeded to walk across the water; from Matthew 14: 23, 24.

> *Vn do he hadde vorlaten de schare,*
>> After He had dismissed them,
> *he ghink vp allenen bedende an enen berghe.*
>> He went up on a mountainside by Himself to pray.

Vn do dat avent ward he allenen dar,
>> When evening came, He was there alone,
> *Aver dat schepeken ward gheworpen in den middle des meres.*
>> but the boat was already a considerable distance from land,
> *vordiddelst den bulghen wente de wynt was en enteghen.*
>> buffeted by the waves because the wind was against it.

Note the common use of the letter 'v' for the letter 'u', and the use of 'gh' where we expect just a 'g'. In the word 'enen', as mentioned above, we would today use 'eenen', but in those days the long 'e' vowel did not yet use the form of a monophthong 'ee'. The word 'bulghen' means "waves", of course, which derives from the concept of waves being 'bulges' in the water.

During the time when Middle Low German was widely spoken, in central and north Germany, the line between where Low German was spoken and where High German was spoken was located much further south than the current boundary line. The current boundary line is called the *Benrath* Line. It is shown on the following map. The discussion will now turn to Low German dialects.

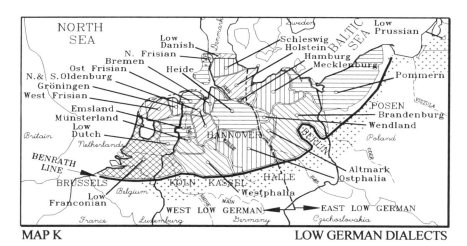

MAP K   LOW GERMAN DIALECTS

403

LOW GERMAN DIALECTS

There is a line that today roughly separates the northern Low German speaking area from the southern High German speaking area. Of course, they also speak High German in the north. The line runs through Benrath, a small village along the Rhine. The *Benrath Line* begins further west of Benrath, in Belgium, just south of Ypres, near Dunkirk. North of there is the Flemish speaking area of Belgium, which language is derived from Old Low Franconian (considered here to be an offshoot of Low Saxon). The Flemish speak their own dialect but write in Dutch. In the south and east of Belgium are the Walloons, descendents of the Celts, who speak dialects of French. There is a small German speaking area in the east of Belgium.

Following the Benrath Line towards the east, it meanders through Aachen, arches up above Cologne through Benrath; then it runs southeast for a while and then northerly again to just below Düsseldorf and Magdeburg, then down to Finsterwalde and north again toward Frankfurt a.d.Oder.

At this point the line encounters enter what is largely a previous Slavic area, at least from the 6th century onward. In the 9th century, Louis the Pious fortified a line of thick hedges and thorn bushes between the Saxons and the Slavs, called the "Limes Saxonia". It was meant to keep the Slavs out. Today there are parts of it still recognizable, such as in the *Sachsenwald* near Hamburg and the *Hahnheide* near Trittau. This line was partly removed in the 12th century, so Germans could migrate eastward and settle in the Slav territory. This emigration included farmers, craftsmen and merchants from all over northern and central Germany.

At this point along the Benrath line the area of West Low German dialects changes now to the area of East Low German dialects. This is shown as a dark dashed vertical line on the map. The area between the Harz Mountains and Magdeburg (Elbostphalisch) is influenced by both German and Slav.

Proceeding eastward now into the previous Slav territory, the *Benrath* line turns north toward the Baltic coast at Danzig and then dips south again to include an area lying between Danzig and the Lithuanian border. At the far easterly end of the Low German area lies the Low Prussian speaking area.

As has been mentioned, this line between Low German and High German was, during the Old High German period, located further south. It once ran through Halle, Leipzig and Elsterwerda, south of Berlin. In and around Halle it was common to hear Low German spoken between 1470 and 1900, although the last official written Low German document appeared about 1417.. This older area, where Low German was once a common language, is shown as a pattern of small crosses on the map. It also includes a part of the Hesse area. In this area they use the term "hond" for the word 'dog' and "schwätzen" for the word 'speak' (as they do in southwest Germany). Around Köln, where they are fond of saying they saying "Rheinisch" instead of German, they use the term "Kallen" for the word 'talk'. In many ways their speech is similar to current Low German. They say 'pass up' instead of 'pass auf', and also use the following words.

met (with)	johr (year)	sonneschien (sunshine)
keene (none)	blieb (stay)	vorbi (gone)

It amazes many today to learn that Berlin was once a.Low German speaking city. They spoke a version of Brandenburg Low German. Berlin dropped Low German in about 1500. As Berlin grew and industrialized, its speech shifted to the Central High German dialect, which was meanwhile evolving around Meissen and Leipzig. Berliners have always had a unique dialect; saying 'shoin' instead of 'schön'. They prefer not using the genitive, even in Standard German. They have an interesting term for 'baker' - Teegaffe (dough-ape), as well as the following words.

schrippe (bread roll)	bulette (meat ball)	bonje (head)
klempner (plumber)	sonnabend (saturday)	Molle (beer)

The ancestry of the West Low German dialects is obviously all German and Franconian. However, the fact that the East Low German area was once Slavic had some influence on the Low German dialects there. However, the 12th and 13th century migration of people from the west to the east had a much larger affect on the current dialects in the eastern portion. Some of the major differences between westerly Low German and easterly Low German will be discussed in the next section.

The following several sections contain *example* words, pertaining to individual Low German dialects. These are given merely to suggest the kind of differences that exists amongst the dialects. It is far from a complete vocabulary. The diversity within a dialect means that some speakers may not recognize the example words given. These examples also do not necessarily represent the exact or current usage of words in a given dialect. These examples were gleaned from various publications or from the works of authors who are connected with a given dialect. In many cases, they reflect word usage that prevailed a century or more ago. First the family of East Low German dialects will be discussed.

EAST LOW GERMAN

The historical culture is also somewhat different in the east.. The difference was exacerbated when East Germany was communist. Centuries ago, in the west a vassel had to promise his *lord* that "as long as I live, I am bound to serve and respect you; your enemies are my enemies". In the east such servitude was more in the form of feudalism, whereby the peasant was more tied to the *land* owned by a noble, than to any one particular noble.

East Low German also was influenced by Low Franconian (via Dutch, Belgian, Ostphalian and Westphalian 12th to 14th century in-migration) and Prussian High

German (next to Lithuania). Some also came from the Hamburg area. This eastern area, generally east of the Elbe and Saale Rivers, was settled for centuries by Slavs. The Romans referred to them as the Venedi, while the Germans called them the Wenden. Until the 12th century it was Slavic all the way west to the Elbe. In the other direction, Low German reached as far east as Danzig, and Low Prussian reached as far east as Königsberg.

It is also true that some Slavs moved in the *other* direction, toward the west, toward the Elbe and Salle Rivers. Their Sorbic influence remains here, in the Lüneburger Wendland. This sort of mixture of Slavic and German influences lead to a 'leveling' process, where certain features from each contributing factor lent something to the final dialects.

In the 18th century, the emerging Standard High German had a strong influence on Low German as well, causing Low German dialects to acquire High German spelling characteristics. More High German loan words were accepted into East Low German than they were in West Low German.

One major difference between west and east dialects is the plural verb ending. In West Low German, the term "we sing" would be said *wi singt*. In East Low German it would be said *wi singen*. The "en" ending of eastern Low German is similar to the Standard German *wir singen*. They also retained some Standard German influence in other ways, such as 'uns' for 'us' (us), which possibly results from the Low Franconian influence. East Low German retains the preterite kind of past tense to a degree, a special form of the past tense that is gone in West Low German.

The major dialects of East Low German are Low Prussian, Brandenburgisch, Mecklenburgisch and Pommersch (Vor-, Middle, and Hinter). The Vorpom-mern area was connected onto Mecklenburg in 1945. The Low Prussian and Pommern areas have lost much of their dialect, due to Polish and Russian domination.

The examples given below, for words in both East and West Low German dialects, are estimates at best. Spelling of words varies so much within a given major dialect area. Major dialect areas have local subareas within them, each subdialect actually having their own name. For example, there is a Wümme Platt subdialect within northern Heide, as well as the Sand Platt subdialect in western Westphalia. They are just too numerous to mention here. The major dialect word examples presented here are meant primarily to show, in general terms, the broad pattern of major dialect differences.

Brandenburg

This region used to be referred to as the Mark; the central portion was called Middle Mark. Mark is an ancient term meaning about the same as 'district'; a marked off area. The northern part was called Nordmark, and it shares some culture with Mecklenburg. In the Prignitz area the dialect is similar to that in Mecklenburg. An area just east of Ostphalia is called Altmark, and still contains some Sorbs (which Germans refer to as

Wends), and the Sorbian dialect is still quite alive there. There is another Sorbian enclave, just north of Berlin. It is known as the Spreewald. The Spree is the river that runs through Berlin.

In Brandenburg, the word for "girl" is *Määken* (compared to *Mädchen* in Standard German and *Mäke* in the Pommern area). Their word for "little" is bitsken, possibly just a derivation of the Standard German word *bischen*. This is similar to the Westphalian (bietken) and Ost Frisian (betken) and Mecklenburg (bisken) word for 'little bit'. The Westphalian, Ostphalian and Ost Frisian impact here (such as using "hei" instead of "he") derives from their history of the Old Low Franconian in-migration. The southern and central parts of Brandenburg were strongly influenced by the Central German dialect of High German to their south. Their *j* letter is pronounced with the *y* sound.

Some emigrants from Flanders and the Netherlands moved to Brandenburg (Böhmerwald and Havelberg), bringing along some of these Low Franconian dialect words.

det instead of dat	dik instead of dich
gein instead of keen (similiar to Standard German 'kein')	
u instead of o	i instead of e

The following words are taken as being somewhat unique to Brandenburg.

baen (leg)	laef (dear)	mudding ('little' mother)
vadder (father)	murer (mason)	dunntomols (at this time)
buckel (back)	rökern (smoked)	modder (mother)
kruschek (wild pear)	kua (cow)	hei (he) sumpf (swamp)

Altmark

Along the westerly edge of Brandenburg, across from Ostphalia, there is a historically Polabisch area. Some of the Slavic terms remain in use there, as they do in the Lüneburger Wendland and Spreewald areas. These are some word unique to this area.

maleitje (raspberries)	jichel (pine needles)
paggeln (knead)	polt (punt boat)

Mecklenburg

In the Mecklenburg region, the diminutive ending is 'ing' (mudding = little mother), rather than the 'ke' or 'ken' ending for Pommern. It appears that people in this area are prone, more than average, to utilizing Standard German words in their dialect. In eastern Mecklenburg and VorPommern they might use the word *kleen* (variation of the Standard German *klein*) for the English word "small". Instead of *snacken* for "talk",

407

they would say *spreken*. From their Slavic history, they have a loan word like Kollatz, meaning wheatbread.

In western Mecklenburg (around Schwerin), the dialect is closer to that of nearby Holstein and Hamburg. However, the majority of the Mecklenburg area has a close similarity to Ostphalisch, as well as Westphalisch and Ost Frisian, due to in-migrations, some as late as the 19th century. Immigrants that came from Westphalia settled around Stargard and Lübeck. The Stargard area also received immigrants from the Altmark.

Lübeck was once the principal trade city, being the base of the Hansa empire. It gave up the principal north German trade city status to Hamburg in the 18th century.

The southern part of Mecklenburg also has dialect similarities to Brandenburg. Part of this is due to their mutual impact from Dutch immigrants ('pütte' for well). The southern half of Mecklenburg was very lightly settled. North Mecklenburg has better loamy soils for farming, as well as an oceanic climate. Wheat and sugar beets are the chief crops. All of Mecklenburg was quite rural. Before 1945, almost 40% of the population were farmers. Half of them belonged to large estates, which easily converted to communist communes. Without heavy outside influence, Mecklenburgers were able to hang on to their dialect fairly well, until they were absorbed into East Germany. This stifled development but it did not promote retention of heritage. There is an old saying that - when the world comes to an end, then go to Mecklenburg, and there the world will end 50 years later.

The following are several Low German words where the spelling is somewhat unique to Mecklenburg.

hei (he)	sei (they)	ick (I)
tau (to)	töög (moved)	heww (have)
twei (two)	sin (his)	min (mine)
sick (himself)	käuhl or keuhl (cool)	breiw (letter)
täuw or töw (wait)	was (was)	schauh (shoe)
brauder (brother)	deip (deep)	nit (nich)
dar (there)	gink (went)	wur (how)
min (mine)	vader (father)	goren (kids)
dunn (then)	vier (four)	brüche (belly)
goln (golden)	sot (salt)	gink (went)
tüschen (between)	mudder (mother)	sturwe (died)
pletten (iron)	keuhj (cows)	tausamme (together)
schaul (school)	dörf (may)	mäke (maid)
gaud (good)	was (was)	

Note the use of 'au' where one might expect to find the Saxon 'o' or the Westphalian 'ao'. There are many words that Mecklenburg shares with the Vorpommern area. One is the word 'töög', meaning to "move into" and another is frigge, which means to

408

"marry". Frigga was the Norse protector god of marriage. The Teutonic counterpart of this god was Frija (which sounds close to the other Low German word for the institution of marriage - freen).

Pommern

Pomerania once strectched all across the Baltic, from Vorpommern and Rügen to Hinter Pommern. The large area between Stettin and Danzig is known as Ost Pommern.

This region, which also was part of the former DDR (East Germany), was originally settled by the Slavs in the 7th century. Denmark's King Canute conquered Pomerania in 1031. The area was devastated. The Slav princes of the Duchy of Pomerania invited German emigrants to come in help rebuild it. They also opened their arms to christianization. The area is now largely Lutheran. They were further colonized by emigrants from Belgium and Holland. Danzig is a Baltic port city, which was once the capital of the Slav province of Vorpommern. It became a German town in 1243. In the 12th and early 13th century the area was by wars between Poles, Swedes, Danes and Germans.

In 1309 this area shifted to German control under the Teutonic Knights, even though a Papal order called for control to be transferred to Poland. The Knights penetrated Poland, where Germans settled 650 districts, and into Lithuania.

During the 30 Years War, in 1626, it was again conquered by Denmark. Sweden was given lower Pomerania by the Treaty of Münster, following the 30 Years War. Brandenburg retained Hinter Pommern. Eastern Pommern (now Vorpommern, around Danzig) was reincorporated into Poland in 1466.

Sweden took full control in 1679 and began settling there, but eventually it went back to Denmark. During the Napoleonic period, when Denmark joined the French and lost, they gave Pomerania to Prussia. Pommern was reconnected by Prussia in 1815. The strong Prussian reforms of 1811-16 were applied in Silesia and in the Pommeran.

Kaschubian is a Polish dialect that once existed in upper Pomerania. The area retained its Kaschubian Slavic background in some ways. One was the retention of large land holds as estates, especially around Stralsund, worked by a large peasant class. The farmland and climate were not suited to good farming, so the area remained poor. They raised rye, oats and potatoes. The Kaschubian Slavic background has left a few distinctive words behind. The Pommern word for 'brüd' (bride), is similar to the Kaschubian 'brutka'. The same goes for Pommern bükweit (buckwheat) and Kaschubian 'buukvita' and for Pommern mohltit (meal time) and Kaschubian 'moltit'.

The Vorpommern and Middle Pommern dialects are fairly similar to that of eastern Mecklenburg, although they use the 'ke' diminutive instead of 'ing'. The most apparent aspect of Hinterpommern words is the loss of the final '-n'. Some have suggested this

could be a Slavic influence, mut more likely it is due to Low Franconian influences
brought by immigrants from West Low German areas.

hüt (today)	köh (cow)	brauder (brother)
schornsteen (chimney)	mitz (cap)	patüffel (potato)
sünnowend (saturday)	nomirrach (afternoon)	morge (morning)
ditt (this)	spreken (talk)	hei (he)
mäke (girl)	klei (small)	johr (year)
froch (ask)	bitske (little bit)	tit (time)
luer (wait)	pier (horses)	kick (look)
mägde (maid)	I (in)	d or dei (the)
t (it)	pomuchel (cod)	tu (to)
räjen (rain)	väl (much)	u (and)
plins (omolet)	luna (firelight)	kruschke (pear)
bratzek (brother)	borma (harrow)	frobel (sparrow)
schwefka (broom)		

A particularly interesting aspect of Pommern is the 'clipping' of word endings.
For example, see words like 'bitske' and 'klei' and 'mäke', where one might expect to
see the letter 'n' at the end. Quite a few words have just one letter, although when
pronounced, the words sound similar to their longer counterparts..

Low Prussian

This area is on the far eastern extreme of the Low German area. It is east even of Ost
Pommern, situated next to the area containing the Kaschubian dialect in Poland. It's
dialect is strongly influenced by Polish from the south and Kaschubian Slav from the
east.

This area was colonized in the 13ᵗʰ century. It's East Middle German langugage
became Low German, as emigrants moved in from the West Low German area. In the
18ᵗʰ century there was an influx of German farmer settlers and Standard German
became the main language.

Here are some representative words, which tend to reflect some High German or
Franconian influence. Their language did not undergo apocope, the loss of the final '-
e', as in the words make (make) and singe (sing).

dröwer (over)	verstaohn (understand)		wiehl (because)
doa (there)	vörzähn (fourteen)		woll (wish)
wihr(was)	joa (yes)		et (it)
werpen (throw)	auf (up)	ös (is)	suke (sow)
straaß (street)	noaber (neighbor)		doa (there)
fru (wife)	e (one)	e (he)	äm (him)
niee (new)	uck (also)	öck (I)	stoah (stand)

410

goah (go)	sinnoawend (saturday)	froach (ask)
joahre (year)	koam (come)	foahr (drive)
vleicht (maybe)	moal (once or time)	woage (wagon)
horchen (wait)	kobbel (mare)	zwei (two)
wie (how)	seed (side)	singe (sing)
kleen (small)	mannke (person)	hadd (had)
uk (also)	baakove (bake oven)	wiefke (little wife)
bute (outside)	beet (little bit)	kolt (cold)

Note some similarity to Ostphalian (especially in the use of 'oa') and some similarity to neighboring Pommern (the '-e' endings and clipped words)

WEST LOW GERMAN

The early West Germanic languages that existed prior to the christian era are usually broken down into Low German and High German. The term Low German includes the dialects west of the Elbe and north of the Benrath Line. Among these are the Old Frisian language and the current Frisian dialects, which are considered as Low German.

Old Frisian

At one time, Old Frisian might well have been a sister language to Old Saxon. The Saxons and Frisians lived adjoining one another, about 3,000 years ago. All the Frisian tribes once inhabitied the ancient homeland of the Germanic tribes; in lower Scandinavia. It may be that, in the pre-Christian era, the Frisians were located in southern Denmark and radiated out from there prior to the period when the other Germanic tribes migrated. This is mere conjecture, but there might have been ancient Frisians in and around Nord Friesland before they came to West or Ost Friesland. They may have, in ancient times, been related to either the Angles or the Saxons.

The Old Frisian tribes were first noticed by the Romans in 12 BC. They were then living along the North Sea. They were given the name Frisii by the historian Tacitus. The West and later the Ost Frisians along the North Sea were part of this family. The Nord Frisian Islands off of Schleswig were ultimately settled by Frisians, at a much later time.

Old Frisian text usually dates back to the 12th or 13th century, which places it far down the time line from the earliest Old Saxon (9th century) or Old High German documents (8th century). The Old Frisian language is therefore not contemporaneous with the languages with which they are often compared (Old Saxon and Old English). For instance, true examples of the Old Frisian language that existed when early Old Saxon language existed are, unfortunately, not available for a true comparison. The Old Frisian language was prominant until about 1400 and still spoken until about 1550.

The Frisians were pagan, until they were forced by the Franks to accept christianity in the 8th century. The following is an excerpt from the Ten Commandments passage of the Bible. The language is 13th century Old East Frisian, which here may be assumed to be closed to Old Frisian. The Old Frisian word 'bod' here means "commandment". The vowels with a breve symbol ^ over them are long vowels

Thet thredde bod:
fira thene sunnandei
end there hêlche degan.

The 3rd Commandment:
Remember the Sabbath day
to keep it holy.

Thet fiârde bod:
minna thîne feder
end thîne môder,
hû thû longe libbe.
Thet fifte bod:
thu ne skalt nenne monslaga dua

The 4th Commandment:
Thou shalt honor thy father
and thy mother
and live long on the earth.
The 5th Commandment"
Thou shalt not kill

Thet sogende bod:
thet thû nowet ne stele.

The 7th Commandment:
Thou shalt not steal

Thet achtende bod:
thet thû thî nowet ne ûrsuere,
ne nên falesk withskip ne drîue.

The 8th Commandment:
Thou shalt not bear false witness
against thy neighbor.

As one reads these commandments in Frisian, the close relationship with both Low German and English is apparent. The similarity has been often noted, and is also reflected in the following list of cognate words.

FRISIAN	OLD ENGLISH	ENGLISH	LOW GERMAN
ding	ðing	thing	ding
sann	sunnan	sun	sünn
muun	monan	moon	maand
hi	he	he	he
dat	dæt	that	dat
diar	ðær	there	dor
hemmel	heofan	heaven	heban
degan	daegan	days	daag
hus	hus	house	hus
hart	heorte	heart	hart

The Runic letter eth (ð) came from Gothic or Primitive German, and its 'th' sound was retained in Old English and Low German, but not in Frisian.

If one investigates all the dialects that existed in the central north German area, English is found to be very similar to Low German, Dutch, Old Saxon and even Old Norse. Part of the reason is that all of these languages derived from the same parent Primitive German language. Another is that the Old Saxon and Old Norse tribes lived near one, and near the Frisians; for centuries. Another is that both English and Low German are direct descendants of Old Saxon. So the similarity amongst all these languages and dialects is to be expected.

The following are words that are somewhat unique to Old Frisian.

wei (way)	efter (after)	feder (father)
fon or fan (from)	us (us)	hit (it)
jif (if)	kuma (come)	leter (later)
melok (milk)	skela (shall)	stenen (stone)
thet (that)	tian (ten)	skrîva (write)
twa (two)	wîf (wife)	wêron (were)
ik (I)	you (thu)	hi or hy (he)
min (min)	wi (we)	your (thin)

This is obviously a West Germanic language. The *v* letter had the *f* sound. Both Old Frisian and Old Norse showed a loss of the letter *n* at the end of words. This and other similarities may prove an old connection to Old Norse or it may be just the influence of Vikings who invaded Friesland during the Viking era.

West Frisian

Because of its location in the north corner of Holland, this language has been influenced by Dutch and Old Low Franconian. It pushed eastward along the North Sea. Frisian also compares well to Old Saxon, because the Saxons were neighbors and combatants. The Saxons pushed the Frisians back again toward Holland. The last stronghold of current West Frisian is in the Dutch Province of Friesland. It has changed quite a bit since the Middle Ages. In the 9th century the language expanded onto the adjoining coastal islands.

The Frisians began losing power in 1500, especially after final establishment of the House of Burgundy portion of the German Empire in 1524. Prior to then, the Frisian tongue was the common language in Friesland. After 1525 A.D. the Frisian city people came into increased contact with the surrounding Dutch, and this developed into a citified (stadsfries - town Frisian) version of Dutch with a Frisian structure. It has since lost ground to both regular Dutch and Frisian. Dutch became the language of the church. Today the Frisians often speak Frisian at home but Dutch elsewhere.

The following contains text which is reported to be a specimen of current West Frisian. It was taken from a text which was entitled *Our Work*, written by Tony Feitsma about 1959.

*Wy binne derfan ùtgien, dat in goede stavering safolle mooglik oanslute moat
by it lûdsysteem fan de tael. Oan elk phoneem moat dus in apart teken
bianderje en elk ûnderskaet teken fortsjintwurdiget in foneem. Dat systeem
wurdt yn elke tinkbere stavering trochkrùst fan de regels fan de ôflieding, de
analogy, de lykfoarmigens en de 'beschaafde uitspraak'.*

One can see how the language has succumbed, over the centuries, to influences from
other languages. It can be transliterated into English as follows.

Our basic premise is that a good orthography must follow the phonetic system
of the language as much as possible. A separate letter must thus correspond to
each phoneme and each different letter stands for a phoneme. In any
conceivable orthography this system is complicated by the rules of derivation,
analogy, uniformity and cultured pronunciation.

There is a concerted and reasonably successful effort in the Dutch Province of Friesland
to teach West Frisian in the schools. In fact, to some extent, it is mandatory to be taught
in certain grades. They use modern multimedia techniques, so as to capture the interest
of small kids. This instructional program has a sort of mascot, a cartoon kid called
Wopke, who is featured in many of the West Frisian language lessons.

> *Wopke, mei dyn keale holle*
>> Wopke, with your little bald head
> *Wopke, dy is neat te fulle*
>> Wopke, nothing is too much for you
> *mei dyn bùkje wat fourùt*
>> with your tummy sticking out
> *rinstu ùs ferhalltsje ùt.*
>> you're running out of this story.

Perhaps it makes more sense to the children. This is how the language can be handed
down to the next generation. The following are several words where the spelling is
somewhat unique to West Frisian, as compared to Low German.

kij (cows)	lam (lamb)	mjitte (middle)
foar (for)	mei (mine)	fiet (feet)
ùs (our)	dei (that)	sjonge (song)
net (not)	ek (I)	erde (earth)
yn (in)	wês (be)	wrâld (world)
better (better)	boarst (chest)	tiisdei (tuesday)
grut (big)	hope (hope)	tsjerke (church)
jier (year)	noas (nose)	sizze (tell)
yn (in)	feie (sweep)	litte (let)
moat (must)	kinne (can)	praten (talk)
sliepe (sleep)	suster (sister)	droech (dry)

wei (way)	gjin (none)	stean (stand)
dei (day)	hus (house)	goed (good)
west (been)	wenje (live)	hy (he)
thredde (third)	bod (commandment)	houn (dog)
doe (then)	beam (tree)	skoen (shoes)
skiep (sheep)	sunnadei (sunday)	degan (days)
tsiis (cheese)	wenji (reside)	kaei (key)
wit (know)	wyt (white)	wiid (wide)
sil (shall)	skriuwe (write)	sille (should)

<u>Nord Frisian</u>

The coast of North Friesland, north of Husum in Schleswig Holstein, is fairly smooth, with several outlying islands. In fact, these islands comprised most of what was the original Nord Friesland. At low tide, the salt mud-flats (Watten) lie above the water and, in some places, connect the islands to the mainland. The temperature is mild, and the coastal farmlands have the highest wheat production in northern Germany.

How and when the Nord Frisian area was settled, by West Frisians or Ost Frisians, is still somewhat of an unanswered question. Why is it called Nord Friesland? Where is South Friesland? It is generally conceded that the combination of West and Ost Friesland together comprise what one might refer to as South Friesland.

It was probably a mixture of West and Ost Frisians that, between the 9th and 12th century, decided to migrate north along the coast and settle the offshore Nord Frisian islands. In those days, the waterlevel was much lower, and these islands were therefore much larger and more inviting for settlement. At the time, the West and Ost Frisian langauges were probably nearly the same. However, today they vary significantly from Nord Frisian. The mainland was probably already settled at the time the offshore Frisian islands were settled. The offshore islands vary in dialect amongst themselves, but more significantly, they vary from the mainland dialect. By and large, they can understand each other.

Since both the islands and the mainland later came under Danish rule, they both have borrowed from the Danish language. This is probably the main reason that the North Frisian dialects vary so much from West Frisian and Ost Frisian. Another reason could be that Nord Friesland was occupied by ancient Frisians (or Angles or Saxons), before the 9th century. However, in that case one would expect more similarity between Old Frisian and Nord Frisian. For comparison, here are both a modern North Frisian and a modern West Frisian (as an example of Old Frisian) version of a passage from the Book of Matthew.

> North Frisian: *De tweelven sånd Jesus üt än kånd ja aw än sää: Gung ai üt aw da hiise jare weege än ai in önj e stääse foon da Samaritane. Gung liiwer tu da farlääsene schäip foon Israels hüs.*

West Frisian: *Dy tolve stjûrde Jezus der op ùt en hy sei harren syn bistel, sizzende: Gean net in wei op nei de heidenen, en gean ghin stêd yn fan Samaritanen; mar bijow jimme leaver nei de forlerne skiep fan it hûs Israël.*

With regard to the Nord Frisian offshore islands, there exist 9 separate dialects. There is the Mooring dialect (east and west), the island dialects of Föhr (east and west) and Amrum, and the somewhat similar Sylt and Helgoland island dialects. Sylt, who enjoys a good tourism trade, is protective of their dialect. This, and their isolation, has helped them to preserve much of their Frisian dialect. On Sylt they say broðer, almost as it sounds in English. The island people can understand the mainland poeple, but cannot easily speak the mainland dialect.

Most things written today appear in the West Mooring dialect. East Föhr people will say brudder (brother), while West Föhr people will say bruller. The word for 'breast" is brast in Fering, brest in Sölring, börs in Halligen and burst in Mooring. In nearby Denmark it is bryst. In Dutch and Low German it is borst.

There are also the Husum and Festland dialects. The Halligen and Festland dialects are said to have come directly from the Ost Frisians, perhaps around the 11th century. Some of the other dialects may have descended more directly from Old Frisian, several centuries earlier. Some Danish has penetrated all the Nord Frisian dialects, except in Helgoland.

Illustrating further the degree of difference among these dialects, it seems that the word "tuesday" is teisdai in Fering, tiisdai in Solring, taisdai in Halunder, täisdi in Mooring, and tirsdag in nearby Denmark. In Dutch it is dinsdag, in Low German it is dingsdag, and in Standard German is dienstag. On the other hand, a very basic word like "finger" hardly changes at all amongst all these languages and dialects.

The southernmost offshore island where a version of Nord Frisian is spoken is Helgoland. Here are some of the unique words used there.

med (with)	fiuw (five)	fiider (further)
wi (we)	djor (year)	dji (you)
iis (our)	full (full)	feer (for)
memm (mother)	hiir (here)	en (and)

The mainland dialects have undergone considerable change due to Low German influence. It isn't unusual for a Nord Frisian to speak Frisian with the parents and siblings, Low German with the spouse, and Standard German with the children.

The following are several Low German words where the spelling may be somewhat unique to Nord Frisian.

416

gäis (geese)	hod (head)	kü (cow)
Tjüsk (German)	fett (feet)	mensken (people)
riiw (drive)	kön (can)	was (was)
diar (there)	snaak (talk)	snä (snow)
jong (young)	uun (in)	miast (almost)
lun (people)	uk (also)	nü (now)
skel (should)	nian (new)	tidj (time)
wilj (wild)	trii (three)	dai (day)
fri (free)	ääben (oven)	sääker (sure)
güül (yellow)	böör (butter)	uug (eye)
skuure (shoe)	broor (brother)	sooben (seven)
biin (leg)	rou (rest)	oan (one)
arm (arm)	tjüsk (german)	ljaacht (light)
hüs (house)	hüüs (hoarse)	koot (cottage)
wus (was)	dåt (the)	witj (white)
hünd (dog)	ej (he)	tu (to)
kii (cows)	swiin (pig)	jå (yes)
åål (elder)	Fraidäi (Friday)	tääte (father)
håne (hens)	scheew (table)	sin (his)
åte (grandfather)	fälj (field)	dränke (drink)
leese (read)	greewe (dig)	naame (take)

As in all Frisian languages, Nord Frisian makes liberal use of vowels and umlauts. In comparison with Low German, Nord Frisian tends to use *ü* in place of *u* very consistently. Also *e* instead of *a* is quite common. It also uses *j* at the end of a word where one might expect a *d* or *t*. They also have three triphthongs, such as uoi ... huois (house) and uoa ... pluoant (plant) and oai ... hoaise (rabbit). The letters *ei* are often written *ej*.

The following is an example of Nord Frisian, taken from an article written by Albrecht Johannsen in a magazine called *Our Own Way*, from Jan.Feb. 1959.. Note the common use of the letter å, probably due to the influence of Danish.

> *Padersdäi wus di wichtiste däi önj di üülje frasche kaläner. Padersdäi gungt e wunter, än e uurs kamt. Dåt iilj, wat di iinj än twuntiste önj e biikenmoune am eenem oufbrånt wårt, wus önj üüljingstide en hiisen brük än schölj da dämoone ferdriwe.*

Here is a rough English translation.

> St. Peter's Day was the most important day in the old Frisian calendar. On St. Peter's Day the winter goes and the spring comes. The bonfire which was burnt on the evening of the twenty first of February was in ancient times a heathen custom and was supposed to drive away the demons.

By way summarizing the Frisian languages, here are the numbers as used in the older Ost Frisian (pre-Low German), West Frisian and Nord Frisian.

ENGLISH	OST FRISIAN	WEST FRISIAN	NORD FRISIAN
one	ên	ien	åån
two	twê	twa	twäär
three	thrî	trije	trai
four	fiüwer	fjouwer	fjouer
five	fîf	fiif	fiiw
six	sex	seis	seeks
seven	soven	sawn	soowen
eight	achta	acht	oocht
nine	niugun	njöggen	nüügen
ten	tian	tsien	tin
eleven	andlova	alve	alwen
twelve	twelef	tolve	tweelwen
thirteen	thredtine	trettsjin	tratäin
twenty	twintich	tweintich	twunti
hundred	hundred	hûondert	hunert

Ost Frisian

This area is located between the Lauwers and the Weser Rivers, along the North Sea. This area has an interesting history, both geographically and linguistically.

In the Middle Ages, the sea flooded great coastal areas in Ost Friesland. Jever was once a port, but is now well inland. At about this time Ost Friesland consisted of a number of small famer run republics, who were responsible for their own local government. They assembled periodically at Aurich, to develop common and consistent societal rules and regulations. As Saxon influence grew in Ost Friesland, this 'local' form of governance began to decline.

The port at Emden became so successful that the City of Hamburg feared its competition and attacked it. The Pirates that were using this port, with full approval of the Ost Friesland government, were harassing Hamburg shipping. The pirates were destroyed by the Hamburg troops, as well as some fine old castles. Prior to WWI Emden was under Prussian control, who made it into a major port again.

The area is culturally divided, based on local allegiance varying between the Catholic Emsland, the Protestant Aurich and the Calvinist Frisians. However, Low German is now spoken by virtually all of them. The current Ost Frisian Low German dialect is not native to the original Ost Friesland.

The West Frisians migrated into Ost Friesland by about the 12th century. The area developed its own Frisian dialect.. The North Saxon type of Low German dialect encroached into the area by about the 15th century. It seems that, in 1464, Ost Friesland was given to the control of the Count of Cirksem, who spoke Low German. Ost Friesland fell to Prussia in 1744, and this cemented their Germanic language and culture.

A few influences of the Old Frisian remain. Two examples are the 3rd person masculine *hum* and feminine *hör*. For a look at what Ost Frisian might have looked like prior to the encroachment of Low German, one should probably look at Old Frisian or West Frisian.

A few parts of the area did not yield to Low German right away. Sometime in the 13th century, a colony of Ost Frisians settled in Saterland, in Oldenburg. This area was accessible only by boat, until a railway was built in 1950 to span the moors. Due to this isolation, even today you may hear a few peat farmers in the uplands of Saterland speaking a language reminiscent of the original Ost Frisian. Ost Frisian also hung on in Harlingerland and Wursten, until the 17th and 18th century. It still could be heard on the small island of Wangerooge until the first half of the 20th century.

The following excerpt from the Lord's Prayer text is one example of an early Ost Frisian.

> *Us foar deer du bäst in 'n Heemel,*
> Our Father, Who art in Heaven,
> *gehilliged wäide din Noome.   Tou us kuume dien Rik.*
> hallowed beThy name. Thy kingdom come.
> *Din Wille Schäl befoulged wäide,*
> *Thy will be done*
> *as in 'n Heeme., soo uk ap de Waareld.*
> as in Heaven, so on the Earth.
> *Un ferreek us use Scheelden,*
> and forgive us our trespasses,
> *soo as wi doo ferreeke doo sik jun us ferfaild hääbe.*
> as we forgive those who trespass against us.

The following are several Low German words where the spelling is somewhat unique to the current Ost Frisian Low German. Many Ost Frisian words are very close to the North Saxon dialect.

moeder (mother)	min (mine)	nit or niet (not)
awend (evening)	bleven (stayed)	geen (none)
ut (out)	west (was)	roup (call)
ferreek (forgive)	jem (them)	schole (school)
bäst (you are)	fon (from)	tau or toe (to)
kleen (small)	hum (him)	waareld (world)
hi or hei (he)	elk (each)	tid (time)
hör (she)	uns (us)	betken (little bit)

tüschen (between)	kauh (cow)	stuur (difficult)
blied (glad)	doo (do)	proten (talk)
süster (sister)	wicht or deern (girl)	din (yours)
spööl (play)	soo (as)	söte (sweet)
säge (doe)	naber (neighbor)	di (you)
tosamen (together)	jahr (year)	sülst (self)
gau (go)	für (fire)	weke (week)
sedel (note)	moj (joy)	famme (young lady)
völ (many)	minsken (people)	proot (talked)

Emsland

This area is south of Ost Friesland, but is historically closely tied to both Ost Friesland and Oldenburg. Being on the border of the Netherlands, it obviously also has dialect in common with Low Dutch.

The dialect here, Emsländisch, could be considered a sub-dialect of Ost Frisian. It is also influenced by its southern neighbor Westphalia. An example would be the phrase wi bünt (we are), which would be wi sünd in Saxon Low German. They say uns (us) or unser (our) instead of us or uus. The Old Low Franconian influence accounts for the use of *uns* (us) rather than the Saxon word *us*. It may also account for the 'en' verb ending, as opposed to the Low German 't or et" ending. However, both Ost Frisian and Emsländish are primarily considered North Saxon dialects.

The following are several Low German words where the spelling is somewhat unique to the Emsländish dialect.

proat (talk)	daet (that)	mot (must)
lewen (live)	use (our)	häi (he)
äin (one)	däil (part)	stäin (stone)
bünt (are)	leep (ill)	misschien (probably)

Groningen

This Dutch province lies just east of the West Frisians; between the West Frisians and Ost Frisians. Up until the 17th century, Groningen still used a West Frisian dialect. This dialect is basically Frisian, but in many respects it has been inundated by Low German. The northern coast especially has become largely Low German, a dialect similar to Ost Frisian.

The following are several Low German words where the spelling is somewhat unique to Groningen.

nait (not)	doar (there)	k (I)	proat (talk)
t (that)	zoll (should)	uut (out)	kinn (can)

420

hou (how)	joar (year)	hai (he)	noar (near)
hom (him)	schoule (school)	vaaire (four)	twij (two)
doe (the)	mie (me)	goan (go)	ain (one)
zekur (secure)	seeg (doe)	sedel (note)	hegen (save)
schuddeldouk (wash rag)	heers (gruel)	schrijven (scream)	

Oldenburg

This is a definitely a North Saxon dialect, located just west of Bremen. It has strong ties to both Ost Frisian and the Heide or Bremen Low German dialects. The southern part has strong ties to the Low German dialect of north Westphalia. In fact, it was once part of Münsterland.

The following are several Low German words where the spelling is somewhat unique to Oldenburg.

uus (our)	wäsen (was)	dar or dr (there)	tau (to)
dütsk (german)	mauder (mother)	frisk (fresh)	jaohr (year)
staoh (stand)	väl (much)	schaul (school)	uck (also)
raver (over)	tauhope (together)	naober (neighbor)	was (was)
bauk (book)	läs (read)	daoge (days)	dei (the)
gaoh (go)	schriew (write)	saoterdag (saturday)	öwer (over)
käönt (can)	päre (horses)	kaom (come)	trügge (back)
bäter (better)	hackels (chaff)	uusen (our)	snack (talk)

These words reflect a consistent use of 'au', 'ao' and 'ä', which places them more in tune with Ost Frisian and Westphalian than with the Heide area.

Westphalian

The Westphalians and Ostphalians are said to come from the ancient Cherusci Tribe, which might explain many of the similarities in their dialects. At one time they were geographically separated by an area call Engern. Engern was once an important religious and political center for the Saxon heathens. At Markloe there was a sacred shrine called Irminsul, and here they would hold their annual meetings (called Dings). As Charlemagne attacked this area, suppressing the Saxons, and making them convert to christianity, the Engern lost it's influence and finally it's identity. After that, the Westphalian and Ostphalian areas absorbed Engern and thus bordered up against each other, primarily separated by the Weser River.

In contrast to most north German areas, Westphalia's primary economic focus for centuries was the textile industry. This industry declined when England developed a larger textile industry. Although initially Westphalia identified with the North Saxon area, since the 16th century it turned south toward Cologne and west toward Holland

and the Rhine area. Thus the dialects along the borders picked up a variety of outside influences, accounting for the variety of dialects in Westphalia today.

In Westphalia the dialects vary considerably in the central, west, north Münsterland), northeast (Lippe), southeastern (Kurkölnische Saarland) and northeastern (Märkischen Sauerland). The Münsterland area is discussed separately.

> In Märkischen Sauerland Platt they may say "johr" for year, "sau" for so, "et" for that, "tau" for to, "gi" for the plural you, and "hius" for house.

> In the *north*, up to Osnabrück, the Platt speaker may say 'straut' for street, "kleen" for small and "klaid" for dress, 'jåår' for year, 'graut' for large, 'paar' for pair, 'auk' for also, 'meer' for more, 'hewwe' for have, and 'pappa' for father. It goes all the way up to the city of Rheine, at the border with Bentheim.

> On the *northeast,* the Lippe dialect is similar to that of the Heide and northern Ostphalia. A few terms common to this dialect are 'fitteka' for disgust, 'heu' for he. 'tohaupe' for together, 'twüdde' for third, and 'gaus' for goose.

> On the *west* it sits right on the border with Holland, and the Sand Platt dialect bears similarity to Low Dutch. Here it contains remnants of the Old Low Franconian influence, such as the 1st and 3rd person plural ending '-en' endings, rather than the Saxon '-et' endings. Westerly Westphalian Platt speakers may say "frä" for free, "gau" for fast, "lö" for people, "klaower" for clover, "minn" for small, "owwen" for oven, "rekkel" for dog, "maiken" for girl, "praoten" for talk, "äten" for eat, "bäter" for better, "naober" for neighbor, "owend" for evening, and "was" for was.

> On the *southeast* it borders the Ostphalian dialect. On the east it borders Ostphalia and has some features in common with that dialect. But Westphalian varies from Ostphalian by using *uo* (bruoken) in place of *o* (broken) or *au* instead of *a*. The Westphalian for 'mi' (me) and 'di' (you) will be 'mik' and 'dik' in Ostphalian. Easterly Westphalia Platt may use "sau" for the word so, "gi" for the word you, and "ower" for the word but.

North and south are basically separated by the Lippe River.

> *South* Westphalia, bordering on the Hessian dialect along the Benrath Line, will often use dem (as in Standard German) instead of den or denn for the dative singular masculine. In Hesse they use the word schwätzen for "talk". In south Westphalia they have words like joore (year), niägen (nine), dräisi (thirty), auk (also), et (that), twai (two) and kumma (come).

The long *u* from Middle Low German becomes *ue* in Westphalian, while *ü* become *üe*. Westphalian will use 'uo' rather than 'o' in a words like 'bruoken' (broken) or 'duorf' (village). In some areas they'll use 'ua' instead.

The Middle Low German's 'a' (an aw sound, which in Platt Düütsch changed to an 'o' letter) changed to an ah sound. For example, moken (maw-ken) in Platt Düütsch is maaken in Westphalian (mah-ken). In both, the short 'a' was lengthened (as in schaap).

Notice the spelling of the word for the English "eaten", which is spelled iäten (rather than eten) in Westphalian. The Old Saxon short vowel *e* became the diphthong *iä* in the Westphalian dialect. Similarly, the word for "know" is wiëten in Westphalian (rather than weten). The Old Saxon short *e* this time becomes the diphthong *ië*.

Amongst the various West Low German dialects, the lengthened 'a' in words like maaken (to make) or chraawen (to dig) is seen only in the Westphalian dialect. The 'ch' letters represent just another way of pronouncing a 'g' sound.

The following are several Low German words where the spelling is somewhat unique to the Westphalian dialect.

pütte (well)	tiid (time)	straot (street)
piärd (horses)	maakt (made)	liäben (live)
uopen (open)	klain (small)	drai (three)
düör (door)	feer (four)	iäten (eat)
wiäten (know)	bliiben (stay)	leef (stayed)
gaoh (go)	wao (who)	säs (six)
knüöckel (knuckle)	iär (her)	daip (deep)
küern (talk)	wiäk (week)	waogen (wagon)
waoter (water)	iälke (some)	hälp (help)
fraog (ask)	staoh (stand)	meer (more)
ächter (behind)	baoll (soon)	äs (as)
noog (enough)	ek or ick (I)	rüe (dog)
trügge (back)	schriewwen (write)	jaohr (year)
miin (mine)	bietken (little bit)	en (in)
wie (how)	hed (has)	suer (sour)
vaader (father)	aobend (evening)	naoh (after)
duorp (village)	küeck (kitchen)	usse (our)
daut (dead)	bruoken (broken)	kuegel (bullet)
naim (take)	süster (sister)	schuller (shoulder)
bedd (bed)	kaise (cheese)	mensken (humans)
dach (day)	fraog(ask)	seggen (say)
emmer (pail)	naidich (necessary)	däärn (thorn)
feugel (bird)	fiif (five)	tain (ten)
säs (six)	feer (four)	drai (three)

et (it)	spraok (speech)	saoterdag (saturday)
van (from)	trügge (backwards)	määr (anymore)
slaop (sleep)	vättein (fourteen)	kören (speak)
knuocken (bone)	tiänn (teeth)	küeck (kitchen)
naomiddage (afternoon)	hiämd (shirt)	boall (almost)

The numeral een (one) distinguishes between male (een) and female (eene), the latter being also the feminine ending in Standard German. The ''g letter is pronounced more like a 'k' sound. The word 'fraog' (ask) in the above list is pronounced much the same, whether you spell it fraag or fraog or frog, as it varies among dialects. The same goes for the words 'staoh' (stand) or 'gaoh' (go). This is exemplar of many differently spelled cognate words in the various Low German dialects.

Münsterland

This area once included most of south Emsland and South Oldenburg, but in this case we're speaking about the area near the City of Münster in Westphalia. Here they'll say 'wasken' instead of 'waschen' (to wash), and 'geis' instead of 'göös' (geese). In Munsterland Platt they may say "dao" for there, "lü" for people, "kääl" for fellow, "üöwer" for over, "mott" for must, and "nie" for new.

Ostphalian

This area includes, on the north, the City of Hannover, the capital of Lower Saxony. In the 17th and 18th century it was the capital city of the Kingdom of Hannover. In the south are the Harz Mountains and Brunswick (Braunschweig). The following is an example of the Brunswick local dialect.

> *Da schlauk hei in sik un sprok: wo vel Dagelöhner had min Vader,*
> > He reflected and said: How many employees had my father,
> *dei Brot dei Fülle hebbet, un ik vorkome vor Hunger.*
> > that had enough bread to eat, so they wouldn't be hungry.

This area is Lower Saxon in origin, and thus is similar to the other Saxon dialects. It is generally located between Hannover on the north and the Benrath Line on the south. It's southern half has been strongly influenced by Standard German. For instance, they might use 'mik' or 'mek' (a version of *mich*) instead of the Low German mi (me). This is due to the fact they retained some of the accusative form. And they might use 'dik' (a version of *dich*) instead of di (you) or use 'jük' instead of ju or jo (you plural). They often pronouce the *j* letter with a *g* sound. The dialect in the eastern portion is sometimes described as Elbostfalisch. Many of their words still have the '-e' ending, such as veele, friue, harre, etc.

The Middle Low German short *o* or short *u* becomes the monophthong oo (boogen).

The following are Low German words where the spelling is a bit unique to Ostphalia.

hei (he)	brauder (brother)	dik (you)
üsch (us)	laupen (run)	gink (went)
sülben (self)	veele (much)	hebbet (have)
brat (bread)	ek (I)	vor (for)
mek (to me)	dek (to you)	jük (you - plural)
ebrocken (broken)	äät (to eat)	mik (me)
snei (snow)	briuk (use)	nai (now)
saine (his)	sieven (seven)	friue (woman)
giegen (against)	use (our)	leiwe (dear)
heil (well)	ierst (first)	daar (there)
soat (seed)	moand (moon)	droi (three)
slapet (sleep)	häuhner (chickens)	seuken (search)
joahr (year)	oabend (evening)	nist (nothing)
harre (had)	hius (house)	diu (you)
döin (yours)	liäve (live)	duivel (devil)
edaan (done)	sau (so)	sitte (sit)
kräog (tavern)	koin (none)	twoi (two)
biur (farmer)	dei (the) luer (people)	seuk (search)
päär (horses)	moleitsche (raspberries)	serwaitsche (bilberry)

Ostphalia, as in Westphalia, uses 'au' (daut) in place of the North Saxon 'oo' (doot). They retained the *ge-* or *e-* prefix in the past participle tense (*e*broken instead of just broken and edaan instead of just daan). They use 'oa' in place of the more common 'aa'. They use 'ei' instead of 'e', as in dei, sei, hei, etc. They use 'iu' instead of 'uu', as in hius, diu, biur, etc. Even with all of these spelling differences, the words sound similar to other dialects when spoken.

We have mentioned that a principal difference between east and west Low German dialects is the ending -'en- (moken) in the east and '-t' in the west (mokt). In Ostphalia it becomes '-et' (maket and slapet and hebbet).

Schleswig

This most northerly part of Germany was for a long time a part of Denmark; as far back as 950. The Danes had always wanted to incorporate all of the duchy of Schleswig. A thousand years ago Danish was the principal language as far south as the River Eider. South Jutlandisch is still spoken near the Danish border, and also throughout southern Denmark. The Treaty of Ripen, of 1460, declared that the duchies of Schleswig and Holstein should be bound together in perpetuity.

In 1806, Napoleon awarded both Schleswig and Holstein to Denmark. But subsequently Holstein was designated a part of the German Confederation. This was a recipe for trouble, since the Germans now had Holstein, but dearly wanted Schleswig as well.

Prussian and Hanoverian troops marched against the Danes, but an armistice was called in 1848, and the troops left Denmark.

In 1863 the new Danish King Christian declared Schleswig to be part of Denmark. Prussian, Saxon and Hanoverian troops moved again, regaining Schleswig and Lauenberg for Prussion.. Holstein was given to Austria. It seems unusual that all of Schleswig should have been taken from Denmark, because it thereby abandoned 200,000 Danes in north Schleswig. So now it came under Prussian rule. In 1920 the Treaty of Versailles provided for a plebiscite vote in *north* Schleswig, and they voted to go back to Denmark. This split up the Schleswig area. Since then, *south* Schleswig has belonged to Germany.

Schleswigsch is considered a North Saxon dialect, although it does often use the 'en' ending for 3 person plural verbs (rather than the 't or et' ending common to West Low German. Schleswigsch has supplanted the old Danish dialect of Jutish. In Flensburg you'll find a minority dialect called Pethu, in addition to the regular Schleswigsch.

The following are several Low German words where the spelling is somewhat unique to the Schleswigsch around Flensburg..

skrift (write)	tiet (time)	güstern (yesterday
wahn (reside)	awend (evening)	bäten (little bit)
lütten (little one)	awer (however)	hüüttodaags (today)
gahn (go)	paar (pair)	Paster (Pastor)
dal (down)	hooch (high)	

Holstein

Holstein was a Duchy of the Holy Roman Empire. It was ruled by Denmark beginning in 1400. Schleswig and Holstein were conqurerd by Prussia in 1864, and then were jointly administered by Prussia and Austria until 1867. In 1945 Schleswig-Holstein became one of the Lands of the German Federal Republic

The easterly edge of Holstein, the former Duchy of Lauenberg, has a minor Slavic history. The area east of Kiel received emigrants from Mecklenburg. This may be reflected in the Polabisch word Plåten, which was once used locally to mean "apron".

This is a North Saxon dialect. However, they vary from standard North Saxon in the use of a long vowel *u* (fru) in place of a diphthong ou (frou). Middle Low German's word for woman was vrouwe, using the diphthong.

The Dithmarsch area is considered to have it own sub-dialect of Holstein. Some of it's local words are the following.

sin (his)	maaken (make)	bäter (better)

van (from)	aaben (oven)	aeten (eat)
gung (went)	väl (much)	waater (water)
gäl (yellow)	waagen (wagon)	süss (six)

The following are several Low German words where the spelling is somewhat unique to the North Saxon dialect of Holstein.

hüttodaags or vundaag (today)		vadder (father)
keem (came)	gören (children)	ook (also)
baven (above)	west (was)	disse (this)
aver (but)	keerl (fellow)	tööf (wait)
mank (among)	köök (kitchen)	avend (evening)
daal (down)	fraag (ask)	retour (back)
gau (fast)	dörv (may)	keed (chain)
tosomen (together)	uns (us)	slaten (locked)
schmacht (hunger)	schleef (rascal)	sien (be)
heegen (preserve)	heers (gruel)	kaat (cottage)

Bremen

Bremen lies on the north bank of the Weser, and was a major river crossing point (east and west) since the 13th century. The historic duchy of Bremen spread all the way north to the North Sea and east over to Hamburg. The City of Bremen joined the Hansa rather late, in 1358. In 1731 Bremen, having been under Swedish control, was finally recognized by Sweden as a free Reichstadt. To gain some of the ocean-going trade that grew in the 18th century, it purchased the land on which to build Bremerhaven in 1827. Bremerhaven became a primary emigration point later in the 18th century, handling much more traffic then than did Hamburg.

This area has strong ties to both Oldenburg and Ost Friesland. For a while Ost Friesland spread over as far as this area, extending almost to Hamburg. They also share a portion of the same North Sea coast, which was once dominated by Frisians.

In the old duchy of Bremen, these words were somewhat unique.

hüüt (today)	güstern (yesterday)	süster (sister)
prammt (stuffed)	ook (also)	vadder (father)
mok (make)	verhierot (marry)	wür (was)
hüt (today)	konn (could)	dissen (this)

Hamburg

In the 7th century, the Saxons built a castle fortification called Hammaburg on the Alster River, a small tributary of the Elbe. Ham was the Old Saxon word for 'river bank'. In 832 a settlement developed alongside, which became the city called Hamburg. It became a Free City (free from taxes and custum duties) on May 7, 1189, thanks to Emporer Friedrich Barbarossa.

Hamburg, "der Hansa Stadt an der Elbe", soon developed into a busy port. But it didn't reach it's regional dominance until the late 18th century. Its marshy area was not a natural port location and it was long overshadowed by Lübeck. In 1520 the Reformation reached Hamburg and it became a Lutheran stronghold. By 1600 it was the largest city in north Germany.

People say there are no less than 4 Low German dialects in the Hamburg area. It was strongly Low German until about 1600, with a bit of English mixed in with their "Hafen" Platt The nearby Finkwarder Platt, made popular by Rudolph Kinau, may be considered one of them.

The following are several Low German words where the spelling is somewhat exemplary of some Hamburg dialects.

üüt (today)	water (water)	torüch (back)	sall (shall)
sülf (self)	vêl (much)	darf (may)	fief (five)
west (was)	hem (him)	sull (should)	hüüt (today)
freuh (early)	goh (go)	stoh (stand)	heur (hear)
moder (mother)	hoben (harbor)	froch (ask)	güstern (yesterday

Heide, Lüneburger

This area's dialect is definitely a North Saxon dialect. Along its southern border, some tend to refer to the dialect as north Ostfalisch. However, the Ostfalisch dialect is significantly different. The term Heide is used to apply generally to the North Saxon dialect area between Hamburg on the north and almost to Hannover on the south. Heide means 'heath'. This 'heath' land was very lightly slightly settled in the Middle Ages. It was not good farmland. The term 'heath' is the basis for the English word heathen. Heide is also an ancient term for 'pagan'. The pagan inhabitants were very independent, and were slow to accept christianity.

It's regional name is the Lüneburger Heide and its ancient name is the Heidmark. The dialect varies somewhat throughout the area, but generally it is similar to the Bremer dialect It is also closely resembles the Holstein dialect and is only slightly less similar to northeast Westphalia and Schleswig, which were all once part of the original Saxon area. It is also fairly similar to the slightly distant Oldenburg, Ost Frisian and even west Mecklenburg dialects.

Poor sandy soils can support crops of rye, potatoes and buckwheat. It has for centuries supported sheep herding, incorporating a special breed of sheep known as the Heidschnucke.

The city of Lüneburg was a principal salt trading City during the Hansa era, and is historically the principal city of the Heide..

On the eastern edge of the Heide lies an enclave, occupied by the Wends, who retained much of their 6th century Slav heritage. It is discussed separately.

The following are several Low German words where the spelling is somewhat unique to Heide.

achter (behind)	snack (talk)	dahl (down)
deern (girl)	foorts (at once)	töv or töben (wait)
wecke (some)	vundaag (today)	kööp (buy)
grübel (brood)	tied (time)	swester (sister)
gistern (yesterday)	jüm (them)	boben (above)
döstig (thirsty)	halen (fetch)	kuul (ditch)
trüch (backwards)	süh (see!)	jümmer (always)
grusel (disgust)	toll (inch)	bomms (crash)

Lüneburger Wendland

In the far eastern corner of the Heide area, along the Elbe, the area heritage was Polabish until the late 17th century. It is now an enclave of Wends and Sorbs, who are attempting to protect their local "dravänopolabish" Slavic language. They spoke a Polabisch dialect until the 17th or 18th century, with such unique words as 'harbait' for 'arbeit' and 'karcke' for 'kirche'. The area around Cottbus, further south, is Low Sorbish. The area around Bautzen is called Upper Sorbish. The wider Sorb area also includes Silesia, now a part of Poland.

The Polabisch word platna, meaning linen cloth (i.e, apron), may have generated the Low German word for ironing, which is pletten.

The Slavic dialects use 'p' where Standard German uses 'f', just as in Low German. The diminutive ending is '-ki', such as in klütki. The area also exhibits the loss of the final '-en' (kok rather than koken). The following are several words where the spelling and usage is somewhat unique to the Wendland area.

rup (up)	tau (to)	pritsch (get away)
harbait (work)	jichel (pine needle)	kubel (bread).
molaiten (raspberries)	kaweke (crow)	potsche (paddle)
aun (chicken)	dach (day)	

Mennonite

There is a dialect used by *some* Mennonites that is considered a form of Low German, called Plautdietsch, although there are many Mennonites consider High German as their mother language. It is significant that Plautdietsch is fundamentally a dialect connected with a religious faith, rather than with with a Germanic tribe or a geographical principality, as is the case with the other Low German dialects. Plautdietsch has traveled widely, to flee religious persecution, and is connected with a number of different countries. This diaspora caused their Low German to become a cumulative product of exposure to wherever this group was located, rather than a product of evolutionary growth in one area.

Mennonite heritage stems from such diverse areas as Prussia, Groningen, Friesland, Belgium, Germany and especially Switzerland. Some Anabaptists, during the Reformation, sought refuge in the Netherlands and Friesland. Their leader was a Frisian called Menno Simons, and in the 16th century they acquired the name Mennonites. Mr. Simons was an Ost Frisian priest, who renounced the Roman Catholic faith in 1536 to become an Anabaptist.

Their mix of High German, Low Franconian, Dutch and Frisian dialects went with them originally as the emigrated east to Hamburg, and then on to the Danzig and the Vistula River delta in the early 16th century. They brought with them some Ost Frisian Low German, however, today most Mennonites have a hard time understanding Ost Frisian. The Vistula was an area with Slavic history, and also exposed them to High Prussian and East Pommeranian dialects. Here the *rural* Mennonites picked up some of the local Low German dialect.

The Dutch language had come along as well, and lived on around Danzig as a church language, until about 1800. In 1788, the first 228 families moved on to the Ukraine, where they were exposed to (and adopted) some Russian and many Ukranian loan words. Some moved further on, to Crimea and even Siberia. At this point the Mennonites spoke a mixture of inherited dialects, in addition to the original Low Franconian-Low German-Frisian mixture. The rural people likely spoke Plautdietsch, while urbanites spoke High German. In the late 19th century and early 20th century, some moved across the ocean to other countries; including the plains states of the United States (primarily Kansas, South Dakota and earlier Pennsylvania) and southern Canada (primarily Manitoba). In the early 20th century some moved to Mexico and South America (Paraguay).

This dialect consistently uses 'au' where other Low Germans uses just 'a'. It uses 'oa' where one often finds just 'o' or 'a'. In this manner, they have similarities with Westphalian and Ostphalian. They use a palatized *k* sound, in the letter combination *kj*. The widespread use of the 'j' letter for the 'g' sound makes their dialect difficult to comprehend. Their palatized *t* sound, in the letter combination *tj,* was probably picked up from Russian. The 'j' letter harkens back to a Frisian and Gröningen dialect.

The following are several words from Plautdietsch.

auleen (alone)   koak (cook)   vää (before)   dickj (thick)

woakj (work)	unja (under)	wota (water)	äwa (over)
oba (but)	moak (make)	bäter (better)	eba (fever)
räajne (rain)	sesta (sister)	daut (that)	laund (land)
kjind (child)	kunn (can)	sikj (self)	huag (high)
woarm (warm)	ekj (I)	si (see)	jeff (give)
et (it)	met (with)	väl (much)	leew (believe)
kjoakj (church)	tjäatj (kitchen)	drock (busy)	kjleen (small)
waig (way)	jing (hang)	joahr (year)	hinja (behind)
räd (talk)	jleewe (believe)	doag (day)	koakj (cook)

RELATED DIALECTS AND LANGUAGES

There are several languages that are tied closely to German. Dutch especially has close ties to Low German. Low Franconian belongs to the Low German branch, and has strongly influenced a number of Low German dialects.

YIDDISH

The term Yiddish is a corruption of the German word *Jüdisch*. It is a mixture of Hebrew and German, as used since the Middle Ages. Over the year it has also been impacted by Polish and Russian. This was the language of the Jewish people for 500 years, especially the exiled Jews of the diaspora. Around the 10th century some Jews in France, who spoke a version of Old French (Judeo-French) and Hebrew, moved eastward towards the Middle Rhine. Here they also picked up Middle High German, which provides a good deal of their Yiddish.

As Jews also settled in Arabia and Persia, they created their own versions of the local languages. In Spain there is a dialect referred to as Judeo-Spanish. (Judezmo). Yiddish might be referred to as Judeo-German.

In the 15th century many Jews moved into eastern Europe, where the language matured. Yiddish was then a literary language, using Hebrew script (earliest documents found are from the 14th century). While Hebrew became the official religious and political language, the average Jew continued to used Yiddish. The religious elite decreed that the Yiddish language was a ghetto language, and should be replaced by Hebrew. Since then, Yiddish has declined in Eastern Europe. The last newspaper published in Yiddish was discontinued in 1998.

The following are a few pronouns in Yiddish, as an example of the language.

I ⇔ ikh	you ⇔ du	he ⇔ er	he ⇔ zi
it ⇔ es	me ⇔ mir	me ⇔ mikh	you ⇔ dikh

LOW FRANCONIAN

Low Franconian is a product of West Franconian. There are some similarities to Standard German, which may not be so surprising since Standard German is a product of East Franconian. As in Standard German, Low Franconian uses a long 'i' and long 'u', where Low German uses, respectively, a long 'e' and long 'o'. Both Central and East Franconian dialects are Central German in origin.

In Low German there is a consistent *t* verb ending for all persons plural. In Low Franconian the 1st and 3rd persons end in *en*. It seems almost as if Low Franconian lies linguistically halfway between Low and High German. In Low Franconian they say 'sei' instead of the Low German 'ji'.

Low Franconian also uses the *ge* prefix quite freely. Old Low Franconian also used the letter 'u' in place of the letter 'v', 'uu' for the letter 'w', ð for 'd', 'c' for 'k', 'e' for 'i', 'f' for 'v', 'u' for 'o' and 'k' for 'ch'.

Below are some examples of west Low Franconian words.

hôre (hear)	gedân (done)	betera (better)
fethar (feather)	namo (name)	jâr (year)
thi (you)	sint (are)	cumit (come)
fuoti (feet)	ist (is)	ôuga
brengan (bring)	bock (goat)	duon (do)
fan (from)	ertha (earth)	fuir (fire)
ic (I)	hie (he)	wuo (how)
of (if)	ruop (call)	sol (salt)'
sprecan (speak)	thuro (through)	undir (under)
uuerk (work)	uuârheide (truth)	thîn (yours)

DUTCH

Dutch is not a dialect, of course, but rather the language of the Netherlands. It has a strong historical relationship to western Old Low Franconian, because both were based largely on a Franconian dialect spoken in Brussels. As in Low Franconian, the letter þ became 'd' about 1100. The Franks brought Old Franconian to the area in the 4th and 5th century. Dutch is still spoken in northern Belgium, but the Flemings would rather refer to it as Flemisch.

Because of its long border with north Germany, it contains similarities to Low German. The east side of the Netherlands (Drenthe and Overijssel) speaks a version of Dutch that has similarities with Low German, and is often referred to as Low Dutch. The river Ijssel is the traditional border between the Saxon influence on the east and the Low Franconian influence on the west. The Dutch keep the '-en' ending on many words, which are dropped in Low Franconian.

An example of Dutch text follows, along with its English translation.

Als woonstad heeft Den Haag door de
　　As a residential town the Hague
mooie om geving ook veel voor
　　has many advantages over
op andere grote steden.
　　other large towns.

The following are several words where, compared to regular Low German, the spelling is somewhat similar in Dutch.

droom (dream)	boom (tree)	koopen (buy)	tien (ten)
ik (I)	jij (you, singular)	hij (he)	ij (she, they)
wiu (we)	jullie (you, plural)	mijn (mine)	mie (me)
boter (butter)	hond (dog)	school (school)	pan (pan)
ook (also)	huis (house)	vrouw (woman)	maar (but)
moeder (mother)	heb (have)	drie (three)	hem (him)

The 'ij' combination of letters, called a ligature, was used in Dutch since the Middle Ages. It is a separate letter on their typewriter.

Afrikaans

The Dutch first settled Cape Town in 1652, as part of the Dutch East India Company settlements. Dutch settlers in South Africa developed the Afrikaans language. This evolved from their natural Dutch, and was originally referred to as Cape Dutch. The British acquired the Cape Colony from the Dutch in 1814, and English became the preferred language. But Afrikaans survived among the Boer people on the farms and ranch settlements. Today Afrikaans is quite strong, and in many areas English is the second language.

Some of the personal pronouns in this language are as follows.

ek ⇔ I	sy ⇔ she	dit ⇔ it
u ⇔ you	my ⇔ me	hom ⇔ him
ons ⇔ we	julle ⇔ us	hulle ⇔ they

The following is an example of current Afrikaans.

Reeds onder die bemanning van die drie skepe waarmee Jan van Riebeeck na die Kaap gekom het, was daar 'n paar Duitsers en in die loop van die 17de en die 18de eeu het 'n ononderbroke stroom Duitse immigrante na die Kaap

gekom, 'n stroom wat tot by die einde van die Hollandse bewind tussen 14.000
en 15.000 Duitsers in die land gebring het.

Here is a rough English translation.

Even among the crew of the three ships with which Jan von Riebeeck came to
the Cape were a few Germans, and in the course of the 17th and 18th centuries
an unbroken stream of German immigrants came to the Cape; a stream which
by the end of Dutch rule brought between 14,000 and 15,000 Germans into the
country. The following are some words somewhat unique to Afrikaans.

agter (behind)   regt (right)   woon (reside)
duk (scarf)   heer (gentlemen)   kaal (bald0
klabjas (whist)   kleintjie (child)   klinker (face brick)
kleinhuisie or uithuisie (outdoor lavatory)

ICELANDIC

This is an early North Germanic language, coming to Iceland when it was colonized by
Norway in 874. The language has changed little since the 9th century. It's been said that
anyone fluent in *Old English* would be able to communicate with modern Icelanders.

The following words are used in Icelandic.

hundur (dog)   husith (house)   kaupa (buy)
hann (he)   ekki (not)   gotunni (street)
mòdir (mother)   ek (I)   hefti (have)

EXAMPLES OF VARIATIONS IN LOW GERMAN DIALECTS

By way of summation, we can look at a small part of the results of a European Science
Foundation project call EUROTYP. In this project they requested that a cross-section of
people describe how a given sentence would be said in their dialect. For example, the
sentence "She is peeling potatoes" came out like this.

Frisian: Hja is oan't jirpelskilen
Dutch: Ze is aan het aardappelschillen
N. Friis (Fering):   hat as uun't eerdaapelskelin
Danish: Hun er ved at skrælde kartofler
Mainland (Moor):   Jü as bai tu kartüfelskälen
Platt Düütsch   Se is bi't kartuffel schelen
Standard German: Sie is am Kartoffelschälen

When comparing the various Low German dialects, it initially appears there are quite a
few differences. How much you see depends somewhat on whether you're looking for

434

differences or looking for similarities. There is an abundance of both. There are some people who see only a small difference in dialects. They are usually people responding to the verbal dialects, having not read much material in the various dialects. Those that have seen other dialects in print often come to the conclusion that there are great differences between the dialects. Both views are true. Those that have read all of the different dialects quickly see beyond the spelling differences and tend to marvel at the many similarities.

The point here is that, when one views the *basic* words, those that come up most often in daily conversation, the differences arise mostly from the spelling variations. And since there is no authority regarding how words <u>must</u> be spelled, the differences are manageable.

The table on the following page contains some of these basic words, although which word a dialect uses is often debatable, even amongst those who speak a particular dialect. One can see some similarities across the board, and others are pertinent to a particular area..

> Notice the word for "brother". The 'd' is silent, and the pronunciation in each dialect is almost identical. In Frisian, it is so silent that it's not even written. Notice also the use of the 'hei' for "he" in both the West and East dialects. However, when pronounced, they are almost identical. The 'hei' is drawn out a bit long. The 'he' in the north is also sometimes dragged out longer. It is perhaps analogous to the differences in a conversation in English held between an Australian, and Englishman and an American.

> The *north* category includes the older North Saxon dialects, one of the West Low German dialects. These four dialects are quite similar. One could also include the Hamburg dialect here. The choice of using the 'o' or the 'a' letter in places represents one of the largest differences, which is actually quite small.

> The *west* category is Saxon and Low Franconian in origin, but all are West Low German dialects. The use of 'hei' for the English word 'he' seems to be consistent in this category. Here the choice of 'e' versus ä favors the latter.

> The *east* category is basically East Low German, which has experienced a myriad of dialectical influences. Brandenburg differs the most here, because it is situated to the south, and includes Berlin, which means it was strongly influenced by Standard German. The Mecklenburg and Pommern dialects are very similar.

> The *related* dialects are basically Frisian, which is part of the Low German branch. They vary the most in spelling, and once one seens the pattern of the differences, they no longer seem so different.

TABLE FIVE
VARIATIONS IN DIALECT

ENGLISH	ask	better	brother	can	dog	eat	father	girl	go	he	year
NORTH											
HEIDE	fraag	beter	broder	kann	hund	et	voder	deern	goh	he	johr
BREM	frog	beeter	broder	kann	hund	eet	vader	deern	goh	he	johr
HOLST	fraag	beter	broder	kann	hund	et	vader	deern	goh	he	johr
SCHLES	fraag	beter	broder	kann	hund	et	vader	deern	gah	he	johr
WEST											
OLDENB	fraog	bäter	braoder	käönt	hund	ät	vadder	deern	goh	he	jaohr
OST FRIS	frog	beeter	broder	kann	hund	eet	vadder	deern	gau	hi	joar
OSTPHAL	fraag	bäter	brauder	kann	hund	äät	vadder	deern	goh	hei	joahr
WESTPHAL	fraog	bäter	brauder	konn	rüe	iät	vaader	wicht	gaoh	hei	jaohr
EAST											
MECKLEN	fraag	beter	brauder	kann	hund	et	vader	dirn	gau	hei	johr
POMMERN	frogg	bäter	brauder	kann	hund	iät	vadder	mäke	gah	hei	johr
BRANDEN	frag	bääter	brauder	kann	hund	äät	vadder	määken	gah	hei	jahr
RELATED											
NORD FRIS	fraag	beter	broer	kön	hünd	et	tääte	deern	gah	ej	djor
WEST FRIS	freegje	better	broer	kinne	houn	ite	heit	faam	gean	hy	jier
STD. GERM.	frag	besser	Bruder	kann	Hund	ess	Vater	Mädchen	gehe	er	Jahr

ENGLISH	a little	make	mine	mother	none	not	our	sister	stand	talk	time
NORTH											
HEIDE	beten	mok	mien	moder	keen	nich	uus	swester	stoh	snack	tied
BREM	beten	mok	mine	mudder	keen	nich	uus	süster	stoh	snack	tied
HOLST	beten	mak	mien	moder	keen	nich	uus	swester	stah	snack	tiet
SCHLES	bäten	maak	mien	moder	keen	nich	use	süster	stah	snack	tiet
WEST											
OLDENB	bäten	maak	min	mauder	keen	nich	uusen	süster	staoh	snack	tied
OST FRIS	betken	mok	min	moeder	geen	nit	uns	süster	stoh	proten	tid
OSTPHAL	bitken	mak	min	mudder	koin	nist	use	süster	stoah	snack	tid
WESTPHAL	bietken	maak	miin	mudder	kein	nich	usse	süster	staoh	küern	tiid
EAST											
MECKLEN	bisken	mok	min	modder	kein	nit	usse	swester	stah	spreken	tid
POMMERN	bitske	mak	min	modder	kein	nit	us	swester	stah	spreken	tit
BRANDEN	bitsken	määk	min	modder	gein	net	uus	swester	stah	spreken	tid
RELATED											
NORD FRIS	beten	maak	mien	memm	keen	nich	us	suster	stah	snaka	tidj
WEST FRIS	let	meitsje	mei	mem	gjin	net	us	suster	stean	prata	tiid
STD.GERM	bischen	mache	mien	Mutter	kein	nich	unser	Schwester	stehe	rede	Zeit

436

The age of the Dinosaurs and ice sheets, a time so long ago that it seems it must have happened on a different planet. However, it happened here and it *is* a part of our history. Both the Dinosaurs and the ice sheets preceded the emergence of mankind in Europe, when *our* history began. It took a long time for the Indo-Europeans and their language to appear in central Europe. Actually, compared to the length of time *since* the Dinosaur, the number of years that have passed since language and civilization came to Europe is like the blink of an eye.

The Indo-European people came originally from either Asia or Africa, many thousands of years ago. Around 6,000 B.C. they were comprised of a collection of tribes living just north of the Black Sea.. A couple of thousand years later they moved west to the Hungarian Plains, near the Danube. They were then quite primitive, near the end of the Stone Age, but had developed a fairly complex language. Soon after, various Indo-European tribes moved northward, eventually entering lower Scandinavia. About 1,500 B.C., their language shifted to Primitive Germanic, and these Germanic tribes became bound together by this new common language. By virtue of the First Sound Shift, the new language differed from the original Indo-European language in certain particular ways. About 500 B.C. they, and their language, soon began spreading throughout northwestern Europe. These barbarians, as history has chosen to call them, initially spread throughout what we now call Germany and Scandinavia and the Netherlands. A number of 'daughter' languages evolved from Primitive Germanic. They were studied by Rask, Jones, Grimm and Verner, and that's how we gained some knowledge about the Indo-European and Primitive Germanic languages.

Just before the christian era, the Gothic and Norse languages broke away from Primitive Germanic. The Goths then migrated far and wide, spreading an Aryan form of Catholicism, which resulted in christianizing many of the barbarians. At about this same time, before the christian era began, the pagan Saxon tribes among them began speaking an evolved version of Primitive German we now call the language Old Saxon. The Frankish tribes had their own different dialect, which they spread as they conquered most of Germany, plus the Netherlands and France. They helped to spread Roman Catholicism amongst many Germanic tribes. The Saxons, along with the Jutes and Angles, invaded England and planted there the seeds for the English language. The Slavic tribes settled in the area east of Germany and planted the seeds for Polish and Russian, amongst others.

About the 4th century the Second Sound Shift created a split off from Primitive German, creating several Old High German dialects. Meanwhile, as has been noted, the Old Saxon language evolved into Old Low German. This sound shift is the reason that Low German and High German began taking different paths. Amongst their many differences, High German words used a 't' while Low German used a 'd' in the corresponding word. Actually, at that time and during the Middle Ages, these languages were surprisingly similar, but the vowel spelling kept changing over time.

In Chapter Two we found why Low German (Platt Düütsch) and High German have a heritage in common with Dutch, Norwegian, Danish, Icelandic, Frisian, Swedish and English. The experts have labeled these various language groups in several ways, but in this summary we'll just refer to them as northerly, westerly and easterly tribal groups.

Before some of these languages developed, the various Germanic tribes spoke a number of separate but similar dialects. The *northerly* Germanic tribal language group includes today's Swedish, Danish, Norwegian, and Saxon Low German languages. Also included are the Frisian dialects of Nord Friesland, West Friesland, Ost Friesland and the Low German dialects of Oldenburg, Bremen, the Heide, Hamburg, Schleswig and Holstein. There are certain ancient relationships here that still exist amongst them, but some have been lost to history. The current Scandinavian languages still use the letter å, which is only faintly visible in northern dialects.

The *westerly* Germanic tribal language group includes the Dutch and Flemish languages. Also included are the dialects of Low Dutch, Westphalian and Ostphalian. Some of these relationships were transported into East Low German, during the 12th century resettlement period.

The *easterly* Germanic language group includes Standard High German language and one could include the easterly dialects of Low German. The latter includes the dialects of Mecklenburg, Pommern, Brandenburg, and the High German dialects of Schwabisch and Bavarian.

The two chapters that contain glossaries, using the North Saxon dialect, reveal a fairly extensive vocabulary. The grammatical analysis in Chapter Four of the Low German vocabulary, and a look at the Standard German and English grammar, shows how similar these languages are to each other. It reveals the similarity between the way nouns are pluralized and verbs are conjugated in the three languages. One can see that the major differences between these languages results from spelling changes over the centuries. This is also the primary differentiating feature among the various Low German dialects.

In Chapter Six the Low German dialects were described, along with examples. The many dialects were categorized in the simplest of term; as North Saxon, Phalian and East German. Attention was drawn to the close relationship between the dialects of the Phalians (West and Ost) and the East Germans. In-migration of 'Phalians' and others from the west into the East Low German areas appears to be the cause.' The dialectical relationship between the area including northern Phalian and Ost Friesland, and the North Saxon area, was brought about by their once being folded into the Kingdom of Hannover (which surrounded Oldenburg). Similarity amongst East Low German dialects also relates to their sharing of a fairly common history.

Within each of these major dialect areas, there are subdialect areas. Sometimes these are just small enclaves where just a few words are handled differently. The major differences began arising as the various tribes migrated and resettled, with each tribe developing their own version of Low German. In so doing, they created these various dialects or subdialects. In many cases, a specific dialect reflects a particular area or people who once actually were a separate country or dukedom; even Kingdom. Each Low German dialect, and the area in which each is used, has its own long and interesting history.

Low German was at its prime during the Hanseatic League period. At that time the language situation was very complex. High German was the secondary language in the north. Major cities used Low German for official documents. The upper class much preferred to speak one of the romance languages; especially French. As High German influence increase, and various interests strove to create a Standard German, Low German began to decline.

Low German had been referred to in High German as nieder duetsch, which directly translates into Low German. But then it became known as 'platt deutsch'. If you look up the term 'platt' in a German dictionary, you'll find it defined as "flat", "trite" or "common". The term 'platt deutsch' (platt düütsch or platt dütsk in Low German) was evidently meant to convey the image of a lower class language. The supposition that it referred to the lowlands of the north is questionable, since there already was a word (nieder deutsch) that covered this. Whatever the intent, Low German speakers of today willingly and proudly embrace Platt Düütsch in Germany and America (where it's often just called Platt). Unfortunately, there are a few that are ashamed to publicly speak any dialect, whether belonging to Low German or High German.

The decline of Low German has affected the number of people that speak the language. But primarily it has affected the literary aspect of the language. This language, once a *major* business and literary language, has existed over 2,000 years. The previous chapters have striven to show that there still exists a more than sufficient vocabulary and grammatical foundation for re-developing a literary Low German. This will be discussed more in the concluding chapter.

Starting millions of years ago, this book has traced European mankind and language through centuries of movement and evolution. It has revealed the very location, in Scandinavia, where all the things German began. In this very same area, the Low German people and their language also came into being, as a primitive and pagan people. They've had to withstand many hardships along the way, which made them resilient and self sufficient. They are somewhat like a fresh baked brotchen; hard on the outside and soft on the inside. Their language has very ancient roots, buried deep in history and tied closely to the land. The language has a gritty and basic simplicity that one might associate with soil. There is an old Low German song called *Anke vun Tharau*, based on a poem written in 1637, that when sung brings a musty and mossy sensation to the nostrils and a feeling of ancient-ness into the heart. Words said in Low

German seem to taste of hard but honest work, simple but fulfilling food, biting but tender sarcasm, light but sensitive humor, along with large doses of respect for their fellow man.

In summary, the uniquely warm and expressive nature of the Low German language thankfully still resonates in several parts of the world. As these areas are beginning to reclaim and support their heritage and language, as well as making efforts to reestablish contact with each other, the prospect for preserving the language shines a bit brighter.

CHAPTER EIGHT
CONCLUSION

The following are a few of the conclusions that one can draw from the discussion in the preceding chapters.

Low German is certainly a simple and direct language. As the saying goes. "Mit Platt Düütsch fallt de muurn". The term 'muurn' here means "walls". In English it says "the walls fall down when you speak Low German". What this means is that when people speak this language, any walls or differences that might exist between the speakers seem to disappear. People tend to trust even strangers when they speak this language. And people don't stay strangers very long. Words in Low German have meanings that are simple; very difficult to misunderstand.

From time to time the elected officials of a couple of north German government bodies (e.g. Schleswig-Holstein and Hamburg) take one session day in the year and set aside a part of it for deliberating government matters in Low German. Invariably, at the end of that evey such day, they come to the same conclusion. Which is: if they spoke it all the time, they would have more agreeable and probably more productive sessions. One wonders how much money that would save.

The language is also highly expressive and descriptive. If one takes a broad look at the Low German vocabulary, one may be struck by the many words that are used for describing personal characteristics. For instance, there are a half dozen or more words for pointing out such human characterisics as "complaining"and "gossiping". There are also a number of terms for representing the "rascally" nature of people, of which about 20 were listed in the introductory chapter

Also of interest concerning this language is the fact that words have shifted in meaning over time -- sometimes two or three times. For instance, the Low German word 'freen' means to marry, but once it meant just to 'court' someone. The word 'bruut' means bride but once meant just 'fiance'. A 'bruutpoor' was, for instance, an 'engaged couple'. In Indo-European days, the word 'appel' meant just any tree fruit, and now it refers specifically to the one fruit. The word 'hochtied' meant just any 'high old time' sort of occasion, and now it refers to one particular occasion. The term 'knecht' used to refer to any young man, and now it means a hired young man. The term 'hals' used to cover all the way around the 'neck' and now it just means 'throat'.

Low German, in its earliest period, was comprised of a number of tribal dialects. For the most part, those dialects still exist. A language this diverse and interesting needs to be preserved. It has an interesting and significant history. By virtue of its Old Saxon language parentage, it is a remarkably old language. Not as old as Greek, perhaps, but it does precede the christian era.

And, during its Hansa period, it was a true literary language. Due to a variety of factors, the concept of Low German as a literary language has been all but lost. The various dialects today, when taken together, comprise at best a verbal language. There are literary products available in some of the Low German dialects, but none of them can represent themselves as a literary Low German language. A literary language is one that has just one way of being written; one standard way way for words to be spelled (with minor exceptions). Such a language can then be read and understood by any Low German person that takes the time to learn to acquire that skill. Such a single Low German language does not exist today.

It is argued here that if the language is to be preserved, then such a Low German literary language needs to be defined and promulgated. Had Low German continued on, from the 16th century on, as a literary language, then consistent spelling guidelines would have evolved on their own, as they did for High German. In which case, we might now have two principal languages in Germany today, as there are in Canada and Belgium, and several in Switzerland.

Of highest importance is the preservation of the language. Closely meshed with that is the need to define one standard language. To accomplish this it would be necessary to ameliorate the different spelling conventions of the various dialects. Such a standard could be flexible. It could accept either 'he' or 'hei' to mean the English word 'he', or accept either the spelling 'et' or 'ät' to refer to eating. However, it would not include a spelling that applied to just one dialect, when other dialects agreed on another and perhaps simpler spelling. Although the spoken versions of many of the dialects of Low German do sound quite similar to each other, their spelling variations make them, for most people, difficult to read. To the ear, the words 'huus' and 'hius' or 'good' and 'guad' sound almost the same. To the eye, they appear as if they could have different meanings.

In many cases, people write their own dialect with words spelled phonetically, or they used available High German or English words and rules. In any event, the variety of spelling has become a handicap for preserving Low German. The term used to describe such spelling rules for a language is *orthography,* which was discussed at length in Chapter Four. The development of such a standard would be used in publishing books, poems, letters and even newspapers, which would certainly strengthen the goal of preservation – without changing or threatening any of the spoken dialects. Being able to publish a newspaper in such a standard language, accessible to all the Low German people, would be a great step forward in preserving the language.

Without a standard method of writing Low German, the currently growing amount of Low German literature finding its way into print is enjoying a sparse audience. Potentially, when you consider all the Low German dialect speakers throughout the world, there is a large potential audience. For most Low Germans, though, the effort to read even their own dialect appears to be challenge enough. A half dozen generations have gone by since reading Low German was a common experience. Even then, what was available to read was written in a particular dialect. Most Low German speakers have never seen their dialect in writing. As much as they would like to read it, it seems to them to be just too daunting a task.

In a few parts of north Germany there are currently ongoing efforts, in schools and at home, to teach Low German to the younger generation. These efforts evolve around their local dialect, and so that dialect's distinctiveness is not a great issue to them. However, the students are not learning anything about the other dialects, nor are the literary highlights of other dialects open up for them. The development of one literary Low German common language would resolve these problems.

For anyone attempting to develop a Low German orthography, these following comments are offered as suggestions. Developing an orthography should involve several representatives, lay and technical, from each of the major dialects. The effort should respect and attempt to incorporate some of the distinctive features found in the majority of dialects, letting them become options that could be used selectively. The effort should provide for, and even should encourage, the continuation of each spoken dialect in its present form. The objective should be to create an overall literary language, containing a "preferred" body of words and grammatical conventions. This language would hopefully become the norm as regards any written material that might be aimed at the Low German public in general.

There is a growing body of written work in Low German. The works of 19th century writers, such as Fritz Reuter, Klaus Groth, etc. have become more widely available. Unfortunately, their writings often employ an *inconsistent* choice of words and means of spelling, even with regard to their own particular dialect. This makes their work difficult for broad enjoyment. Contemporary writers are laboring, in a variety of ways, to fill some of the gap. There are more poems, songs, books, and plays in print every year. The songs and books are, unfortunately, not widely available and the dialectical variations in which they are written serve only a very narrow audience. When seen on television, a play purported to be in Low German will usually utilize a "missingsch" (mixed) form of Low German. It will be heavily laced with Standard German words, in an attempt to reach a commercially viable audience. Various towns support Low German theater, but this involves only their own dialect. They are to be lauded, but again, the audience is limited to a small portion of the potential audience.

As has been suggested, creating a single standard Low German literary language would require finding a compromise amongst the major dialects. It would have to capture as much as possible the richness and enormous pleasure that one hears and feels when speaking or listening to today's various dialects? This will require compromises. Room should be left for using "local" words, but they should be kept to a minimum. This would preserve some of the "flavor" that makes Low German so special, but also speak to the need to reach the whole audience. Room should be left even for some "loan words", for filling those needs for which Low German words aren't readily available. A form of identification, such as italics, might be used to set these words off from the basic standard Low German text. One advantage of this might be to reduce the temptation for authors to *create* word spellings to make some words seem like Low German words.

The "local" dialect should continue to be written with its own local spelling conventions, for the enjoyment of "local" readers. The audience for such writings would intentionally be limited to those dialect speakers. Works of general interest should be written with a literary standard Low German, to make it possible for them to be read by all Low German speakers and anyone else making the effort to learn to speak or write Low German.

Using a literary Low German would mean that poems, books, songs and plays could reach an international Low German speaking audience. This audience could even include persons that are interested, but have never before used any dialect of Low German. They would know that their efforts to learn Low German would be rewarded by then having access to a wide 'readable' source of documents.

In addition to a literary Low German, preservation of the language certainly requires some other individual efforts. People who speak the language should make an effort to include it more in their everyday life. It would be fun to use it sometimes in everyday correspondence with other speakers of Low German. It would be interesting to try and write poems, if only for your own enjoyment. Teaching the grandchildren a few words would be fun for everybody concerned. Low German speaking people everywhere should make some effort toward teaching some of their Low German dialect to their children and grandchildren. Even a handful of words would help to instill some appreciation of the history of Low Germans and their language in future generations.

Experts that publish technical works can play a stronger role in preservation, by more directly sharing their important work with the average Low German speaker. They should strive to make their work more understandable by the public, or perhaps co-publish a version of their work in words that the average person can understand.

People should take steps to revive their historical penchant for songs and plays in the language, and share their common interests by forming and supporting related community organizations. Speaking of the *community* aspect, citizens should look for opportunities to draw attention in their community to German cultural values, such as the writings of Goethe and Schiller, or the music of Brahms, Beethoven, Schumann or even the Austrians Mozart and Schubert. This could be extended to include supporting the teaching of Standard German in local High Schools and Parochial schools. Teaching Low German in Elementary Schools may well have to be confined to schools in Germany.

As the history of the Low German people and their language has been reviewed, it has become apparent that such a long and resplendent history shouldn't be allowed to recede into nothingness. There are still tens of thousands of people who speak the language, scattered throughout the world. However, it is also certain that what took almost **three thousand years** to develop may disappear in the next generation.